Energy and the Transformation of International Relations

Energy and the Transformation of International Relations:

Toward a New Producer–Consumer Framework

Edited by
ANDREAS WENGER
ROBERT W. ORTTUNG
JERONIM PEROVIC

Contributors
MONICA ENFIELD
BASSAM FATTOUH
MIKKAL HERBERG
TANVI MADAN
JOHN ROBERTS
ROGER TISSOT
MICHAEL E. WEBBER

Published by the Oxford University Press
for the Oxford Institute for Energy Studies
2009

OXFORD

UNIVERSITY PRESS

Great Clarendon Street, Oxford OX2 6DP

Oxford University Press is a department of the University of Oxford.
It furthers the University's objective of excellence in research, scholarship
and education by publishing worldwide in

Oxford New York

Auckland Cape Town Dar es Salaam Hong Kong Karachi
Kuala Lumpur Madrid Melbourne Mexico City Nairobi
New Delhi Shanghai Taipei Toronto

with offices in

Argentina Austria Brazil Chile Czech Republic France Greece
Guatemala Hungary Italy Japan Poland Portugal Singapore
South Korea Switzerland Thailand Turkey Ukraine Vietnam

Oxford is a registered trade mark of Oxford University Press
in the UK and in certain other countries

Published in the United States
by Oxford University Press Inc., New York

© Oxford Institute for Energy Studies 2009

The moral rights of the author have been asserted
Database right Oxford Institute for Energy Studies (maker)

First published 2009

British Library Cataloguing in Publication Data

Data available

Library of Congress Cataloguing in Publication Data

Data available

Cover designed by Clare Hofmann
Typeset by Philip Armstrong, Sheffield
Printed by Information Press, Eynsham, Oxfordshire

ISBN 978-0-19-955991-6

1 3 5 7 9 10 8 6 4 2

CONTENTS

ILLUSTRATIONS

Figures

CONTRIBUTORS

Monica Enfield is Manager, National Oil Company Strategies Service, PFC Energy.

Bassam Fattouh is Senior Research Fellow at the Oxford Institute for Energy Studies.

Mikkal Herberg is BP Foundation Senior Research Fellow for International Energy at the Pacific Council on International Policy.

Robert Orttung is a senior fellow at the Jefferson Institute and a visiting fellow at the Center for Security Studies at the Swiss Federal Institute of Technology (ETH) in Zurich.

Jeronim Perovic is a visiting fellow at the Center for Security Studies at ETH Zurich and a scientific collaborator with the Department of History at the University of Basel.

John M. Roberts is the Energy Security Specialist for Platts energy services.

Tanvi Madan is Harrington Doctoral Fellow, L.B.J. School of Public Affairs, the University of Texas at Austin.

Roger Tissot is an energy fellow at the Institute of the Americas (www.iamericas.org/) and a partner in the Brazil-based consulting firm Gasenergy (www.gasenergy.com.br).

Michael E. Webber is Assistant Professor, Mechanical Engineering; Associate Director, Center for International Energy & Environmental Policy; Fellow, Strauss Center for International Security and Law; all at the University of Texas at Austin.

Andreas Wenger is Professor of International and Swiss Security Policy and Director of the Center for Security Studies (www.css.ethz.ch) at ETH Zurich.

ACKNOWLEDGMENTS

The research presented here was originally undertaken for a conference entitled 'Energy and the Transformation of International Relations: Global Perspectives,' which took place 26–27 October 2007 at ETH Zurich. Based on discussions during the conference and comments from the editors following the collapse in oil prices in Fall 2008, the contributors revised their chapters at least twice.

We would particularly like to thank the participants of ETH energy security events who provided useful comments to the authors in preparing the resultant chapters. They were Pami Aalto, Margarita Balmaceda, Michael Bradshaw, Kyrre Elvenes Braekhus, Stefan Brem, Christian Cleutinx, Stacy Closson, Michael Da Costa, Stefan Dörig, Matteo Fachinotti, John Gault, Roland Götz, Tim Guld, Philip Hanson, Graeme Herd, Jan Kalicki, Sergei S. Kolchin, Viacheslav Kulagin, Ivan Kurilla, Andrei Makarychev, Silvia Mathis, Elena Merle-Beral, Tatiana Mitrova, Andrew Monaghan, Julia Nanay, Indra Overland, Nina Poussenkova, Liliana Proskuriakova, Peter Rutland, Oliver Schelske, Peter Sparding, Bill Tompson, and Peter Zweifel. We would like to thank Christopher Findlay for his editorial help and Frank Haydon for creating the maps. We are also grateful to Jennifer Gassmann and Silvia Azzouzi for excellent logistical help in Zurich. Despite the support of colleagues, the editors remain solely responsible for any errors in the text.

LIST OF ABBREVIATIONS

ANP	Agencia Nacional do Petroleo (Brazil)
ANWR	Alaska National Wildlife Refuge
b/d	Barrels per day
BBC	British Broadcasting Corporation
bcm	Billion cubic metres
BEE	Bureau of Energy Efficiency (India)
BNEA	Bolivia Northeast Argentina gas pipeline
boe	Barrels of oil equivalent
BP	British Petroleum
BPS	Baltic Pipeline System
BTC	Baku–Tbilisi–Ceyhan pipeline
BTU	British Thermal Unit
CAFE	Corporate Average Fuel Economy
CCS	Carbon Capture and Storage
CIL	Coal India Limited
CNOOC	China National Offshore Oil Company
CNPC	China National Petroleum Corporation
CO_2	Carbon dioxide
CPC	Caspian Pipeline Consortium
CREZ	Competitive Renewable Energy Zones
CTL	Coal-to-Liquids
DOE	Department of Energy (USA)
E&P	Exploration and Production
ECLAC	United Nations Economic Commission for Latin America and the Caribbean
ECOWAS	Economic Community of West African States
EIA	Energy Information Administration (USA)
EISA	Energy Independence and Security Act (USA)
EITI	Extractive Industries Transparency Initiative
EPA	Environmental Protection Agency (USA)
EPACT 2005	Energy Policy Act of 2005 (USA)
EPE	Energy Policy for Europe
ERI	Energy Research Institute (China)
ESPO	East Siberia–Pacific Ocean pipeline
EU	European Union
FBR	Fast Breeder Reactor
FDI	Foreign Direct Investment

FIT	Feed-In Tariffs
FT	*Financial Times*
FY	Fiscal Year
GCC	Gulf Cooperation Council
GDP	Gross Domestic Product
GECF	Gas Exporting Countries' Forum
GHG	Greenhouse Gases
GNP	Gross National Product
Gt	Gigatonne
GW	Gigawatt
HDI	Human Development Index
IEA	International Energy Agency
IEF	International Energy Forum
IMF	International Monetary Fund
IOC	International Oil Company
ITER	International Thermonuclear Experimental Reactor
ITT	Ishipungo, Tambococha, Tiputini oil project (Ecuador)
kb/d	Thousand barrels per day
LNG	Liquefied Natural Gas
LPG	Liquid Petroleum Gas
mb/d	Million barrels per day
MOU	Memorandum of Understanding
mpg	Miles per gallon
MPNG	Ministry of Petroleum and Natural Gas (India)
MT	Million tons
Mtce	Metric tons carbon equivalent
Mtoe	Million tons of oil equivalent
MW	Megawatt
NAFTA	North American Free Trade Agreement
NDRC	National Development and Reform Commission (China)
NEA	National Energy Administration (China)
NEC	National Energy Commission (China)
NIOC	National Iranian Oil Company
NNPC	Nigerian National Petroleum Corporation
NOC	National Oil Company
NOGC	National Oil and Gas Companies
NRDC	National Resource Defense Council
NSG	Nuclear Suppliers' Group
OECD	Organization for Economic Cooperation and Development
ONELG	Office of the National Energy Leading Group (China)
ONGC	Oil and Natural Gas Corporation

OPEC	Organization of Petroleum-Exporting Countries
OVL	ONGC Videsh Limited
OWEM	OPEC World Energy Model
P&O	Peninsular and Oriental Steam Navigation Co.
PDVSA	Petroleos de Venezuela S.A.
Pemex	Petróleos Mexicanos
PRD	Party of the Democratic Revolution (Mexico)
PRI	Institutional Revolutionary Party (Mexico)
PSA	Production Sharing Agreement
QP	Qatar Petroleum
R&D	Research and Development
RPS	Renewable Portfolio Standards
RTS	Russian Trading System
SCO	Shanghai Cooperation Organization
SCP	South Caucasus Pipeline
SED	Strategic Economic Dialogue
SENER	Mexico's Secretary of Energy
SEPA	State Environmental Protection Agency (China)
SLOC	Sea Lines of Communication
SO_2	Sulphur dioxide
SPR	Strategic Petroleum Reserve
tcf	Thousand cubic feet
tcm	Thousand cubic metres
TCP	Trans-Caspian Pipeline
TGI	Turkey–Greece-Interconnector
UGSS	United Gas Supply System
VLCC	Very Large Crude Carrier
WEO	World Energy Outlook
WMD	Weapons of Mass Destruction
YPFB	Yacimientos Petroliferos Fiscales Bolivianos

PART I

INTRODUCTION

CHAPTER 1

THE CHANGING INTERNATIONAL ENERGY SYSTEM AND ITS IMPLICATIONS FOR COOPERATION IN INTERNATIONAL POLITICS

Robert Orttung, Jeronim Perovic, Andreas Wenger

The current global energy system is not sustainable. Addressing this problem will be a source of change in the larger international political system and will reflect larger changes in that system.

The world is witnessing a major transformation in the nature of the relationship between producers and consumers of energy. The old system, which existed from about 1980 until 2003, was characterized by relatively cheap energy, energy consumption largely concentrated in the West, producers with excess capacity, little awareness of the consequences for the environment of burning fossil fuels, and a general lack of interest in promoting causes such as energy efficiency and alternative sources of energy to replace the traditional reliance on coal, oil, and natural gas.

Numerous changes in markets, politics, and environment mark the new system as being different from the old. First, the energy markets are now characterized by extreme price volatility, investment insecurity, and the rise of large new consumers in Asia. Since approximately 2003, oil prices rose from $20–$30 a barrel to a high of $147 a barrel (July 2008) before dropping below $50 by the end of 2008. The rapid changes in prices and a volatile political environment in many of the producing countries meant that investors had difficulty in defining whether they wanted to proceed with large energy production projects, or if it makes more sense to wait for an undefined future date. Developing countries like China and India have greatly increased demand for energy and opened up new markets, meaning that producers no longer have to rely solely on customers in the West.

Second, in political terms, state-run national oil companies (NOCs) now have much greater power while energy production is increasingly concentrated in a small number of countries. Unlike in the old system, when a few Western private international oil companies controlled the bulk of the world's oil, now, around four-fifths of the known oil and gas reserves are in the hands of state-owned NOCs. Working with these companies has become very important for private companies, in order to gain access to global reserves and to make sure there is enough investment to keep up with the rise in global demand. It is the NOCs that now define the terms of engagement when it comes to actual collaboration with producers. Over time, the Middle East is expanding its importance as an oil producer, while Russia is becoming increasingly powerful as a gas supplier. The result is more assertive producers and increasingly heterogeneous consumers.

Third, there is also a new awareness of the phenomenon of global warming and its potentially catastrophic effect on the planet. With the long-term trend toward generally higher energy prices and increased concern about the environmental consequences of burning fossil fuels, there is growing demand for promoting energy efficiency and developing renewable sources of energy. Energy consumers, and many producers, now realize that the days when enhancing energy security was simply a matter of increasing the size and diversity of supplies are over. Now energy security also means implementing policies designed to reduce the demand for energy. The need to adopt such conservation naturally imposes difficult choices on national and international leaders. Each country has to decide how to reduce its own demand, and the international community has to decide how to split the burden between the USA, the European Union (EU), and developing countries such as China and India.

Whether the search for energy security will lead to greater international conflict or cooperation remains an open question. The outcome hinges on what kind of energy policies countries pursue. If they seek simply to increase supplies of fossil fuels, then countries will inevitably come into conflict as they chase after ever-declining resources. However, if countries focus on the demand-side, seeking to increase energy efficiency and alternative sources of energy, then they there will be many more opportunities for cooperative action. Additionally, both consumers and producers share an essential desire to maintain the stability of the energy system. Disruptions and shocks would ultimately hurt the interest of all parties involved. In this context, climate change represents a truly global challenge that will require international efforts to resolve. The development of new efficiency technologies and alternative energy sources also provides great opportunities for cooperation.

This introductory chapter will lay out what has changed since 2003 in the global energy system. These changes make it necessary to re-examine the producer–consumer relationship. It will then briefly describe the overall energy situation, providing the reader with the numbers to summarize levels of reserves, production, and consumption. Finally, it will offer a roadmap of the chapters that make up the rest of this book.

Key Changes in the Energy Producer–Consumer Framework Since 2003

The current energy situation represents a dramatic break from the past and deserves extensive analysis. This section will look at three kinds of change: changing markets, the changing political conditions for producer–consumer cooperation, and the greater awareness of global warming.

Changing Markets

A key change in the energy markets from the 1980s and 1990s era of cheap oil is the incredible amount of price volatility beginning around 2003. Prices rose dramatically from that time until the middle of 2008, and then just as dramatically dropped below $50, although they did not return to their previous levels and remained historically high. This volatility is bad for both producers and consumers because it makes it extremely difficult to plan business activities. With a lack of clarity in prices, investors are unsure where they can best place their funds, making it difficult to develop new sources of fossil fuel as well as finding funding for alternative energy and efficiency projects.

The rise of China and India as major energy consumers means that there are now three types of players in the system: producers, traditional consumers within the OECD area (the USA, Europe, and Japan), and new consumers (China, India, and other Asian countries). We will refer to these three groups frequently throughout the following chapters. Each of these three groups has its own set of interests.

The producers represented in this book demonstrate two key trends: a growing concentration of location in production, and greater energy nationalism. The Middle East countries are the main oil producers, while Russia is the key source of natural gas, especially for Europe. The smaller, but increasingly important, producers in Latin America and Africa make it possible for some of the major consumers to diversify their supplies. However, these countries, particularly those in South America, reflect the growing trend of resource nationalism. Africa also shows some signs of resource nationalism, but it is an outlier in that it is open for business to the international oil companies and, due to the lack of local development, the vast majority of its oil is available for export.

The traditional consumers, represented in this book by the USA and Europe, have interests that differ from the producers and the new consumers. The traditional consumers are Western countries that are wealthy compared to the rest of the world. The USA's key interaction with the international energy sphere is through the global oil market, since it has significant domestic sources of energy. The USA (along with Russia) is a country that simultaneously is a major producer and consumer of energy. Accordingly, its relationships with Saudi Arabia and China are critical for shaping the contours of international energy flows. Europe is a less important energy player. In contrast to the USA, it is dependent on both the global oil and natural gas markets, and is particularly vulnerable to Russia. Europe has gone a lot farther in terms of developing energy efficiency and alternative sources than the USA.

The new consumers include China and India and other rising Asian powers. These developing countries are going through profound transformations, as rural residents move into the city and for the first time have heated homes and access to cars and motorcycles. The result is a massive new demand for energy. In fact, China's growing energy needs make it the main driver of world demand. China's current energy situation is unsustainable, and it has therefore become a major international player, as its need for additional energy drives it to find new supplies in Asia, the Middle East, Africa, and Latin America. Though its expansion has not been as rapid as China's, India is also a major source of growing energy demand on a global scale. Accordingly, it often competes with China for new sources of energy, though, in some cases, its NOCs have learned to cooperate with Chinese companies so that they do not simply bid up prices for available resources.

Changing Political Environment

Despite the increasing importance of Africa and Latin America, energy production is increasingly concentrated in the Middle East and Russia. Middle Eastern producers will provide the major new sources of oil, while Russia takes advantage of its extensive gas reserves.

At the same time, producing countries have greatly increased their reliance on state-controlled national oil companies. Many countries felt that the market did not serve all interests equally. To better protect their specific interests, Norway, Russia, China, India, Venezuela, and countries in the Middle East have, among others, used their states to exert greater power over their natural resources. As a result, today state energy monopolies control the vast majority of oil and gas reserves. NOCs control 77 per cent of the world's oil reserves, international oil companies (IOCs), like ExxonMobil, the Royal Dutch Shell Group, BP, and ChevronTexaco control 10 per cent, NOCs and IOCs jointly control 7 per cent, and Russian oil companies control 6 per cent.[1] Nevertheless, despite their limited access to reserves, the IOCs lead the pack as the world's largest energy producers. The increased role of the state in global energy markets means that governments that are not necessarily friendly to Western interests have a much greater say in the international sphere.

These developments naturally create new worries for the consuming countries. Politicians in the consuming countries often like to score easy points by making populist calls for energy independence. Such efforts set up an energy dilemma in which efforts by consumers to reduce their dependence on producers naturally provoke similar responses among the producers to reduce their reliance on the consumers, ultimately establishing an unhappy spiral as both sides work away from each other.

The system seems destined to create increased competition and conflict as long as both sides focus on supply-side solutions and seek to increase their access to fossil fuel deposits. However, by emphasizing a greater focus on the demand-side, particularly by promoting energy efficiency and the development of alternative sources, it will be possible to engage in greater cooperation. The difficulty here is that demand-side policies are a function of domestic politics, and therefore efforts to affect demand depend heavily on the domestic choices of a country's political system. Ultimately, however, domestic coalitions will have to reach across national borders to form the kind of international networks which will be needed to address complex problems such as global warming.

Greater Awareness of Global Warming

A third change that is transforming the producer–consumer energy framework is the greater worldwide awareness of global warming. There is now an international consensus that the use of fossil fuels is causing climate change. Traditional consumers, new consumers, and producers are responding differently to the problems posed by the changing climate, but all three groups have made the issue part of their policies.

The traditional consumers now realize that their current energy policies are unsustainable. They accept that it is not possible to simply seek out new sources of oil and natural gas. Instead, it is necessary to focus on greater energy efficiency in order to reduce demand and to develop alternative sources of energy that can eventually replace fossil fuels.

The EU, in particular, has taken the lead in this direction, while the USA resisted such change during the Bush administration. However, the USA looks set to change course, as President Barack Obama has defined a strong interest in addressing climate change. The Europeans have set deadlines for concrete reductions in greenhouse gases by ratifying the Kyoto Protocol and adopting even more stringent limits on their own. Several EU countries have emphasized energy efficiency and have invested heavily in alternative sources of energy, such as wind power. The Americans, by contrast, have been unwilling to accept such stringent limits, fearing that it would hurt the business climate and limit the competitiveness of American business. However, shortly after coming into office, the Obama administration announced plans to introduce a cap and trade system to reduce greenhouse gas emissions as well as other environmentally-friendly measures.

To the dismay of the producers, the traditional consumers frequently assert that a combination of reduced demand through greater efficiency, and more extensive use of alternative sources will make it possible for them to reduce their dependence on the traditional energy-producing countries. Thus, while most forecasts predict rising energy demand, many producers worry that their traditional consumers will ultimately make good on their efforts to find alternative sources of energy, thereby reducing fossil fuel consumption needs.

The new consumers, like China and India, also accept the facts of climate change, but their populations want to enjoy the benefits of their new-found wealth. As a result, they are quickly growing in ways that produce increasing amounts of greenhouse gases. These economies are often extremely energy inefficient, so their growth has a relatively large impact on the environment. However, they argue that they should not be forced to give up the benefits of their growth, particularly when their standards of living are still not on the same level as Western countries. As a result, the issue of global warming is important in these countries, but it is embedded in more urgent questions of economic growth and the achieving of world-class living standards. Accordingly, they think that Western countries should take the lead in making the transition to an energy system that will be more environmentally sustainable.

Producers accept the problem, but are seeking ways to address it while ensuring that the world continues to rely primarily on fossil fuels. Saudi Arabia and other OPEC members, for example, stress the benefits of carbon capture technology, arguing that it allows consumers to use fossil fuels in an environmentally-friendly way.[2] Additionally, they have a common interest with the consumers in increasing the importance of energy efficiency. Greater efficiency in both producing and consuming countries will allow them to continue exploiting existing oil and gas fields while postponing investments to develop new fields. These new fields will naturally be more expensive to operate because they are in remote locations with inhospitable climates that are far from customer use centres. The producers ultimately share the consumers' interest in reducing CO_2 emissions because their countries will also be affected by the impact of global warming.

Global Energy Trends: Facts and Figures

This section seeks to lay out the basic facts of the energy situation so that it will be possible to place each of the subsequent chapters that deal with individual regions or countries in a global context.

Global Patterns

In 2006, the world produced 11,741 million tons of oil equivalent (Mtoe), up 92 per cent from 1973, when the figure was 6,115 Mtoe. Production of all types of energy, oil, natural gas, coal, nuclear, and renewable sources, grew during this period. In the 2006 total primary energy supply mix, oil made up 34.4 per cent, coal 26.0, gas 20.5, nuclear 6.2, combustible renewable and waste 10.1, and hydro 2.2.[3]

The countries with the largest reserves and production of oil, natural gas, and coal are listed in Tables 1.1–1.6. In terms of oil reserves, the Middle Eastern states, Venezuela, and Russia are the clear leaders, as shown in Table 1.1. If tar sands are included, Canada also joins these ranks. Russia and Saudi Arabia are the biggest crude oil producers, as shown in Table 1.2. Overall, OPEC produced 42 per cent of the world's crude oil in 2006.

While oil supplies are limited, there is no danger of the world running out of oil in the short term. The development of new technologies has made it possible to recover more oil from existing fields than was previously thought possible. Additionally, as the price of oil rises, new sources that have not been economically viable become so.

Russia, Iran, and Qatar have the largest natural gas reserves, as shown in Table 1.3. However, the largest producers of natural gas are Russia, the USA, and Canada, as shown in Table 1.4. Other countries, including those in the Middle East, do not produce nearly as much as these leaders.

The USA, Russia, China, Australia, and India have the world's

Table 1.1: Regions and countries with the largest oil reserves year end 2007

Region and Country	Reserves billion barrels	Share of total %
North America	**57.1**	**4.6**
Canada	27.7	2.2
USA	29.4	2.4
Latin America	**123.4**	**10.0**
Venezuela	87.0	7.0
Mexico	12.2	1.0
Brazil	12.6	1.0
Europe and Eurasia	**143.7**	**11.6**
Russia	79.4	6.4
Kazakhstan	39.8	3.2
Norway	8.2	0.7
Azerbaijan	7.0	0.6
European Union	6.8	0.5
Middle East	**755.3**	**61.0**
Saudi Arabia	264.2	21.3
Iran	138.4	11.2
Iraq	115.0	9.3
Kuwait	101.5	8.2
United Arab Emirates	97.8	7.9
Qatar	27.4	2.2
Africa	**117.5**	**9.5**
Libya	41.5	3.3
Nigeria	36.2	2.9
Algeria	12.3	1.0
Asia Pacific	**40.8**	**3.3**
China	15.5	1.3
India	5.5	0.4
World	**1237.9**	**100.0**

Notes: North America does not include Mexico.

Source: British Petroleum, *BP Statistical Review of World Energy,* June 2008
www.bp.com/statisticalreview

Table 1.2: The world's largest crude oil producers 2007

Country	mb/d	Share of 2007
Saudi Arabia	10.4	12.6
Russia	9.9	12.6
USA	6.9	8.0
Iran	4.4	5.4
China	3.7	4.8
Mexico	3.5	4.4
Canada	3.3	4.1
United Arab Emirates	2.9	3.5

Table 1.2: *Continued*

Country	mb/d	Share of 2007
Venezuela	2.6	3.4
Kuwait	2.6	3.3
Norway	2.6	3.0
Nigeria	2.4	2.9
Iraq	2.1	2.7
Algeria	2.0	2.2

Source: British Petroleum, *BP Statistical Review of World Energy*, June 2008
www.bp.com/statisticalreview

Table 1.3: Regions and countries with the largest natural gas reserves year end 2007

Region and Country	Reserves trillion cubic metres	Share of total %
North America	**7.61**	**4.3**
Canada	1.63	0.9
USA	5.98	3.4
Latin America	**8.10**	**4.6**
Venezuela	5.15	2.9
Europe and Eurasia	**59.41**	**33.5**
Russia	44.65	25.2
Turkmenistan	2.67	1.5
Uzbekistan	1.74	1.0
Kazakhstan	1.90	1.1
Ukraine	1.03	0.6
Azerbaijan	1.28	0.7
European Union	2.84	1.6
Middle East	**73.21**	**41.3**
Iran	27.80	15.7
Qatar	25.60	14.4
Saudi Arabia	7.17	4.0
United Arab Emirates	6.09	3.4
Iraq	3.17	1.8
Africa	**14.58**	**8.2**
Nigeria	5.30	3.0
Algeria	4.52	2.5
Asia Pacific	**14.46**	**8.2**
Australia	2.51	1.4
Indonesia	3.00	1.7
Malaysia	2.48	1.4
China	1.88	1.1
India	1.06	0.6

Source: British Petroleum, *BP Statistical Review of World Energy*, June 2008
www.bp.com/statisticalreview

largest coal reserves, as shown in Table 1.5, while China and the USA are the largest producers, followed by Australia, and India, as shown in Table 1.6. In 2006, coal was the world's fastest growing hydrocarbon, largely driven by China, according to the 2007 British Petroleum Statistical Review of World Energy.

Table 1.4: The world's largest natural gas producers, 2006

Country	Billion cubic metres	Share of total
Russia	607.4	20.6
USA	545.9	18.8
Canada	183.7	6.2
Iran	111.9	3.0

Source: British Petroleum, *BP Statistical Review of World Energy*, June 2008
        www.bp.com/statisticalreview

Table 1.5: Countries with the largest coal reserves, year end 2007

Country	Billion tons	Share of total
USA	247	28.6
Russia	157	18.5
China	115	13.5
Australia	77	9.0
India	56	6.7
South Africa	48	5.7
Ukraine	34	4.0
Kazakhstan	31	3.7

Source: British Petroleum, *BP Statistical Review of World Energy*, June 2008
        www.bp.com/statisticalreview

Table 1.6: Top coal producing countries, 2007

Country	Mtoe	Share of total
China	1289.6	41.1
USA	587.2	18.7
Australia	215.4	6.9
India	181.0	5.8
South Africa	151.8	4.8
Russia	148.2	4.7
Germany	51.5	1.6

Source: British Petroleum, *BP Statistical Review of World Energy*, June 2008
        www.bp.com/statisticalreview

The USA is by far the largest energy consumer in the world. With just 4.6 per cent of the world's population, it accounts for 22.5 per cent of the world's overall energy consumption. Likewise, the USA is the world's largest petroleum user, followed by China and Japan, as shown in Table 1.7. Currently, the world uses about 85 million barrels of oil a day (mb/d), according to the International Energy Agency's (IEA) 2007 *World Energy Outlook.*[4] The USA is also the largest natural gas consumer, followed by Russia, which is a major producer, as shown in Table 1.8. China currently leads the world's coal consumption, as shown in Table 1.9. Even with high prices since 2003, energy consumers generally continued to expand their usage until the economic crisis of 2008 hit.[5]

Table 1.7: Major world petroleum consumers, 2007

Country	Million tons	Share of total
USA	943.1	23.9
China	368.0	9.3
Japan	228.9	5.8
India	128.5	3.3
Russia	125.9	3.2
Germany	112.5	2.8
South Korea	107.6	2.7
Canada	102.3	2.6
Saudi Arabia	99.3	2.5
Brazil	96.5	2.4
France	91.3	2.3
Mexico	89.2	2.3
Italy	83.3	2.1
Spain	78.7	2.0
United Kingdom	78.2	2.0
Iran	77.0	1.9

Source: British Petroleum, *BP Statistical Review of World Energy*, June 2008
www.bp.com/statisticalreview

If the pre-crisis trends continue once the economy recovers, by 2030 the world's energy needs will be 50 per cent higher than they were in 2007, according to the IEA. China and India account for 45 per cent of this growth. Of the three major fossil fuels, coal use is likely to increase most rapidly by 2030, mainly driven by China and India.

Future Trajectories and Environmental Impact

According to the 2008 IEA reference scenario, the world's energy needs are going to expand greatly through 2030, from the 8.1 Mtoe consumed

Table 1.8: Major world natural gas consumers, 2007

Country	Billion cubic metres	Share of total
USA	652.9	22.6
Russia	438.8	15.0
Iran	111.8	3.8
Canada	94.0	3.2
United Kingdom	91.4	3.1
Japan	90.2	3.1
Germany	82.7	2.8
Italy	77.8	2.7
Saudi Arabia	75.9	2.6
China	67.3	2.3
Ukraine	64.6	2.2
Mexico	54.1	1.8
Uzbekistan	45.6	1.6
Argentina	44.1	1.5
United Arab Emirates	43.2	1.5
France	41.9	1.4
India	40.2	1.4
Indonesia	33.8	1.2
Malaysia	28.3	1.0

Source: British Petroleum, *BP Statistical Review of World Energy*, June 2008
www.bp.com/statisticalreview

Table 1.9: Major world coal consumers, 2007

Country	Mtoe	Share of total
China	1311.4	41.3
USA	573.7	18.1
India	208.0	6.5
Japan	125.3	3.9
South Africa	97.7	3.1
Russia	94.5	3.0
Germany	86.0	2.7

Source: British Petroleum, *BP Statistical Review of World Energy*, June 2008
www.bp.com/statisticalreview

in 2006 to the 17.7 Mtoe predicted in the reference scenario, or to the 15.8 Mtoe in the alternate scenario, which assumes that currently planned energy savings measures are actually implemented.[6] If current policies continue, fossil fuels will remain the dominant source of energy until 2030, accounting for over 80 per cent of the overall increase in energy demand between now and 2030. While the share of oil will drop, it will remain the largest single source in the global energy mix over the next quarter of a century or so.[7]

As of 2007, the USA and China are approximately tied as the world's largest producers of carbon dioxide (CO_2) in energy consumption, followed by Russia, Japan, India, and Germany. China's emissions are rapidly increasing as its economy continues to surge forward. The world produced 28 Gt of CO_2 in 2006[8] and this output could reach 42 Gt by 2030 if current trends continue.[9] Government action to limit CO_2 production could keep it to 34 Gt according to the IEA. While this is higher than today's output, it is not as bad as it could be if no measures are taken. Increased efficiency is accepted as the best way to reduce demand for energy, and the inefficient economies of China and India are the most likely to produce quick gains by incorporating new efficient technologies.

Roadmap for the Book

The following two chapters in the introductory section lay out the main issues of the book. The next section examines the issues facing the producer countries. Subsequently, we look at the consumers. Each of the regional or country chapters examine how changes in the international energy system affect the prospects for international cooperation and conflict. The concluding chapter ties together all of these observations to examine the overall prospects for cooperation and conflict.

In his introductory chapter 'Changing Markets, Politics, and Perceptions: Dealing with Energy (Inter-) Dependencies', Jeronim Perovic argues that recent developments in markets, politics, and perceptions mean that the traditional relationship between energy producers and consumers is now undergoing change. The key differences since 2003 include a rise in price volatility, which means that both consumers and producers must deal with the consequences. With great uncertainty about future prices, cooperation is difficult to organize. A second change is the rise of Asian consumers, who now compete with traditional consumers for new sources of energy, and provide producers with new markets outside the West. A third change is the rise of resource nationalism, as states in producing countries start to exert much greater power, and national oil companies increasingly take control over resources from international oil companies.

Despite their growing power, producers do not feel confident that demand for their energy will remain strong. While Western states argue for additional investments to expand production capacity, they also work hard to reduce their need to import energy, by increasing domestic energy efficiencies and developing alternative sources to the usual oil and gas.

Consumers are mainly concerned about secure supplies at affordable prices. They now feel more at risk than they did previously, particularly as they face new concerns about use of the 'oil weapon' and resource nationalism. They fear that the newly powerful state-run national oil companies will not invest enough to meet inexorably growing energy demands. Moreover, the consumers are concerned that terrorists will attack vulnerable energy infrastructure.

The challenge today is to find a new balance between producers and consumers that encourages mutual interdependence. Perovic offers several ways to proceed. First, he stresses the role for enhanced dialogue between producers and consumers, particularly including the new consumers China and India. Second, he stresses the need to identify ways for better cooperation between NOCs and IOCs. Third, he argues that the West must stop trying to assert its energy independence, and instead focus more attention on better managing the evolving producer–consumer relationship, which should stress the numerous ways the two sides can work together to mutual advantage.

In his companion introductory chapter 'Changing Energy Use Patterns: Increasing Efficiency, Adopting Alternative Sources', Robert Orttung points to global climate change as having a growing impact on the producer–consumer relationship. The growing awareness of climate change means that many individuals in producing and consuming countries alike are coming to the realization that a fossil-fuel-based energy system is no longer sustainable. As a result there is a much greater push for increased energy efficiency and for the development of renewable energy sources. Increasing energy efficiencies is a solution that can be implemented relatively quickly in the short term, while successfully pursuing the search for alternative energies will take much longer. These policies are largely domestic, but they have clear international implications, particularly in that they create some apprehension within producing countries that demand for their product will drop.

The global threat of climate change provides a strong impetus for cooperation, since all countries face this problem. However, achieving such cooperation will not be easy as the producers, traditional consumers, and new consumers all have different interests. Representatives of the three groups of countries have a different sense of who should do what and when. Undoubtedly, the obstacles to collective action are enormous. In the political realm, they include many of the current tax and subsidy systems which are in place. In the economic sphere, the key is the high price required to make the transition from the current energy system to one based on alternative sources. There are also difficult technical issues, since each new source of alternative energy comes with trade-offs. For example, increasing ethanol production based on corn increases the cost of food.

The chapter argues that even if domestic policies in these areas are effective, we will still need to have international governance to make the link between energy security and climate change. It must be clear to fossil fuel producers that they will benefit from improved efficiency. In fact, producers will benefit because greater efficiency will help improve their environment while extending the benefits they can derive from their resources. Since energy-producing countries are among the most inefficient energy users in the world, greater efficiency will also allow them to put more resources into diversifying their economies. While the relatively rich traditional energy consumers are prepared to move ahead, new consumers do not have the resources to do so. This situation could provide the USA and Europe with opportunities to engage countries like China and India in a variety of new cooperative efforts. The existing international institutions, such as the IEA, are not sufficient, and it will be necessary to develop new possibilities to make the link between energy security and climate change, to ensure a joint response to this problem. Leadership by example and increased information exchange among countries will be crucial.

The next section of the book examines energy producing regions and countries. In his chapter 'How Secure Are Middle East Oil Supplies?' Bassam Fattouh lays out the perspective of the world's most important energy producer. He asserts that in the light of the Middle East's record as a reliable supplier, consuming countries exaggerate the threat to Middle Eastern production. Instead, he argues that a more useful approach is to assess under which circumstances the region would cease to act (willingly or unwillingly) as a reliable supplier, the chances of these events occurring, and, in the event of a disruption, how big the impact is likely to be on oil supplies and productive capacity. He finds that, with the exception of the US invasion of Iraq in 2003, most recent major oil disruptions took place in OPEC countries outside the Middle East.

Fattouh examines the possibilities of wars and conflicts, political instability, the rise of Islamists, anti-colonial feelings, terrorist attacks, oil export restrictions, and the closure of oil transit choke points, and concludes that the probability that any of the events will occur is quite low. Since conventional analysis assigns a high probability that these events will take place, with severe consequences in terms of output and productive capacity, the potential threats from the Middle East are overstated. Fattouh also notes that Middle Eastern countries are addressing investment concerns by working to increase capacity, with Saudi Arabia planning to increase oil output and Qatar working to increase oil and gas production capacity. However, Saudi Arabia is unlikely to reproduce the spare capacity it had in the mid-1980s unless there is a significant drop in world demand.

Fattouh concludes that efforts to reduce dependency on Middle Eastern oil may prove unrealistic and counter-productive, since there are few good alternatives to this source of energy supply in the short- to medium-term. If the consuming countries want to ease the impact of supply disruptions, their best bet is to develop their strategic reserves, which is the only concrete and effective tool available to them.

In their chapter on 'Russia's Role for Global Energy Security', Jeronim Perovic and Robert Orttung start by pointing out that Russia is the world's largest oil and gas producer and its largest gas exporter. Russia is currently the main supplier of gas to Europe, and aspires to play a much more important role in Asia. Russia is likewise the main export route for energy producers in Central Asia (Kazakhstan, Turkmenistan, and Uzbekistan). Overall, Russia hopes to strengthen its already strong position in Europe, retain its predominance in Central Asia, and diversify its energy sales as much as possible into Asia.

Russia faces three challenges in trying to attain these goals, which require a large increase in production. First, the Russian state is playing a much larger role in the energy sector, and it is not clear that it will be able to manage production growth to meet the rapidly increasing requirements of Europe and Asia. Currently, the state-controlled energy companies Gazprom and Rosneft lack sufficient capital and technical know-how to complete new upstream projects, while insecure property rights and state pressure prevent outside companies from investing. A second problem is that Russia's state monopolies are concentrating their investment in distribution pipelines, particularly in European countries, rather than creating new production capacity, because they see higher profits in distribution than production. A third issue is that Russian domestic gas consumption is likely to increase over time, leaving less gas for export.

Addressing the challenges in the Russian energy sector will have a great impact on the level of conflict and cooperation with Russia's neighbours. Russian and European energy cooperation has been increasing in recent years, but growing political tensions between the EU and Russia threaten to undermine these ties. In relations with Central Asia, Russia is no longer able to import relatively cheap gas from these countries, enabling it to export its own gas to Europe at a much higher price. While continuing their relationships with Russia, the Central Asians are now demanding higher prices and looking for alternative partners, such as China, who will help them diversify away from dependence on Russia. Russia sees Asian energy markets as a way to diversify its sales away from their current extensive dependence on Europe, and as a stimulus in developing eastern Siberia and the Russian Far East. However, little progress has been made so far in developing the fields or in building pipelines, because China has not been willing to pay an acceptable price for Russian energy, while Japan, technically at war with Russia since the end of WWII, has been unable to reach agreement with Russia for new supplies beyond the existing projects on Sakhalin. In this light, Europe appears to be a more reliable partner.

In 'Africa in the Context of Oil Supply Geopolitics', Monica Enfield points out that Africa produces energy for export to North American, European, and Asian demand centres without consuming much energy itself. The continent has significant upside potential for exploration, and is almost unique in that it is generally open to foreign investment by IOCs. African oil exports to Europe are replacing declining North Sea output. In the wake of 9/11, the USA is also interested in increasing supplies from the continent. African crude is high quality and therefore in great demand in Asia, where the less complex refineries prefer the kind of simple oil found in Africa.

Emerging trends in Africa are having an impact on oil supply geopolitics. Africa suffers from the resource curse, and African oil producers have not used their wealth effectively to promote development in their countries. Accordingly, the continent suffers from low levels of democracy, high conflict, financial problems, and extensive corruption. Additionally, increased resource nationalism in Africa is now driving the countries to seek greater returns on their assets from the IOCs operating there, as well as increased investments by outsiders in other parts of the economy. Community activists inside Africa are increasingly demanding that the existing rentier states distribute resource benefits more equitably among all stakeholders. Despite these greater demands, nationalizations of the types seen in Latin America are unlikely, because African companies do not have the resources to develop local reserves.

Africa is having an increasing impact on global markets and international relations. Instability in Africa has the ability to restrict the flow of resources to consuming countries. Tightening fiscal terms and higher local content requirements driven by resource nationalism will affect the timing and pace of development projects that outsiders can operate. Africa has also become a stage for potential conflict between traditional consumers and new consumers, as both the USA and China seek to lock up new sources of oil. Nevertheless, there is room for cooperation. China relies on the USA's ability to keep maritime shipping lanes open in order to receive its energy supplies. Africa is also playing a role in providing more energy to Europe, thereby relieving European concerns about Russian supplies. Since Africa's reserves are relatively small, its increased production will not create much of a threat to the larger producers in the Middle East and Russia.

Roger Tissot's chapter 'Energy Security in Latin America', points out that the region's reserves are slightly less than those found in Africa, but much less than the Middle East's available reserves. Nevertheless, Latin America is particularly important as a key supplier to the USA. The key trends defining the energy situation in the region are: declining reserves in key producers such as Mexico and Colombia; increasing resource nationalism in Venezuela, which holds 70 per cent of the region's oil reserves and nearly 60 per cent of its natural gas; and the rise of indigenous movements that have sought greater control over resource wealth, particularly in such countries as Bolivia and Ecuador.

These trends within Latin America have strong implications for the way in which the continent interacts with the rest of the world. The rise of Latin American NOCs has made it difficult, but not impossible, for IOCs to operate in the region. Likewise, the way in which the individual countries have responded to globalization has greatly affected their influence on international energy markets. Anti-globalizers like Venezuela's Hugo Chavez have attacked US and IOC interests, but provide new openings to NOCs and new consumers like China. In contrast, soft-globalizers like Brazil have adopted a much more pragmatic approach, ending national oil company Petrobras' monopoly and attracting foreign investment to the country. Pro-globalizers, such as Mexico, Central America, Chile, Peru, and Colombia, have sought to work much more closely with the USA, though Mexico has so far blocked private access to its energy sector. Ultimately, the result is that the USA is facing many challenges to its traditional dominance in the region.

The third section of the book examines the situation of energy consuming countries. In his analysis of US energy policy, Michael Webber begins with the observation that the USA is the largest energy user by far, in overall terms and on a per capita basis. Currently the USA imports one-third of its energy, with most of these imports coming from global oil markets, which is the USA's main point of contact with the global energy system. The USA is also one of the world's largest energy producers and a leader in developing innovative technology for energy efficiency and alternative sources.

Because the USA is such a large consumer of energy, its future policy choices have an enormous impact on international politics, Webber argues. If the USA decides to pursue more supply-side solutions, seeking to import more energy from international markets, then it is more likely to come into conflict with a variety of traditional and new consumers also looking for more energy. If, instead, the USA begins to push demand-side solutions, such as increasing efficiency and finding alternatives to oil on the basis of technological innovation, then there will be much greater opportunity for international cooperation with the other consuming states. However, producing states will be more likely to oppose such changes, and it will be necessary to find a way of working with them as well. Additionally, US politicians have been increasingly calling for 'energy independence'. While perhaps attractive to American voters, such appeals could prove alienating to the rest of the world (producers and consumers alike) and upset the current system of mutual dependencies.

The USA, particularly during the Bush administration, has also had major disagreements with Europe and others over the seriousness of climate change and what steps should be taken to address it. Europe, for example, has made energy more expensive than it is in the USA, through its taxation policies. The future US approach toward global warming will also have a major impact on the level of conflict or cooperation in the international energy system. Barack Obama's victory in the 2008 presidential elections suggests that the USA will seek to become a leader in addressing climate change, but doing so will require overcoming the efforts of powerful interest groups.

In examining 'Energy Challenges for Europe', John Roberts points out that the 27 countries of the EU are collectively the third largest energy consumer in the world. Even though Europe's overall energy demand is shrinking, domestic supplies are drying up even faster, and Europe will increasingly find itself reliant on imports, particularly imports of natural gas from Russia. At the same time, Europe has set ambitious goals for protecting the global environment, increasing energy efficiency, and developing alternative sources of energy.

On the supply side, the major concern for Europe is the reliability of Russian natural gas, particularly since Russia shut off supplies to Europe at the beginning of 2006 and 2009. The main problem is the asymmetry between the two sides: While Europe favours open markets, Russia's system emphasizes a strong state. Accordingly, because of the problems with Russia, Europe is seeking to diversify supplies by increasing imports from other areas, including North Africa, the Caspian, Central Asia, and potentially Iran. On the demand side, Europe is trying to cut its reliance on imports, whether from Russia or other countries, by reducing its overall need for energy.

In the sphere of international relations, Europe's major task is to improve ties with Russia. In fulfilling this goal, Europe can draw on the possibility of offering long term investments for the development of Russian energy in exchange for long term Russian commitments to supply energy to Europe. The EU can offer Russia access to its wealth, recognize Russia's energy security concerns, and help Russia improve its poor energy efficiency record. In moving forward, however, the EU will have to demand more economic reform in Russia, including the obtaining of Russia's agreement to the principles of the Energy Charter Transit Protocol.

In 'Fuelling the Dragon: China's Energy Prospects and International Implications', Mikkal Herberg assesses the impact of China's rapidly growing demand for energy. China is already the world's second largest energy consumer after the USA, and its swiftly growing needs are transforming international energy markets. Like the USA, China has mainly focused on increasing its energy supplies. Since coal, a heavy polluter, makes up 70 per cent of China's commercial energy mix, China managed to surpass the USA as the world's largest emitter of greenhouse gases in 2007. With its continuing growth and the accompanying pollution, China's current energy use picture is not sustainable, meaning that within the next decade it will have to adopt new policies requiring better demand management, more efficiency, and the production of fewer greenhouse gases.

China faces enormous challenges in reducing its voracious demand for energy while maintaining its high growth rates. China's industrial structure, growing consumer demand, and concern about slowing the economic and job growth machine make it difficult to change energy policies. China has no choice but to increase its dependence on international energy markets. Accordingly, China has encouraged its companies to participate in a 'go out' policy to invest in oil supplies globally. Such policies naturally have the potential to increase conflict, as other countries also try to gain control of the same supplies. Tensions have increased in USA–China relations, for example, because of Chinese efforts to work with Iran and Sudan. In Asia, China's emergence has increased fears among Japan, South Korea, and India of a growing competition to control energy supplies.

Nevertheless, there are many opportunities for international cooperation. China has so far focused on gaining physical control of more energy supplies through national company equity investments. A more effective approach would be to secure access to global supplies rather than ownership. Through this approach, there is more potential for cooperation with the IEA and other international organizations. China may have more opportunities for cooperation with Russia, as it develops its East Siberian resources. Additionally, there are extensive opportunities for cooperation if China starts to take seriously the need to reduce overall energy demand. The key for cooperation here is for Europe, the USA, and China to link the issues of energy security and climate change into one package.

In 'India's Quest for Energy', Tanvi Madan points out that India is expected to overtake Japan and Russia as the world's third largest energy user by 2030. Like China, India relies heavily on domestic coal, but is increasingly dependent on the world market for supplies of oil and gas. In fact, India is now more dependent on oil imports than the USA or China.

India wants to be a strong, independent country with a seat at the international table. Like China and the traditional energy consumers, India is seeking to secure greater supplies abroad. In fact, India is trying to pursue a variety of goals simultaneously, and these sometimes come into conflict. Thus, for example, India wants to improve a strategic partnership with the USA, but that goal sometimes conflicts with its interests in the potential Iran–Pakistan–India pipeline or with increasing energy supplies from Myanmar, Sudan, and Venezuela. Pursuing each of these goals necessarily involves trade-offs and India must make its choices with limited resources.

India generally supports a policy of international cooperation, but it is not clear how such a policy will evolve. It is unlikely that India will try to form an Asian 'axis of oil' to compete with the IEA. Such a grouping would inevitably include China, and there is not yet a sufficient level of trust between the two countries for there to be extensive cooperation. Indian politicians (particularly the Communists), who do not trust the USA, suggest working more closely with Russia, but again this relationship is always viewed against the larger set of international ties, and India does not want to sacrifice improving relations with the West. India's leaders do not feel threatened by the international energy order, but they do want to be included in it more directly. Joint efforts to improve energy efficiency and develop alternative sources may provide grounds for cooperation. In short, India is trying to keep all of its options open.

Andreas Wenger's concluding chapter ties together these regional and country analyses to examine the prospects for future conflict and cooperation in world energy markets. Overall, if traditional and new consumer countries focus mainly on increasing their supplies, there is likely to be increased competition and conflict. However, if consuming countries place a greater focus on demand reduction through greater efficiency and alternative sources, then there will be greater opportunities for cooperation. Emphasizing whether countries choose supply or demand-side solutions highlights the link between domestic politics and international efforts. Moving toward a more sustainable energy system will depend on domestic choices regarding the balance between demand and supply-side efforts. Different political systems will produce different solutions at the national level. Therefore the EU and USA should lead by example at the international level, by trying to stimulate demand-side solutions in their relations with new consumers and producers.

The governance framework must be expanded, and stability will depend on three conditions, according to Wenger. First, there must diversity of supply, demand, and type of fuel throughout the entire system. Second, there must be expanded cooperation between traditional and new consumers, particularly China and the USA. Finally, it is necessary to adopt a new producer–consumer framework.

This new framework emphasizes that both producers and consumers have an interest in improved resilience of the global oil market. Strengthened dialogue and greater information sharing should improve coordination of strategic reserves, address investment problems, and develop cooperation to protect the entire supply chain. These efforts should take place at both the state and corporate levels. A crucial aspect of this process will be to ensure that producers see that they have an interest in increased efficiencies throughout the system, because reducing their own domestic demand will increase their export potential and help diversity their economies away from a heavy reliance on fossil fuels.

Notes

1   Amy Meyers Jaffe, 'The Changing Role of National Oil Companies in International Energy Markets', Presentation at the James A. Baker III Institute for Public Policy, Rice University, 1 March, 2007. www.rice.edu/energy/publications/docs/NOCs/Presentations/Hou-Jaffe-KeyFindings.pdf

2   See, for example, the 'Riyadh Declaration', adopted by The Third Summit of Heads of State and Government of OPEC Member Countries in Riyadh, Kingdom of Saudi Arabia, on 17–18 November 2007. Declaration published in: *OPEC Bulletin*, 12/2007, 32–5, (here page 35). www.opec.org/library/OPEC%20Bulletin/2007/pdf/OB122007.pdf.

3   International Energy Agency, *Key World Energy Statistics 2008*, IEA, Paris, 2008, 6.

4   IEA, *World Energy Outlook 2007*, IEA, Paris 2008

5 See British Petroleum, *BP Statistical Review of World Energy*, June 2008, www.bp.com/statisticalreview.

6 IEA, *Key World Energy Statistics 2008*, 28 and 46.

7 IEA, *Key World Energy Statistics 2008*, 46.

8 IEA, *Key World Energy Statistics 2008*, 44.

9 IEA, *World Energy Outlook 2007*, IEA, Paris, 2008, 192.

CHAPTER 2

CHANGING MARKETS, POLITICS, AND PERCEPTIONS: DEALING WITH ENERGY (INTER-) DEPENDENCIES

Jeronim Perovic

The financial crisis that hit the world in autumn 2008 might go down in history as 'a defining moment for economic globalization'.[1] What started as a crisis on the US mortgage market and on Wall Street soon took on international dimensions as it affected the whole global financial system, leading to an economic downturn in the USA, Europe, and Asia. The extent of the crisis took many by surprise, as it indicated just how globalized the world financial system had become, and how fragile it was, given that an event in one sector and one part of the globe would be able to have such a dramatic impact on other sectors and other regions. The crisis also demonstrated the power of perception: once people – or rather the media – decided that there was a crisis and it was going to turn worse, even the massive state aid packages were unable to prevent stock markets all over the world from crumbling.

Another truly international market in which events both global and local can have a dramatic impact is the oil market. The price of oil depends on the balance of demand and supply, which is, however, not only sensitive to market forces, but political turmoil in producer countries, regional conflicts, harsh winters, the ups and downs of the US dollar (the currency that oil is traded in), and developments in global stock markets. Oil makes up almost 40 per cent of the world's energy consumption and is the single largest commodity traded on the global market; in 2006, crude oil had a share of 17 per cent in total global trade.[2] The oil market is unique, as oil is a commodity of central strategic importance to virtually all of the world's national economies. However, its price is hard to forecast, being subject to extreme volatility. In 2008 a barrel of oil traded for $100 in January, $147 in July and then fell below $40 in December.[3]

In a volatile market environment with almost no price predictability, producers and consumers alike must deal with the consequences. Before the autumn 2008 crisis, when the global economy was booming and supply for energy was tight because demand was rising fast, even a very minor local event – like an attack on a Nigerian oil pipeline – was able to drive the price of oil up. After the crisis, when demand fell and oil reserves piled up, not even the Organization of Petroleum Exporting Countries' (OPEC) decision to cut production by a historic 4.2 mb/d (decided at the OPEC meeting on 17 December 2008) had a significant impact on the commodity's price.[4]

Dependencies between buyers and sellers are an inherent condition of global trade and the international division of labour. However, the global context in which producers and consumers operate has been subject to continuing changes. Working together in this context has never been easy. In fact, the modern history of the producer–consumer relationship has been quite turbulent. The single most dramatic upheaval in the energy market occurred in 1973, when OPEC decided to withhold oil shipments to the USA and some of its Western allies because of their support of Israel in the Yom Kippur War. The embargo led to a 400 per cent increase in the price of oil, ultimately triggering recessions in a number of Western economies. In the long-run, however, the oil weapon was ineffective. Among other things, the high oil price led to overproduction, which ultimately brought prices down, and the massive inflow of petrodollars spurred inflation in the producers' economies. Eventually, the price of oil stabilized at a relatively low level. During much of the 1980s and 1990s, buyers gained the upper hand in the oil market and, at times, even resorted to economic sanctions against sellers.

From about 1999, oil prices started to rise again, but climbed sharply only after the USA-led invasion of Iraq in spring 2003; from this point onwards, conditions in the energy market have been changing, not as suddenly and dramatically as in 1973, but more fundamentally. Because global demand for oil was expected to grow faster than production, the energy market tightened and oil prices were high. While Organization for Economic Cooperation and Development (OECD) countries were the major destination market for Middle Eastern oil until recently, today China and other Asian countries have expanded the number of potential customers and thereby diversified demand. But even as demand rose, observers worried that a number of key producing states were under investing in the energy sector due to a combination of poor management practices and a surge in 'resource nationalism'. In fact, around four-fifths of the known global oil and gas reserves are today in the hands of national energy companies. In the high-price environment of 2003–08, power, it seemed, had definitely shifted back towards producers. Yet perceptions changed again after the financial crisis hit in autumn 2008, when, amidst falling oil prices, it became clear that no side was really able to shape developments on a market so tightly interconnected and so heavily exposed to 'glocalizing' forces.

Despite extreme interdependencies among producers and consumers, cooperation between these key actors continues to be highly problematic. Both producers and consumers are interested in the stability of the system, yet they each have different perceptions of what constitute key threats to the system, which ultimately also lead to different policy prescriptions to protect against these threats.

To be sure, consumers have worked with oil-rich producer-states in the Middle East, the post-Soviet space, Latin America, and elsewhere regardless of whether the regimes in these countries were democratically organized or adhered to Western-style liberal market principles. Yet, especially during the high-price market environment of 2003–08, many countries increasingly perceived dependency on these states as a security threat. The anxiety in the West was not so much grounded in concern that there was too little oil on the market – in fact, the producers increased their production considerably during the boom years 2003–08 in order to satisfy growing demand – but the perception that growing dependency would leave consumers at the mercy of producers who *might* use their power and increasing wealth for a variety of non-commercial purposes – building up their military, deploying energy as a 'political weapon' against neighbours, buying up strategic assets in consumers' countries, or expanding domestic state security services in order to crack down on local civil societies. The producers criticize the Western consumers for misreading their intentions and insist they are mostly interested in a stable demand for their energy at the highest possible price. Also, what the West has pejoratively labelled 'resource nationalism' is a policy that producers claim will put their oil wealth to the best use for society's overall interests.

Regardless of whether the threats to the energy market are more perceived than real, the fact remains that producer–consumer relations are out of balance and the challenge is to find a new equilibrium that would ensure stable relations. If such an equilibrium cannot be reached, there is a real danger of what one observer has called the 'energy security dilemma'. Such a dilemma might occur when the two sides continue to feel insecure vis-à-vis each other and begin to make preparations in case the other intends to threaten it. These preparations create extra suspicion and provoke additional measures in order to better prepare for an eventual threat. Translated into energy relations, such preparations would result in an intense race to diversify purchases and sales away from each other – despite the fact of existing mutual dependencies.[5]

Thus, the way ahead is not further diversification away from each

other, but deepening existing interdependencies and finding new mutually beneficial ways of engaging with each other. Anything else might
further endanger the stability of the international energy market with
negative consequences for all parties involved. A successful partnership
requires, first and foremost, a deepened understanding of the nature of
interdependencies between producers and consumers. In order to avoid
misreading each others' intentions, there needs to be reliable information, not only on hard data regarding current and future demand and
supply volumes, but also on the larger national development strategies,
interests, and perceptions. Moreover, any new producer–consumer
governance model also needs to include the new Asian fossil fuel
importers, which have come to play an increasingly important role on
the global energy market.

This chapter starts by explaining in the *first* section the main characteristics of the global energy market as it evolved since 1973. The
second section analyses the changes that occurred over the past several
years and considers the economic and political consequences; it also
looks at changes taking place in public attitudes. The *third* section
considers the producers' perspective when analyzing the threats and
risks inherent to the new energy system. The *fourth* section looks at the
consumers' perspective. The *fifth* section then identifies intersections
of interests between producers and consumers in order to consider,
in the *sixth* section, some ideas on how to move beyond the current
producer–consumer stalemate.

Characteristics of the old system

The old system described here refers to the situation as it evolved after
the 1973 oil shock, when OPEC decided to embargo oil supplies to the
USA and some of its allies, through 2003, when prices started to rise
rapidly. The oil shock led to a sharp increase in oil prices, ultimately
spurring recessions in Western economies. Yet, while the producer
countries gained from high oil prices in the short run, overproduction
and a drop in global demand brought the price of oil down in the long
run. Ultimately, the system did not favour producers who were heavily
dependent on the Western export market. Moreover, Western states
were important for maintaining the stability of the market because
their armed forces helped ensure regional security – especially via the
USA military alliance with Saudi Arabia – and guaranteed the security
of the maritime routes for oil supplies.

On 17 October 1973, the members of OPEC[6] decided to embargo oil shipments to the USA and other states that backed Israel during the so-called Yom Kippur War. The embargo sent shock waves throughout the global oil market. At the time of the event, OPEC controlled over 50 per cent of global oil production, and its market leverage was considerable. Practically overnight oil prices increased by a factor of four. The embargo had economic repercussions not only for those directly targeted, but for the oil-importing countries in general. At this time, Europe did not have any substantial domestic production and imported all of its oil. Sixty per cent of Europe's oil originated from the Middle East. Due to high oil prices, the world financial system, which was already under pressure from the breakdown of the Bretton Woods agreement, suffered recession and high inflation, a situation that persisted until the early 1980s.[7]

The 1973 oil crisis showed Western consumers quite clearly how sensitive the market was to political crises and how precarious it was for the OECD-importing countries to be over-dependent on foreign oil, especially from the Middle East. The sense of vulnerability and exposure to foreign pressure was accompanied by another trend in the energy market: the nationalization of production and reserves in oil-rich countries. Up until the point when some Arab countries started nationalizing their oil industries in the 1960s, seven Western oil companies – the so called 'seven sisters' – controlled some 85 per cent of global oil and gas reserves.[8] During nationalization, many oil-producing states in the Middle East set out to gain control over their resources. This process accelerated after the 1973 crisis, when many Middle Eastern countries, among them Saudi Arabia, managed to completely nationalize their oil industries. The big Western oil companies were thus increasingly losing control over Middle Eastern oil reserves and production.

In retrospect, however, the Middle Eastern oil producers lost some of their market leverage due to the measures undertaken by the Western importing nations. Among these was the creation of the International Energy Agency (IEA) in 1974 as a forum in which Western oil importers could share information and discuss measures to prevent oil supply shocks; in this respect, a major achievement was the IEA's decision to create strategic oil reserves in each of the member states in order to withstand interruptions for up to 90 days.[9] Another major effect of the 1973 oil crisis was a reduction in demand for Middle East oil due to the development of non-OPEC oil production. Europe's dependency on Middle East oil decreased when new fields in the North Sea came online. In parallel to this, the Soviet Union emerged as a major alternative supplier of oil and gas. Non-OPEC oil was also coming online from new fields in Mexico, Canada, and Latin America. Ultimately,

OPEC's share in global oil production declined. In 1985, non-OPEC production reached the historically high level of 71 per cent of world total oil production.[10]

As a direct consequence of the 1973 oil crisis experience, Europeans and Americans also managed to significantly reduce their economies' oil intensity – the amount of oil used to generate each dollar's worth of gross domestic product (GDP) – by developing alternative sources of energy (including nuclear and natural gas) and increasing energy efficiency. It is important to note here, however, that while the US economy also lowered its oil intensity, it lagged significantly behind Europe's and Japan's efforts. Energy efficiency and the development of alternative energy, combined with a global recession, caused a reduction in demand which led to falling crude oil prices. Prices spiked during periods of turmoil in the Middle East, such as during the Iranian revolution of 1979 or the initial phase of the Iran–Iraq war in the early 1980s, but remained otherwise relatively stable, although at a higher price level than before 1973. This general picture is especially accurate for the period 1986–1999, which became known as the era of 'cheap oil'. Prices for oil reached a historic low of US$12 per barrel in January 1999. During this time, some of the oil-rich countries (Venezuela, Iran, Kuwait) reversed their previous policies and again opened up to foreign capital.[11]

A key element for guaranteeing the stability of the post-1973 system was the alliance between the USA and Saudi Arabia. This alliance was – and in fact remains to this day – vital for security of supply. In order to provide balance against a potential Iranian (and later Iraqi) threat, the USA guaranteed the security of Saudi Arabia, and US Marines protected the global oil supply routes. In return, Saudi Arabia shipped oil to the global market and made sure it maintained a high level of spare capacity – the difference between total liquids production capacity and actual output – in order to smooth out supply interruptions. Events in 1991 demonstrated the stability of the system when a USA-led coalition liberated Kuwait from Iraqi occupation. This invasion did not lead to any serious supply crisis since OPEC – driven by a Saudi initiative – agreed to increase production for the year in order to smooth out interruption shocks, ultimately keeping prices moderate.

The relative stability of the post-1973 system was thus due to a simple convergence of interests: The Middle East was interested in preserving the Western market for its oil. In return, the West took increasing control over economic and military security in the Middle East region. In addition to the USA–Saudi alliance, energy relations between Europe and the Soviet Union, which became increasingly important after 1973, were without problems, and remained largely trouble-free even after the collapse of the Soviet Union in 1991.

It is thus no surprise that energy has not been high on the security agenda of Western states for the past quarter of a century or so. The balance of the energy market was clearly in favour of consumers. If anything, it was the Middle Eastern oil producers who felt dependent on their Western customers, and it was these customers who frequently used energy sanctions as an instrument of foreign policy, blocking targeted countries from trade or investment.[12] Sanctions were imposed at different times against countries like Iraq, Iran, or Libya. As long as there was enough oil in the market, disputes with these countries did not affect prices greatly, and the system remained relatively stable.

Changing conditions: Energy security in the years of high oil prices

Beginning around the time of the 2003 Iraq war, the post-1973 system began to disintegrate due to changes in markets, politics, and perceptions. The major change in the market was the entrance of Asian consumers, which resulted in a tightening of supplies against ever-rising global demand. The heightened demand led to the erosion of spare capacity, which meant that the market could not smooth out interruptions easily. In addition, there were fewer investment opportunities for Western private energy companies in the traditional producers' markets since state-run National Oil Companies (NOCs) took control over the bulk of the world's remaining oil and gas. This situation drove up the price of oil and generated massive new wealth for producing countries and their companies. Only with the sharp drop in oil prices towards the end of 2008 did the picture start changing again.

Oil prices started to rise in 1999 once the impact of the Asian financial crisis, which had reduced global demand, had faded. The price for oil began to rise sharply and steadily from mid-2003 onwards, thanks largely to the loss of Iraqi production capacity following the US-led invasion and subsequent occupation, low inventories in the USA and other OECD countries, and the start of economic growth, which led to a rise in demand. At the same time, demand for oil grew at a rapid pace among Asian countries, particularly China. China became an oil importer only in 1993, yet by 2006 it had to import almost half of its total consumption. If the country's economy continues to grow at the high rate of past years, the IEA expects that China will account for about 30 per cent of the total growth in world energy demand up to 2030. According to 2007 IEA estimates, China and India together will account for 45 per cent of the total increase in world primary energy consumption (coal, oil, gas, nuclear, hydro, renewables) during the period up to 2030.[13]

OPEC therefore raised its output levels to meet fast-growing global demand for oil, which led to the erosion of excess production capacity. The low level of spare capacity provided the foundation for the high oil price environment between 2003 and 2008. A dearth of spare volumes meant that the market had little flexibility in adjusting to changes in demand. When Venezuelan oil workers went on strike in 2002–3, the USA, which then imported some 15 per cent of its oil from Venezuela, had been able to replace this oil via imports from other places. The existence of spare capacity then meant that the impact on prices was only moderate. After the invasion of Iraq in March 2003 and the steep drop in Iraqi oil production, however, excess capacity reached a historic low because most countries, including Saudi Arabia, were producing at near maximum capacity. Given the limited spare capacity, the whole system of energy flows became extremely interdependent – and vulnerable. In February 2006, for example, al-Qaeda affiliated terrorists carried out an unsuccessful attack on Saudi Arabia's Abqaiq oil refinery, the world's largest oil processing centre. The news of the plot was enough to push the oil price up by several dollars per barrel.[14]

Recent years of high oil prices saw another trend in the market, the resurrection of what Western commentators somewhat disparagingly label 'resource nationalism'. In a number of key producing states, including Russia and Venezuela, governments tightened conditions by calling off production sharing agreements (PSAs) and joint ventures, retracting concessions and licenses, and, in some cases, expropriating property outright. By 2005, national oil companies (NOCs) controlled a staggering 77 per cent of known global oil reserves. Private international oil companies (IOCs) had unrestricted access to less than ten per cent of the world's oil and gas resource base. Partially or fully privatized Russian companies owned an additional six per cent, (state-owned) NOCs and IOCs jointly exploited the rest on the basis of partnership agreements.[15]

Seven state-controlled companies became key global players in oil and gas – and in fact now comprise the 'new seven sisters', according to a *Financial Times* (FT) article published 11 March 2007. On the basis of resource volumes, output levels, company ambition, domestic market size, and industry influence, the FT included Saudi Arabia's Aramco, Russia's Gazprom, China's CNPC, Iran's NIOC, Venezuela's PDVSA, Brazil's Petrobras, and Malaysia's Petronas in its list. According to FT data, in 2007 the new seven sisters controlled about one-third of the world's oil and gas production and reserves. In contrast, descendants of the original seven sisters – the USA's ExxonMobil and Chevron, and Europe's BP and Royal Dutch Shell – produced only about ten per cent of the world's oil and gas, and held a meagre three per cent of its reserves. With high oil prices, the IEA estimated that state-controlled companies from the emerging world would grow even more powerful. In contrast to the previous 30 years, when publicly traded companies within the OECD produced over 40 per cent of all oil, during the next 30 years, 90 per cent of production could originate from a relatively small number of NOCs in the developing world.[16]

Between 2003 and 2008, oil money bolstered the financial position of producers, and provided them with new opportunities in the world market. In fact, the years of high fossil fuel prices witnessed a reverse globalization trend, with developing countries buying up assets in Western economies. From a Western perspective, this development acquired a political dimension if governments controlled the money invested, either through state-owned companies or via state funds.

Russia's dramatic change of fortune after 1999 is a case in point. In 1999, when the price for Urals crude hovered around $10 per barrel,[17] it took Russia three months to earn $2 billion; in 2007, Russia earned a similar amount of money from crude exports in less than a *week*.[18] The companies retained some of the funds and reinvested them in projects, both inside and outside the country. However, the state collected the lion's share of the profits in the form of taxes, duties, and fees and channelled them into state funds. In 2004, Russia set up an oil stabilization fund which accumulated $157 billion by January 2008.[19] At the same time, Russia also built up nearly $600 billion in foreign exchange reserves by the middle of 2008, making Russia the world's third-largest holder of such reserves after China and Japan at the time.[20] Russia's experience mirrored a general trend that saw the massive accumulation of wealth from oil and gas sales. Approximately 40 sovereign wealth funds managed $2.5 trillion around the world at the beginning of 2008.[21]

Not only were the conditions within the international financial market changing due to high energy prices, but oil wealth also started to affect entire regional balance-of-power systems, not least because of the massive rearmament of some oil-rich states. Largely thanks to oil income, Russia set out to rebuild its military after years of decline. It increased spending to US$34.7 billion in 2006 (up from US$19.1 billion in 2000) and in 2007 launched a US$189 billion programme to modernize its military in the period up to 2015.[22]

Russia was far from alone in buying new weapons. Azerbaijan, also in the post-Soviet space, has dramatically increased its military spending, largely thanks to oil export revenues. Baku's military expenses increased by 51 per cent during the period between 2004 and 2005 and by 82 per cent in 2006. In 2007, the military budget rose to $1.1 billion and to $1.85 billion in 2008. In response to Azerbaijan's military build-up, its neighbours Georgia and Armenia have also increased their defence spending.[23] The balances of power were also shifting in the Persian Gulf, where many countries dramatically increased military spending. In fact, the Persian Gulf countries represent some of the biggest military spenders in the world. In 2006, Saudi Arabia spent US$1,152 per capita on defence, or a total of US$29 billion – one of the highest per capita rates in the world.[24]

All these changes stirred considerable concern in the West and brought the issue of energy security to the top of the political agenda. According to *Transatlantic Trends 2007*, an annual opinion survey comparing American and European attitudes on transatlantic relations, 88 per cent of Americans and 78 per cent of Europeans in 2007 considered energy dependence to be a threat which was likely to affect their personal life. Interesting in this respect is that Americans and Europeans seem to be equally worried about a more assertive Russia: 59 per cent of those surveyed in Europe, and 58 per cent of Americans are concerned about 'Russia's role as an energy provider'.[25]

On top of growing public concern over foreign energy dependence, many people in the West also feared that peaceful means would not be sufficient to sort out competition for energy resources. According to the results of a 2006 *BBC World Service* survey in 19 countries, 77 per cent of respondents feared that energy shortages and rising prices would destabilize the global economy. Notably, 72 per cent believed that competition for resources would give rise to more conflicts.[26]

Ultimately, however, it was not high energy prices that triggered an economic downturn in the Western consuming countries (later engulfing the Asian energy consumers), but a home-made crisis which started in the US mortgage market. In early 2008, 'the fastest-growing bet' in the oil market was 'that the price of crude will double to $200 a barrel' by the end of 2008.[27] Instead, the financial crisis and global economic slowdown brought the price down from a $147 high in July to under $40 dollars in December, as demand for oil fell sharply and spare capacity grew. Should the economic crisis continue, spare capacity could, according to Cambridge Energy Research Associates, reach as much as 7 mb/d, or 8 per cent of demand, by 2010 (compared with less than 3 per cent in 2007).[28] Future oil prices depend on global economic growth, as well as many other factors, which include the ability of consuming countries to expand energy efficiency and to increase their use of renewable energy sources.

While many believed that power had shifted to the producers during the high oil price environment between 2003 and 2008, with the beginning of the financial crisis and lower oil prices, both consumers and producers felt that the extreme price volatility was a major problem, and power a relative thing in a system which was so highly interconnected. Amidst the financial chaos, the steep fall of the oil price did not really come as a relief, but as an additional worry about a trading system that seemed out of control. Extreme price volatility creates major dilemmas for future business planning and investment in the energy sector 'because the more volatile the oil price, the more cautious the investment planning of oil companies'.[29] If, however, companies do not invest in new production now, there might be a bottleneck in the future – meaning that the market could become tight once the economic recovery starts and demand increases. Old threat perceptions and fears of dependency have not vanished, in the light of continuing instability in the Middle East and Russia's unpredictability as an energy supplier to Europe. The ultimate goal for the Western consumers was, and remains, more diversification and less reliance on foreign energy imports. Yet after the experiences of autumn 2008, oil price volatility can now be added to the list of threats connected to the fuzzy notion of 'energy security'.[30]

The common denominator among all parties in the energy market is thus to maintain the stability of the system, reduce volatility, and enhance predictability through more transparency and information exchange. Yet before examining proposals for a new model of cooperation between producers and consumers, it is essential to better understand how producers and consumers each view the key threats to market stability. As the following sections show, there are significant differences between how producers and consumers perceive these threats.

Key challenges from a producers' perspective

Each producer has interests and views which depend on the specifics of the country's domestic and international situation. Yet the common interests of all the major fossil fuel exporters is to have secure demand for energy at the highest possible price.

There is a range of strategies which producers pursue to maintain security of demand: diversifying energy supplies to new costumers,

keeping maximum control over their energy sectors while also securing sufficient domestic and foreign investment to maintain or increase
production, diversifying economies away from the raw materials sector
in order to prepare for drops in demand or price shocks, and investing
new energy wealth in projects both inside and outside their countries.
On top of all this, some producers – especially in the Middle East, Latin
America, and in the post-Soviet space – are also very keen to invest in
their military in order to emerge as more independent security actors.

Diversification of consumers is both a result of recent market development and a conscious strategy of the producers: The rise of the
Asian consumers brought about a change in the supply structure and
opened new markets and possibilities for producers. Asia's entrance
to the global oil market in about 2003 has not changed the way the
market operates. A large share of the oil is still traded on global spot
markets and sold to the highest bidder. The novelty is that an ever
growing share of the oil (and gas) produced is now going east instead
of west; the entrance of Asia thus enhanced competition and brought
the oil price up after 2003. In this regard, the rise of Asia was definitely
advantageous from the producers' perspective. Yet another more concrete benefit for producers is that diversity has increased their export
options and enhanced their security in case of a drop in demand caused
either by a recession in the traditional Western markets, an increase in
energy efficiency, the use of alternative energies, or a combination of
all factors. Naturally, there is little that producers can do in the worst
case, a general drop in global demand – as happened in the aftermath
of the global financial crunch beginning in autumn 2008.

The amount of energy investment is another key concern for producers. Producers face a major dilemma here. They need to avoid
investments in capacity expansion which end up remaining idle and
affecting the price of oil negatively. Yet they also need to make sure
they meet rising demand in order not to alienate their costumers. As
noted by Mohamed Hamel, head of OPEC's Energy Studies Department, 'OPEC is facing large uncertainties over how future oil demand
plays out and over the amount that it will eventually need to supply'.
Thus, depending on different demand scenarios, OPEC projections of
the amount needed for upstream investment requirements up to 2020
vary between US$230 billion and US$500 billion.[31]

Aleksei Miller, CEO of Russia's giant gas monopoly, Gazprom, was
more explicit about his company's interests. He stated at the annual
shareholders meeting on 30 June 2006: 'Gazprom prepares its gas balance basis for the future and the gas production plans in accordance
with the needs of only those partners who had concluded respective

long-term contracts already today. The gas will not be produced until it is sold'.[32]

However, after the price of oil fell in the second half of 2008, attracting foreign investment has yet again become a more pressing concern for NOCs, as their financial reserves are melting away quickly. Demand for natural gas is high and rising in Europe, and Gazprom has secured sufficiently large customer commitments in Europe to justify investing in new production, yet the company's shares, once valued at over $300 billion before the crisis hit in autumn 2008, had fallen about 75 per cent by January 2009, sending Gazprom from the world's number three firm to number 35.[33] Gazprom, which has been quite restrictive in allowing the participation of foreign investors with regard to some of its new key upstream projects in recent years, might thus now show more inclination to open up to foreign investment in the future as it needs Western money to make sure new gas comes online before overall production, which mainly comes from old fields in Western Siberia, starts to decline.

The same might happen in other oil-producing countries. A telling example is Venezuela, whose president, Hugo Chavez, is now silently courting Western oil companies once again (including Chevron, Royal Dutch Shell, and Total), after having pushed them out of the country in previous years.[34]

Energy-producing countries need foreign investment in light of the financial crisis, yet the national governments in many of the oil and gas producing countries also want to maintain control over the energy sector through state-controlled NOCs. From the producers' perspective, energy is a good too strategic to be left to market forces alone. Having the state engaged in planning investment, output volumes, and directions of energy flows ensures a more guided, long-term development of the energy sector. More importantly, however, state control is vital in order to control rents generated from energy sales. NOCs are seen as the driving economic forces in developing economies and are often assigned important social and macro-economic functions. Often, governments seeking popular support, force NOCs to sell their energy at subsidized prices on the domestic market and finance various state programmes in the economic and social spheres.

Diversifying their economies away from the raw materials sector has emerged as yet another increasingly important goal for producers. The desire to increase diversification is particularly strong among the traditional Middle Eastern producers, who have had trouble dealing with large financial inflows in the past. During the 1970s and 1980s, Saudi Arabia and other countries of the Middle East first experienced inflation, and then a deep recession, following the collapse of oil prices in the mid-1980s. In the 1990s, GDP began growing again because of the Saudi regime's relatively successful efforts to diversify the country's economy. In order to prevent inflation, economic planners now invest much more oil money into the non-oil sector, with an emphasis on long-term industrial programmes, than was the case in the past. Other oil-rich countries in the Middle East region have also sought to diversify their economies, and are today better prepared for negative price effects.

Despite these efforts, however, Middle East economies are still heavily dependent on oil. The International Monetary Fund (IMF) reported that in 2005, oil export revenues accounted for around 90 per cent of total Saudi export earnings, 70–80 per cent of state revenues, and 44 per cent of the country's GDP.[35] A prolonged low price for oil would ultimately affect countries in the region severely.

Although Russia does not rely on oil to the same extent as Saudi Arabia, the drop in the oil price in the second half of 2008 had a negative impact on Russia's economy. According to the World Bank, Russia's oil and gas sector accounts for 20 per cent of GDP, over 60 per cent (64% in 2007) of its export earnings and 30 per cent of all foreign direct investment.[36] Russia suffers from symptoms of 'Dutch disease', since the years of high energy prices saw rapid growth in imports combined with much slower development of domestic industry.[37] The government acknowledges this problem and has been actively seeking to promote the non-energy sector (for example the IT sector, the aviation industry, nanotechnology, etc.); yet progress has been rather modest so far.[38]

Before the financial crunch in autumn 2008, a safe way to bolster the economy against the negative impact of high rents was to invest the money in state funds or in projects abroad. While Western countries often viewed such business expansion with a certain amount of suspicion – especially when state actors seemed to be driving the expansion – producers saw investing abroad as a good way to manage their high profits from fossil fuel exports, thereby avoiding inflation in their own countries; an approach also practiced by Western state-owned oil companies like Norwegian Statoil. The forerunners of this process were large state-owned companies like Russia's Gazprom or Saudi Aramco, but other companies were following suit. After the financial crisis began, governments in the producer countries began drawing heavily on their accumulated oil rents in order to support their economies and stabilize the financial systems. In just half a year, Russia's reserve fund fell from a peak of $598 billion on 8 August 2008 to $427 billion on 9 January 2009 (and some observers claim it may well have shrunk by more than half during this time).[39]

Just as the producers were taking control over the energy sectors in their countries and expanding their economic activities into the downstream market, so they were increasingly trying to take security into their own hands by engaging in massive rearmament programmes. Recent years saw an increase in military spending in all the major oil producing regions, the Middle East, Eurasia, and Latin America. Middle Eastern states were rearming against the background of shifting balances of power due to the US invasion of Iraq and fears that Iran would be able to play a stronger role in the region.

While states like Saudi Arabia, Bahrain, Kuwait, Oman, Qatar, and the United Arab Emirates are – for the time being – interested in maintaining a strong military alliance with the USA in order to safeguard against regional imbalances, they are also increasingly interested in raising their own military profile in order to emerge as more independent players, and not to be seen by their own populations as mere puppets controlled by the West. Other oil-rich states – like Russia – became more directly engaged in building up their military, in order to preserve their 'sphere of influence' and did not show any particular eagerness in forming a military alliance with the West. When Georgia attempted to retake the separatist region of South Ossetia by force in August 2008, Russia felt sufficiently confident not only to push the Georgian forces out of South Ossetia, but also to invade Georgia proper, only to backtrack when threatened with EU sanctions.[40] Still other countries – for example Iran and Venezuela – were using oil money to enhance their role as regional centres of power.

Key challenges from a consumers' perspective

If producers are generally concerned with secure demand for energy at the highest possible price, consumers are largely concerned with secure supplies at affordable prices. During the high-price era between 2003 and 2008, Western consumers have followed the shifts in producer–consumer relations with concern, viewing the changes that took place as threatening the stability of existing economic, political, and security arrangements – a system that so far served the interests of Western consumers well.

Not since the 1973 oil crisis has the West felt more exposed to the many potential risks which might result from the present situation. The debate in the West has been loaded with negative rhetoric stressing the risk of the 'oil weapon', the resurgence of 'resource nationalism', the danger of financing terrorism through 'wealth transfer' from the West to the Middle East, and the potential threat presented by Middle Eastern or Russian financial investments for national security.

Naturally, the West is not a unitary actor, and different governments have been reacting very differently, depending on their specific interests and position within the energy market. The USA, for example, has been much more outspoken about the dangers of dependency on Middle East oil and Russia's energy policy than most European governments. Yet the main trendline in the West, as reflected in the Western press and in public opinion polls, follows the same negative undertones.

One of the most frequently debated threats relates to the geopolitical consequences of energy wealth, namely that producer countries could use energy as a weapon by stopping deliveries, thereby causing economic difficulties in the consuming countries. In the USA, memories of the OPEC oil embargo of 1973 shape the discussion. Asked how to address the 'threat' of energy dependence, the *Transatlantic Trends 2007* survey found that 54 per cent of those polled in the USA would agree with the proposition that the best approach to enhance energy security is to reduce dependence on energy-producing countries, even if prices were to rise.[41] During the 2008 presidential campaign, candidate Barack Obama pointed out that US presidents had been promising to reduce the country's dependence on foreign energy for the past 30 years, even as foreign dependence increased, and he intended to make good on those promises.

Europeans associate the 'energy weapon' less with Middle East oil than with the behaviour of Russia.[42] According to European Commission figures, 27 per cent of the European Union's oil consumption and 24 per cent of gas consumption are of Russian origin. The EU imports 30 per cent of its oil and 44 per cent of its gas from Russia.[43] The European voices calling for diversification away from Russia increased in volume following the temporary shutdown of Russian gas deliveries to Ukraine in January 2006 and in January 2009. These shutdowns caused immediate shortfalls in gas supplies to a number of European countries.[44]

In relation to a potential energy delivery embargo, the West views the increasing diversification on the demand side with some concern. The problem associated with the development of a more diversified demand structure is not so much the fact of the diversity itself, but the combination of diversified demand with potentially low spare capacities and limited investment opportunities. Should Russia, for example, build oil and gas pipelines to China and link these pipelines to the existing energy transportation system, it might – at least in theory – be in a position to redirect some energy from West to East, leaving Europe with little choice but to look for other sources of energy (if these sources are available) or pay higher prices for Russian energy. For gas in particular, Europe fears the building of a gas cartel among its major outside suppliers. Hypothetically, an agreement on prices between Algeria and Russia, which together make up for currently 70 per cent of total EU gas imports, would substantially increase these countries' leverage vis-à-vis Europe.

The growing demand from Asian countries, combined with low spare capacity, might have a negative impact on the West's ability to effectively enforce sanctions on certain 'unfriendly' producers. Under a situation of tight global supplies and high prices, as existed between 2003 and 2008, Iran, for example, would be expected to have far greater leverage to counter-sanction major oil-consuming nations by cutting back its oil exports. Western nations now have enough spare capacity to increase shipments to offset potential Iranian cutbacks, so prices would be unlikely to rise sharply. Yet once the global recession is over and demand is rising again, Iran might either choose to sell less, and earn more, or sell to places other than the West – like China – thus circumventing a potential Western-led embargo. At least under conditions of high oil prices, broad economic sanctions, comparable to the isolation of Iraq in the 1990s, are no longer a feasible option. [45]

A further major concern in the West is related to growing state control over the energy sector and restricted access for Western private companies in the upstream sector of producing countries. Despite statements from OPEC to the contrary, the Western consumer countries are not assured that OPEC will invest enough, and sufficiently fast, to meet growing global demand. In Europe, the most frequently cited example concerns the slow progress in the development of new gas fields. While Russia's major traditional fields in West Siberia are all declining, many experts in the West believe that Gazprom is investing too little too slowly to make sure that new fields, such as the gigantic Shtokman offshore field in the Barents Sea, or the fields on the Yamal peninsula, are developed on time. Because of Russia's current financial crisis, Gazprom and many other Russian energy companies, are now in need of foreign money; however, it remains to be seen to what extent the economic rationale to open up to foreign investment will eventually outweigh political considerations to maintain tight control over the nation's energy sector.

In the Western view, a further major obstacle to sufficient investment is related to the increasing role of state players in the energy market. The suspicion with which the West views the role of NOCs is based on the fact that many of the state-owned companies are not operating as effectively as privately owned ones. According to the results of 15 in-depth case studies of NOCs conducted by the Baker Institute Energy Forum at Rice University in Houston, Texas, together with the Japan Petroleum Energy Center, average technical efficiency of NOCs is only 60–65 per cent of the efficiency of the big international private energy companies.[46]

The expansion of state-owned companies and investments from producing countries are also often viewed with suspicion. Fuelled by national security concerns over terrorism, strong opposition from the US Congress in spring 2006 prevented a United Arab Emirates-based maritime company from concluding the acquisition of London-based Peninsular and Oriental Steam Navigation Co. (P&O), which has operations at six major US ports, including New York and Baltimore.[47] The politicization of Europe–Russia energy relations since the shutdown of Russian gas to Ukraine in early 2006 has been accompanied by growing resistance to Russian investment in Europe's energy market. When Gazprom announced its intentions to enter the UK retail market through the acquisition of Centrica, the owner of British Gas, in 2006, an alarmed British government warned it would scrutinize and eventually block any takeover move for this UK gas company.[48]

Western states are particularly concerned about the security of energy infrastructure, which is vulnerable to attacks by terrorists, military actions, and natural disasters. Attacks in Saudi Arabia in 2006, the Russian invasion of Georgia in 2008, and the incidence of hurricanes on the US coast have all raised various questions about crucial energy supply lines and processing facilities.

Likewise, Western consumers fear increasing authoritarianism within producer states, particularly in Latin America and the post-Soviet area. High oil prices have not caused this, but they have certainly made it easier for political rulers to repress nascent civil society movements and to prevent the development of a political opposition critical of the regime. Between 2003 and 2008, Russia's increasingly authoritarian elites focused on getting a larger share of hydrocarbon revenues, rather than on promoting long-term sustainable economic development.[49] Non-democratic regimes in the Middle East leave little room for political opposition. Young people, many of whom are unemployed, are politically disenfranchised and largely anti-Western in their views, and thus represent easy prey for radical Islamist organizations.

The West is especially concerned about countries that combine authoritarianism with a military build-up, particularly when the countries are major energy suppliers to world markets but otherwise pursue their own agenda in international affairs. The USA and some of its Western allies are interested in maintaining a strong military presence in the Persian Gulf, both directly through the US navy and military bases, and indirectly through massive military assistance. In July 2007, for example, Washington offered the member states of the Gulf Cooperation Council (Saudi Arabia, Bahrain, Kuwait, Oman, Qatar, and the United Arab Emirates) a US$20 billion arms sales package, the bulk of which will go to upgrading Saudi Arabia's military capabilities – a move that provoked considerable political opposition in Washington at the time.[50] In September 2007, Saudi Arabia signed a major arms deal with Great Britain for the purchase of 72 Eurofighter Typhoon jets for US$8.84 billion.[51]

However, the Western presence is increasingly unpopular, not only with large segments of Middle Eastern populations, but also among citizens of Western countries themselves – especially against the background of the Iraq war. The USA also faces challenges from regimes in oil-rich countries, such as Venezuela or Iran, which pursue an increasingly confrontational course. Elsewhere in the world, the USA and Europe are engaged with Russia in a struggle for power and influence over resources in the energy-rich Caspian region. While Azerbaijan is now firmly tied into the Western orbit and directly connected to Western markets via a pipeline to Turkey, the Central Asian states of Turkmenistan, Kazakhstan, and Uzbekistan are still heavily dominated by Russia and depend on Russian pipelines for the bulk of their exports going west.

A somewhat separate issue of concern is the combination of resource wealth with failing state structures in the third world. In war-torn countries like Nigeria, Sudan, or Angola, oil money can directly feed conflict by favouring those parties which are in control of production. The unbalanced distribution of resources can lead to wars between different ethnic or tribal groups. This situation is a cause of concern as it has a negative impact on world energy prices. It is also a direct security concern when the workforce is threatened (including the kidnapping of foreign workers) or when energy infrastructure is attacked; but these security concerns are more local, and the West potentially has considerable leverage if it decides to protect energy facilities and infrastructure through its military.

Risk assessment in an interdependent market

In the following section, we analyse some of the concerns that we have discussed in the previous two sections in order to determine how likely the real and perceived threats to market stability are to happen. Thus, we assess issues such as the possibility of producers dictating prices and trade conditions on the energy market, the energy weapon, the investment issue, the connection with terrorism and infrastructure protection.

The high oil prices between 2003 and 2008 provided producers with additional opportunities and means to play an increasingly important role in the global economy, as well as in international political and security affairs. At the same time, however, the new power did not greatly enhance the producers' actual *leverage* over the consumers, since the relationship has remained essentially an interdependent one. The main danger for producer–consumer stability does not lie in the clash between two seemingly conflicting sets of interests, but in misreading the nature of the interdependencies in the energy, market and in growing mutual mistrust.

It is certainly true that OPEC's importance for global fossil fuel supplies is unlikely to diminish in the near future given that the cartel controls approximately 70 per cent of currently known global oil and gas reserves. Still, these resources do not automatically translate into increased direct influence over prices. In fact, observers note that OPEC has lost much of its cartel power over the years, given that the organization currently controls only about 40 per cent of global oil production, and members display little unity among themselves.[52] It is telling that in both the era of high prices and low excess capacity (2003–2008) and in the current era of low prices and high excess capacity (since autumn 2008), OPEC did not play a significant role in setting oil prices.

In the area of natural gas, key producers are unlikely to be able to form a cartel that can control prices since there is no global gas market comparable to the oil market. The gas market is largely regionalized. Some 90 per cent of gas is traded via pipelines, and producers and consumers work out the terms of their gas supply deals in long-term bilateral agreements. This system gives producers a substantial amount of freedom in dealing with their clients in order to work out the best possible deals. In order to institutionalize their cooperation, gas producers set up the Gas Exporting Countries' Forum (GECF) in 2001; yet it is telling that this forum, whose heterogeneous membership includes both LNG and pipeline producers, still functions essentially as an informal discussion club and is unlikely to move in the direction of OPEC as long as the gas market remains essentially a regional market and each member follows its own distinct agenda.[53]

In light of the economic slowdown and decreasing demand, in October 2008 the three gas-producing countries Russia, Iran, and Qatar took a decision to form a 'big gas troika'. Although some Western observers were quick to portray this as yet another effort towards the creation of a new 'gas-OPEC',[54] the goal, according to Gazprom CEO Aleksei Miller, is not to set prices, but to better coordinate activities of the three countries and their energy companies in an ever more globalized gas market.[55] For Europe, this is not dramatic, but it still might have an impact if these three gas producers, possibly also including Algeria, agree on some sort of arrangement in order to avoid engaging in direct competition on the European gas market. The fact that Algeria has a large outstanding debt to Russia related to weapons purchases might weaken its ability to push ahead with projects that are not in Russia's interest.[56]

Contrary to widespread public perception, it does not seem very likely that OPEC, or other major fossil fuel exporters, would consider using energy as a weapon directly against their own costumers, since doing so would further encourage OECD-countries to move away not only from imported fossil fuels but oil altogether – thus provoking a similar chain reaction as occurred after the 1973 oil crisis. Such a move could potentially cost OPEC its most lucrative market.

If producers stopped oil exports to Western countries, for example during a war in the Middle East, it would certainly send shock waves throughout the industrialized world; at the same time, there are a number of reasons why the oil weapon would not be very effective. For one, relatively low oil intensity in Europe makes this market far less vulnerable to the energy weapon than during the 1970s. The USA imports more oil from abroad than 30 years ago, but only about 11 per cent from Persian Gulf countries.[57] In addition, strategic reserves would smooth out oil cuts from the Middle East, at least for several months. At the same time, the options for Middle Eastern countries to diversify their exports away from their traditional buyers are limited. China is a ready buyer, but not eager to become too dependent on one source of supply either.

In certain cases there are also simple technical and/or infrastructural reasons why it is not possible for a country to sustain a blockade for a long period: For example Venezuela, despite its fierce anti-US rhetoric, cannot easily stop shipping oil to its northern neighbour, because only US refineries have the capability to refine heavy Venezuelan crude. Iran would be able to ship oil and gas to Asia if there were a Western embargo, yet Europe remains a lucrative destination, especially for Iranian gas, since the Europeans need to find new gas suppliers against the background of declining domestic gas production, sharply increasing demand, and an uncertain outlook for Russian gas production.

Russia's energy leverage over Europe also has limits. A hypothetical halt to Russian energy deliveries to Europe would hurt Europe, but it would potentially hurt Russia much more. Around two-thirds of Russian gas and oil exports go to EU member states, the rest to other European countries and the CIS states (only a small fraction is presently exported to other countries). The EU in 2005 accounted for some 56 per cent of total Russian exports and around 45 per cent of total imports. Compared to this number, the significance of Russia for Europe is small: Russia in 2005 accounted for only about ten per cent of EU overall imports and was responsible for a little more than six per cent of EU exports.[58]

A halt to oil deliveries would hurt Europe less than an interruption to gas supplies, simply because all of the gas that Europe imports from Russia is through pipelines. The physical connection between consumer and producer is weaker in oil, where the bulk is imported in tankers, and shortfalls could theoretically be balanced out via imports from other places. Yet even in the realm of gas, Russia has limited manoeuvring room. All of Russia's export trunk pipelines are currently oriented towards the West and towards Europe; plans to diversify to Asia are on the table, but the pipelines, if they are ever built, will not be operational in the short term and will then – according to Russia's plans as laid out in its official energy strategy up to 2020 – make up for only about 10–15 per cent of Russia's gas export share.[59]

The question of investment is certainly at the heart of the producer–consumer debate. The problem, it seems, is not that producers are unwilling to invest, but they are unwilling to give away information on their investment plans because this might have an unfavourable impact on prices. If the Western consumer *knew* that there were enough reserves and enough investment to exploit these reserves, such certainty might drive energy prices down. At the same time, producers, even during the high-price period between 2003 and 2008, were never interested in creating a situation that would drive their clients away. In fact, it is telling that OPEC had, over the past years, made efforts to appear in a benign light vis-à-vis its Western clients. OPEC's commitment to meet rising demand is, according to the organization's own information of April 2007, underpinned by some 140 projects totalling more than US$120 billion, thus making sure crude capacity will increase by around five mb/d to almost 40 mb/d in 2010.[60] Also, Gazprom has sought to be viewed as a more transparent company and has started to publish some of its investment figures regularly on its website.[61]

With an eye toward future investments, the West has criticized producers, arguing that state-owned companies are not the most suitable actors to improve the efficiency of their energy sectors and to make sure that there is enough investment to keep production up. Producers argue that the 'performance' of a company should not only be measured against technical criteria, but with regard to the larger socio-political and domestic economic functions which NOCs perform in their countries.

Moreover, there are clear differences among the individual state-owned companies, and the degree to which companies are subjected to politics differs from country to country. Companies like Norwegian Statoil, Malaysian Petronas or Saudi Aramco are fairly efficient and competitive. However, other companies, such as the Nigerian NNPC or the Venezuelan PDVSA, are clearly more ideologically oriented, and their behaviour on the market is indeed heavily constrained by political considerations that their country's leaders impose.[62] PDVSA in 2005, for example, was obliged to spend US$7 billion to finance state programmes in the areas of education, health, nutrition, and job creation.[63] Still other companies are reforming and adapting; Russia's Gazprom, for example, which was obliged by the state to sell its gas on the domestic market at around 20 per cent of world market prices in 2006, might have more incentives to increase efficiency if the government implements its plan, adopted in November 2006, to gradually increase this price to market levels.[64]

With regard to the connection between wealth transfer and support for transnational terrorism, one cannot exclude the possibility that some oil money does indeed end up in the pockets of terrorists. Money spent by governments to help Islamic schools or organizations inside or outside the Middle East can at least indirectly support radical tendencies. At the same time, it does not make sense to emphasize the connection between wealth transfer and terrorism heavily. Terrorists can operate effectively without large sums of Western petrodollars. Also, most of the states in the region are actively engaged in the fight against terrorism since they worry about attacks on their infrastructure in the same way as consuming countries.

What in the West was pejoratively labelled as 'wealth transfer' during the period of high oil prices was in fact not a one way street. Petrodollars were not money 'lost' to the Western consumer. At least part of this money flowed back into the global economy as investment. The bulk of the money, however, benefited regional economies by creating new jobs and investment opportunities – which also opened up possibilities for US and European companies.[65] Indeed, it is precisely here that producers saw inconsistencies in the West's line of argument: Between 2003 and 2008 the West stressed that it wanted to liberalize energy markets in order to have open access to energy reserves and production, but it did not really open its own market for investment. This could be seen in the West's reluctance to allow large-scale investment by state funds in Western stocks and bonds, because of national security concerns.[66]

The danger of a terrorist attack on energy infrastructure is real, but the likelihood and impact of such an attack should be placed in context. In Saudi Arabia, two-thirds of crude oil production is processed in one huge refinery (located at Abqaiq); yet this large refinery is very well protected and would require major military preparations on the part of terrorists to carry out a successful attack. Should terrorists indeed succeed in damaging or even destroying such a refinery, global supply would immediately drop several percentage points. Rogue states or terrorists could also attempt to target critical oil supply and distribution chains; 90 per cent of Middle East oil passes through the Strait of Hormuz (17 mb/d), Bab el Mandeb (3.0 mb/d), and the Suez Canal–Sumed pipeline (3.8 mb/d) – passages for which there are limited alternatives.[67] Despite the heavy presence of US Marines in the region, blocking the Strait of Hormuz with sea mines would be relatively easy for Iran in case of war with the USA. However, Iran is certainly not in a position to sustain such an action for a long period of time, but the immediate (psychological) effect for the market would potentially be considerable.

This is not to suggest that the current situation does not bear considerable risks. However, some of the major risks that are currently debated, such as the establishment of a natural gas price cartel or the application of the energy weapon, appear rather farfetched when analysed in economic terms. Others, like terrorist attacks on energy infrastructure, are more probable and would be psychologically very significant (yet only if they coincide with low excess capacities), but would not actually affect the global supplies of oil or gas over a longer time period. Moreover, it is precisely in the area of protecting the energy infrastructure where the interests of both producers and consumers are most obviously connected.

A real danger for producer–consumer relations is growing mutual mistrust due to the highly politicized debate on energy security. In the sensitive field of energy, especially during times when prices are high and competition for scarce resources is increasing, politics and perceptions play an important role. Ultimately, when consumer and producer do not trust each other, they try to diversify away from each other, resulting in an 'energy security dilemma', as described above. This spiral is all the more worrying if diversification away from each other is accompanied by other aggravating trends in producing states, such as increasing authoritarianism, anti-Western movements, or military build up. These developments are not directly related to energy relations, but would probably have a negative impact on relations in rather unpredictable ways.

Ensuring market stability and stabilizing producer–consumer relations

The stability of the energy market hinges on delicate balances in a highly interdependent web of relationships. Power in the system shifted toward the producers between 2003 and 2008, but returned again to consumers after the price of oil fell sharply in the second half of 2008. Finding the right equilibrium between producers and consumers against the background of extreme price volatility and an uncertain outlook for demand and investment requires diplomatic efforts as well as closer cooperation at the business level. There also must be a reassessment in the sphere of security and military alliances.

It is, first and foremost, through enhanced dialogue that the long list of real and perceived problems in producer–consumer relations can be addressed and misconceptions removed. This dialogue should be intensified within existing institutional frameworks which include producers and consumers, such as the International Energy Forum at the international level, or the EU–Russia Energy Dialogue or the EU–OPEC Energy Dialogue at regional levels.[68]

It will be important to include newly emerging energy consumers, initially China and India, in any such dialogue. For example, China's role and intentions have to be understood correctly in order for the West to work together with the country. Rather than presenting the emergence of China *a priori* as a threat to the energy market, the West needs to identify those areas of cooperation where interests coincide. While Chinese NOCs might use different methods than IOCs to acquire licenses and to cooperate with other state-run companies, China, like all other parties in the global energy market, is also essentially interested in maintaining a stable and secure supply of oil at affordable prices. One concrete place to engage with China is in African conflicts. In Sudan, for example, where Chinese companies are heavily engaged, unrest hurts all players on the international market, by driving away investors, bringing down profits and pushing up prices.

In the area of business relations, one way to develop producer–consumer ties is to better explore the many possible ways to engage in mutually beneficial relationships among IOCs and NOCs. Despite setbacks due to re-nationalization, business has already started to adjust. It is important that IOCs and Western business understand that they will not be in a position to dictate the terms of the relationship with NOCs in producing countries, regardless of whether energy prices are high or low. This has become evident in the case of Russia, where the state has effectively managed to nullify PSAs signed with foreign companies during the 1990s; in 2007, Russia's then-president Vladimir Putin criticized these PSAs as 'colonial' in nature.[69] Business has to find niches and forms of cooperation. There are already various models of successful partnerships.[70]

In Russia, the rules of the game have changed in favour of state-owned Gazprom in the gas area and Rosneft in the oil sector. For both technical and financial reasons, however, it is essential for these companies to cooperate with foreign companies in order to develop difficult and capital-intensive projects like those on the Yamal peninsula, in the Barents Sea, East Siberia, the Far East, or in Russia's harsh northern territories.[71] IOCs are now prevented by law from control-ling majority stakes in large oil and gas projects – i.e. those which are classified as 'strategic' – but they can still take part as minority stakeholders, namely as service providers or through the provision of specific technical functions. The Shtokman offshore project in the Barents Sea, one of the world's largest natural gas fields, is a case in point: after Gazprom declared in November 2006 that it intended to exploit this gigantic field on its own, it invited foreign companies back in as minority stake-holders in mid-2007.[72]

The Saudi Arabian case shows that although IOCs are not allowed to take part in oil production, they are welcome to join in gas produc-tion – an industry that is only now emerging in Saudi Arabia. Also, there are numerous other possibilities for Western companies to profit from new possibilities in the emerging markets in Saudi Arabia and in other states of the Persian Gulf. One area with a very large invest-ment potential is construction. Here, foreign companies are welcome. Another, largely unexplored, field of cooperation is in increasing energy efficiency or in developing renewable sources of energy.[73]

Increasing interdependencies also means taking into account mon-etary flows from producers to consumers: businesses from the Middle East and Russia have, during the high-price era between 2003 and 2008, invested heavily in the downstream market of Europe and the USA. Some NOCs have been slowly turning from purely national companies into companies with international outreach. It is in this area where the IOCs could form partnerships with NOCs, for example through the establishment of joint ventures, and thus assist NOCs in their foreign activities. In return, IOCs might get a share in projects in the NOC country. The foreign expansion of NOCs is increasing mutual inter-dependencies, and raises the stakes for all sides. The more a company owns in the whole chain of supply, the higher the stakes and the more it is interested in keeping the energy flowing.

This is not to suggest that the USA and Europe should simply open their doors to investment from these countries without requiring some degree of reciprocity. Also, the West needs to make sure that invest-ments from abroad – be it from NOCs or state funds – are made in a transparent way and are subject to the rule of law. However, the mere fact that the companies are investing in producer nations is a positive development, since it increases the interconnectedness between produc-ers and consumers; increased business cooperation could spill over into politics and have overall positive effects for international relations.

The global energy market is heavily exposed to forces beyond the confines of the economy. The price fluctuations over the past years are the clearest indication of the fact that the market alone is not able to guarantee the smooth functioning of international energy relations. How the energy system and producer–consumer relations develop in the future will thus depend also on how states deal with crises which are not necessarily related to the energy market. Most importantly, it will depend on how states deal with the situation in key producing regions of the globe, especially in the Middle East. Conflict prevention and regulation are as much an element of enhancing the stability of the energy market as business cooperation between NOCs and IOCs or the institutionalization of dialogue between producers and consumers.

It is thus also through political and military relations that the interna-tional community should strive to maintain stability within the broader energy system. The USA and its allies are still the dominant military force, and play the key role for the international and regional balances of power – be this in the post-Soviet space, where the USA has been seeking to contain Russia in the Caspian region, or in the Middle East, where Washington and its allies try to guarantee stability and security through their military presence and via their military alliances with key states of the region, including Saudi Arabia. There has been much criticism that the USA through its actions – namely in Iraq – has in fact undermined, rather than fostered, stability; therefore, the task for the new administration of President Obama will be to address the key challenges emerging from energy regions such as the Middle East and post-Soviet Eurasia in a way that promotes the establishment of stable long-term relations.

Notes

1   Peter Mandelson, 'In Defence of Globalisation: We Need Another Bretton Woods to Lessen the Risks but Keep the Benefits of World Financial Markets', *The Guardian*, 3 October 2008. www.guardian.co.uk/commentisfree/2008/oct/03/globalisation.globaleconomy

2   Enno Harks, *Der globale Ölmarkt: Herausforderungen und Handlungsoptionen für Deutschland*, SWP-Studie S 11, Stiftung für Wissenschaft und Politik, Berlin, 2007, 10–13.

3   For a history of the oil price: Energy Information Administration (EIA), World Crude Oil Prices, http://tonto.eia.doe.gov/dnav/pet/pet_pri_wco_k_w.htm

4   151st (Extraordinary) Meeting of the OPEC Conference in Oran, Algeria, 17 December 2008. www.opec.org/opecna/Press%20Releases/2008/pr172008.htm

5   Andrew Monaghan, 'Dilemma Energicheskoi Bezopasnosti', *Pro et Contra* 10, nos. 2–3, March–June 2006, 16–31. Published in English as 'Russia–EU Relations: An Emerging Security Dilemma', www.carnegieendowment.org/files/EmergingDilemma1.pdf; also: Jeronim Perovic and Robert Orttung, 'Russia's Energy Policy: Should Europe Worry?', *Russian Analytical Digest*, no. 18, April 2007, 2–13, (page 6 here).

6   OPEC is an organization that currently includes 12 oil exporting countries. OPEC was founded in 1960. Original OPEC members included Iran, Iraq, Kuwait, Saudi Arabia, and Venezuela. Between 1960 and 1975, the organization expanded to include Qatar (1961), Indonesia (1962), Libya (1962), the United Arab Emirates (1967), Algeria (1969), and Nigeria (1971). Angola joined the organization in 2007.

7   For general background on the history of oil and the 1973 oil crisis, see Daniel Yergin, *The Prize: The Epic Quest for Oil, Money, and Power*, Simon & Schuster, New York, 1991; Leonardo Maugeri, *The Age of Oil: The Mythology, History, and Future of the World's Most Controversial Resource*, Praeger, Westport, Conn., 2006.

8   The 'seven sisters' included at the time: Standard Oil of New Jersey, Royal Dutch Shell, Anglo Persian Oil Company, Standard Oil of New York, Standard Oil of California, Gulf Oil, and Texaco. See Sampson, Anthony, *The Seven Sisters: The Great Oil Companies and the World They Shaped*, Viking Press, New York, 1975.

9   On the history and role of the International Energy Agency (IEA), see William F. Martin and Evan M. Harrje, 'The International Energy Agency', in *Energy and Security: Toward a New Foreign Policy Strategy*, eds. Jan H. Kalicki and David L. Goldwyn, Woodrow Wilson Center Press, Washington, 2005, 97–116.

10 EIA, 'Non-OPEC Fact Sheet', *Country Analysis Briefs*, June 2005, www.eia.doe.gov/emeu/cabs/nonopec.html

11 Amy Meyers Jaffe and Ronald Soligo, 'Impact of the Reopening of Persian Gulf Upstream Sectors to International Investment in International Oil

Markets', Study published by the James A. Baker III Institute for Public Policy of Rice University, May 2000. www.rice.edu/energy/publications/docs/JES_ImpactReopeningPersianGulfUpstreamSec.pdf

12 Edward L. Morse and Amy Myers Jaffe, eds., *Strategic Energy Policy: Challenges for the 21ˢᵗ Century*, Council on Foreign Relations Press, New York, 2001, 12.

13 IEA, *World Energy Outlook 2007: China and India Insights*, IEA, Paris, 2007, 118.

14 'Intelligence Brief: Saudi Arrests Demonstrate Threat to Energy Markets', *PINR News Report*, 1 May 2007. http://pinr.com/report.php?ac=view_report&report_id=645&language_id=1

15 'The Changing Role of National Oil Companies in the International Energy Market', *Baker Institute Policy Report*, no. 35, published by the James A. Baker III Institute for Public Policy of Rice University, April 2007. www.rice.edu/energy/publications/PolicyReports/BI_Study_35-1.pdf

16 Carola Hoyos, 'The New Seven Sisters: Oil and Gas Giants Dwarf Western Rivals', *Financial Times*, 11 March 2007. www.ft.com/cms/s/2/471ae1b8-d001-11db-94cb-000b5df10621.html

17 EIA, 'Petroleum Navigator', http://tonto.eia.doe.gov/dnav/pet/hist/wepcuralsw.htm

18 Clifford Gaddy, 'US–Russia Economic Relationship: Implications of the Yukos Affair', Testimony before the House Financial Services Subcommittee on Domestic and International Monetary Policy, Trade and Technology, Washington DC, 17 October 2007.

19 'Russia Oil Fund Rises to $156.8 bln on Jan 1', *Reuters*, 9 January 2008, http://uk.reuters.com/article/oilRpt/idUKL0971670520080109

20 'Russian Oligarch $260bn Meltdown in Private Wealth', *Times Online*, 28 January 2009. http://business.timesonline.co.uk/tol/business/economics/article5607618.ece

21 'Russia Opens the Door to Investing in the West', *International Herald Tribune*, 1 February 2008, 13.

22 'Russia', SIPRI 2006 database (http://www.sipri.org/contents/milap/milex/mex_database1.html); 'Russia to Put 50 Topol-M Missile Systems on Duty Before 2015', *RIA Novosti*, 7 February 2007, http://en.rian.ru/russia/20070207/60345412.html

23 International Crisis Group, 'Nagorno-Karabakh: Risking War', *Europe Report*, no. 187, 14 November 2007; Farid Guliyev, 'Oil Wealth, Patrimonialism, and the Failure of Democracy in Azerbaijan', *Caucasus Analytical Digest*, no. 2 (January 2009), 2–5. www.res.ethz.ch/analysis/cad/details.cfm?lng=en&id=95426

24 'Saudi Arabia', SIPRI 2006 database (www.sipri.org/contents/milap/milex/mex_database1.html)

25 *Transatlantic Trends: Key Findings 2007*, 8–10. http://www.transatlantictrends.org/trends/doc/TT07KFR_FINAL.pdf

26 The results of this study can be viewed at: 'BBC World Service 19 Nation Poll on Energy, Questionnaire and Methodology'. www.worldpublicopinion.org/pipa/pdf/jul06/Energy_Jul06_quaire.pdf

27 Grant Smith, 'Oil $200 Options Rise 10-Fold in Bet on Higher Crude', *Bloomberg*, 7 January 2008. www.bloomberg.com/apps/news?pid=2060108 7&refer=home&sid=ayQXcHVStlP8

28 Cambridge Energy Research Associates, '"Recession Shock" Hits the Oil Market; Are Future Shocks and Oil Market Volatility Inevitable?', (executive summary), 19 December 2008, 5. www.cera.com/aspx/cda/public1/news/ pressReleases/pressReleaseDetails.aspx?CID=10002

29 Ibid., p. 8.

30 See also: Robert W. Orttung and Jeronim Perovic, 'Energy Security', in *The Routledge Handbook for Security Studies*, eds. Myriam Dunn Cavelty and Victor Mauer, Routledge, London, 2009 (forthcoming).

31 Mohamed Hamel, 'OPEC: Dialogue Between Producers and Consumers', Speech delivered to the Side Event of Vienna-based intergovernmental organizations at the UNCSD-15, New York, 7 May 2007. www.opec.org/ opecna/Speeches/2007/DialogueProdCons.htm

32 Aleksei Miller, 'Gazpropm–Strategy for the Energy Sector Leadership', Speech at the Annual Shareholders Meeting, Moscow, 30 June 2006. www. gazprom.ru/eng/articles/article20334.shtml

33 'Behind the Russia–Ukraine Gas Conflict', *BusinessWeek*, 3 January 2009. www.businessweek.com/globalbiz/content/jan2009/gb2009013_045451. htm?campaign_id=rss_topEmailedStories; 'Russia Pushes To Grow Gazprom's Reach, Control', *NPR.org*, 5 January 2009. www.npr.org/templates/ story/story.php?storyId=98874958

34 'Quietly, Chávez Reopens the Door to Western Oil Firms', *International Herald Tribune*, 15 January 2009. www.iht.com/articles/2009/01/15/america/ venez.php

35 EIA, 'Saudi Arabia', *Country Analysis Brief*, February 2007. www.eia.doe.gov/ emeu/cabs/Saudi_Arabia/Background.html

36 World Bank, *Russian Economic Report*, no. 13, December 2006. http:// ns.worldbank.org.ru/files/rer/RER_13_eng.pdf

37 See: Stephan Barisitz and Simon Erik Ollus, 'The Russian Non-Fuel Sector: Signs of the Dutch Disease? Evidence from EU-25 Import Competition', in *Focus on European Economic Integration*, 1/2007, CEEC Research Platform, Oesterreichische Nationalbank, 2007, 150–166. www.oenb.at/de/img/ feei_2007_1_barisits_ollus_tcm14-58444.pdf

38 For additional information, see Philip Hanson, 'The Sustainability of Russia's Energy Power: Implications for the Russian Economy', in *Russian Energy Power and Foreign Relations; Implications for Conflict and Cooperation*, eds. Jeronim Perovic, Robert W. Orttung and Andreas Wenger, Routledge, London, 2009, 23–50.

39 Philip Hanson, 'Oil and the Economic Crisis in Russia', *Russian Analytical Digest*, no. 54, February 2009, 2–4, (page 3 here). www.res.ethz.ch/analysis/ rad/details.cfm?lng=en&id=95992; Anders Aslund, 'Crisis Puts Putinomics to the Test', Moscow Times, 24 December 2008. www.petersoninstitute. org/publications/opeds/oped.cfm?ResearchID=1086

40 Jeronim Perovic, 'Caucasus Crisis: Implications and Options for the

West', *CSS Analysis in Security Policy* 3, no. 39 (September 2008). http://
se1.isn.ch/serviceengine/FileContent?serviceID=47&fileid=839B
8F81-2970-2DBC-3130-21CF0D11CFCF&lng=en

41 *Transatlantic Trends: Key Findings 2007*, p. 10. http://www.transatlantictrends.
org/trends/doc/TT07KFR_FINAL.pdf

42 For example: Walter Mayr, 'Putin's Cold War: Using Russian Energy as a
Political Weapon', *Der Spiegel (English Online Edition)*, no. 2, 9 January 2006.
www.spiegel.de/international/spiegel/0,1518,394345,00.html

43 European Commission (EC), *The European Union and Russia: Close Neighbors,
Global Players, Strategic Partners*, European Commission External Relations,
Brussels, October 2007, 13. http://ec.europa.eu/external_relations/library/
publications/34_eu_russia.pdf

44 For an overview on the Russia–Ukraine gas conflict of January 2009: 'The
Russian–Ukrainian Gas Conflict', *Russian Analytical Digest*, no. 53 (January
2009). www.res.ethz.ch/kb/search/details.cfm?lng=en&id=95596; Jeronim
Perovic, 'Farce ums Gas: Russland, die Ukraine und die EU-Energiepolitik',
Osteuropa 59, no. 1 2009, 19–35.

45 Jeffrey J. Schott, 'Economic Sanctions, Oil, and Iran', Testimony before the
Joint Economic Committee, United States Congress Hearing on 'Energy
and the Iranian Economy', Washington, DC, 25 July 2006.

46 'The Changing Role of National Oil Companies (NOCs) in International
Energy Markets', The Baker Institute Energy Forum at Rice University,
Houston, March 2007. www.rice.edu/energy/publications/PolicyReports/
BI_Study_35-1.pdf

47 Jonathan Weisman and Bradley Graham, 'Dubai Firm to Sell US Ports
Operations', *The Washington Post*, 10 March 2006, 1.

48 'Russia's Gazprom Eyes British Gas', *BBC News*, 26 April 2006. http://
news.bbc.co.uk/nolpda/ifs_news/hi/newsid_4945000/4945366.stm

49 Robert W. Orttung, 'Energy and State–Society Relations: Socio-Political
Aspects of Russia's Energy Wealth', in *Russian Energy Power and Foreign Relations: Implications for Conflict and Cooperation*, eds. Jeronim Perovic, Robert W.
Orttung, and Andreas Wenger, Routledge, London and New York, 2009,
51–70.

50 'Administration's Plan for Large Arms Sales to Saudis Stirs Reservations in
Congress', International Herald Tribune, 18 September 2007.

51 'Saudi Arabia Reaches Agreement with Britain to Buy 72 Typhoon Jets',
International Herald Tribune, 17 September 2007.

52 EIA, 'OPEC', *Country Analysis Briefs*, 8 August 2006. www.eia.doe.gov/emeu/
cabs/opec.html; Bassam Fattouh, 'OPEC Pricing Power: The Need for a
New Perspective', *OIES Working Papers WPM*, no. 31, Oxford Institute for
Energy Studies, March 2007. www.oxfordenergy.org/pdfs/WPM31.pdf

53 Moira Herbst, 'Why a Gas Cartel Could be a Bust', *Business Week*, 9
April 2007. www.businessweek.com/bwdaily/dnflash/content/apr2007/
db20070409_886425.htm

54 Ariel Cohen, 'OPEC Redux: Responding to the Russian–Iranian Gas Cartel', *Heritage Foundation WebMemo*, no. 2118, 28 October 2008. www.heritage.

org/research/energyandenvironment/upload/wm_2118.pdf

55 The interview with Aleksei Miller, CEO of Russia's Gazprom, on Channel One on 1 November 2008 is available in English at www.gazprom.com/eng/articles/article33041.shtml

56 Matteo Fachinotti, 'Will Russia Create a Gas Cartel?', *Russian Analytical Digest*, no. 18, April 2007, 14–16. www.res.ethz.ch/analysis/rad/details.cfm?lng=en&id=29825

57 EIA, *Petroleum Supply Monthly*, August 2007. Data is for January–December 2005. 'Persian Gulf' here includes Bahrain, Iran, Iraq, Kuwait, Qatar, Saudi Arabia, and United Arab Emirates.

58 European Commission (EC), *The European Union and Russia: Close Neighbors, Global Players, Strategic Partners*, European Commission External Relations, Brussels, October 2007, 13 and 26–31. http://ec.europa.eu/external_relations/library/publications/34_eu_russia.pdf

59 Ministerstvo Promyshlennosti i Energetiki Rossiiskoi Federatsii (MPE RF), *Energeticheskaya strategiya Rossii na period do 2020 goda* [Energy Strategy of Russia for the period to 2020], approved as decree no. 1234-r by the Russian government on 28 August 2003. Available (in Russian) at: www.minprom.gov.ru/docs/strateg/1/. Also: Nina Poussenkova, 'Russia's Future Costumers: Asia and Beyond', in *Russian Energy Power and Foreign Relations: Implications for Conflict and Cooperation*, eds. Jeronim Perovic, Robert W. Orttung, and Andreas Wenger, Routledge, London and New York, 2009, 132–154.

60 Fuad Al-Zayer, 'The Future of Oil and Gas and the Resultant Challenges and Opportunities for NOC', Speech at the World National Oil Companies Congress, London, 25–6 April, 2007. http://212.27.106.6/opecna/Speeches/2007/WorldNOCsCongress.htm

61 Gazprom's English website is at www.gazprom.com

62 See the respective case studies at: www.rice.edu/energy/publications/nocs.html

63 See the case study on PDVSA: David R. Mares, 'Venezuela's PDVSA and World Energy Markets: Corporate Strategies and Political Factors Determining its Behavior and Influence', in: 'The Changing Role of National Oil Companies (NOCs) in International Energy Markets', The Baker Institute Energy Forum at Rice University, Houston, March 2007. www.rice.edu/energy/publications/docs/NOCs/Papers/NOC_PDVSA_Mares-Altamirano.pdf

64 'Russia Approves Plan to Double Domestic Natural Gas Prices', *International Herald Tribune*, 30 November 2006. www.iht.com/articles/2006/11/30/business/rusgas.php

65 Stanley Reed, 'The New Middle East Oil Bonanza', *BusinessWeek.com*, 13 March 2006. www.businessweek.com/magazine/content/06_11/b3975001.htm

66 See, for example, the article by deputy US Treasury Secretary, Robert M. Kimmitt, 'Public Footprints in Private Markets: Sovereign Wealth Funds and the World Economy', *Foreign Affairs*, 87, No. 1, January–February 2008, 119–30.

67 EIA, 'World Oil Transit Chokepoints', *Country Analysis Briefs*, November 2005. www.eia.doe.gov/emeu/cabs/World_Oil_Transit_Chokepoints/Full. html; EIA, 'Persian Gulf Region', *Country Analysis Briefs*, June 2007. www. eia.doe.gov/emeu/cabs/Persian_Gulf/Full.html

68 See: Robert Skinner, 'Energy Security and Producer–Consumer Dialogue: Avoiding a Maginot Mentality', OIES Background Paper presented at the Government of Canada Energy Symposium, Ottawa, Sheraton Hotel, 28 October 2005. www.oxfordenergy.org/presentations/SecurityOfSupply.pdf

69 See the chapter on Russia by Perovic and Orttung in this book.

70 Valérie Marcel, 'Investment in Middle East Oil: Who Needs Whom?', *Chatham House Reports*, London, February 2006. *www.chathamhouse.org.uk/ files/3304_vmfeb06.pdf*

71 Michael Bradshaw, 'Striking a New Deal: Cooperation Remains Essential', *Pacific Russia Oil & Gas Report*, Summer 2007, 9–14, (page 14 here).

72 For up to date developments around Shtokman: www.oil-and-gas.net/index. php?page_id=3630

73 See the chapter 'Changing Energy Use Patterns' by Robert Orttung in this book.

CHAPTER 3

CHANGING ENERGY USE PATTERNS: INCREASING EFFICIENCY, ADOPTING ALTERNATIVE SOURCES

Robert W. Orttung

In order to reduce their dependence on imported energy and non-renewable fossil fuels, many consuming countries are adopting domestic policies aimed at increasing energy efficiency and expanding the use of new alternative energy sources. While these policies seek to address domestic needs, they will have a significant impact on international politics, particularly in relation to producing countries, and the nature of that impact will be determined by the kind of policies both consumers and producers adopt. These changes can provide numerous benefits for all countries: making it easier to achieve adequate supplies by reducing overall demand, addressing the problem of climate change, and reducing the political tensions created by a growing number of consumers chasing after an ever dwindling supply of hydrocarbons. Nevertheless, despite the obvious benefits, making the transition from the existing energy supply system to a new one will be a difficult and expensive process.

There is a growing global consensus that current energy usage patterns are not sustainable. This realization is a dramatic break from past beliefs and assumptions. Using fossil fuels at today's rate is producing global warming that most scientists and politicians believe could, if unchecked, lead to catastrophic consequences for the Earth's environment. However, climate change is a slow moving process. There is still time to change policies and adopt viable solutions.

To address the situation, countries must reduce carbon dioxide (CO_2) emissions as part of a larger international process. Thanks to recent trends in globalization, Western countries outsource much of their production to China and other low-cost manufacturers that rely heavily on coal. Dependence on coal generates large amounts of CO_2, which affects the climate for everyone. Such practices epitomize the kind of problems that cannot continue indefinitely without lasting consequences.

Inevitably, for countries to switch to new systems of energy supply means changing existing relationships. Such changes will not happen quickly. Currently renewable energy sources make up only 5 per cent of global power usage.[1] It will take decades to significantly expand the use of energy-saving technologies and renewable energy supplies. Without proper preparations, such changes may be destabilizing for the international system, as consumers seek new supplies and producer countries lose their current customers. However, in the long term, all countries will be better off if the international community can develop a more sustainable energy system that does not do significant damage to the environment.

The first priority is to increase energy efficiency, and while reducing demand is easier than finding new supplies, making such changes requires significant up-front investments. To date, the USA has done a poor job of addressing such needs, while the EU and Japan have made more progress. Once these investments are made, they can produce clear advantages, since increasing efficiency can spur economic benefits – the new technology mastered in this process can be transferred into new markets.

Although most countries have not given high priority to energy efficiency, they have increased their efficiency over time in practice.[2] Table 3.1 displays the energy intensity figures for the entire planet as well as in major countries and regions around the world for 1995 and 2005. Overall, the world succeeded in reducing the amount of energy required to produce a unit of Gross National Product (GNP) during the 10 years from 1995 to 2005. Of the major consumers, the USA is least efficient and uses somewhat more energy than the Europeans. China is about halfway between the USA and Europe. Major energy producers, such as the Middle East and the former Soviet Union, are

Table 3.1: World energy intensity: total primary energy consumption per dollar of GDP using purchasing power parities, 1995, 2005 (BTU per US dollar)

Region/Country	1995	2005
World	9,335	8,035
USA	11,352	9,113
C. & S. America	6,556	6,792
Europe	8,112	7,177
Former Soviet Union	20,776	14,681
Middle East	14,150	15,037
Africa	6,962	6,365
China	9,763	7,906
India	5,215	4,001

Source: US Energy Information Administration, *International Energy Annual 2005*, posted October 1, 2007 www.eia.doe.gov/pub/international/iealf/tablee1p. xls

extremely inefficient energy consumers, with the situation in the Middle East worsening during this period.

Policies aimed at increasing efficiency and developing renewable sources are largely functions of domestic politics and rarely overlap into the area of foreign policy. However, these demand-side adjustments have international implications, in the same way that efforts to find greater supplies of oil and gas do. The impact affects the level of conflict and cooperation. In particular, current fossil fuel producers fear that they will lose their customer base or that demand will become discontinuous, further exacerbating drops in demand due to economic cycles. While consumer countries will not become completely independent of foreign oil and gas, as many politicians proclaim is their goal, they may be able to make significant cuts in their consumption requirements. However, the likelihood of such changes should not be exaggerated, as energy usage is expected to remain considerable for the foreseeable future. The 2008 International Energy Agency (IEA) reference scenario estimates that global primary energy demand will expand 1.6 per cent each year between 2006 and 2030, based on the assumption that governments continue their current policies. According to alternate scenarios, which pay greater attention to reducing CO_2 output, the rate of growth would be 1.2 per cent or even less.[3] Much also depends on the price of energy in the future and the state of the global economy. Given the rapid rise and sudden drop in oil prices over the course of 2008, it is difficult to predict how energy prices will fluctuate in the future. While low prices naturally benefit consumer countries, they have the unfortunate side effect of reducing interest in increased efficiency and alternative sources of energy.

Similarly, there is enormous potential to cut greenhouse gas emissions through increasing energy efficiency and adopting alternative sources of energy. If policies currently under consideration are put into effect, then the world could potentially cut its production from 41 Gt CO_2 in 2030 to 33 Gt, according to estimates by the IEA.[4] Increased efficiency in terms of electricity and fossil fuel use would deliver as much as 78 per cent of the savings, while the rest would come from the use of nuclear power and a variety of renewable energies.[5]

Western leaders often portray reduced dependence on foreign oil and gas as a universal good, but such an outcome would cause dislocation among producer countries, forcing them to adapt to the reduced demand for their output. In a situation in which there is less need for oil and gas, producing countries would have much less influence than they do today. However, because all countries could benefit from increased efficiency levels, the introduction of such innovations also creates opportunities for international cooperation. Such reorderings of the world energy system have been predicted in the past, particularly in response to the energy crisis following the Arab oil embargo in the 1970s. Then, in response to the shut off of energy supplies, improved efficiency levels caused temporary reductions in demand. However, with the reappearance of cheap energy, US consumers quickly returned to previous levels in terms of consuming oil, gas, and coal, though European and Japanese consumers maintained some efficiency measures. The situation is now different, because there is growing consensus that the use of hydrocarbons is causing global warming and is therefore unsustainable at current levels. There is also an awareness that hydrocarbon supplies will not last forever. While the 'peak oil' literature may have been too alarmist in predicting the imminent end of the Earth's oil supplies, energy planners recognize that hydrocarbon supplies will eventually run out and, sooner or later, energy consumers will have to find a different way of fuelling their economies.[6]

Despite the politicians' rhetoric, the IEA figures cited above suggest that talk of achieving 'energy independence' is not realistic because the Organization for Economic Cooperation and Development (OECD) countries will continue to remain dependent on imported oil and natural gas. In this sense, there is no major threat to producers because even if consumers adopt a strong programme aimed at cutting usage, energy imports will continue to grow at least until 2015. Any changes in usage are necessarily going to be incremental over time. Accordingly, they can be managed to reduce any possibility of deleterious influence on the producing countries. In this sense, the adoption of greater efficiency and alternative sources of energy does not really present much of a threat to producing countries.

This chapter will first lay out the most important characteristics of the old system of international energy supply and consumption, and then examine what is new and changing. A key focus is on the possibilities for increasing efficiency and the use of alternative fuels. The second section lays out the difficulties of making the transition from the status quo to a new type of energy system at the national level. The final section examines what the implications of improved efficiency and the adoption of alternative sources will be on potential conflict and cooperation in the international political system.

The Old and New International Energy Systems

The traditional energy system, which was in place until prices started rising precipitously after 2000, took advantage of cheap and abundant fossil fuel energy sources. This system discouraged energy efficiency and the search for alternative sources. As prices rose and a consensus began to build that it was necessary to address climate change, there was growing interest in new technologies. Despite this interest, however, taking action proved difficult because traditional consumers in the West, new consumers in China and India, and the producers all came at the problem from a different perspective. Progress has been slow and halting.

The Traditional System of Energy Supply and Consumption

The traditional energy system drew on abundant supplies of cheap oil, deflecting attention from efficiency and alternative sources. With the economics of plentiful supplies encouraging consumption, the environmental movement largely remained on the fringes of society. Readily available inexpensive sources of energy meant that there was no real need to look elsewhere. The 1973 Arab oil blockade changed the situation temporarily, but its impact was short-lived. The result was that fossil fuels made up nearly 87 per cent of global energy consumption in 2006.[7] Oil, natural gas, and coal provide most of the energy people use to heat their homes and offices, fuel cars, run factories, and grow food. Among the major energy consumers, several European countries have taken the lead in introducing efficiency and alternative energy source policies, frequently outstripping actions adopted in the USA. This divergence became clear in the 1980s, when the impact of the 1973 oil crisis wore off in the USA. While Americans benefit from extensive resources, stress a more individualistic culture, and have a historic aversion to high taxes and government intervention, Europeans typically have fewer natural resources, are more community minded, and are more generally willing to accept state intervention. Accordingly, the Europeans have been willing to impose high energy taxes on their populations, holding down consumption, while American politicians have refused to take such a step.

Since petroleum supplies were relatively cheap and abundant for most of the twentieth century, policy-makers and consumers gave little thought to increasing efficiency and developing alternative sources of energy. Oil is well entrenched in the current system because it is a convenient source of fuel, given its high-energy content and the ease with which it can be shipped around the world. The infrastructure to transport oil is extensive, since energy consumers are usually located far from production sites.[8] The interdependencies created by the enormous costs of this infrastructure have forced countries to cooperate with each other, even though they are engaged in a variety of other political and economic disputes. Venezuela, for example, has continued to provide oil to the USA even though President Hugo Chavez has launched a broad array of anti-American initiatives. Likewise, the Soviet Union and Iran continued to supply oil to the West even during the highpoints of their conflicts.

When the Organization of Petroleum-Exporting Countries (OPEC) imposed an oil blockade on the USA, raised prices to other customers by 70 per cent, and cut production in 1973, it had a large impact on consumer attitudes toward energy at the time. The high prices and short supplies forced consumers to think about ways to conserve energy and find alternative sources for the first time. Several oil price shocks followed. Between 1978 and 1983, US petroleum consumption dropped from 18.8 to 15.2 mb/d.[9] The Europeans also made adjustments. They imposed a high tax on gasoline, resulting in pump prices for European drivers that are far higher than those in the USA. France began investing heavily in nuclear power as an alternative to dependence on international oil flows, and now generates 78.1 per cent of its electricity from such reactors.[10] The decision to concentrate on nuclear technology and invest heavily in it created a legacy that still influences France's energy use today.

With a few exceptions, such as France's nuclear investment, these changes in behaviour did not last long, particularly in the USA. By the mid-1980s, prices had dropped again and the West was able to secure continued access to cheap energy, because it was essentially the only consumer of the world's existing supplies. Drivers, home owners, and business managers went back to their old ways, using energy with little regard for the extent of supplies or the impact on the environment. Since cheap oil was available from the later 1980s until about 2004, few made energy efficiency a high priority.

Price is the key determinant. The higher the price of oil, the greater the interest in improved efficiency and alternatives. As the price of oil climbs, alternatives become more cost effective. However, as soon as the price comes down, lessons learned are usually forgotten. This phenomenon has been repeating itself with great regularity in the recent past. Californians, for example, failed to keep in place the energy savings they achieved following the electricity crisis of 2000 and 2001, when the state faced brownouts. Once the drama ended in 2002 and more supplies were available, half of the earlier savings disappeared.[11] The sudden oil price drop of 2008 naturally again raises the spectre that consumers will return to profligate energy use, though the poor state of the economy suggests that there are also strong drivers for conservation.

Even though price was the main determinant in energy policy, the USA and European countries developed different policies in response to the crisis caused by the 1970s oil shocks. John Ikenberry's important work examining national responses to the energy crisis suggests that these differences are a function of state strength: the relatively strong French state invested heavily in nuclear power, while the much weaker US state focused on market responses that required little state intervention.[12] In other words, the capacities of each state defined what measures it could take in addressing the challenges presented by the crisis. In responding to today's crisis, a variety of other factors are at play as well. In the political sphere, European governments are much more capable of imposing high taxes on their populations, a possibility that is typically considered political suicide within the US system. The legacy of the Goldwater–Reagan anti-big government philosophy remains strong in the American psyche.

The politics of economic and budgetary issues are also at play. The US political process has made it extremely difficult even for well-intentioned politicians to set in place long-term policies to deal with issues such as promoting energy security, when price concerns are not an immediate issue. For example, maintaining a major Research and Development (R&D) programme for alternative energies would require consistent funding and support. Despite growing interest in the issue, however, 30 years after being opened by President Jimmy Carter, the US's National Renewable Energy Laboratory barely had enough money to get by.[13] As discussed below, beginning around 2000 Germany was able to make a much stronger commitment to solar power, and greatly increased its role in the German energy supply system.

Under the status quo global energy system, the role for alternative energy sources has been small. These technologies were undeveloped and have not provided a cost-effective alternative to traditional fuel sources such as oil, natural gas, and coal. Only heavy government subsidies and the involvement of individuals interested in the early adoption of innovative new technologies have spurred the development of these sources.

What is New?

Higher prices, tighter supplies, the rise of China and India, the increasingly popular view of energy as a security issue, and growing concern about the environment are driving much greater interest in efficiency and alternative sources. However, it will be difficult for traditional consumers in the West, new consumers in China and India, and producers to address the common climate challenge, since they all come to the problem from different perspectives.

Since 2003 several changes have transformed the traditional energy system. First, rapidly growing demand for energy has led to higher prices, so the era of relatively cheap oil is over. Even the dramatic price drop in the second half of 2008 did not return prices to their historically low levels, and prices are expected to climb when the global economy picks up again. Second, the depletion of oil and gas fields in the West, and the concentration of production in the Middle East has increased dependence on this region. At the same time, in the wake of the 9/11 terrorist attacks, many in the West now view energy as a security issue, since Western money funds petrodictators in Saudi Arabia, Russia, Venezuela, and elsewhere, who use the money against Western interests.[14] Third, the rise of new consumers like China and India has made it possible for producing countries to sell their oil and gas to others besides their traditional customers in the West. However, it remains unclear how much energy these countries will want, and how much they will be willing to pay for it. With the combination of these concerns, policy makers now recognize that the traditional system of energy supply is no longer sustainable.[15]

These three trends are driving traditional consumers in the USA, Europe, and Japan to place a much higher priority on energy efficiency and alternative sources, which introduces new kinds of uncertainty into energy markets. While the oil price drop in 2008 may delay the move toward efficiency and alternative sources, there is little doubt that it will happen in the long term. Producers view this new interest in reducing consumption as a threat to their demand security. With key customers seeking alternative sources of energy, producers have expressed concern that the demand for their energy will be unstable in the future. Under these conditions, there is a drifting apart of producers and consumers, as interest in mutual dependence drops.

This drift is all the more pronounced because consumers often do not recognize the international consequences of their plans. For example, a proposal for a major increase in US reliance on solar power, published in *Scientific American*, made the far-fetched claim that ending US oil imports would 'eas[e] political tension in the Middle East', without explaining how the cause and effect are logically connected.[16]

With the growing consensus that climate change is a reality, however, there is a strong impetus for cooperation to prevent extensive environmental damage to the planet. The environmental impact of energy usage frames the problem as a common one facing producers, traditional consumers, and new consumers alike. Nevertheless, leveraging the potential opportunities will be difficult. There are different perceptions on the three sides as to who should do what and when. In particular, China and India are not ready to adopt the efficiency and alternative energy practices of the developed world. They feel that they should not be made to carry the burden for addressing this issue, particularly when consumption patterns in the West have been mainly responsible for causing it. The traditional consumers are even further split amongst themselves on how seriously they take the issue of climate change. In the USA, the issue of global warming is extremely political, with the left, identified most prominently with former Vice President Al Gore, issuing warnings about the problem, while the right frequently dismissed the issue. Despite these political cross currents, public opinion polling evidence suggested that a majority of Americans were concerned about the environment and were willing to pay for changes in the way they use energy.[17]

The US federal government under the Bush administration paid little attention to climate change, but numerous state and local governments responded with efforts to save energy and to reduce reliance on fossil fuels.[18] President Obama expressed much greater concern about this issue, and sought to cooperate with other countries in addressing it. Even with a growing consensus about the need for action, policy change will be very slow because, in addition to the enormous infrastructure costs, the political process has not supported reform. American politicians across the spectrum are reluctant to ask their constituents to make the kind of sacrifices they say that they are ready to make. At the same time, status quo energy interests have also been able to protect their position within the corridors of Washington.

In contrast to the USA, among traditional consumers, the EU has set its energy policy goals as promoting security, ensuring sustainable economic development, and protecting the environment. Unlike the Bush administration, European leaders made climate change a key priority. Also in contrast to the USA and many of the developing countries, Europe pledged to implement commitments made during the Kyoto process, which sets limits on greenhouse gas emissions. In contrast to their American and developing country counterparts, the Europeans called for aggressive efforts to cut down on emissions. The Europeans have also gone beyond the limited requirements of the Kyoto process. In March 2007, the EU members committed themselves to a major policy innovation that integrates energy and environmental concerns. The EU sought to take a leadership position on these issues by declaring that it would save 20 per cent of energy consumption, compared to projections for 2020, increase to 20 per cent the share of renewables in overall energy consumption, and cut greenhouse gas emissions by at least 20 per cent by 2020.[19] The EU has vowed to try to reach these goals regardless of what other countries do.

While the Europeans have always taken a leading position on environmental issues, they have not always been able to achieve unity. They are now partly driven by the rise of an assertive Russia, that has demonstrated a willingness to use its energy to achieve political goals, particularly against its neighbour Ukraine. Fear of being dependent on an assertive Russia has helped the Europeans find common cause in pushing for increased efficiency and alternative energy sources. Europe is particularly vulnerable to Russian threats because it receives 24 per cent of its total natural gas and 27 per cent of its oil from its eastern neighbour.[20] When Russia cut off natural gas supplies to Ukraine at the beginning of 2006 causing gas shortages in Europe, Europeans woke up to a new reality in which they were dependent on the whims of the Kremlin for their energy supplies. Previously, the Europeans had seen little need to question Russia's reliability. The even longer gas dispute of 2009 only confirmed Europe's growing concerns.

New consumer countries like China naturally emphasize economic advancement over environmental concerns. They want the chance to build up their economies, prioritizing economic growth over environmental protections, just as the West had done when it first went through the process of industrialization. Since China's most abundant and easily accessible source of energy is coal, it is developing this resource as part of its policy to meet its energy needs. As a result, it surpassed the USA as the largest greenhouse gas emitter in 2006.[21]

However, the extensive pollution caused by coal is forcing a re-examination of policies. While Chinese leaders are still focused on increasing energy supply, they are also beginning to consider its consequences. For example, on 4 June 2007, China released its first national climate change plan.[22] The document lists the ways that China will address climate change through mitigation, research, and public awareness campaigns. While the plan does not include enough programmes for China to address global warming adequately, its adoption shows that the leaders of the world's largest developing country are now taking the issues of global warming seriously.[23] In its 11th five-year plan, China has committed itself to cutting its energy intensity to 20 per cent below 2005 levels by 2010. Likewise, the National Renewable Energy Law of 2005 set a target for producing 16 per cent of primary energy from renewable sources by 2020, up from about 7 per cent at the time of adoption.

The energy-producing countries have their own take on how to deal with global warming. Saudi Arabia is actively promoting carbon capture and storage technologies as a way to address the problem, because such technologies would deal with the environmental issues without requiring countries to curtail their use of fossil fuels. The Saudis argue, reasonably, that oil and gas will be with us for many decades into the future, so it makes sense to make them more environmentally friendly. According to their logic, cleaner fossil fuel technologies are 'compatible with current energy infrastructures and would not lead to costly and disruptive change'.[24] Western advocates do not always place this form of technology as their highest priority, stressing instead the development of alternative energy sources. Nevertheless, through forums like the EU–OPEC Roundtable on Carbon Dioxide Capture and Storage, the two sides can potentially find ways to unite efforts in mutually advantageous ways.

Increasing Use of Efficiency-Enhancing Technology and Alternative Sources

The growing consensus around the need to cut CO_2 emissions is driving greater interest in a host of new technologies. Countries seeking to reduce their dependence on fossil fuels face a difficult set of choices in picking the best way to move forward with energy efficiency and alternative fuel technologies. Certainly, there is no single easy answer that will radically change the energy supply system. Rather, each country will have to compile a set of partial solutions that makes the overall system work. In the short term, increasing energy efficiency is the best solution, while alternative sources can be developed over the longer term.

Increasing energy efficiency should be a top priority for all countries, because it offers the quickest way to reduce demand for energy and minimize damage to the environment.[25] A United Nations Foundation report issued in the summer of 2007 called on the G8 countries to double 'the global historic annual rate of energy efficiency improvement to 2.5 per cent per year from approximately 2012 through 2030'.[26] The report estimated that the money invested in making these improvements would be paid back within 3–5 years thanks to the energy saved as a result of the new technologies. The IEA makes similar declarations for the efficacy of investing in greater efficiency. It claims that 'Every additional dollar invested in more efficient electrical equipment and appliances mitigates paying more than two additional dollars in investment in power generation, transmission and distribution lines'.[27]

Several technological innovations propelled the improvement in energy efficiency described in Table 3.1. Improved energy saving technology in refrigeration, air conditioning, and heating have made such appliances much more efficient than they used to be.[28] There have also been improvements in building standards. In terms of automobile efficiency, an area that is particularly important since the transportation sector consumes a considerable amount of energy, Europe, Japan, China, and Australia have outstripped the USA.[29]

Increasing energy efficiency is not simply a matter for energy experts. Great savings can be gained, for example, through better information management, improved scheduling and shipping, and other aspects of business organization that rely heavily on greater information availability. The USA, in particular, was able to increase energy intensity in the period from 1997 to 2001 at an average of 2.7 per cent per year due to increased use of these information-based technologies.[30] Buildings that can sense when rooms are occupied and then automatically turn off lights when they are not in use could save large amounts of electricity that are currently wasted. Even more effective are systems that can sense the level of daylight entering through windows and adjust the lighting accordingly. Wal-Mart reported a two-year payback when it installed such systems in its stores.[31]

This section has shown how the energy system has changed over time, particularly in light of rising prices and the growing consensus about climate change. The result is an increased interest in energy efficiency and alternative sources. Adopting such changes is a function of national level policies. The next section examines the difficulties of implementing energy efficiency and alternative energy technologies at the national level.

National-Level Obstacles to Securing the Use of Efficiency Enhancing and Alternative Energy Technologies

There are numerous political, economic, and technological obstacles to the implementation of new efficiency and alternative energy possibilities. In the political sphere, the central issues are taxes, subsidies, and regulations encouraging the use of energy-saving technology. The main obstacle in the economic sphere is the high cost of buying new efficient equipment to replace previous models. In the technological sphere, countries have to balance the role of the state and private sector to stimulate innovation, scientists must overcome a number of technical challenges, and policy-makers must make choices among various alternative energy sources, weighing the advantages of each new technology against its inevitable downsides.

Political Issues

The political issues work at a variety of levels. At the individual level, implementing efficiency and alternative energies requires changes in personal behaviour regarding energy consumption. On one hand, this behaviour can be influenced by government policies (taxes, subsidies, and regulations) and market incentives that encourage individual citizens to save energy or to convert to alternative sources. On the other hand, such changes can result from individuals acting on their own, because they are willing to spend part of their disposable income on energy saving or alternative technologies. While there is some debate on whether individual actions add up to significant change, climate change activists feel that every little bit helps.[32]

At the national level, among the traditional consuming countries, Europeans have been much more focused on efficiency and alternative sources than their American counterparts. In 2000 Germany passed a Renewable Energy Law that allowed it to double renewable energy generation, bringing usage up to 12.5 per cent by mid-2007, three years earlier than planned. Germany is the world leader in installed wind-power capacity, and has the largest photovoltaic market, even though the country gets much less sunshine than some of its southern neighbours.[33] Between 1992 and 2004, Denmark increased its use of renewable fuels from 3 per cent to 24 per cent. The government guaranteed an above-market price for the energy, spurring investment because businesses were assured of a return. In both cases, the governments passed the higher costs on to consumers.[34]

Historically, American consumers have favoured big cars, paying little attention to their environmental consequences. American carmakers knew their market and produced vehicles to meet these needs. Environmental groups in the country that sought to force changes were never strong enough to counter the power of this consumer–corporate nexus.[35] European and Japanese publics and auto makers were typically more aware of the need to promote efficiency and to take environmental considerations into account. For example, the British Motor Corporation introduced the Morris Mini in the 1950s. This utilized a sideways-mounted engine, a front-wheel drive system, accommodated four passengers, and was extremely efficient.[36] American companies did not adopt this technology until the late 1970s. Detroit's foreign competitors were able to win a significant share of the American market, satisfying those buyers who sought greater fuel efficiency.

More recently, there have been signs of change. At the end of 2007, President Bush signed a major energy bill into law, entitled the Energy Independence and Security Act of 2007, that will force American home owners to replace incandescent lights with compact florescent lights beginning in 2012; auto fleets will be required to meet an average of 35 miles a gallon by 2020 (a 40 per cent increase from the existing standard of 25 miles per gallon, which was adopted in 1975); and production of biofuels will be increased to 36 billion gallons a year by 2022, five times current production.[37] Additionally, by the end of 2008, General Motors and Chrysler had to accept federal bailout money to survive; the money came on the condition that they revised their products to meet efficiency and environmental concerns.

Another key issue for politicians is to reduce current subsidies to fossil fuel producers. These subsidies artificially lower the costs of fossil fuels and perversely encourage their use. In 2005, the IEA estimated that non-OECD countries provided as much as $250 billion in direct energy consumption subsidies to residences and factories.[38] Indirect subsidies are much harder to calculate, but one estimate suggests that they are $30 billion to $50 billion annually in the USA alone.[39] These estimates are high because they include such costs as defence, transportation, and tax expenditures that are not specific to energy. For example, the USA spends as much as $44.4 billion annually simply to secure the oil trade in the Persian Gulf.[40] US direct government expenditure subsidies were approximately $2 billion in FY 1999.[41] Reducing subsidies would have the effect of raising some fuel prices, but with the beneficial impact of increasing incentives for greater efficiency and alternative energy use. Naturally, efforts to remove such subsidies will be blocked by the interest groups that currently benefit from them. For example, Congress could not pass the 2007 US energy bill until it removed a tax package that would have eliminated benefits for the largest US oil and gas companies.[42]

While subsidies for alternative energy may make sense as a way to expand their usage, even some of these are not rational. US corn farmers who turn their crop into ethanol receive federal subsidies even in years when they are prospering and do not need the support. However, Congress does not seem interested in making changes, especially since such a reform would mean that less money would flow to Iowa, traditionally the first state to cast a vote in the US presidential primary marathon, and therefore one with extraordinary political weight.[43]

Such resistance could be reduced by ploughing the money saved from reducing subsidies back into energy-saving efforts in the affected areas. President Obama has sought to build support for alternative energy by making it a central part of his economic stimulus package.

Economic Issues

Overturning the status quo will be expensive.[44] Often the technology to increase energy efficiency exists, but the high cost of installing new equipment presents an enormous obstacle to making the transition from the current dependence on fossil fuels to a new system. Much depends on the future price of oil and the availability of credit, both of which are hard to predict as banks around the world struggle to survive. Not surprisingly, it has often been hard to muster the political will to make the investments now to reap rewards in the future. For example, the UK government *Stern Review on the Economics of Climate Change* argues that spending relatively small amounts now to counter global warming will save the planet from a much larger price tag later.[45] Nevertheless, the report came under attack from critics who sought to avoid even these lower expenses.

The new technologies are typically not cost competitive with the old ones. Paying for R&D, and the production of pilot and demonstration plants, is expensive and requires companies to overcome what is described as the 'mountain of death' for potential new technologies.[46] Funding the resources to surmount these difficulties usually requires government subsidies. Installing solar units for business or residential use only makes sense for the end user if the state pays for part of the equipment needed, and provides other tax incentives. While there may be less interest in investing in new energy technologies during an economic downturn, government spending to stimulate the economy can prioritize 'green technologies' and create new sources of capital.[47] President Obama's administration included $16.8 billion for energy efficiency and renewable energy in the $787 billion February 2009 economic stimulus package.[48] Japan is currently one of the few places where government subsidies have greatly stimulated solar installations, but it has extremely high electricity costs, making it easier for solar power to compete.[49]

Although fossil fuels are still cheaper than the currently existing alternatives, the balance is starting to shift in favour of alternatives, particularly with the high cost of oil and gas, according to a February 2007 analysis in the *Wall Street Journal*.[50] For example, wind power electricity cost 80 cents per kilowatt hour in 1980, 10 cents in 1991, and now is typically down to 6–9 cents, which is getting close to the cost of generating electricity from coal, about 3–5 cents. Generating electricity with solar panels has cost 35–45 cents, but a new technology focused on 'concentrating solar power' will bring the price down to 9–12 cents. These improved figures mean that alternative energies will likely soon become cost competitive, so that private industry can play a larger role. Moreover, foundations like Google.org are working to achieve the goal of cost-effective energy from green sources.

Technological Issues

Technological challenges also present an obstacle to implementing higher efficiency levels and bringing alternative sources of energy online. Part of the solution is in applying already existing technologies. A 2007 report by the McKinsey Global Institute found that the estimated annual growth in energy demand could be cut by more than half by using currently available technologies.[51] Even if the technology already exists, implementing change will take time: approximately 10 years to substantially replace the automobile stock and 50–70 years to replace buildings.

Another part of the solution comes from developing new technologies. Innovation requires an intelligent mixture of state and private actions. State funding is necessary to support the basic scientific research behind technological advances. However, in the USA, critics point out that federal R&D efforts are performing poorly because they are fragmented and unfocused. Assuming that the state can make the underlying basic science available, private investors can then take over to commercialize research findings. The government's job is to create an environment in which innovation can flourish.[52]

As soon as private industry sees an opportunity for profit, it can play a role in stimulating innovation. In Silicon Valley venture capitalists and technology firms are making large investments in alternative technology solutions. Most prominently, financier Vinod Khosla has backed a variety of new ideas. Companies like Cypress Semiconductors have gone from making computer chips to constructing solar panels.[53] Private companies are also investing in the basic science. In February 2007 BP made a 10 year, $500 million commitment to the University of California, Berkeley, the Lawrence Berkeley National Laboratory, and the University of Illinois at Urbana–Champaign for energy research. Billionaire Richard Branson is investing in synthetic fuels that could potentially be used in his Virgin Atlantic airline.[54] 'Venture capital in energy has reached a critical mass', according to energy expert Daniel Yergin.[55]

In stimulating innovation, different countries have different state capacities which they can use. Brazil is frequently cited as a successful example of a consuming country that was able to use ethanol to replace 40 per cent of its oil consumption for transportation fuels, through a concerted national effort beginning in the 1970s.[56] The Brazilian ethanol industry benefited from a number of advantages, such as guaranteed purchases by the state-owned oil company Petrobras and fixed gasoline and ethanol prices, where ethanol sold for 59 per cent of the gasoline price at the pump.[57] Such tools would not be available in the USA where there is no state-owned oil company or price controls. Brazil's programme remained effective even after the government dismantled its fiscal and price supports. Of course, it is not necessary to exactly reproduce this experience to develop a similar industry elsewhere in the future.

Today, the technological problems involved in developing alternative energy sources further are enormous. Solar power, for example, is seen as one of the best sources of electricity in the future because sunlight is an abundant resource that can be consumed with few consequences for the environment. Currently, however, it provides less than 1 per cent of electricity worldwide and only 0.01 per cent of the US electricity supply.[58] Even in 25 to 30 years it is not expected to contribute more than a few per cent. To be effective, the technology needs to capture the sun's energy and transform it into electricity more efficiently, and there need to be better ways of storing that energy once it is captured.

In the area of biofuels, the biggest challenge facing scientists now is 'how to break down cell wall material, which is a combination of cellulose and lignin, in a more cost-effective, energy-efficient way'.[59] Ultimately, the goal is to produce cellulosic ethanol from Miscanthus, a 13-foot tall grass that grows much faster, causes less soil erosion, and requires less water and fertilizer than other plants. Cellulosic ethanol is chemically identical to ethanol produced from corn starch or sugar, but it is much more readily available. It differs from the other sources because it requires a more difficult chemical process to make the ethanol.

Nanotechnology, in which scientists work at the level of the atom, offers huge promise and is expected to create a $3 trillion worldwide industry by 2014. In the energy sphere, nanotechnologies could potentially transform the power grid by replacing copper wire with carbon nanotubes, which can carry 1,000 times as much electricity without losing heat in the process.[60] Nanotechnology may also hold the answer for improving the efficiency of solar panels to provide cheap electricity.[61] Products using nanotechnology are already coming on the market, but

Table 3.2: Advantages and disadvantages of various fuel technologies

Technology	Advantages	Disadvantages
Increasing Efficiency	Easiest 'source' of new energy; lower fuel bills pay off initial investments	Initial investments can be expensive; rebound effect (energy savings may encourage new uses which ultimately increase total energy use)
Oil	Cheaper than many other sources; proven technology; convenient; extensive infrastructure in place; could be environmentally-friendly through carbon capture technology	Supplies running out; creates greenhouse gases; sends money to adversarial regimes; promotes corruption, authoritarianism in producing countries
Natural Gas	Abundant supplies; less impact on the environment than oil; pipelines link Russia and Europe; could be sold as LNG on global market	Supplies located in authoritarian countries; causes greenhouse gases; extensive investment needed for drilling and transportation; creates strong dependencies when sent via pipeline
Coal	Abundant in some consuming countries; relatively cheap	Dangerous to mine; dirty; emits extensive greenhouse gases
Biofuels	Renewable, domestic source; second generation sources (cellulose) could provide more energy while overcoming the problems associated with first generation sources (corn)	Using corn increases food prices; uses extensive land; drains aquifers; exacerbates fertilizer runoff; crops may damage soil; accelerates deforestation; damages biodiversity; cellulosic ethanol is not yet economically feasible
Geothermal	Using underground heat sources provides renewable, cheap electricity in some locations, such as the Pacific ring of fire; very effective in Philippines;[62] using 55° Fahrenheit temperatures underground can help with heating in winter, cooling in summer	Using underground heat requires consistent management effort to utilize effectively; taking advantage of 55° F for residential uses is expensive

Table 3.2: *Continued*

Technology	Advantages	Disadvantages
Nuclear	Domestic source; proven, cost-effective technology; no greenhouse gases	Expensive to build new plants; Radioactive waste; increased chance of proliferation; water used for cooling heats rivers, therefore limited application in the summer when electricity demand is high[63]
Solar	Abundant supply; no greenhouse gases	More expensive than conventional electricity generation; doesn't work at night; need to improve sunlight gathering efficiency, increase energy storage; solar panel production produces toxic waste
Wind	Generates electricity from renewable sources when oil is over $40/barrel	Unsightly turbines; danger to wildlife; takes up rural land; need to transport from area of production to consumer centres
Heavy Oil, shale oil, tar sands	Available in the USA and Canada (also Venezuela, Australia, Brazil, China, and Russia); expands known oil reserves	10 times as expensive as producing a barrel of oil from Saudi Arabia; production process is energy and water intensive; high greenhouse gas output; negative environmental consequences
Ocean waves	900 times as much energy in moving water as air	High cost to capture energy
Algae	Some algae can be converted into biodiesel or jet fuel; grows faster and in less space than other biofuel crops; could be located anywhere; could consume pollution	High cost of production ($20 a gallon); many years until commercially viable
Fuel Cell (Combining hydrogen and oxygen to produce electricity)	CO_2 emissions can be concentrated, with hydrogen used in cars and houses; far more efficient than a typical battery	Extremely expensive to separate hydrogen from other elements and transport it

Source: Compiled by the author from numerous sources.

many questions remain about their safety, and their environmental and health impacts.

As the information in Table 3.2 shows, there are a wide variety of possibilities for providing alternative sources of energy. None of them is a perfect solution, and all of them incur a variety of trade-offs in implementation. Biofuels, for example, could provide a renewable source of domestically-produced energy, but they also have an impact on food prices and on the environment in which they are produced.

Overcoming these obstacles will require extensive political will and economic investment. In the political sphere, national leaders will have to make a concerted effort to address the issues of taxes, subsidies, and regulations. These reforms will then make it possible for investors to pay for the development of new technologies to meet the potential offered by increased efficiency and alternative sources. Making the technologies a reality will require intensive efforts by states and private sectors to develop the basic science and then to bring the new innovations to market. However, the successful development of these new technologies at the national level could have negative consequences at the international level if not handled correctly. The next section will examine these challenges.

Energy and International Politics

This third section examines the international consequences of the introduction of efficiency and alternative energy technologies at the national level. While greater efficiency and new sources can serve consuming countries' interests by reducing their dependence on outside supplies, such changes can create tensions in the international system by depriving producing countries of their customers. This section examines ways of avoiding such conflicts. It lays out common interests among producers and consumers, particularly focusing on the establishment of a balanced energy system, the overall benefits of increasing efficiency, and fighting climate change. Subsequently, it focuses on ways to facilitate international cooperation. It examines the obstacles to such cooperation and then suggests ways to overcome them.

Shared Interests among Producers and Consumers

In a simplistic analysis, energy relationships between producers and consumers are a zero-sum game: producers want the highest price possible, while consumers seek to pay as little as they can. In fact, there is much more room for cooperation. Such shared objectives come in terms of common interests in establishing a balanced international energy system, increasing energy efficiency, and fighting climate change.

The traditional international energy system basically worked for the interests of both producers and consumers. Consumers received reliable and affordable supplies of energy, while producers were well compensated for their natural resources. The system functioned reliably, despite the existence of political conflicts that often divided producers and consumers.

The key to ensuring the stability of the new energy system will therefore be to make sure that it meets the needs of the traditional consumers, new consumers, and producers. Achieving this commonality of interests will be largely a function of investments. The consuming countries will have to invest heavily in increased efficiency and alternative sources, to ensure that they are able to meet their energy needs in the future. Likewise, the producing countries will have to use their current windfall gains to secure their economic future for a time when they are no longer in a position to sell hydrocarbons. The drivers in ensuring that these investments are made appropriately will be efforts to benefit economically from the new technologies, and concern to end climate change.

Both consuming and producing countries share an interest in promoting greater energy efficiency. Consuming countries obviously want to reduce their demand for imported fuel to limit their current high reliance on exporting countries that are often working against Western interests.[64] Given their generally more advanced economic and technological bases, the consuming countries have typically taken the lead in developing new technologies. Most of the innovations discussed in this chapter have come from the USA and Europe, as they have sought to make advances with this type of technology.

Although oil producing countries naturally benefit from maintaining the world's current dependence on hydrocarbons, they can also benefit from technologies to improve efficiency. As noted earlier, many of the energy-producing countries are currently among the most energy inefficient in the world. Russia wastes enormous amounts of energy with its aging infrastructure, centralized residential heating system, and flaring of natural gas at oil well sites.[65] Russian residential and industrial consumers benefit from subsidized energy prices, so using resources efficiently is not a priority. Developing more sources of hydrocarbons is going to be very expensive, because the resources are located in poorly accessible far northern and eastern Siberian regions that are a long way from the ultimate customers. Over the long-term, the country would be better off finding ways to use current and future supplies more efficiently, since doing so would reduce costs for infrastructure, transportation, and the environment. Iran, likewise, is an extremely inefficient energy user. It has long subsidized gasoline prices. Even though it is a petroleum exporter, it must rely on imports of gasoline, because it does not have enough refineries to meet domestic demand. Currently, these countries are heavily reliant on the presence of their abundant resources. To ease their own dependence, they may seek to invent their own solutions, or benefit from the new technologies being developed in the consuming countries.

Naturally, to achieve these gains in energy efficiency, countries must overcome the key obstacles to change. They must be willing to make investments now that have payoffs in future years. Willingness to make these investments fluctuates with the price of oil, so carrying out such investments will require strong political will. Producing countries that fear they will ultimately lose their customer base will also have to take extensive action to prepare for their futures.

Framing energy security issues in terms of climate change makes it possible to promote international cooperation and to overcome the political, economic, and technology challenges listed above. With a warming planet and the resulting consequences, all countries face a common threat that requires joint work to address it. Nevertheless, energy consumers will have to make expensive new investments in efficiency and alternative technologies to deal with climate change.

The stakes are high. Beyond the improved environmental conditions and extended life of their resource endowments, by investing in different types of high technology, producing countries can start diversifying their own economies away from fossil fuels into areas that are more sustainable and profitable over the long term. Abu Dhabi, OPEC's fourth largest producer with 10 per cent of the world's oil reserves, is one country that sees the benefit of this logic. It is investing heavily in renewables, such as solar, wind, and hydrogen power, and working with the Massachusetts Institute of Technology to develop experience in a variety of alternative energy fields.[66] The emirate is a big consumer of power for its air conditioners and swimming pools, and sees the new sources of energy as a way to reduce its own dependence on fossil fuels.

New consumers such as China and India will also need to be convinced that defining energy security in terms of climate change is in their interests. In contrast to traditional consumers in the relatively rich West, new consumers do not have the resources to pay the costs associated with developing and implementing greater energy efficiency and alternative sources of fuel. Beyond any concern for the environment, China does not want to become dependent on foreign sources of energy. As a result, it is implementing tough fuel efficiency standards and working hard to develop electric and hydrogen-based cars.[67] Since the populations of China and India are not major energy users now, on a per capita basis, it is possible that they will be able to learn from the experiences of the Western countries and adopt energy-efficient technologies without first having to rely on existing wasteful technologies.

Traditional consumers are already farthest along in their readiness to adopt climate change as a framework for energy security. Their energy usage patterns are those primarily responsible for the problem, and they have the most resources available to address it. The USA and EU should also accept the fact that addressing climate change along the above lines is a good way for them to engage in cooperative activities with new consumers like China, and with producing states.

Facilitating International Cooperation

Despite the shared interests between producers and consumers, there are numerous obstacles to international cooperation. As noted above, consumers want to change, but doing so will be expensive. Producers will be even harder to convince. Energy producing countries face enormous challenges at home as they try to diversify their economies and manage the social impact on their populations. Many also have unstable political systems that may not be able to survive the stresses such changes will bring. Likewise, the producers will need to import new technologies from the West to spur the economic and social development they must undergo, to compete in the 21st century economy.

What will it take to overcome the political, economic, and technological obstacles and foster change in the international energy system? It is not enough to have national solutions, and it will be necessary to stimulate international approaches as well.

Governance at the international level is necessary to leverage common national interests among the producers and traditional and new consumers. Such international-level action is necessary because all of the benefits discussed here only come over the long term. States might not be willing to take on such costs on their own without external stimulus. As we have seen, it will be difficult for all of the consumers and producers to make such commitments. Energy producers fear that change in the existing energy system will threaten their ability to sell energy. New consumers do not have enough resources to continue their economic growth while simultaneously increasing energy efficiency and reducing environmental impact. Traditional consumers have more resources at their disposal, but fear changes in the energy system that potentially threaten their own prospects for business growth.

There has been considerable discussion about either expanding one of the existing international institutions to deal with this issue, or creating a new one. One idea is to give more powers to the IEA, which was set up in 1974 by the OECD as a way for Western countries to coordinate their actions in response to the Arab oil embargo. Currently, the IEA's key job is to prevent disruptions in the supply of oil. It also promotes alternative energy sources and seeks to coordinate international energy policy among the traditional consuming countries. A key issue now is to bring in new members from among the new group of consuming countries, such as China and India, to expand its reach and ability to address global problems. A major obstacle to such an expansion, however, is that to join the IEA, countries must be members of the OECD, with open markets, democratic political systems, and respect for human rights.[68] Other possibilities, such as expanding the powers of the International Energy Forum (IEF), established in 2003 to promote dialogue between producers and consumers at the ministerial level, have been criticized because the IEF allows oil producing countries to veto its activities.[69]

It is not necessary to create new international institutions.[70] Rather, it will be better to foster self-help approaches within the current system. As states in the three camps see other states leading by example, they should be able to use existing diplomacy and opportunities for information exchange to adopt the best technologies for their own purposes. The media, Internet, and international forums are best placed to help spread effective ideas on how best to conserve energy and develop alternative sources.

Conclusion: Energy, Climate, and International Cooperation

National efforts to develop greater efficiency and alternative sources of energy offer enormous possibilities for international cooperation while creating a more sustainable international energy system for the planet. Traditional consumers, new consumers, and producers can benefit from them. Consumers benefit by reducing their dependence on energy imports, while producers can extend the benefits they derive from their resources, while also diversifying their economies.

Despite this potential, achieving the benefits of technological innovation will require overcoming enormous political and economic obstacles.

Most importantly, producer countries will have to be convinced that they will be able to prosper under the new energy system. Making such assurances realistic will require overcoming doubts that demand for their exports, whether fossil fuels now or new products in the future, will remain strong. Additionally, both consumers and producers will have to believe that investments in greater efficiency and alternative sources will pay off in the future.

Addressing the challenges of global warming requires the contribution of all countries, whether energy producers or consumers. Research is accumulating which suggests that the planet is heating even more quickly than earlier estimates, with consequences that are becoming increasingly apparent. The imperative of focusing on climate change comes against a backdrop of numerous other problems, including volatile economies, terrorism, proliferation of nuclear weapons, poverty, hunger, and disease. Such pressing concerns make it hard for political leaders to focus attention on energy and climate issues. Nevertheless, pursuing the economically advantageous opportunities offered by co-operation is the only way to begin addressing the challenges.

Notes

1   'Renewable Energy Policy Network for the 21ˢᵗ Century', *Renewables 2007 Global Status Report*, REN21 Secretariat Paris and: Worldwatch Institute, Washington, DC., 2008, 6.www.ren21.net/pdf/RE2007_Global_Status_Report.pdf
2   Nathan E. Hultman, 'Can the World Wean Itself from Fossil Fuels?', *Current History* 106: 703, November 2007, 378–9.
3   International Energy Agency, *World Energy Outlook 2008: Executive Summary*, OECD/IEA, Paris 2008, 13. www.worldenergyoutlook.org/docs/weo2008/WEO2008_es_english.pdf
4   IEA, *World Energy Outlook 2008*, 13.
5   Laura Cozzi, 'World Energy Outlook 2006', presentation at 'Global Perspectives on Energy Security', Swiss Re Centre for Global Dialogue, 8–9 March 2007.
6   Kenneth S. Deffeyes, *Beyond Oil: The View from Hubbert's Peak*, Hill and Wang, 2005, and Richard Heinberg, *The Party's Over: Oil, War and the Fate of Industrial Societies*, revised and updated edition, New Society Publishers, Gabriola Island, Canada, 2005.
7   Calculation based on Energy Information Agency figures. www.eia.doe.gov/pub/international/iealf/table18.xls
8   Frank Verrastro and Sarah Ladislaw, 'Providing Energy Security in an Interdependent World', *The Washington Quarterly* 30:4, Autumn 2007, 97.
9   US Department of Energy, Energy Information Administration, 'History

of Energy in the United States, 1635–2000'. www.eia.doe.gov/emeu/aer/eh/frame.html

10 Ariana Eunjung Cha, 'China Embraces Nuclear Future', *Washington Post*, 29 May 2007.

11 Craig Canin, 'California Illuminates the World', *OnEarth*, Spring 2006, www.nrdc.org/onearth/06spr/ca1.asp

12 G. John Ikenberry, 'The Irony of State Strength: Comparative Responses to the Oil Shocks of the 1970s', *International Organization* 40:1, Winter 1986, 105–37.

13 Clifford Krauss, 'Energy Research on a Shoestring', *New York Times*, 25 January 2007.

14 Thomas Friedman, *Hot, Flat and Crowded: Why we need a green revolution – and how it can renew America*, Farrar, Straus, and Giroux, New York, 2008, (esp. chapter 4).

15 Concluding Report to General Conference by Gareth Evans, President, International Crisis Group, as Chair of International Atomic Energy Agency (IAEA) Scientific Forum 2007, Vienna, 20 September 2007. www.crisisgroup.org/home/index.cfm?id=5089&l=1

16 Ken Zweibel, James Mason, Vasilis Fthenakis, 'A Solar Grand Plan', *Scientific American*, January 2008. www.scientificamerican.com/article.cfm?id=a-solar-grand-plan

17 Josef Braml, 'Can the United States Shed Its Oil Addiction?', *The Washington Quarterly* 30:4, Autumn 2007, 124.

18 For a list of these initiatives, see www.pewclimate.org/what_s_being_done/in_the_states

19 For an overview, see European Union Activities: Energy, http://europa.eu/pol/ener/overview_en.htm

20 European Commission (EC), *The European Union and Russia: Close Neighbours, Global Players, Strategic Partners*, European Commission External Relations, Brussels, October 2007, 13. http://ec.europa.eu/external_relations/library/publications/34_eu_russia.pdf

21 Bloomberg News, 'China overtakes US in greenhouse gas emissions', *International Herald Tribune*, June 20 2007. www.iht.com/articles/2007/06/20/business/emit.php

22 'China and Climate Change', www.pewclimate.org/policy_center/international_policy/china.cfm

23 Joanna I. Lewis, 'China's Climate Change Strategy', *China Brief* 7:13, 27 June 2007.

24 Welcoming Remarks to EU/OPEC Roundtable on Carbon Dioxide Capture and Storage (CCS) by Dr. Majid Al-Moneef, Saudi Arabia's Governor to OPEC, Riyadh, Sandi Arabia, 21 September 2006. www.opec.org/home/Press%20Room/EU-OPEC%20presentations/Al-Moneef%20welcoming%20remarks.pdf

25 Jonathan Elkind, 'Building a Secure Energy Future: A Challenge for New Presidential Leadership', Brookings Institution, 28 August 2007. www.brookings.edu/papers/2007/0828energysecurity_Opp08.aspx

26 United Nations Foundation, 'Realizing the Potential of Energy Efficiency', July 2007. www.globalproblems-globalsolutions-files.org/unf_website/PDF/realizing_potential_energy_efficiency.pdf

27 Laura Cozzi, 'Global Energy Scenarios: Running Out of Time', in *Our Energy Future: An Economic, Geopolitical and Risk Perspective*, eds. Esther Bauer, Fritz Gutbrodt, Oliver Schelski, Rushlikon: Swiss Re Centre for Global Dialogue, 2007, 15.

28 Arthur Rosenfeld, Pat McAuliffe, and John Wilson, 'Energy Efficiency and Climate Change', *Encyclopedia of Energy*, vol. 2, Elsevier Press, Amsterdam 2004, 373.

29 See Arthur H. Rosenfeld, 'Successes of Energy Efficiency: The United States and California', presentation 2 May 2007. www.energy.ca.gov/2007publications/CEC-999-2007-023/CEC-999-2007-023.PDF

30 Rosenfeld, McAuliffe, and Wilson, 378.

31 See Thomas D. Crowley et al, *Transforming the Way DoD Looks at Energy: An Approach to Establishing an Energy Strategy*, LMI, Washington, April 2007, E-19.

32 Liza Mundy, 'Can One Household Save the Planet?', *Washington Post Magazine*, 17 February 2009.

33 See the 27 August 2007 Capitol Hill presentation of Dr. Christine Worlen. www.gmfus.org/event/detail.cfm?id=418&parent_type=E

34 Leila Abboud, 'Alternative Approaches', *Wall Street Journal*, 12 February 2007.

35 Jack Doyle, *Taken for a Ride: Detroit's Big Three and the Politics of Pollution*, Four Wall Eight Windows, New York, 2000, 8.

36 Doyle, 442.

37 Steven Mufson, 'House Sends President an Energy Bill to Sign', *Washington Post*, 19 December 2007 and Steven Mufson, 'Power Switch', *Washington Post*, 20 January 2008.

38 International Energy Agency, *World Energy Outlook 2006*, OECD/IEA, Paris, 2006, 278. www.iea.org/textbase/nppdf/free/2006/weo2006.pdf

39 UN Foundation, *Realizing the Potential of Energy Efficiency*, 23.

40 Of course, such figures can only be an estimate. See the discussion in Milton R. Copulos, *America's Achilles Heel, The Hidden Costs of Imported Oil: A Strategy for Energy Independence*, The National Defense Council Foundation, Washington, DC, 2003, 32.

41 www.eia.doe.gov/oiaf/servicerpt/subsidy/executive_summary.html. For more detailed analysis on calculating subsidies, see the information provided by Earth Track. www.earthtrack.net/earthtrack/index.asp?page_id=201&catid=73

42 Steven Mufson, 'House Sends President an Energy Bill to Sign', *Washington Post*, 19 December 2007.

43 Dan Morgan, 'Corn Farms Prosper, but Subsidies Still Flow', *Washington Post*, 28 September 2007.

44 Heinberg, 183.

45 Stern Review on the Economics of Climate Change. www.hm-treasury.gov.

uk/sternreview_index.htm

46 See the discussion in Patrick Avato and Jonathan Coony, *Accelerating Clean Energy Technology Research, Development, and Deployment: Lessons from Non-energy Sectors*, Word Bank, Washington, 2008, 15–6.

47 Van Jones, *The Green Collar Economy: How one solution can fix our two biggest problems*, HarperCollins, New York, 2008 advocates a green new deal.

48 See the text of the law at: http://frwebgate.access.gpo.gov/cgi-bin/getdoc. cgi?dbname=111_cong_bills&docid=f:h1enr.pdf. The provisions for energy efficiency and renewable energy are on page 24 of the pdf.

49 'Tilting at windmills', *Economist*, 18 November 2006, 73. After Japan removed subsidies for the solar cells, the number of installations began to decline. See Devin T. Steward and Warren Wilczewski, 'How Japan Became an Efficiency Superpower', Policy Innovations, 3 February 2009. www.policyinnovations. org/ideas/briefings/data/000102

50 Rebecca Smith, 'The New Math of Alternative Energy', *Wall Street Journal*, 12 February 2007.

51 McKinsey Global Institute, *Curbing Global Energy Demand Growth: The Energy Productivity Opportunity*, May 2007. www.mckinsey.com/mgi/publications/ Curbing_Global_Energy/index.asp

52 Vijay V. Vaitheeswaran, 'Oil', *Foreign Policy*, November/December 2007, 30.

53 'Tilting at windmills', *Economist*, 18 November 2006, 71; John Markoff, 'Forget Computers. Here Comes the Sun', *New York Times*, 14 April 2006; Annys Shin, 'Internet Visionaries Betting On Green Technology Boom', *Washington Post*, 18 April 2006.

54 Michael Specter, 'Branson's Luck', *New Yorker*, 14 May 2007, 124.

55 Clifford Krauss, 'Investing in algae as an alternative to oil', *International Herald Tribune*, 6 March 2007.

56 John V. Mitchell, *A New Era for Oil Prices*, Chatham House, London, August 2006, 21.

57 Amory B. Lovins et al., *Winning the Oil Endgame: Innovation for profits, jobs, and security*, Rocky Mountain Institute, Snowmass, CO, 2005, 105.

58 British Petroleum Statistical Review of World Energy 2007. www.bp.com/ liveassets/bp_internet/globalbp/globalbp_uk_english/reports_and_publica- tions/statistical_energy_review_2007/STAGING/local_assets/downloads/ pdf/statistical_review_of_world_energy_full_report_2007.pdf and Andrew C. Revkin and Matthew L. Wald, 'Solar Power Wins Enthusiasts But Not Money', *New York Times*, 16 July 2007.

59 'Clean Energy: A personal and institutional crusade: A Conversation with Nobel Laureate Steven Chu', *The Promise of Berkeley*, Spring 2007, 4.

60 Robin Marantz Henig, 'Our Silver Coated Future', *OnEarth*, Fall 2007.

61 Michael Barnes, 'Harvesting Light', *Catalyst*, Fall 2006, 12.

62 Blaine Harden, 'Filipinos Draw Power from Buried Heat', *Washington Post*, 4 October 2008.

63 James Kanter, 'Global warming imperils its potential solution', *International Herald Tribune*, 27 May 2007. During the summer months in France, nuclear

plants have to curtail output or shut down.

64 John Deutch and James R. Schlesinger, *National Security Consequences of U.S. Oil Dependency*, Council on Foreign Relations Independent Task Force Report no. 58, 2006, 26.

65 International Energy Agency, *Optimising Russian Natural Gas: Reform and Climate Policy*, OECD/IEA, Paris, 2006.

66 Hassan M. Fattah, 'Abu Dhabi Explores Energy Alternatives', *New York Times*, 18 March 2007.

67 Vaitheeswaran, 28.

68 See Erica Downs, 'The Brookings Foreign Policy Studies Energy Security Series: China', December 2006, 49–50. www3.brookings.edu/fp/research/energy/2006china.pdf

69 See David Goldwyn and Michael Granoff, 'Additional View', in John Deutch and James R. Schlesinger, *National Security Consequences of U.S. Oil Dependency*, Council on Foreign Relations Independent Task Force Report no. 58, 2006, 61.

70 See, for example, 'The illusion of global negotiation solutions', in Hermann Scheer, *Energy Autonomy: The economic, social, and technological case for renewable energy*, Earthscan, London, 2007, 154–7.

PART II

PRODUCERS

CHAPTER 4

HOW SECURE ARE MIDDLE EAST OIL SUPPLIES?

Bassam Fattouh

During the 1980s and 1990s, energy security declined in importance as oil prices fell and spare capacity stood at high levels. This situation reversed in the following decade, when energy security became a priority on the policy agendas of most oil-importing countries once more. High oil prices, threats of terrorist attacks, instability in many oil-exporting countries, and the rise of so-called 'oil nationalism' raised serious concerns about oil supply security. In the background, fears grew that the world may be running out of oil, with many observers predicting an imminent oil supply crunch[1] and raising doubts about the size of proven oil reserves in the Middle East and elsewhere.[2] These doom-laden predictions gained popular credence when market conditions tightened and oil prices skyrocketed towards $145/barrel in the first half of 2008. Although the subsequent economic downturn shifted the focus more to the impact of the crisis on global oil demand, fears of future supply shortages due to the retrenchment of investment in the oil sector still feature high in the policy debate.[3]

Given that the Middle East is endowed with the bulk of the world's oil reserves and is responsible for a large share of global oil production, the security of Middle East oil supplies is central to the oil security debate. In fact, some analysts consider the most important facet of energy security is 'limiting vulnerability to disruption given rising dependence on imported oil from an unstable Middle East'.[4] Others equate the improvement of energy security with reducing dependency on Middle East oil. In his State of the Union Address in 2004, US President George Bush declared that 'America is addicted to oil, which is often imported from unstable parts of the world' and that breakthroughs in technology will help the USA 'reach another great goal: to replace more than 75 per cent of our oil imports from the Middle East by 2025'.[5] In their new energy plan for America, US President Barack Obama and Vice President Joe Biden announced that within a decade, the USA will aim to 'save more oil than we [Americans] currently import from the Middle East and Venezuela combined'.[6]

The fact that high dependence on Middle East oil creates serious grounds for concern should come as no surprise. The region has experienced numerous disruptions, some causing large losses of supplies, such as the fallout from the Iraqi invasion of Kuwait, which resulted in a cumulative loss of 420 million barrels during the period 1990–1991 (see Table 4.1). The region has witnessed wars, civil conflicts, invasions, revolutions, and terrorist acts. This list is usually widened to include potential sources of instability, such as the unresolved Palestinian question and the Arab–Israel conflict, the rise of anti-US feelings,[7] the revival of Shi'a Islamism;[8] the rise of radical Islamism,[9] the threat from an al-Qaeda that has recently 'risen from the grave',[10] the possible emergence of Iran as a nuclear power, the instability of political regimes, and the problem of youth unemployment in many Gulf States.[11]

Table 4.1: Global oil disruptions caused by events in the Middle East (1951–2004)

Date of oil supply disruption	Duration (months)	Average gross shortfall (mb/d)	Reason for oil supply disruption
03/1951–10/1954	44	0.7	Iranian oil fields nationalized May 1 following months of unrest and strikes in Abadan areas
11/1956–03/1957	4	2.0	Suez War
12/1966–03/1967	3	0.7	Syrian transit fee dispute
06/1967–08/1967	2	2.0	Six Day War
05/1970–01/1971	9	1.3	Libyan price controversy; damage to tapline
04/1971–08/1971	5	0.6	Algerian–French nationalization struggle
03/1973–05/1973	2	0.5	Unrest in Lebanon; damage to transit facilities
10/1973–03/1974	6	2.6	October Arab–Israeli War; Arab oil embargo
04/1976–05/1976	2	0.3	Civil war in Lebanon; disruption to Iraqi exports
05/1977	1	0.7	Damage to Saudi oil field
11/1978–04/1979	6	3.5	Iranian Revolution
10/1980–12/1980	3	3.3	Outbreak of Iran–Iraq war
1990–1991		420[12]	Gulf Crisis
03/2003–09/2004	*Continuing*	1.0	Iraq war and continued unrest

Sources: Energy Information Administration, *International Energy Outlook* 2007 (Paris: OECD, 2007) and Paul Horsnell, *The Probability of Oil Market Disruption with an Emphasis on the Middle East.* Working paper published by James A. Baker Institute for Public Policy, September 2000.

Despite these various potential sources of instability, it has not been all bad news when it comes to the security of Middle East oil supplies. The Middle East and, in particular, the Gulf States continue to act as the main supplier of oil to global markets. In many instances the region has played the role of a swing producer, absorbing supply shocks from within and outside the region. For example, the available spare capacity in Saudi Arabia filled the large shortfall of oil caused by Iraq's invasion of Kuwait. Recently, some Gulf States (especially Saudi Arabia) have invested heavily in their upstream sectors with the aim of increasing their productive capacity.[13]

Finally, if one examines more recent history, the major oil disruptions in the last decade originated from OPEC members outside the Middle East and non-OPEC members in other parts of the world (the exception is the US invasion of Iraq in 2003). The region did not witness any civil unrest or strikes (such as those in Venezuela), successful militant attacks on oil installations (as in Nigeria), or tense relations with importing countries (as in the case of Russia). Furthermore, the region did not experience any major disruptions due to technical failures, hurricanes, or other weather-related events. Despite this robust performance, many countries feel unease, and sometimes a sense of mistrust in relying on Middle East oil. Unfortunately, the events surrounding the 1973 oil crisis and the embargo imposed by Arab countries had a lasting effect on the oil security agenda, despite the fact that the oil cuts were for a short duration and the event was an exception, rather than the rule, in the long history of oil.

In light of the Middle East's record as a reliable supplier, the argument that consuming countries should reduce dependency on Middle East oil may prove unrealistic, costly, and counter-productive. This chapter argues that a more useful approach is to assess under which circumstances the region would cease to act (willingly or unwillingly) as a reliable supplier, the chances of these events occurring and, in the event of a disruption, how big the impact is likely to be on oil supplies and productive capacity.

In the first part of this chapter, we discuss the roots of energy security concerns and provide a broad definition of energy security that focuses on potential factors and events that cause disruption to oil flows. In the second part, we assess the types of potential oil flow disruption, and conclude that potential threats to oil supplies from the Middle East are over-stated. The third part analyses the under-investment problem in the oil sector; we argue that the investment problem has many facets and cannot be attributed to a single factor. Rather than making this issue a high priority, energy policy has not been successful in defining how to create an environment which is more conducive for increasing investment in the oil sector in the Middle East and elsewhere. In the last section, we conclude that measures to enhance oil independence from the Middle East are impractical, extremely expensive, and often reduce rather than enhance a country's energy security. Oil importers can pursue oil substitution policies and undertake efficiency measures to reduce dependency on oil. However, these are long-term measures. If oil-importing countries are concerned about short-term supply disruptions from the Middle East, then the maintenance of strategic reserves is the only concrete and effective national policy available to them. This policy, however, is suboptimal and what is needed is to invest in building a sustainable producer–consumer framework that could help prevent importers and exporters from pursuing inefficient and counterproductive energy policies.

Oil Security and Dependency on Middle East Oil Supplies

Unlike the 1970s when oil dominated the energy policy debate, the concept of energy security has been broadened to include the security of other sources of energy, such as gas and electricity.[14] In this respect, oil is by far the most tradable fuel and therefore presents fewer problems in terms of security when compared to other, less tradable fuels. Energy security has also become intertwined with environmental concerns which place restrictions on the use of fossil fuels. Despite these new aspects of energy security, oil still occupies a central place in the policy debate. Such a prominent position is expected, since although the importance of oil as a percentage of GDP has declined in most developed countries in the last 30 years, it still constitutes the world's most important source of energy.

According to the 2008 BP statistical review, oil constituted around 36 per cent of global energy consumption in 2007 followed by coal (29 per cent) and natural gas (24 per cent).[15] Furthermore, the transportation and aviation sectors, the lifelines of any modern economy, are still totally reliant on oil, while no other fuels have been able to cut into this market. Around 98 per cent of the energy used for road and air transportation (the dominant forms of transportation) is based on fuels derived from oil.[16] Given the dominant position of oil in the world's economy, it is also widely believed that high and volatile oil prices can have damaging effects on economic growth, with many studies showing that oil price shocks have preceded most recessions in the USA and other OECD countries.[17] Furthermore, high oil prices can induce global imbalances, especially for developing countries.[18] Thus, unlike other commodities, securing oil supplies and avoiding oil price shocks are essential for an efficient and smoothly-functioning global economy.

At the root of oil security concerns is the concept of 'oil dependency'. Due to a geological accident, oil is found and extracted in one part of the world and consumed in another. A small group of countries, predominately in the Middle East, is endowed with the bulk of the world's oil reserves and is responsible for a large share of global oil production. According to the 2008 BP Statistical Review, in 2007 the Middle East claimed 30.8 per cent of global oil production and around 61.0 per cent of the world's proven reserves. On the other hand, the USA, EU, Japan, and China dominate global oil consumption. In 2007, these countries made up approximately 57 per cent of world consumption and the USA by itself accounted for almost a quarter of global oil consumption. Although some of these countries are important oil producers, domestic production accounts for only about one-quarter of their consumption, forcing them to rely on oil imports to fill the gap. Trade movements in 2006 indicate that the Middle East exported more than 20 mb/d, while Europe, Japan, and the USA imported more than 32 mb/d. Oil dependency is likely to increase in the future for North America, Europe, and Asia as they possess less than 10 per cent of the world's proven reserves.

Dependency, however, is not a sufficient condition to elicit concerns about energy security. Relying on oil imports would not constitute a source of concern if oil continued to flow smoothly from surplus to deficit areas. Thus, in addition to oil dependency, an underlying theme is that the regular flow of oil to importing nations may be subject to disruptions. This conjunction of the concepts of oil dependency and vulnerability to serious disruptions in oil supplies constitutes the basis for energy security concerns, and is reflected in widely-used definitions of energy security. Daniel Yergin defines it as the 'availability of sufficient supplies at affordable prices'.[19]

It is interesting to note that in addition to disruption, these definitions incorporate the concept of 'affordable prices'. This concept of affordability is, however, very ambiguous, as affordability tends to vary widely across countries: what is affordable to one country may not be affordable to another.

From the view of oil exporters, the above definitions are biased, in the sense that they only consider energy security from the oil importers' perspective. Very low oil prices, which are affordable to consuming countries, may undermine the energy security of oil-exporting countries since oil revenues represent the main source of income for these countries. From a producer perspective, low oil prices constitute a major threat to their security. Thus, major oil exporters have been asking for 'reasonable prices' and security of demand in the face of concerns about security of supply.

This chapter analyses energy security in terms of potential factors, or events disrupting the flow of oil through the supply chain, without considering affordability. It is important to stress the following features of our definition. First, there are many causes of disruption, including technical failure, weather-related events (such as hurricanes and storms), strikes, terrorist attacks on oil facilities, wars and civil strife, regime change that may restrict the capability of a country to export, and a deliberate restriction of exports. The dynamics of supply and demand in the oil market may also result in market dislocations, with considerable impact on oil supplies. In the worst possible scenario, global oil supply might fall short of global oil demand due to a lack of investment, or inexorably declining output past the point at which peak output has been reached.[20] Furthermore, the oil market can experience a reduction in available supplies due to a change in the policy of exporters.

Second, among all the various causes for oil supply disruptions, the 1973 Arab oil embargo, which sought to reduce US support for Israel, still looms the largest in Western consciousness. Since that traumatic experience, analysts frequently point out that Middle Eastern states can use their oil production as a political weapon against the West, seeking to force the USA and Europe to meet Middle Eastern political demands. Ironically, since the 1970s, the Middle East oil exporters have not sought to use their energy exports as a way of obtaining political concessions, and politics has not been a major cause of oil supply disruptions.

Third, disruptions and dislocations can occur at any segment of the supply chain. The supply chain from the resource holder to the end user is very long and includes refining, international and local transportation, storage, and delivery facilities.

Fourth, disruptions can also originate from consuming countries. For instance, strikes in importing countries can result in serious interruptions. Furthermore, the dependence of oil-exporting countries on oil revenues implies that consuming nations can use sanctions to target specific countries. Unilateral and multilateral sanctions have been widely used against oil-exporting countries, with the USA the most active in using sanctions as a tool of foreign policy to induce behaviour change in regimes.[21] Multilateral sanctions under the UN umbrella can be very harmful, as they have the effect of curtailing oil exports from the targeted country. Multilateral sanctions adversely affect the country's productive capacity by limiting foreign investment and technology transfer in the oil sector. Unilateral sanctions, on the other hand, do not necessarily affect the flow of oil from the country under sanction. Typically, unilateral measures cause temporary inconvenience, as the oil exporter establishes new trade partners and seeks new customers.

However, if unilateral sanctions are maintained for a long time, they would ultimately affect the productive capacity of exporters.[22]

Finally, the impact of disruptions is not uniform. Some disruptions, such as those caused by technical failures, occur often but have limited impact on global oil supplies and productive capacity. Disruptions, such as those due to natural disasters, occur infrequently but their impact on oil supplies can be significant in the short- to medium-term. Some disruptions are less regular, but their impact might have both short-term effects on oil supplies and long-term effects on productive capacity.

The discussion above shows that the realm of energy security is very broad given the many factors that can cause shortfalls in oil supplies, the different impact that disruptions and dislocations may have on oil supplies and investment, and the fact that some of these disruptions may originate in consuming nations and that energy security applies to the entire supply chain. To focus the discussion, we now concentrate on those events which may undermine the security of Middle East crude oil supplies, namely the geopolitical factors and the under-investment issue.

Types of Potential Disruptions of Middle East Oil Flows

Although disruptions may occur at any point of the oil supply chain due to a wide range of factors, it is the politically-driven threats to oil supplies that have dominated the energy security debate and the imagination of policy makers. In this debate, the Middle East features prominently. In the following discussion, we look at how reliance on the Middle East raises a number of concerns, starting with the least likely (though most frequently discussed) and moving to the more likely. Among the fears most commonly expressed are those that oil producers will use the oil weapon; transit choke points will be cut off; oil-exporting countries from the region could be hit by wars or internal conflicts; oil-exporting countries may witness long periods of instability that could cripple their oil industry; terrorist networks will succeed in destroying oil installations and pipelines; and oil exporters' policies may cut the supply of oil.[23] We shall explore each of these in detail.

The oil weapon

Analysts who worry about the oil weapon argue that the double de-pendence on oil and stable oil prices implies that oil exporters possess a very powerful weapon with which they can 'blackmail' oil-importing governments in order to obtain political concessions. This argument may suggest a lack of understanding of the nature of the oil market. Not only can the oil weapon prove costly for the country using it, but restricting oil exports would typically be ineffective and counterproductive.

To begin with, the oil weapon cannot be targeted against a specific country or group of countries. This is due to the nature of the market where oil is easily and widely traded. Countries that are not blacklisted by producers can obtain oil and then redirect it to countries under the embargo. Adelman makes this point forcefully when he argues that 'whether a supplier loves or hates a customer (or vice versa) does not matter because, in the world oil market, a seller cannot isolate any customer and a buyer cannot isolate any supplier. But conventional wisdom…is that Middle Eastern nations wield an "oil weapon" that they can use to punish the USA or any other nation.'[24]

For an oil embargo to be effective, it should therefore result in a total cutback of global oil supplies. If the loss of oil due to the embargo is counteracted by increases in supplies from somewhere else, the embargo would have a temporary effect on oil market supplies or prices. It would only benefit other producers that have the ability to fill the shortfall. Hence, the effectiveness of an oil weapon depends to a large extent on whether market conditions are tight and on a country's ability to convince or pressure other producers to also implement supply cuts – something which is very difficult to achieve. Disagreement on oil embargos and export cuts is the norm rather than the exception. Agreement on export cuts occurred just once: in 1973, when a large group of Arab producers decided to cut exports to countries 'committing aggression or participating in aggression of sovereignty of any Arab state or its territories'.[25]

It is also worth stressing that the oil weapon is indiscriminate, in the sense that it does not distinguish between friend and foe. A successful use of the oil weapon that results in the cutback of total global oil production and sharp rises in oil prices would have an adverse impact on all countries, regardless of whether they are poor or rich, a friend or an enemy. It is always possible to devise schemes to compensate friendly regimes, but they are difficult to implement in practice.

Furthermore, many argue that oil producers are highly dependent on oil revenues and hence cannot support production cutbacks for a long time. However, a successful use of the oil weapon can push prices to high levels, such that a rise in total revenues can compensate for losses due to the decline in production. The 'dependency on revenues' argument for not using the oil weapon is true only in the unlikely event that the country stops exporting oil altogether. Although revenues may increase in the short run, the long-term effects can be damaging and long lasting, and can undermine the interests of other oil exporters. Observers point out that 'an oil shock can be a terrible experience for the industrial countries, but is not a fatal blow. As soon as they perceive the long-term nature of such a shock they react, and their reaction can turn into a permanent nightmare for any producers. Any structural reaction implies not only reduction in demand, but also much more money devoted to research and development of alternative sources of energy or investment in new oil producing countries.'[26]

The discussion above suggests that only very extreme circumstances would push any country to use the oil weapon, and probably only with limited effects. Unfortunately, however, in the academic literature and the popular press, the oil weapon is portrayed as a ready tool for blackmailing the West. It is also unfortunate that some oil exporters, such as Iran, declare from time to time that they are prepared to use the oil weapon whenever faced with political confrontation. Such announcements continue to cast a shadow over the oil market.

Closure of oil transit choke points

The use of the oil weapon can also take the form of closing oil trade routes. A maritime tanker fleet transports the bulk of oil supplies: more than 1.9 billion tons of petroleum products a year, constituting around 62 per cent of all petroleum products. Pipelines or trains and trucks carry the remainder (38 per cent), but usually over small distances.[27] International oil shipping lanes must traverse a variety of chokepoints, defined as locations 'that limit the capacity of circulation and cannot be easily bypassed, if at all. This implies that any alternative to chokepoints involves a level of detour or use of an alternative that translates into significant financial costs and delays.'[28]

The Straits of Hormuz and Malacca constitute the world's most important oil chokepoints, with almost 30 mb/d flowing through these passageways. Oil tankers can avoid the Straits of Malacca, but only at very high cost and longer journey times. It is virtually impossible today to divert oil transit away from the Straits of Hormuz. The only significant outlet is the Saudi pipeline to Yanbu on the Red Sea, but this pipeline can only handle around 4.8 mb/d. The closure of the Straits of Hormuz therefore represents the ultimate nightmare for the oil market, as this chokepoint links the Persian Gulf oilfields to the rest of the world.

Many believe that the narrowness of shipping lanes and the difficulty of manoeuvring oil tankers make the Straits of Hormuz vulnerable to politically-motivated disruptions. However, history suggests otherwise. In what was known as the Iraq–Iran 'Tanker War', there were 554 attacks on oil tankers in the Straits of Hormuz, which resulted in the deaths of 400 sailors and the wounding of 400 more. These attacks did not completely block transit. Even at its most intense, the fighting disrupted no more than 2 per cent of the ships passing through the Persian Gulf.[29]

In the current tension between the USA and Iran over the latter's nuclear programme, Iran has threatened to block the straits of Hormuz. It is, however, very difficult to envisage a scenario in which an aggressor would block the Straits of Hormuz for a long period of time. Doing so would defy international conventions and increase Iran's isolation. The closure of this oil transit route would alienate Iran's allies in Asia and elsewhere, as the adverse impacts of the blockade would spread across the globe. In other words, the use of this 'weapon' is completely indiscriminate, and if Iran attempted to block international shipping, it would face a very wide and powerful coalition opposed to it. There are also doubts about whether Iran can physically block the Straits of Hormuz. There are four possible ways in which the Straits of Hormuz could be blocked: by placing military artillery on one of the islands located near the shipping channels; by using mines; by sinking vessels in the shipping channel; or by imposing a naval blockade. El-Shazly and Blair and Lieberthal assess these possible ways, and conclude that none of them is militarily feasible.[30] Only very extreme circumstances would therefore push Iran to use this option, and even then it may not succeed in achieving its objective of disrupting oil supplies.[31] There are therefore serious costs and risks associated with the use of the oil weapon. It is not always effective; it is indiscriminate; and it cannot be sustained for a long period of time.

Wars and conflicts

In the last 50 years or so, the Middle East has witnessed many devastating wars: the 1956 Suez Canal war; the 1967 and 1973 Arab–Israeli wars; the Iran–Iraq war in the 1980s; the Iraqi invasion of Kuwait in 1990; and most recently the US and British invasion of Iraq. Notwithstanding the ongoing violence in Iraq, some of the conflicts that have engulfed the region are not likely to re-emerge any time soon. For instance, state-to-state warfare between Arab countries and Israel is highly unlikely given that Egypt and Jordan have signed peace agreements with Israel. Syria, another neighbouring country, has not yet concluded a peace deal with Israel, but it considers peace as its strategic priority.[32] Although the tension between Iran and Israel is likely to continue, it is unlikely to escalate into a full-scale regional war. Most probably these two countries will engage in proxy conflicts, such as the

Hezbullah–Israeli war in Lebanon during the summer of 2006. Iran's nuclear ambitions could present serious challenges for other countries in the region, especially the Gulf States, but it is highly unlikely that any of these states would contemplate waging a war against Iran in the manner of Saddam Hussein in the 1980s, or have the ability to do so.[33]

However, other types of conflicts could emerge. A direct USA–Iran confrontation cannot be ruled out. The Sunni–Shi'a tension in Iraq could spread to other parts of the region. The Palestinian and Israeli conflict has reached a turning point with the Hamas control of the Gaza strip and the sharp divisions within the Palestinian camp. The possible emergence of an independent Kurdish state could have serious implications within Turkey and for its future role in the region. The risk that the region may witness some sort of disturbance therefore remains high.

The impact of wars and civil conflicts on oil supplies is twofold. First, such events usually result in medium- to long-term supply losses, as they reduce the ability of countries to produce and export oil. Second, they affect the long-term productive capacity of countries by hindering investment. The US invasion of Iraq is a prime example of these impacts. In 2003 many oil experts, both Iraqi and non-Iraqi, expected that Iraq's oil production would return to its pre-Kuwait invasion level of 3.5 mb/d one or two years after the Baathist regime had been overthrown. Other more optimistic observers projected that 'a totally rehabilitated and sanctions-free Iraq' could increase its production capacity 'beyond' 8 mb/d,[34] competing with or even replacing Saudi Arabia's prominent position in the oil industry. The reality, however, has been quite different. Six years after the invasion, and despite a more stable security situation in the last couple of years, Iraq has failed to increase its productive capacity. The dispute between the various political factions in Iraq has hindered the passage of a new hydrocarbon law because there are still disagreements over how to distribute oil revenues, and which body has authority to conclude agreements with foreign oil companies. The Iraqi case shows that wars and civil strife not only result in short-term loss of oil supplies, but also adversely affect long-term productive capacity by preventing maintenance and hindering investment, especially if wars and civil conflicts tear the social fabric of the nation.

Regime instability

There is a general perception that governments in the region, especially in the Gulf, are highly unstable. The key question for many researchers is not whether these regimes will be toppled but 'the scope of the violence of their demise and who wields the violence'.[35] A widely-discussed scenario is potential turmoil in Saudi Arabia (but also in other Gulf States). A common argument is that Saudi Arabia faces serious political, economic, and social challenges and that it is only a matter of time before the Saudi regime is toppled under these pressures.[36]

It is true that the stability of these Gulf States has not been perfect. For instance, in Saudi Arabia the royal family has been challenged on more than one occasion: a coup attempt in 1960; the Juhayman revolt and the seizure of the holy mosque in 1979; sporadic protests by the Shi'a minority in the 1980s;[37] and, more recently, a series of terrorist attacks against government and civilian targets. Saudi Arabia also faces many socio-economic challenges manifested in high unemployment among its youth, extensive reliance on foreign labour, increasing internal pressures for political reform and more inclusive participation rates, and the need to strike a balance between the demands of the reform-minded and the religious elements within Saudi society. The mechanism for succession within the royal family also poses further challenges. Nevertheless, the Al-Saud family has proven *resilient* when faced with these *challenges* and the royal family still holds firmly onto power. [38] By most accounts, the armed forces and the religious class remain loyal to the ruling family and so far it is difficult to see an alternative to the current regime,[39] especially given that opposition in Saudi Arabia has always been fragmented, a situation which is likely to persist in the foreseeable future.[40]

Of course, the past is not necessarily a good predictor of the future, and one cannot rule out the possibility that the region may witness violent regime changes. However, the focus should not be on regime instability or regime change *per se*. Instead, the focus should be on whether the new regime would alter existing oil policy in such a way that it engages in a deliberate restriction of oil exports. While one may wish to assign a high probability for a regime change, it is reasonable to assign a low probability (or even zero probability) that a new regime would deliberately curtail oil production and exports. A new regime may decide to direct its exports away from the USA or Europe, but given that the oil market is one great pool, this diversion would have limited effects on the functioning of the oil market.

It is more likely that consumer nations would decide to impose an oil embargo on the country if they did not approve of the new regime in power. Similarly, even if one allows for the possibility of extreme Islamists gaining power,[41] it is difficult to envisage a situation in which Islamists in power would stop conducting business or trading with the West, or voluntarily curtailing their oil exports.

Nevertheless, any form of political instability or regime change is likely to affect long-term productive capacity, as it may induce sanctions, social unrest, changes in the social fabric, and lead to changes in the investment environment and tolerance of foreign investment. Iran is a classic example: despite a social revolution that saw the replacement of a Western-friendly regime with an anti-Western regime, oil continued to flow from Iran to the West even at the climax of the Islamic revolution, although at half of its capacity. The reduction in Iran's oil capacity was not the result of a deliberate policy of restricting oil exports,[42] but was due to a combination of factors, including the Iran–Iraq war, sanctions, and underinvestment due to the unattractive business environment.

Terrorist attacks on oil facilities

In the last decade, oil installations, pipelines, and tankers have been subject to numerous terrorist attacks. Perhaps the most spectacular was the attack by an explosives-laden boat on the Very Large Crude Carrier (VLCC) Limburg, carrying a cargo of around 400,000 barrels of crude off the shores of Aden. Following this attack, Al-Qaeda issued a warning that this incident 'was not an incidental strike at a passing tanker but...on the international oil-carrying line in the full sense of the word'. The attempt to hit the Abqaiq oil processing terminal in Saudi Arabia in 2006 provided fuel for counterfactual scenarios in which Al-Qaeda succeeded in destroying Saudi Arabia's oil facilities with disastrous economic and social implications.

Concerns that terrorist attacks could force the oil industry to its knees are, however, exaggerated. Terrorist attacks usually have temporary effects and damage is rapidly repaired. Despite numerous threats,[43] only a few have been translated into attacks, highlighting the difficult logistical challenges involved in hitting oil installations. Furthermore, the degree of vulnerability is not the same across all parts of the oil supply chain. For example, it may be relatively easy to blow up a pipeline. However, the impact is minimal as attacks on pipelines usually result in limited losses. In the Saudi context, an attack on a pipeline would have no impact, as there is plenty of spare capacity in the transport infrastructure, which makes it straightforward to bypass the damaged pipeline. To cause large disruptions, terrorists therefore need to cause damage to key installations, such as oil processing complexes, or to set oilfields ablaze. Hitting such key targets is very difficult and should not be compared to attacks on a pipeline. Given the importance of the oil industry to the Saudi economy, bottlenecks are heavily guarded.

However, terrorist attacks on oil targets remain a menace to the oil market. Although their impact is limited, terrorist attacks affect the psychology of market players and tend to place a premium on oil prices.

Oil Exporters' Policy

Paul Horsnell argues that supply discontinuities (defined as changes in the oil export policy of the producer country which cause sharp changes in the oil price) are 'far more common than disruptions, are often longer lasting and in terms of barrels removed are normally of a greater magnitude'.[44] He notes that over the period from 1999 to early 2000, OPEC's withdrawal of oil supply amounted to a greater loss than the Gulf crisis, with the withdrawal exceeding 1 billion barrels. Middle East exporters, mainly Saudi Arabia, played the leading role in implementing these cuts. In fact, for many observers, OPEC production policy constitutes a threat to the global economy. Adelman argues that 'the real problem we face over oil dates from after 1970: a strong but clumsy monopoly of mostly Middle Eastern exporters cooperating as OPEC. The biggest exporters have acted in concert to limit supply and thus raise oil's price…The output levels they establish by trial-and-error are very unstable. OPEC has damaged the world economy, not by malice, but because its members cannot help but do so.'[45]

Although OPEC output policy has an impact on oil supplies, and often looks like a disruption, these withdrawals should be placed in their proper context. OPEC production quotas are implemented when the market is perceived to be oversupplied, and when oil prices have fallen below what OPEC considers 'acceptable'. In other words, OPEC cuts are very often a reaction to weak market conditions. In its attempt to fine-tune the market, OPEC policy may cause oil prices to overshoot if exporters overreact and engage in excessive cuts. In other instances, OPEC's decision-making process may induce volatility. Given the uncertainties of demand and supply, the lack of reliable and timely data about consumption, production, and inventory levels, and the unreliability of short-term forecasts, it is difficult for OPEC to anticipate the direction of the market. Even if it could do so, implementing a mutually agreeable policy can prove to be very difficult because of OPEC's structure. The organization is a coalition of a heterogeneous group of countries facing distinct economic, social, and political challenges and with no incentive to share information. OPEC has no monitoring system to oversee production and shipments and, more importantly, no punishment mechanism to deter cheaters. This structure, which is unable to generate clear signals to the market, may induce considerable uncertainty about future oil supplies, contributing to oil price volatility.[46]

This lack of precision in controlling the market should not, however, obscure the fact that cuts are usually implemented in reaction to weak market conditions. One may wish to evaluate the costs and benefits of OPEC's actions, but considering OPEC cuts as a threat to security is farfetched. Production cuts are not designed to act as an instrument to restrict the flow of oil supplies to achieve political objectives, but rather as a tool for oil market management. Furthermore, energy security should be broadened to include the perspective of the oil exporters. Since oil revenues constitute the main source of income for Middle East exporting countries, very low oil prices comprise a source of insecurity which would eventually force them to react. In fact, one could argue that failure to react to low oil prices may undermine the ability of the Middle East exporters to act as reliable suppliers; low oil prices may induce economic and social unrest, which in turn can undermine the security of oil supplies to the rest of the world.

Given the large geopolitical uncertainties surrounding the Middle East, it is best to analyse the risks of disruption using a probabilistic approach, and to differentiate between their impact on oil supplies and long-term productive capacity. Table 4.2 lists each of the events discussed above, the probability of it occurring, and its impact on output loss and long-term productive capacity.

Table 4.2: Assessment of event probability and impact on oil supply and productive capacity

Event	Probability	Impact on global oil supplies	Impact on productive capacity
Export restrictions	Very low	Low	Low
Closure of trade routes	Very low	High	Low
War and civil conflicts	Low/Medium	High	High
Political instability, regime change, revolutions	Low	Low	Medium/High
Successful terrorist attacks on oil facilities	Low	Low	Low
Production cuts	High	High	Low

The picture is rather mixed. The probability of any of the above events occurring is quite low. Should one of them happen, there would be wide variation in its potential impacts on oil supplies and productive capacity. However, when it comes to the Middle East, energy policy seems to attach a high probability to any of the above events occurring. In addition, the general perception is that these events would always result in large expected losses in terms of output and productive capacity. In this way, the potential threat to oil supplies from the Middle East is over-stated.

Energy Security and Investment in Middle Eastern Oil Sectors

In addition to politically-induced disruptions, the dynamics of the oil market may cause a serious reduction in oil production. In a worst case scenario, oil supply could drop well short of demand. Such an outcome can occur in two ways: either as a result of peak oil[47] or due to lack of investment, preventing the oil industry from maintaining and expanding its productive capacity to meet oil demand.[48]

The issue of underinvestment in the oil sector has become central to the energy policy debate.[49] Given that the bulk of oil reserves are in the Middle East, the issue of investment in the oil sectors of the region receives special attention. Many international organizations, such as the International Energy Agency (IEA) and Energy Information Administration (EIA), project that most of the increase in global demand for oil would be met by OPEC and especially the Middle East producers within OPEC. This would require that these Middle East oil exporters increase their investment outlays or open their oil and gas sectors to foreign investment.

Obstacles to investment in the Oil sector

For most of the 1980s and 1990s, investment in the oil and gas sectors of Middle Eastern countries was stagnant. There were a few countries, such as Qatar and Algeria, that embarked on a heavy programme of investment in the mid-1990s but these were exceptions. Many factors explain why investment in the oil sectors stagnated in the past two or three decades and why, despite the rise in oil prices, some Middle Eastern countries are still showing reluctance to undertake rapid and large expansion programmes.

The large spare capacity and the oil price decline in the 1980s and most of the 1990s threw the industry into deep recession, reduced the attractiveness of existing investment plans, and adversely affected the incentive to invest. These problems were accompanied by widespread demand pessimism and exaggerated expectations of non-OPEC supply. Geopolitical instability and wars have also prevented capacity expansion in many Middle Eastern countries. For example, the Iran–Iraq war, the Iraqi invasion of Kuwait, and the US invasion of Iraq have limited the capacity of Kuwait, Iran, and Iraq to channel investment into their oil sectors. Economic sanctions against Iran, Libya, and Iraq limited their access to technology and foreign capital and hindered any serious capacity expansion.

In addition, the relationship between the owner of the natural resource (i.e. the government) and the national oil company, which extracts the resource, can be highly inefficient, yielding sub-optimal rates of investment in the energy sector. In most countries in the region, the national oil company does not determine its capital budget. Such decisions are usually subject to general governmental budgetary require-ments, rather than available investment opportunities in the oil sector. Relying on external factors implies that the capital budget for national companies is quite tight, and frequently prevents them from undertaking new projects. Such difficulties are likely to continue, as many Middle Eastern economies are capitalizing on oil revenues to achieve economic diversification, which is badly needed to create the necessary growth to absorb the high number of young people entering the labour market. Addressing these concerns means that oil company budgets seeking to increase investment must compete fiercely with other economic and social projects. Thus, unlike international oil companies whose main objective is to maximize shareholder value, national oil companies are expected to play a role in the development and diversification of their local economies.

In most Middle Eastern and North African countries, foreign invest-ment in the oil sector remains a highly sensitive political issue. Project Kuwait is a classic example. In 2003, Kuwait's Supreme Petroleum Council (SPC), the body responsible for setting general petroleum sector policy, approved Project Kuwait, a strategy for the development of the Kuwait Oil Sector up to 2020. Project Kuwait would allow international oil companies to invest in upstream production in five northern oil fields near the border of Iraq, to increase their production from the current level of 650,000 b/d to 900,000 b/d. However, the project has made little progress since Kuwait's National Assembly continues to resist foreign investment in the country's oil sector.

Investment is also complicated by the relationship between the governments and/or national oil companies and the international oil companies. International organizations, such as the IEA, identify restric-tion of access to reserves in the Middle East as an important barrier to investment. However, access is not the main issue, since such access is effectively restricted only in Saudi Arabia and Kuwait, with the latter developing plans to open its sector to foreign investment through Project Kuwait. What matters most is the nature of the relationship between the two parties. Experience has shown that even in countries where access to reserves is allowed, there may be important obstacles that could delay or prevent investment by international oil companies. As markets have tightened and we again make a transition from a buyer's to a seller's market, the terms and conditions demanded by the owners have been hardening over time. Iran is a good example. Iran has not been able to attract foreign investment on a large scale partly because of sanctions and partly because of unattractive contractual terms.

Furthermore, oil prices have often been volatile, blurring the distinction between transitory and permanent price movements. As suggested in the literature regarding irreversible investment under uncertainty, the large investment outlays in oil projects and the irreversible nature of these investments have the effect of increasing the value of the option to wait. There is, thus, a case for delaying the investment until new information about market conditions arrives, especially information about expected global demand and oil supplies from other countries. For the oil industry, the option to wait is very valuable. After all, the decision to defer rather than invest immediately, or increase production, is more profitable than to invest and increase production in the face of falling global demand. In other words, it is more profitable for all oil investors (national and private companies) to err on the side of under-investing.

Finally, the potential uncertainties facing the oil market in the current context have become more complex, especially the uncertainty concerning importing countries' responses to the climate change challenge. Like any other region, Middle Eastern countries are increasingly becoming more concerned about the potential economic and social impacts of climate change (water shortages, land degradation, rising sea levels, etc.). However, for Middle East oil exporters, climate change exerts an additional potential impact by affecting the market for fossil fuels, which constitutes their main source of income. Their main concern is the potential impact of the response measures of importing countries on the demand for oil, where it is feared that subsides supporting alternative sources of energy, such as renewables, nuclear, coal, and ethanol, and high carbon taxes can cause both a reduction in oil demand and oil prices.[50] The parties to the UN Framework Convention on Climate Change Annex I refuse to take these arguments at face value. They argue that it is true that oil demand might decline when emission reduction measures are adopted, but that decline is likely to be much larger in other sources of energy, such as coal. Furthermore, oil-producing countries are well positioned to benefit from Clean Development Mechanism schemes.[51]

Regardless of the arguments and counterarguments, considerable uncertainty remains about the potential impact of climate change policy on oil demand, which, in turn, may affect oil exporters' willingness to engage in large and rapid capacity expansion programmes. For instance, using OPEC's World Energy Model (OWEM) as a basis for the reference case, Ghanem et al. examine the implications of measures to reduce the emissions of greenhouse gases, in accordance with the Kyoto Protocol.[52] In their initial scenario, each of the three OECD regions would impose a carbon tax that is sufficient to reach their own Kyoto emissions targets, which would result in a fall in OECD demand of 6.5 mb/d by the year 2010, compared to the reference case. Many other models have examined the economic impacts on implementation of the Kyoto Protocol and reached similar conclusions in terms of the loss of oil market share, though the estimated loss varies depending on the models' underlying assumptions, such as the elasticity of demand, and to what extent OPEC is able to counteract the impact of response measures. The main disagreements are in policy conclusions, specifically whether OPEC can prevent induced revenue losses by managing its production,[53] or whether oil-importing countries can take certain measures to minimize the adverse economic impacts on OPEC members.[54]

Thus, the investment problem in the oil sector has many facets, and cannot be attributed to a single factor. Given the various dimensions of the underinvestment problem, energy policy has not been successful in tackling the issue of increasing investment in the oil sector.

Unlike the experience of the past two decades, and despite the large uncertainties surrounding the oil market, some Middle Eastern exporters have responded to the investment challenge, and have embarked on large projects aimed at generating new additional production capacity. Leading examples are Saudi Arabia's current plans to increase its oil production capacity and Qatar's plan to increase its oil and gas production capacity. In the last few years, Saudi Arabia has been investing heavily in its energy sector, especially in upstream oil, with the aim of increasing the Kingdom's capacity from its current level of around 10.8 mb/d to 12.5 mb/d in 2009 at a cost of $20 billion.[55] Similarly, Qatar Petroleum (QP), the Qatari national oil company, has embarked on a new five-year plan (2006–2010) with the intention of expanding its capacity in crude oil production, natural gas, gas to liquids, refining, and petrochemicals. Despite these recent success stories, some observers, such as the IEA, argue that the current investments are small compared to what is needed to meet the anticipated increase in global demand, especially given that the region did not invest in the energy sector during the previous two decades. Furthermore, observers often note that investment in the energy sector has not been uniform across Middle Eastern countries with some, such as Kuwait and Iran, lagging behind.

Investment, spare capacity and the security margin

An important aspect of the current energy security system has been the availability of spare capacity. The maintenance of spare capacity or a 'security margin' in the oil supply chain by a few Middle Eastern oil exporters has on many occasions helped to fill the shortfall caused by spectacular disruptions. However, since the mid-1990s, this large spare capacity has been in continual decline, and by 2004 and 2005 it reached very low levels. The issue at this juncture is whether this spare capacity could be re-established.

To address this issue, it is important to first stress that the large spare capacity in the mid-1980s was not the outcome of policy decisions aimed at providing a security margin for global oil markets. Instead, it was a residual outcome, as global demand for oil fell and non-OPEC supply rapidly increased. Due to the inability or unwillingness of national oil companies to invest unless security of demand was guaranteed, the ability of oil-exporting countries to provide a security margin has diminished. The exception is Saudi Arabia, where the declared policy is to maintain a volume of spare capacity of 2 to 3 mb/d. The maintenance of this spare capacity is essential to establish Saudi Arabia's leadership in international oil markets as the supplier of last resort, and thus it has always formed an integral part of the Kingdom's oil policy. Although this target set by Saudi Arabia could be achieved, spare capacity of 2 mb/d to 3 mb/d comprises around 3 per cent of global demand. Furthermore, there are limits on how much Saudi Arabia is willing to invest in providing new spare capacity. Recently, the Kingdom has been raising the issue of whether it should bear the costs of maintaining spare capacity on its own. Thus, in the current context, unless there is a reduction in oil demand, it is highly unlikely that spare capacity will reach the unprecedented levels it achieved in the mid-1980s. The loss of spare capacity will have strong implications for both the functioning of the oil market and for the energy security agenda.[56]

Concluding Remarks

This chapter has argued that, with only a few exceptions, the Middle East has been a reliable supplier of energy to the world market. The threats to these supplies, frequently cited by outside observers, are exaggerated with little connection to reality. Accordingly, the measures adopted by consuming countries to enhance oil independence from the Middle East are not necessary and often work to undermine their energy security.[57] First, due to geological realities, the independence of importing countries is not achievable, at least in the short- to medium-term. Second, politically-induced oil disruptions in the Middle East have been the exception rather than the rule in the long history of the oil market. As such, consumers have no reason to seek independence from the Middle East because the Middle East is in fact a reliable partner. Third, reducing dependency on Middle East oil implies higher dependency on other exporting countries, which may be unstable and suffer from the same or even worse problems than those that plague the region. Fourth, policies aimed at reducing dependency on the Middle East can backfire, as these countries may not then feel pressure to invest to increase production. In fact, it is an irony that many Western governments call for reducing dependency on the Middle East, while at the same time urging Middle Eastern producers to increase investment in their oil sector to meet the expected rise in demand. The implications of such mixed signals are to slowdown current investments and delay investments in new projects, undermining the energy security agenda.

Given the nature of the threat regarding supply disruptions as described in this chapter, a more rational response for the consuming countries is the maintenance of strategic reserves. Such reserves represent the only concrete and effective instrument available to them. Energy importing countries can straightforwardly deal with any shortfall of oil supplies due to political instabilities, wars, and terrorist attacks by calling on strategic reserves. Strategic reserves provide time for governments to determine whether the causes for disruption are short-term, and to consider the available options. Critics note that the guidelines under which these reserves should be released are unclear and outdated. A common argument is that on many occasions in the past, oil-importing countries have been reluctant to release strategic reserves to calm the market, inflicting unnecessary costs on their economies. These shortcomings do not, however, negate the effectiveness of this policy instrument in dealing with oil disruptions. An important objective of energy security should be to revise the guidelines under which stockpiles could be released. The so-called 'producer–consumer' dialogue should aim at coordinating efforts in the area of strategic reserves, for example by coordinating efforts on the volume of strategic stocks that should be kept, the timing of filling and releasing of strategic stocks, and whether additional countries should seek to hold strategic stocks.

National policies based on strategic reserves and other policy measures, however, are not optimal and what is urgently needed is to invest in building a more sustainable producer–consumer framework that could work internationally and at different price levels. A more realistic assessment of the potential threats to oil supplies from the Middle East, refocusing the energy security agenda towards policies aimed at relieving investment bottlenecks and creating a more conducive environment for investment in the energy sector, would go a long way toward establishing a more productive and sustainable producer–consumer dialogue. It is hoped that in the future such a dialogue could help importers and exporters avoid pursuing inefficient and counterproductive energy policies.

Notes

1   Colin J. Campbell and Jean H. Laherrère, 'The End of Cheap Oil', *Scientific American*, March 1998, 78–83.
2   Matthew Simmons, *Twilight in the Desert: The Coming Saudi Oil Shock and the World Economy* Wiley, Hoboken, 2005.
3   Paul Stevens, *The Coming Oil Supply Crunch. Chatham House Report*, August 2008. www.chathamhouse.org.uk/publications/papers/view/-/id/652/
4   William F. Martin, Ryukichi Imai, and Helga Steeg, *Maintaining Energy Security in a Global Context: A Report to the Trilateral Commission*, Trilateral Commission, June 1996.
5   BBC, 'State of the Union: Full Text'. http://news.bbc.co.uk/1/hi/world/americas/4668628.stm
6   Barack Obama and Joe Biden: New Energy for America. www.barackobama.com/pdf/factsheet_energy_speech_080308.pdf
7   Julia E. Sweig, *Friendly Fire: Losing Friends and Making Enemies in the Anti-American Century*, Public Affairs, New York, 2006; Tom Regan, 'Polls show anti-American feelings at all time high in Muslim countries', *The Christian Science Monitor*, 22 February, 2007.
8   Rime Allaf, Ali Ansari, Maha Azzam, Rosemary Hollis, Robert Lowe, Yossi Mekelberg, Soli Özel, Gareth Stansfield, and Mai Yamani, *Iraq in Transition: Vortex or Catalyst?*, Chatham House, London, September 2004; Vali Nasr, *The Shia Revival: How Conflicts within Islam Will Shape the Future*, WW Norton, New York, 2006; Vali Nasr, 'When the Shiites Rise', *Foreign Affairs*, 85:4, July–August 2006. For an alternative view of the Shi'a revival, see M. Terhalle, 'Are the Shi'a Rising?' *Middle East Policy*, XIV:2, Summer 2007.
9   Michael J. Mazarr, *Unmodern Men in the Modern World: Radical Islam, Terrorism, and the War on Modernity*, Cambridge University Press, Cambridge, in press.
10 Bruce Hoffman, 'The Global Terrorist Threat: Is Al-Qaeda on the Run or on the March?', *Middle East Policy*, XIV: 2, Summer 2007.

11 Daniel L. Byman and Jerrold D. Green, 'The Enigma of Political Stability in the Persian Gulf Monarchies', *The Middle East Review of International Affairs*, 3: 3, September 1999.

12 Cumulative effect.

13 Bassam Fattouh, 'The GCC Oil Sector Market Developments', in *Gulf Yearbook* 2006–2007, Gulf Research Centre, UAE, 2007.

14 Daniel Yergin, 'Ensuring Energy Security', *Foreign Affairs*, March–April 2006.

15 British Petroleum, *BP Statistical Review of World Energy*, June 2008, 41. www.bp.com/productlanding.do?categoryId=6929&contentId=7044622

16 Olivier Appert and Philippe Pinchon, 'The Future Technical Development of Automotive Powertrains', in *Oil in the 21ˢᵗ Century*, R. Mabro, ed., Oxford University Press, Oxford, 2006.

17 Donald W. Jones, Paul N. Leiby, and Inja K. Paik, 'Oil Price Shocks and the Macro-economy: What has been learned since 1995', *Energy Journal*, 25: 2, 1–32.

18 International Monetary Fund, *World Economic Outlook*, IMF, Washington, April 2006.

19 Yergin, 'Ensuring Energy Security'. Kalicki and Goldwin similarly define energy security in terms of 'provision of affordable, reliable, diverse and ample supplies of oil and gas and their future equivalents and adequate infrastructure to deliver these supplies to market'. See Jan H. Kalicki and David L. Goldwin, *Energy and Security – Toward a New Foreign Policy Strategy*, Woodrow Wilson Center Press, Washington DC, 2005, 9.

20 Paul Horsnell, *The Probability of Oil Market Disruption with an Emphasis on the Middle East*, Working paper published by James A. Baker Institute for Public Policy, September 2000.

21 Michael E. Canes, 'Impacts of Oil Sanctions in World Markets', *American Petroleum Institute Issue analysis*, 101, December 1997.

22 For instance, the Iran–Libya Sanction Act (ILSA) imposed by the USA against Iran and Libya (it no longer applies to Libya) prohibited international oil companies from investing in the oil sectors of these countries, curtailing their long-term production capacity.

23 Similarly, Cordesman and Al-Rodhan identify the following key geopolitical uncertainties: stability of oil-exporting nations; terrorism in the Gulf and oil facilities security; embargos and sanctions; ethnic conflict and strife (Anthony Cordesman and Khalid Al-Rodhan, *The Changing Risks in Global Oil Supply and Demand: Crisis or Evolving Solutions?*, First Working Draft, Center for Strategic and International Studies, September 2005). They also include proliferation of WMD, which is not discussed here.

24 M. A. Adelman, 'The Real Oil Problem', *Regulation*, 27:1, Spring 2004, 16–21.

25 Stephen J. Randall, *United States Foreign Oil Policy since World War I*, McGill Queen's University Press, Montreal, 2005.

26 L. Maugeri, *The Age of Oil: The Mythology, History, and Future of the World's Most Controversial Resource*, Praeger Publishers, Westport, CT, 2006, 262–3.

27 Jean-Paul Rodrigue, 'Straits, Passages and Chokepoints: A Maritime

Geostrategy of Petroleum Distribution', *Les Cahiers de Geographie du Quebec*, 48: 135, 2004, 357–374.

28 Rodrigue, 359.

29 D. Blair and K. Lieberthal, 'Smooth Sailing: The World's Shipping Lanes Are Safe', *Foreign Affairs*, May/June 2007.

30 Nadia El-Sayed El-Shazly, *The Gulf Tanker War: Iran and Iraq's Maritime Swordplay*, Palgrave Macmillan, Hampshire, 1998); and Blair and Lieberthal, 'Smooth Sailing'.

31 This does not imply that US military attacks on Iran will not have any impact on oil markets. If the USA decides to attack Iran's nuclear sites, the flow of oil would be disrupted as oil tankers would avoid passing through the Straits of Hormuz during the military strikes. Iran's production would most likely halt. This would cause panic in the oil market as countries would compete for oil access causing oil prices to shoot to very high levels. The impact of this, which should not be confused with the use of the oil weapon, would be temporary and its effects could be mitigated by the use of OECD strategic and industrial reserves. The oil weapon may come into effect after attacks if Iran retaliated by cutting its oil exports. The impact of such a move would depend on the size of the cut and whether the shortfall is counteracted by the use of strategic reserves and/or Saudi Arabia's spare capacity.

32 Syria has on many occasions expressed willingness to engage in peace negotiations with Israel. For example, in her visit to Syria, Nancy Pelosi declared that the Syrian president Bashar al-Assad was ready to 'resume the peace process' (See the editorial 'Pratfall in Damascus: Nancy Pelosi's foolish shuttle diplomacy', *Washington Times*, 5 April 2007). More recently, the Syrian Vice-President Faruq al-Shara announced that 'Syria is looking at all the options, but its priority is peace'. However, it seems that any peace agreement will have to wait (Stephen Zunes, 'Divide and Rule: U.S. Blocks Israel–Syria Talks', *Foreign Policy in Focus*, 6 May 2007).

33 Thomas R. Mattair, 'Mutual Threat Perceptions in the Arab/Persian Gulf: GCC Perceptions', *Middle East Policy*, XIV: 2, Summer 2007.

34 Fadhil J. Chalabi, 'Iraq and the Future of World Oil', *Middle East Policy*, VII: 4, October 2000.

35 Samuel Huntington, *Political Order in Changing Societies*, Yale University Press, New Haven, 1968.

36 Michael Scott Doran, 'The Saudi Paradox', *Foreign Affairs*, January/February 2004. Baer concludes 'sometime soon, one way or another, the House of Saud is coming down' (Robert Baer 'The Fall of the House of Saud', *The Atlantic Monthly*, 291: 4, May 2003).

37 Fouad Ibrahim, *The Shi'as of Saudi Arabia*, Saqi Books, London, 2006.

38 Byman and Green argue that stability has been maintained by a combination of six strategies: strong security services; cooperation of potential dissidents; divide and rule strategies; ideological flexibility; token participation and accommodative diplomacy (See Daniel L. Byman and Jerrold D. Green, 'The Enigma of Political Stability in the Persian Gulf Monarchies', *The*

Middle East Review of International Affairs, 3: 3, 1999; Joseph Kostiner, ed., *Middle East Monarchies: The Challenge of Modernity*, Lynne Rienner Publishers, Boulder and London, 2000; and Michael Herb, *All in the Family: Absolutism, Revolution, and Democracy in the Middle Eastern Monarchies*, State University of New York Press, New York, 1999.

39 See Herb, *All in the Family* and Mohammed Ayoob, 'The Middle East in 2025: Implications for US Policy', *Middle East Policy*, XIII: 2, Summer 2006.

40 Daryl Champion, 'The Kingdom of Saudi Arabia: Elements of Instability Within Stability', *Middle East Review of International Affairs* 3: 4, December 1999.

41 Doran argues that in recent history, extremist movements in the Muslim world have failed to assume power and would probably not be successful in maintaining power for a long period of time. He notes that 'in the last two decades, several violent groups have challenged regimes such as those in Egypt, Syria, and Algeria, but in every case the government has managed to crush, coopt or marginalize the radicals' (see Michael Scott Doran, 'Somebody Else's Civil War', *Foreign Affairs*, January/February 2002). He attributes this failure to the fact that radical political Islam is not a unified movement. However, he warns that 'the new tactic of targeting America is designed to overcome precisely this weakness of political Islam' and that this new tactic 'by tapping into the deepest emotions of the political community, smacks of brilliance, and – much to America's chagrin – will undoubtedly give political Islam a renewed burst of energy'. See also Emmanuel Sivan, 'Why Radical Muslims Aren't Taking over Governments', *Middle East Quarterly*, December 1997.

42 In fact, rather than using the oil weapon, in the early years of the revolution, Iran refused to respond to OPEC's call for output cuts, producing above its assigned quotas.

43 For example, in February 2007 a faction affiliated with al-Qaeda extended the call, urging Muslim militants to attack oil facilities all over the world because 'in the long run, America might be able to lessen its dependence on Middle East oil and would be satisfied with oil from Canada, Mexico, Venezuela, and other new producers or double its dependence on alternative energy resources; therefore, oil interests in all regions that serve the USA and not only in the Middle East, should be attacked', *The Guardian*, 15 February 2007.

44 Horsnell, *The Probability of Oil Market Disruption with an Emphasis on the Middle East*, 7.

45 Adelman, 'The Real Oil Problem'.

46 Bassam Fattouh 'OPEC Pricing Power: The Need for a New Perspective', in *The New Energy Paradigm*, Dieter Helm, ed., Oxford University Press, Oxford, 2007.

47 Peak oil considerations have fuelled concerns about energy security and have given rise to calls for oil substitution. Peak oil, however, will not be discussed in this paper.

48 Horsnell, *The Probability of Oil Market Disruption with an Emphasis on the Middle*

East.

49 It is important to stress that the so-called underinvestment problem not only applies to crude oil production, but generally includes shortages of refining capacity, pipeline systems and storage facilities. See Bassam Fattouh and Robert Mabro, 'The Under-Investment Problem in the Oil Sector', in *Oil in the 21ˢᵗ Century*, Robert Mabro, ed., Oxford University Press, Oxford, 2006.

50 Jacqueline Karas and Tatiana Bosteels, *OPEC and Climate Change: Challenges and Opportunities*, Chatham House, London, 2005.

51 Karas and Bosteels, *OPEC and Climate Change*.

52 Shokri Ghanem, Rezki Lounnas and Garry Brennand, 'The impact of emissions trading on OPEC', *OPEC Review*, 23 June 1999, 79–112.

53 Jon Barnett, Suraje Dessai and Michael Webber, 'Will OPEC Lose From the Kyoto Protocol?', *Energy Policy*, 32: 18, December 2004, 2077–88; and Ulrich Bartsch and Benito Müller, *Fossil Fuels in a Changing Climate: Impacts of the Kyoto Protocol and Developing Country Participation*, Oxford University Press, Oxford, 2000.

54 Jonathan Pershing, 'Fossil fuel implications of climate change mitigation responses', in Lenny Bernstein and Jiahua Pan, eds., *Sectoral and Economic Costs and Benefits of GHG Mitigation*, Intergovernmental Panel on Climate Change, Bilthoven, 2000.

55 Fattouh, 'The GCC Oil Sector Market Developments'.

56 Bassam Fattouh, 'Spare Capacity and Oil Price Dynamics', *Middle East Economic Survey*, XLIX: 5, 30 January 2006.

57 Adelman emphasizes this point from a different perspective arguing that 'it does not matter how much oil is produced domestically and how much is imported. Presidents may declare that there is an 'urgent need' to cut imports and boost 'energy independence' – no one ever lost political support by seeing evil and blaming foreigners. The facts are less dramatic. Imports do not make any importer 'dependent' on any particular exporter, or even all of them taken together. Therefore, direct or indirect spending to reduce imports is a waste of resources'. (Adelman, 'The Real Oil Problem'.)

CHAPTER 5

RUSSIA'S ROLE FOR GLOBAL ENERGY SECURITY

Jeronim Perovic and Robert W. Orttung*

Russia is the world's largest oil and gas producer and its largest gas exporter. It is the world heavyweight in gas, holding about a third of global gas reserves. Although it has only about 6 per cent of global oil reserves, it produces around 12 per cent of the world's oil and rivals Saudi Arabia's output.[1]

Russia is the main supplier of gas and oil to Europe, with producer and consumer maintaining a strong, inter-dependent relationship. According to European Commission figures, Russia provides 27 per cent of the European Union's (EU) oil consumption and 30 per cent of its oil imports. The Russian share in EU gas consumption stands at 24 per cent and Russia accounts for some 44 per cent of EU gas imports.[2]

Despite the breakup of the Soviet Union, Russia remains closely tied into the oil and gas markets of the post-Soviet space. It is the sole energy exporter to many of the Eastern and Central European countries, as well as to its immediate neighbours Belarus and Ukraine. It also remains a main export route and a market for energy from Kazakhstan, Turkmenistan, and Uzbekistan. Russia is, likewise, an important consumer of Central Asian gas.

Aspiring to become a player on Asian energy markets, Russia is planning to explore and develop East Siberian oil and gas fields and to build a network of oil and gas pipelines in the East to deliver future output to China, Japan, and other consumers. Sakhalin Island's oil and

*   This chapter partly draws on research sponsored by the research project 'RUSSCASP – Russian and Caspian energy developments and their implications for Norway and Norwegian actors', financed by the PETROSAM program of the Research Council of Norway. The project is carried out with the Fridtjof Nansen Institute, the Norwegian Institute for International Affairs, and Econ Pöyry as consortium partners and also includes other institutions and researchers as participants.

   The authors would like to thank Julia Nanay and the participants of the conference on 'Energy and the Transformation of International Relations: Global Perspectives and the Role of Russia', held at ETH Zurich on October 26–27 2007, for their helpful comments.

gas developments are already able to supply some oil to Asia. In February 2009, Sakhalin-2 started producing Russia's first liquefied natural gas (LNG). Once the project is fully on stream, it could supply some 5 per cent of global LNG.[3] Russia's National Energy Strategy foresees that by 2020 the share of oil exported to Asia will rise to 30 per cent, up from the current 3 per cent. The Energy Strategy also envisages that 15 per cent of Russian gas exports will go to Asia in the future.[4]

Russia's energy importance extends beyond oil and gas. It has the world's second largest coal reserves after the USA. Additionally, Russia has the potential to develop various renewable energy resources, including hydro, solar, and biomass. Russia is also a major net-exporter of electricity to a number of its post-Soviet neighbours, as well as some European countries (Finland, Poland, Turkey, the Baltic States), and China. Russia is the world's fourth largest power producer (after the USA, China, and Japan) with a potential to significantly expand electricity exports to Europe – provided that the grids between Russia and Europe are synchronized to allow power transmission.[5]

Russia's declared goal is to expand its role as an energy supplier to both traditional and new markets and tighten its control over oil and gas flows in the post-Soviet space. It is still the dominant force in Eurasian energy, but the region has seen some important changes. After 1991, new players and centres of production emerged, and new transport routes allowed some of them to circumvent Russia in selling energy to foreign customers; on the western side of the Caspian from Azerbaijan through Georgia and Turkey to Europe, and on the eastern side of the Caspian from Kazakhstan to China and from Turkmenistan to Iran. Russia's reputation as a reliable partner of Europe suffered when it shut natural gas flows to Ukraine in the winters of 2006 and 2009, prompting European leaders to call for efforts to diversify away from Russian supplies, and for the introduction of legislation which would make it more difficult for Russian companies to buy assets in the European energy market. Finally, Russia has made only limited progress toward its goal of becoming an important energy supplier to Asia.

Given Russia's immense energy resources and its strong position within the energy structure of the post-Soviet and European energy spaces, the country's future moves will inevitably have an impact on the energy situation in both of these areas, as well as in Asia. The key question is not whether Russia will be important, but what role it will play for energy security. Will Russia use its energy wealth as a political tool vis-à-vis its neighbours or as a means to do business? Will it try to play Europe and Asia against each other in the future? Will it bring enough new oil and gas supplies online to be able to feed European and Asian markets? What is it doing now to increase gas supplies for the future?

This chapter discusses the major trends of Russia's energy strategy in the oil and gas sphere, and highlights some of the challenges involved. In the first section, we lay out Russia's goals within the international energy context. In the second section, we highlight three key challenges, which we believe define Russia's role in the Eurasian and global energy market: the role of the state, allocation and volume of investment, and the reform of the internal energy market. In the third section we look at implications for Russia's external relations with Europe, the Central Asian energy-rich states, and Asia. We then draw some conclusions and consider trends for the future.

Russia's potential and its goals in the Eurasian energy context

Russia wants to achieve three major goals within the larger European and Asian energy markets: First, it wants to remain the single most important supplier of energy to Europe by maintaining current volumes of oil exports and increasing gas exports. Second, it seeks to maintain control over energy flows from the energy-producing Caspian states, Turkmenistan, Kazakhstan, and Uzbekistan. Third, it strives to become a leading supplier of energy to East Asian markets and beyond.

Figure 5.1 lays out a rough estimate of Russia's gas and oil exports and imports, as well as energy flows that are circumventing Russia. The size of the arrows represent the approximate size of the flows, though they are not to scale. The question marks in the figure indicate that there are a number of uncertainties as to whether Russia will be able to achieve its goals in terms of future volumes of energy flows.

The questions of which way energy flows in the future, and in what volumes, depends on a host of factors, not all of which Russia is able to control. In the oil sector, the most significant change from the past is the opening of the Baku–Tbilisi–Ceyhan (BTC) pipeline in July 2006. This pipeline, which was constructed with the strong backing of the US government, is the first major oil pipeline circumventing Russia; it runs from Baku through Georgian territory to the Turkish port of Ceyhan, and was designed initially to transport Azeri oil, but has enough capacity to also ship crude from other Caspian producers, especially Kazakhstan (see the maps in the appendix to this chapter).[6] Other major developments in the oil sphere since 1991 include the opening of an oil pipeline from Kazakhstan to China, which became

Gas flows

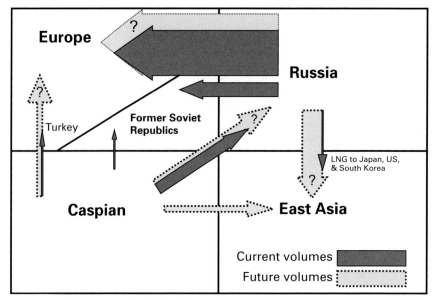

Oil flows

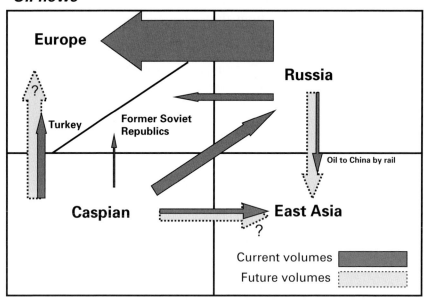

Note: The sizes of arrow do not reflect actual volumes of oil and gas and are approximate estimates by the authors.

Figure 5.1: Current and future energy flows

operational in mid-2006 transporting 90,000 barrels per day (b/d), with the capacity to increase to 200,000 b/d.[7]

Otherwise, however, Caspian energy still flows mainly north through Russia, which has also built additional new export infrastructure, the most important of which so far is an oil pipeline which runs from Kazakhstan to the Russian Black Sea port of Novorossiisk. This pipeline is operated by the Caspian Pipeline Consortium (CPC), an international grouping of companies. Since its inauguration in 2001, the CPC transports mainly Kazakh oil through Russian territory westwards, and thus makes sure the bulk of this country's oil continues to flow via Russia and not through the BTC line.[8]

In the gas sphere, the major Eurasian pipelines still run through Russia. Russia has also built some new transportation routes, including the Blue Stream pipeline, which was an effort to block other pipeline projects, as it transports Russian and Caspian gas to the Turkish gas market. So far, the only major gas pipeline circumventing Russia is the South Caucasus Pipeline (SCP), which follows the BTC line and started to ship gas at the end of 2006. However, this pipeline is running below capacity because, so far, it has only transported gas from the first phase of production from the Shah Deniz field in Azerbaijan, and this field has been absorbing most of its gas for domestic consumption.[9] The only other planned pipeline project circumventing Russia is a gas pipeline transporting Turkmen gas through Uzbekistan and Kazakhstan to China with a capacity of up to 30 billion cubic metres (bcm) per year. The first gas from Turkmen fields is expected to flow in 2009.[10] In 2008, construction started on a parallel gas pipeline from Kazakhstan to China, which will connect to the Turkmen–China gas pipeline and is expected to ship small volumes of gas in 2010, to be expanded in later years.[11] Uzbekistan also agreed to feed gas into the new Central Asia–China pipeline system.[12]

Given rising demand for fossil fuels over the next quarter of a century, Russia, with reserves much larger than those of its energy-rich Caspian neighbours, will remain the key player in the region, especially in the sphere of natural gas. Table 5.1 provides data showing the scale of Russia's dominance. What is unclear, however, is to what extent Russia will be able to increase gas exports to Europe, to satisfy increasing domestic gas demand, and also to enter the East Asian gas market. Moreover, given that the country's old gas fields face declining production, many analysts doubt that Russia is investing enough in new fields in order to prevent a supply shortage in the near future.[13]

Another uncertainty exists with regard to Central Asian gas, which is important for Russia in order to keep up existing levels of gas exports

Table 5.1: Caspian oil and gas reserves (figures for 2006)

	Proven oil reserves		Proven natural gas reserves	
	billion barrels	% of world total	trillion cubic feet	% of world total
Russia	79.5	6.6	1682.07	26.3
Kazakhstan	39.9	3.3	105.9	1.7
Azerbaijan	7.0	0.53	46.66	0.7
Uzbekistan	0.6	*	66.01	1.0
Turkmenistan	0.5	*	100.96	1.6

Source: *BP Statistical Review of World Energy*, June 2007, p. 6 and p. 22.

against the background of its declining fields. Although Russia has been able to tie the three gas producers, Turkmenistan, Kazakhstan, and Uzbekistan, to Russia via infrastructure and agreements on gas purchases, there is tough competition from Europe and China, both of whom are seeking access to Central Asian gas via the construction of new pipelines circumventing Russia. Turkmenistan, Kazakhstan, and Uzbekistan have already concluded agreements with China on gas supply via new pipelines that will not cross Russia (see the maps in the appendix to this chapter).

Russia's position in the Eurasian oil market is still dominant, but the market is already more diversified than the gas market, and the chances of further diversification appear to be better. Again, one key uncertainty is whether Russia will be able to increase production in order to deliver substantial volumes of oil to the Asian market without diverting some oil away from Europe. Experts doubt that Russia will be able to achieve this goal; while Russia's major oil fields in West Siberia and other parts of Russia are mature and declining, Russia has so far invested very little in the exploration of new fields in East Siberia, which is the natural source of supplies for exports to China and other Asian markets.

Three challenges

We will now consider Russia's ability to meet the increasing gas and oil demands of Europe and Asia by analysing the following three key challenges: the impact of increasing Russian state control over the energy sector for production and growth; investment in the energy sector – in particular Russia's focus on the downstream sector instead of increased production – and its possible consequences; the effects of domestic market reforms, especially the impact of rising gas prices.

The interplay among these issues will have a significant impact on the future of Russia's role for global energy security and particularly on its energy relations with Europe, its ex-Soviet neighbours, and Asia.

Increasing state control over the energy sector

The growing role of the state is reducing Russia's oil and gas output. The state companies Gazprom and Rosneft lack the capital and technical capacity to carry out new production projects. State tax policy, unstable property rights, and state pressure have limited the role of international oil companies (IOCs) to that of junior partners.

Looking back from the end of Vladimir Putin's second term as president, the privatization of Russia's oil sector during the 1990s was, to a certain extent, an effort to emulate the USA, where private companies run the industry. In Europe during this period, the trend was also toward privatizing a number of the big state companies. In most oil-producing countries, however, it is the state that controls reserves and production of oil and gas through state-owned companies. In fact, national oil companies (NOCs) today control approximately 80 per cent of global oil and gas reserves.[14]

Putin and his key allies used the extensive powers of the Kremlin to rectify what they considered to be the 'mistakes' of the privatization period in the 1990s, when Russia handed control over strategic assets to private business people at bargain prices, and sold some of its most lucrative oil fields to foreign companies. Especially during Putin's second term in office (2004–08), the Kremlin sought to correct past policies by re-establishing state control over all the larger 'strategic' oil and gas fields. Putin himself, in an interview with *The Times* on 4 June 2007 called the Production Sharing Agreement (PSA) over Sakhalin-2 signed with Shell in the 1990s a 'colonial agreement', which did not serve Russia's national interests.[15]

Many analysts agree, however, that privatizing the industry had helped to increase Russian petroleum output by the end of the 1990s. After a slump in output in the early and mid-1990s, Russia's private oil barons took advantage of the after-effects of the August 1998 financial crisis and the increase in oil prices after 2000 to rejuvenate existing oil fields and to apply modern technology to explore new fields in difficult terrain, boosting output from around 6 million barrels of crude oil per day (mb/d) in 1997 to almost 10 mb/d in 2007.[16] Russian crude exports increased to around 4 mb/d of crude by 2007 (5 mb/d if oil products are added).[17]

Growth in oil production slowed, approximately following the nationalization of Russia's biggest private oil company, Yukos, a process

that started in 2004. As of 2007, the share of oil production coming
from state-controlled companies has increased to around 40 per cent of
Russian oil production, meaning that private companies still control a
significant share of output, especially compared to other oil-producing
countries.[18] In reality, however, the state has a number of tools which
allow it to exert extensive control over Russia's entire oil supply by virtue
of the fact that it has tight control over the regulatory environment,
the taxation regime, transportation monopolies (through state-owned
pipeline company Transneft), as well as licenses and the operating
environment.

Whether or not the stagnation in production growth can be ascribed
to increasing state control, however, is difficult to say. Recent empirical
studies on the effectiveness of state-owned companies from various
producing states indicate that they operate, on average, less effectively
than private companies.[19] In the case of Russia, Yukos had evolved
into the most successful and transparent private oil company until it
was dismantled.

A key challenge for Russia is the problem of underinvestment in
the exploration and development of new oil fields. Russia's remaining
private oil companies lack long-term incentives to make these investments. When oil prices and rents were high between 2003 and 2008,
companies were concerned about property rights, leading them to make
as much fast money as they could, not worrying about what happened
in the future.

A 2007 analysis from Moscow's Alfa Bank argues that rising costs
and high taxes make Russia's entire oil sector unprofitable over the
long-term if the state does not reorganize the tax regime in favour
of producers.[20] Natural Resources Minister Yuri Trutnev sought to
counter this tendency by declaring in April 2007 that companies may
soon have to pay taxes in relation to the potential of the reserves that
they control, not simply to their actual production. In other words,
Trutnev wants companies to engage more actively in the exploration
and development of new fields.[21] At the same time, Moscow has also
announced financial incentives (usually tax breaks) for firms that invest
in Russia's eastern territories.[22]

In the remote fields of East Siberia and the Far East, the expansion
of state ownership over private companies is unlikely to encourage
more investment. As the Sakhalin projects have shown, tapping these
deposits requires substantial up-front investment and the application of
the latest technology. Both Gazprom and Rosneft, the so-called 'national
champions' in the gas and oil sectors, do not, at the moment, have the
capacity to develop such projects on their own. The investment issue

has become even more pressing since the sharp decline in profits from oil and gas exports following the collapse of the oil price in the second half of 2008. Some of Russia's major oil companies, which felt the impact of falling prices immediately, announced a reduction in their investment programmes in autumn 2008.[23]

Russia's key state companies gained control over many major private projects and companies during the second half of Putin's term as president, yet in light of the global financial crisis, they urgently need access to private capital in order to fully fund all the projects. Also, they need to strike new deals with technologically-sophisticated IOCs, as well as with private Russian companies; otherwise, the potential to develop difficult projects like those in East Siberia, the Far East, and Russia's North might not be fully realized.[24]

At the same time, international oil companies like BP, Chevron, ExxonMobil, Shell, Total, and others, which have the managerial know-how, technical capabilities, and deep pockets, are increasingly reluctant to invest in risky and expensive projects without the tax and other contract incentives required. Contract sanctity is an important issue and the breaking of the Sakhalin-2 PSA with Shell has created uncertainty for all future investors, with no guarantee that large investments in new greenfield developments will be secure.

The situation is similar in the gas sector, which was, however, never privatized to the same extent as the oil sector. About 85 per cent of gas production is controlled by Gazprom, which is 51 per cent state owned. Gazprom is Russia's largest company. It is the sole owner of Russia's gas pipelines and has the exclusive right to export gas via pipelines to foreign markets. As a result, non-Gazprom producers, the so-called independent gas producers, depend on Gazprom for the transmission of their gas. It is these independents, however, that will play a key role in Russia's future gas production. In fact, independent producers have accounted for basically all the growth in the gas sector in recent years; Gazprom accounted for negative or zero growth, as Figure 5.2 shows.

A key assumption in determining Russian production figures is that the share of gas produced by independent producers will increase. According to Russia's Energy Strategy until 2020, independent producers could produce up to 20 per cent of Russia's total output by 2020, up from 12 per cent in 2002 (with roughly half of the gas coming from non-Gazprom gas producers and half from oil companies).[25] This figure corresponds with the International Energy Agency (IEA) outlook, which considers 'non-Gazprom production' essential (whether by independent gas producers or via Central Asian gas). Additionally, Gazprom must bring new fields online if it wants to meet its 2006 strategic goal of

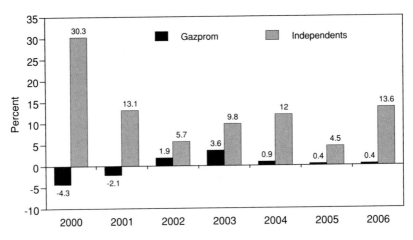

Source: Institute of Energy Policy, Moscow

Figure 5.2: Annual gas production growth rates

increasing production from 547.9 bcm/y in 2005, to 560 bcm/y in 2010, and to 590 bcm/y in 2020.[26]

Allowing independent producers to flourish would be good news. However, the question remains whether Gazprom and the Russian government will permit the independents such freedom, and there are indications that Gazprom seeks to strengthen control over them. This desire is evident from the fact that Gazprom is actively seeking to buy into other private gas companies (e.g. Novatek) and in its policy to use access to its gas pipelines as leverage against other companies.

A case in point is the Kovykta project, currently the richest gas project in East Siberia, with the potential to develop into a springboard for the establishment of a unified gas supply system in the Russian east. With potential annual production estimated at 40–45 bcm per year, Kovykta could produce enough gas to satisfy 15–20 per cent of the non-contracted gas demand of China and South Korea by 2020. The project is operated by Rusia Petroleum, in which TNK–BP – until June 2007 – had a 62.4 per cent share. While production for the domestic market has been underway for some time, Gazprom effectively stalled international sales, including the construction of an export pipeline to China, until it was able to gain a controlling share in this project. By the end of June 2007, after months of intense pressure, TNK–BP agreed to sell its stake in Rusia Petroleum for a figure between just $700 million and $900 million (pending a final agreement) – a very modest amount for a majority share in a project which could be worth well over $20 billion once completed.[27]

Russia forced similar concessions in Sakhalin-2, which was the only PSA that lacked the participation of a Russian company. On 21 December 2006, the Russian state forced foreign companies to hand over part of their stakes to Gazprom for $7.45 billion. In order to get the foreign partners to give up their stakes, Moscow threatened them with the enforcement of the country's environmental legislation, alleging that project activities had violated it. Once the deal was complete, these environmental concerns disappeared.

More investment in distribution pipelines than productive capacity

The performance of Russia's energy sector will depend largely on the amount of domestic and foreign investment which is allocated to it, and where these investments go: to upstream or downstream projects; the modernization of transportation lines; to East or West Siberia or to offshore projects in the north of Russia; or to the oil, gas, coal, or nuclear sectors. It is also important when these investments take place: now or in 15 years time. Naturally, there simply is not enough money to meet all these needs at once.

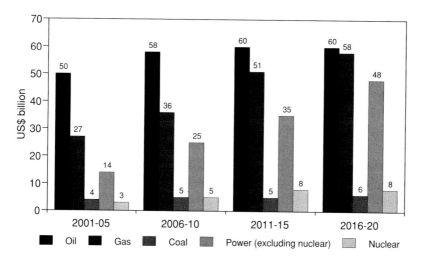

Source: Ministerstvo Promyshlennosti i Energetiki Rossiiskoi Federatsii (MPE RF), *Energeticheskaya strategiya Rossii na period do 2020 goda*, approved as decree no. 1234-r by the Russian government on 28 August 2003, www.minprom. gov.ru/docs/strateg/1/

Figure 5.3:   Investment required according to Russia's Energy Strategy up to 2020 (minimal estimate)

Russia's Energy Strategy estimates that as much as $172 billion must be spent in the gas sector alone between 2003 and 2020 in order to meet the stated objectives of increased gas production of 14–22 per cent (from 595 bcm/y in 2002 to 680–730 bcm/y in 2020). The figures for other sectors are no less impressive: oil: $228 billion; coal: $20 billion; electricity: $122 billion; and nuclear: $24 billion (see Figure 5.3).

While Russia's Energy Strategy thus requires investments of around $566 billion up to 2020, the IEA estimates that Russia's energy sector will require investments of over a trillion US dollars by 2030.[28] Daniel Simmons and Isabel Murray estimate that Russia's gas sector alone needs $18 billion of investment each year, for every year until 2030, in order to meet production targets, with most of this investment in production assets.[29]

In recent years, however, Russian investment has been focused more on downstream than upstream production projects. Transneft has made the most significant investments, constructing new oil export infrastructure. Gazprom, too, is focused on planning new export pipelines, buying up energy assets in transit countries, entering downstream markets of consuming countries in the West, and taking over the gas assets of foreign-partnered projects in Russia. Gazprom is also determined to become a major LNG producer and exporter. Such trends are evident in Gazprom's $20.1 billion investment programme for 2007 (approved in December 2006), as depicted in Figure 5.4.[30]

Despite the fact that Asia has become more important in Russia's overall international energy strategy, Russian energy companies have

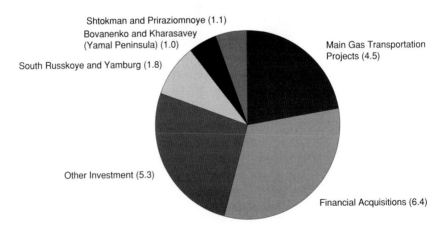

Source: www.gazprom.ru

Figure 5.4: Gazprom's investment programme for 2007, US$ billion

focused mainly on the traditional European market. The dominant strategy so far has been to build new export pipelines backed by long-term contracts, in order to strengthen dependencies by locking consumers into energy purchases many years into the future. Thus, Gazprom seeks to secure its sales before it knows when, and to what extent, it will be able to actually fill the pipelines. Also, by building new pipelines, Russia seeks to reduce its dependency on traditional transit routes through Ukraine and Belarus, which currently transport the bulk of Russian oil and gas to Europe, but have become risky because of tensions in bilateral relations and unsettled price issues. Finally, by building new pipelines, Russia is effectively undermining other pipeline projects, mainly those aimed at accessing Caspian oil and gas, circumventing Russian territory.

Russia has devoted extensive resources to this strategy. In the gas sphere, the new major alternative pipeline routes include the Nord Stream natural gas pipeline linking Russia directly to Germany through the Baltic Sea. Two projects are under consideration that would challenge the EU's favoured Nabucco pipeline project, which is planned to carry natural gas from Azerbaijan, Central Asia, and Iran to Europe. These projects, an extension of the Blue Stream gas pipeline from Turkey, and a new South Stream gas pipeline from Russia under the Black Sea to Bulgaria, parallel Nabucco and would serve the same markets. In the oil sphere, Russia is championing a plan to construct an oil pipeline from Bulgaria's Black Sea port of Burgas to Alexandroupolis in northern Greece. Additionally, work has begun to increase the capacity of the Baltic Pipeline System (BPS), opening up an alternative to the Druzhba pipeline through Belarus, as a route for oil.[31] (See the corresponding maps in the appendix to this chapter.)

A primary concern about Russian downstream activity is that there is too little investment in the upstream sector, with a risk that Russia will not be able to fill oil and gas pipelines and meet its contractual obligations. While Gazprom is not very transparent regarding information on how much it is investing in upstream production, publicly available figures suggest that there has been too little upstream investment for major new gas fields to come online soon. Of particular concern are the Shtokman and Yamal fields, which are very important for European energy security since the bulk of Russian gas shipped to Europe in the future is meant to come from these fields.

The level of overall investment has been growing, but not much has gone into upstream production. The $20.1 billion investment programme for 2007 assigned only about $1 billion to projects on the Yamal peninsula. In mid-2007, the investment programme grew to nearly $30 billion largely due to the purchase of stakes in Sakhalin Energy, Belarussian pipeline operator Beltransgaz, and Mosenergo, the Russian capital's generating company.[32] In December 2008 the Gazprom board approved a further 12 per cent increase.[33] Among the priority projects are the pre-development of projects on the Yamal peninsula and Shtokman, and the construction of corresponding transportation infrastructure.

It remains to be seen whether this increased investment comes fast enough to prevent stagnation, or even a decline in future gas production. The total investments allocated for the Bovanenkovskoye gas field on the Yamal peninsula in 2008 were $4.3 billion, of which only $2.3 billion was going into upstream development, the rest was for building a gas transportation system and for the Obskaya–Bovanenkovoye railway, according to Former Deputy Energy Minister Vladimir Milov.[34] While Gazprom announced in December 2008 that it plans to spend about RUR 210 billion ($7.5 billion) in 2009 on the 'Yamal mepaproject' and expects actual production to begin in 2011, with large volumes coming online in 2015 (75–115 bcm/y in 2015, 135–175 bcm/y in 2020, 200–250 bcm in 2025, 310–360 bcm/y in 2030), Milov doubts that Gazprom will be able to achieve these production targets at the current pace. Uncertain prospects also cloud the future of the gigantic Shtokman field, another important gas project in shaping the future of exports to Europe, where investments are expected to amount to $12–14 billion in just the first stage. In early 2009, however, Shtokman remained in the early stage of development.

Moreover, due to Gazprom's serious financial problems beginning with the 2008 oil price fall and economic downturn in Russia, it remains unclear whether the company will be able to stick to its ambitious investment plans. While Gazprom CEO Aleksei Miller declared in November 2008 that the company might have to seek state help in order to fund its projects, First Deputy Prime Minister Igor Shuvalov suggested in December 2008 that Gazprom should cut back its investment plan for 2009 by 25 per cent, which Gazprom eventually did.[38] The Russian newspaper *Kommersant* reported on 25 February 2009 that the Gazprom board had decided to reduce its investment programme from RUR 920.5 billion to RUR 713 billion.[39] At the time of the decision, this sum equalled only about $20 billion, given that the rouble–dollar exchange rate dropped from a ratio of 28:1 in early December 2008 to 35:1 by late February 2009.

The financial crisis might also have a negative impact on energy development in East Siberia and the Far East. Russia has long announced plans to emerge as a major player on the Asian market, and in 2007 the government approved the 'Eastern Program' with Gazprom as the main coordinator.[40] Yet Russian energy companies have so far invested relatively little in the development of new fields in East Siberia. At the moment, there is no transport infrastructure in place to ship large volumes of either oil or gas. In September 2007, Russia sent some 264,000 b/d to China via rail.[41]

Apart from the Sakhalin oil and gas projects, other major projects – like Kovytka – are still in the development phase. The investment requirements to exploit the region as a whole are simply enormous. Given the harsh climate, recovering oil and gas in East Siberia is two to three times more expensive than in West Siberia. In the oil sector alone, the Russian government plans to invest some $26.5 billion for exploration up to 2020. Russian researcher Alexei Kontorovich, from the Siberian Branch of the Russian Academy of Sciences, estimates that another $14.5 billion will be needed to reach the production target of 80 million tons of crude from East Siberia by 2030 (and these figures do not include support for Sakhalin production.)[42]

If the fields of East Siberia are to be developed, construction of an extensive pipeline infrastructure to East Asia is of paramount importance. This goal, however, has also proved to be more complicated than anticipated. Negotiations with Japan and China have been going on since the early 1990s, but it remains uncertain when the pipelines will be built and operating.

Trajectories of domestic energy market reform

Another big challenge, with a potentially very large impact on Russia's future role as an energy supplier, is connected to developments in Russia's domestic energy sector. Gas dominates Russia's energy consumption, making up 54 per cent of Russia's total energy mix in 2006. While there are efforts to reduce Russia's gas consumption by promoting nuclear and coal, experts predict that the absolute volume of gas used domestically is very likely to increase further in the future, as Figure 5.5 indicates.

At the same time, Russia uses gas and other fossil energy extremely inefficiently. Russia uses more than twice as much energy to produce a unit of GNP as the EU, although it is making slow improvements. According to the Russian Ministry of Industry and Energy, Russia could save a substantial part of its current energy use if adequate efficiency measures were introduced. Although Russia claims that it burned off 15 bcm/y of gas at its oil wells in 2005, satellite pictures suggest that in reality it flared as much as 60 bcm/y. The amount of these flares

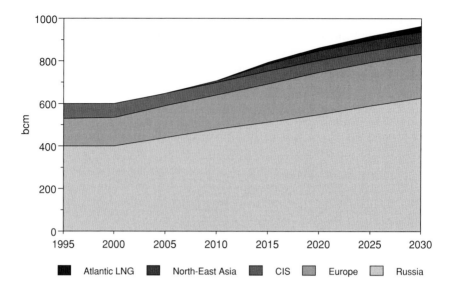

Source: Calculations based on data from Tatiana Mitrova, Center for International
         Energy Market Studies, Russian Academy of Science, Moscow.

Figure 5.5: Projected Russian gas consumption to 2030

is increasing as oil production grows. Additional gas supplies are lost
in transit because of Russia's aging pipeline system.[43] Moreover, much
of the energy devoted to heating Russian homes is wasted because the
heat is centrally produced and then transported, with significant losses
along the way.[44]

One of the key problems is the continuing subsidization of gas on
the domestic market. If a serious reform and break-up of Gazprom is
unlikely in the near future, a gradual price increase for domestic gas can
be expected in the years to come. On 30 November 2006, the Russian
government announced a plan to gradually increase gas for domestic
consumers to well over $125 per 1,000 cubic metres by 2011 (at the end
of 2007, Russian domestic natural gas prices were around $45 per 1,000
cubic metres).[45] This increase means that gas prices should, in the words
of the then Russian Minister for Economic Development and Trade
German Gref, reach 'the same level of profitability as exports' by 2011.[46]

A gas price increase will certainly have a large impact on the Russian
energy market, but its impact on production and exports is difficult to
assess. Gazprom in 2006 received about five times more for selling energy
to European customers than it did on the subsidized domestic market. As
long as gas remains so cheap, domestic demand will grow and less will
be available for export. A rise in domestic prices will increase efficiency

efforts, and will probably boost the development of other energy sources, including coal, nuclear, and, potentially, renewables.

Overall, the result of a price increase could produce contradictory effects for gas exports: it could mean that while independents will increasingly supply the domestic market, Gazprom will send its gas to the foreign market; on the domestic market, Gazprom-produced gas would thus be replaced by independent gas producers and possibly also by other energy sources, thus leaving more gas for export. At the same time, higher prices could also have a contradictory effect as they might reduce Gazprom's incentives to expand gas exports or to engage in risky and expensive new development and exploration projects. If Gazprom decides to sell more on the domestic market once prices are raised, this could ultimately leave less gas for export.[47] Much will depend on the development of the oil price. If the low oil price environment after autumn 2008 continues to persist, gas will also be sold much more cheaply on the international market, ultimately further reducing Gazprom's incentives (as well as abilities) to invest in large and expensive new projects.

The country also has a large potential in the development of renewables. Russia's Energy Strategy to 2020 suggests that as much as 30 per cent of the country's energy needs could be met using alternative sources, if these were developed to their full potential. Russia currently gets only about 3.5 per cent of its energy supply from renewable sources, including its numerous hydroelectric dams.[48]

Implications for Russia's external relations

The challenges outlined are interconnected. Development in one area will ultimately have an impact on developments in other areas. The question of how Russia's external energy relations will be affected is determined by interactions between these domestic developments, but it also depends on the situation in the country's international environment. In the following section, we will analyse Russia's energy relations in three major directions: Europe, the post-Soviet Central Asian states, and Asia. The kind of relations Russia manages to establish with its neighbours will greatly impact its role as an international energy power.

Russia's relations with Europe

Russia's energy relations with Europe need to be understood against the background of economic dependencies, as well as general political

trends. While Russia is dependent on Europe economically, and cooperation in this sphere has flourished in recent years, political relations
have worsened. The tension created due to this rift will affect relations
in the long term.

Europe depends on Russia for a substantial part of its oil and gas
consumption. In all other aspects of EU–Russia trade relations, it
is Russia that depends much more on Europe than the other way
round. In 2006, sales of oil and gas alone accounted for a quarter
of Russia's GDP, three-fifths of its exports, and nearly half of federal
budget revenues.[49] The bulk of this income is generated from exports
to the EU: around two-thirds of gas and oil exports go to EU member
states, the rest to other European countries and the CIS states (a small
fraction is exported to other countries). However, not only is the EU
Russia's most important destination for oil and gas, it is also its most
important trading partner: 56.2 per cent of Russian exports went to the
EU in 2005. The EU accounted for 44.8 per cent of Russia's imports.
Conversely, Russia accounted for only 10.1 per cent of the EU's overall
imports, and is responsible for a meagre 6.2 per cent of EU exports.[50]

Russia is important to Europe as the single biggest supplier of oil and
gas, yet Europe's dependency needs to be put into perspective. Europe
imports some 30 per cent of its oil from Russia, but Russia's leverage is
still limited due to the nature of the oil market. Unlike the gas market,
most of the oil is shipped to Europe via tanker. The Druzhba pipeline
transports about a quarter of Russian crude, the rest is directed to
maritime ports (the majority to the one in Primorsk), from where it
can be shipped to any place in the world. Should Russian production
stagnate or decline, or should Russia divert considerably more of its oil
to the Asian market, Europe could theoretically turn to other suppliers.

Europe has less room for manoeuvre in the case of gas, which is a
different story for three reasons. First, the natural gas market is largely
a pipeline market, and Russian gas to Europe is shipped through
pipelines only (Russia has only small volumes of gas available as LNG
from Sakhalin-2 which can be shipped by tanker, and plans to increase
LNG volumes from the Shtokman gas condensate field). Second, Europe
receives 44 per cent of the gas it imports from Russia, so its dependency
is considerably greater than it is for oil. Third, Europe's demand for
gas is expected to increase much more substantially in the near term
than its demand for oil.[51]

Europe is thus hardly in a position to do without Russian gas in the
future. Yet although Russia's importance as a gas supplier to Europe
will increase in terms of *absolute* volumes, its *relative* weight will ultimately diminish. According to Energy Information Administration (EIA)

forecasts, while oil demand in OECD Europe is unlikely to increase by 2030, European gas import demand might increase substantially. Projections with regard to future gas demand and supply are dependent on the level of economic growth, development of energy efficiency and renewables, and the use of energy prices as policy measures, yet the requirements for the gas imports of the EU and Turkey combined could well amount to some 480 bcm/y, or 65 per cent more than was consumed in 2005. To meet these needs, Norwegian production and purchases on the growing international LNG market could contribute around 100–120 bcm/y each, thus the IEA estimates that pipeline gas from Russia, North Africa, the Caspian, and the Middle East is needed to supply a further 240–280 bcm/y (up from 175 bcm/y in 2005).[52]

If this scenario reflects reality, then one thing is certain: Russia alone will not be able to meet this increasing demand even if the most optimistic scenarios about Russian gas production and export capabilities hold true. Russian gas exports will stagnate at a very high level and Russia will remain the single biggest supplier, but Europe will have to look for alternative suppliers, such as North African countries, Central Asia, Iran, and Qatar. Thus, according to the IEA 2008 reference scenario, the share of CIS gas exports (the bulk of which consists of Russian gas exports) to the European OECD countries (EU-27 together with non-EU members in East and South East Europe as well as Turkey, Switzerland, and Norway) will fall from the current 58 per cent to about 32 per cent in 2030, while the share of imports from Africa to European OECD countries will increase from the current 37 per cent to 54 per cent.[53]

Given Russia's dependence on Europe, as well as the fact that it will face competition from other gas exporting countries, it is Europe that clearly has greater potential leverage. Yet for political reasons, Europe has so far not used this leverage. As long as European countries do not want the EU to speak with a single voice in energy policy, but prefer to deal with Russia on the basis of individual bilateral relations and agreements between energy companies, the EU cannot bring its potential to bear. This fragmentary approach is particularly evident in the area of reciprocity, which has been a major point of friction between Russia and the EU for some time.[54]

The EU has been insisting that if Russian energy companies are allowed into the EU downstream energy market, then EU companies should also be allowed to enter the Russian downstream market, which is currently monopolized by Gazprom and Transneft. The EU has thus for years tried in vain to convince Russia to ratify the Energy Charter Treaty, which would, among other things, imply an opening up of

Russia's energy market, thus potentially undermining Gazprom's and Transneft's energy transportation monopolies. In summer 2007, in a move to increase the pressure on Russia, the EU Commission proposed breaking up big utilities that control power supply, generation, and transmission; this effort is directed at some of Europe's own big energy companies, but would also effectively bar foreign companies such as Gazprom from controlling European networks unless they play by the same rules as EU companies, and their home country (in this case Russia) has an agreement with Brussels.[55]

It is far from clear whether this proposal will be implemented, since doing so would generate fierce resistance not only from Russia, but from powerful interest groups within the EU. So far, the rows in Russia's relations with Europe have not proven to be impediments to the general level of business cooperation and day-to-day politics. Investment and trade volumes are booming, and Gazprom has successfully negotiated contracts on long-term gas deliveries with a number of energy-related companies, including Italy's Eni S.p.A. and Gaz de France (GdF) in 2007. Moreover, European companies are being invited back into Russia's oil and gas upstream development sector, as the case of Shtokman indicates. Although in 2006 Gazprom declared that it intended to develop the project on its own, in 2007 it invited two foreign companies, Total and Statoil, in as minority stake holders.[56]

In contrast to these positive trends in economic relations, however, political relations have worsened. The trigger point was Russia's shut down of gas deliveries to Ukraine in January 2006. Even if Russia's action in January 2006 was directed at Ukraine only, Russia ultimately accepted that by stopping deliveries to Ukraine, it might hurt some of its European gas costumers, in the likely case that Ukraine redirected deliveries destined for Europe – which it ultimately decided to do. Russia's assertive move against Ukraine came at a time when the overall political context was already charged negatively against Russia. These general atmospherics were only partly to do with Russia's energy behaviour, they were also concerned with the West's image of Russia as an increasingly authoritarian and anti-democratic power. Even though the Soviet Union–Russia had been a reliable supplier for the past 30 years, the question for Europe ultimately was whether it wanted to remain a partner with this kind of Russia.[57]

In January 2009, when Russia once more stopped delivering gas to Ukraine and European clients, leaving half of Europe shivering for almost two weeks, Russian and Gazprom representatives again put the blame entirely on Ukraine. Gazprom declared that the crisis proved the unreliability of Ukraine as a transit route, and urged European support in building alternative routes around transit states (namely the Nord Stream and South Stream pipeline projects).[58] Gazprom's reputation may have suffered tremendously in the eyes of many Europeans, yet the response from the EU and its member states was not coordinated, and it is unlikely that the future will see major changes in European policy towards Russia, as long as policy is driven by the interests of individual states and companies vis-à-vis Russia. Several European countries and companies have long supported Gazprom's pipeline ambitions; accordingly, Germany is unlikely to abandon its support for Nord Stream, while Italy and a number of southeast European countries will continue to favour South Stream. This support, of course, does not mean that these pipeline projects, both of which face daunting financial, legal, and political obstacles, will be realized soon, nor does it mean that these same European countries will not also seek to support other pipeline projects (such as Nabucco) and energy suppliers.[59]

Russia's relations with Central Asian gas producers

Energy is the defining element in Russia's relations with the energy-rich states of Central Asia. Just as Russia needs independent gas producers to fill the growing gap from its declining fields, it counts on gas inflow from Central Asia in order to keep export volumes up at a time when Gazprom's production growth is flat. From an economic point of view, it is cheaper for Russia to buy up Central Asia's gas at (relatively) low prices than invest in expensive fields in its north. From a geopolitical perspective, Russia maintains an influential position in Central Asia as long as energy ties are kept strong.

Since all the major Central Asian gas pipelines go through Russia, it has so far been easy for Russia to 'convince' the Central Asians to keep selling their gas to Russia below market prices. In 2006, Gazprom purchased about 60 bcm/y from Central Asia, a significant amount, but one which is unlikely to increase any time soon, especially if Turkmenistan, which provides the bulk of these supplies, is not able to increase its production substantially in the near future.[60] It can be expected that over the next few years Russia will be able to at least maintain Central Asian imports at this level, and not forfeit any ground to other competitors for these supplies. In the mid- to long term, however, other countries – particularly China, but potentially also Europe – will emerge as powerful competitors for Central Asian gas.

The scale of Russian direct investment in the region is modest, particularly in comparison to the investments made by other countries. Russian foreign direct investment in Kazakhstan, for example, amounted to only $930.5 million (or 3.1 per cent of total foreign direct investment) for the period between 1993 and September 2004. The three largest foreign investors, the USA, Great Britain, and Italy, accounted for almost $15 billion (50.73 per cent). However, Russia has so far been very good at securing long-term contracts on gas deliveries. Also, from 2005 onwards, there has been a marked upturn in Russian investment in the region. Russia's private oil company Lukoil, for example, has emerged as one of the leading foreign companies in upstream projects in Kazakhstan.[61]

The most important regional partner for Russia in terms of gas is Turkmenistan. President Gurbanguly Berdymukhammedov of Turkmenistan has confirmed the previous gas deal signed by his predecessor in 2003, giving Russia an almost exclusive right to import gas from Turkmenistan, at least until 2009. Under the deal, Turkmenistan sold Gazprom up to 60 bcm of gas in 2007, 60–70 bcm in 2008, and up to 80 bcm in each of the following years (in 2006, Gazprom imported 42 bcm of gas from Turkmenistan). After 2009, the two sides agreed to enter negotiations for a long-term contract, preferably up to 2028. In March 2008, however, in a surprise move Gazprom declared that it would pay European prices for Central Asian gas beginning in 2009. Consequently, not only Turkmenistan, but also Uzbekistan and Kazakhstan, announced they would no longer aim for long-term agreements but negotiate gas prices and the terms of their gas sales with Russia in annual contracts.[62] Thus the times when Russia virtually blackmailed Turkmenistan to sell its gas for $44 per thousand cubic metres, with only half of the price paid in cash and the rest through barter are gone. In November 2007, Turkmenistan and Gazprom had already agreed to raise the price of Turkmen gas from $100 per 1,000 cubic metres in 2007 to $130 in the first half of 2008 and to $150 in July–December 2008.[63] Starting in 2009, Gazprom is paying $340 per 1,000 cubic metres for Turkmen gas (a price that will fall in the second quarter of 2009 should oil prices remain low).

This jump clearly indicates the importance Gazprom attaches to Central Asian gas, and also shows that Russia is ready to offer a good price in order to outbid international competitors. Despite Turkmen commitment to Russia, however, President Berdymukhammedov indicated that he wants to leave his options open by not ruling out the construction of a pipeline under the Caspian Sea in the future. Also, the Turkmen president signed an agreement with China on gas deliveries and the construction of a pipeline to China in mid-July 2007 which would see 30 bcm/y from new field developments in eastern Turkmenistan flowing to China in the next decade.[65]

The Central Asian gas producers have thus empowered their position vis-à-vis Russia. At the same time, however, they will also have to raise production substantially in order to meet their contractual obligations: Turkmenistan's current total output stands at about 60 bcm/y, thus the country will have to increase production substantially to meet its targets of increasing gas supplies, not only to Russia, but also China and other potential partners in the future.[66] Russia is seeking much smaller amounts from other Central Asian countries.

In order to gain direct access to Caspian gas, Europe and the USA favour the construction of a pipeline, the Trans-Caspian Pipeline (TCP), under the Caspian Sea, which would then connect to the markets of Turkey and Europe. This project is opposed by Russia on environmental and legal grounds (the legal status of the Caspian, and whether it is a sea or a lake, has not yet been resolved by the five countries around it). Instead, Russia has agreed to expand existing pipeline capacities from Central Asia (Central Asia Centre gas pipeline, running from Turkmenistan through Uzbekistan and Kazakhstan to Russia) and has also committed itself to the construction of a new pipeline following a route along the Caspian coast for transporting mainly Turkmen gas.

In the near future, the EU and the USA thus cannot count on substantial amounts of Caspian gas flowing directly westward. Only Azerbaijan will transport gas in this direction through the newly opened Baku–Tbilisi–Erzurum pipeline (also known as the South Caucasus Gas Pipeline). There is little hope that large amounts of Kazakh gas will fill the pipeline. A substantial part of Kazakhstan's additional gas production, at least over the next decade or so, will be absorbed by exports to Russia's Orenburg processing plant, a planned petrochemical facility, and its domestic market. Since Kazakhstan's largest gas field, Karachaganak, is located in the north of the country near Russia's border, it is more convenient to transport gas via the existing transportation networks.

China, rather than the EU or USA, is very likely to emerge as the major competitor for Central Asian gas. In addition to the deal with Turkmenistan, China signed a memo with the Uzbek leadership in April 2007 announcing the intention to build a 530 km natural gas pipeline to China with a capacity of 30 bcm/y.[67] Additionally, China agreed with Kazakhstan to the construction of a natural gas pipeline from Kazakhstan to China. Kazakh gas shipments to China will only be feasible if Karachaganak succeeds in implementing large output increases, beyond what is committed already to Orenburg. The plans are ambitious (construction on the pipeline started in 2008 and the two sides have announced that first gas will flow in 2010), yet given the limited export capacities in Kazakhstan, it is uncertain as to exactly when large amounts of gas will flow to China. In any case, it is seems only a matter of time before China will be able to draw larger amounts of gas (and oil) from Central Asia eastwards.[68]

Russia's relations with Asia

Russia has declared expansion into the Asian market to be a priority of its energy strategy. The development of the energy sector of East Siberia and the Far East is important, because Russia sees it as an opportunity to encourage the engagement of this region with the lucrative markets of Asia. Russia does not want to become merely an exporter of raw material for Asia, and is reluctant to provide the fuel for growth in this region, but energy is seen as the means of starting the development of a region which has faced economic and social hardship and demographic decline since the collapse of the Soviet Union. The other driver behind Russia's move towards Asia is diversification. Just as energy importers seek to diversify their supplies in order to become less dependent on a single source, producers seek to diversify exports and enter new markets in order to enhance security of demand.

Exactly how much oil and gas East Siberia holds is uncertain, but volumes could be enormous, especially for gas. One estimate, from a report by the Japanese Economic Research Institute for North East Asia, holds that East Siberia contains up to 18 per cent of Russia's oil and up to 29 per cent of Russia's natural gas, without taking the Sakhalin reserves in Russia's Far Eastern region into account.[69] According to a recent estimate by TNK–BP, East Siberia has proven oil reserves of about 7 billion barrels, but since only 5 per cent of the oil-producing zones have been explored so far, the reserves could well be 75 billion barrels. This amount would equal the proven reserves for the entire country, or a quarter of the reserves of Saudi Arabia.[70]

The only projects in the Russian east that are starting to produce are those on Sakhalin Island. It is also still not clear where Sakhalin energy will go, however. Sakhalin-2 has produced oil since 1999, which is shipped to international markets. With the construction of a major LNG terminal at Sakhalin-2, officially inaugurated by President Dmitry Medvedev in February 2009, Russia will be able to serve different markets; yet it has in fact already contracted most of its gas from Sakhalin-2 to Japan, South Korea, and the USA. First shipments of Russian LNG from Sakhalin-2 are expected in spring 2009.[71] While oil from the Sakhalin-1 project is already shipped to world markets (most of it to East Asia), Russia is still undecided where the gas from Sakhalin-1 will go. While ExxonMobil, the project operator, favours the construction of a pipeline to China, one of the minority shareholders, Gazprom, in an obvious attempt to increase control over Sakhalin-1, argued that the gas destined for China from this project should be rerouted in order to supply gas to the Russian Far Eastern regions.[72] Gazprom has also been considering constructing a gas pipeline from Sakhalin-1 to Japan, but is it unclear if and when this project will be realized.[73]

Apart from the considerable technical and financial obstacles to developing this region, there are broader economic and geopolitical trade-offs related to Russia's Asian strategy. In the following analysis, we will illustrate these obstacles by looking at the different planned pipeline projects.

In the oil sector, the major proposed pipeline is the East Siberia–Pacific Ocean pipeline (ESPO). This project has been the subject of intense lobbying from the Japanese and Chinese governments for first access to Russian oil deliveries.[74] In the summer of 2006, Russian officials announced that China would have access to the oil pipeline first. The initial phase is the construction of a 4,100 km long pipeline trunk through Russian territory from Irkustk Oblast to Skovorodino in the Amur region, just 70 km away from the Chinese border. From there, the remaining segment will connect to the Chinese city of Daqing, where the Chinese oil industry is concentrated; this segment will be constructed by China. Only after this will the stretch to Russia's Pacific coast be finalized, allowing Japan to have oil shipped from this relatively close location.[75] Russia's decision to serve China first was prompted by fear that otherwise, China might intensify its search for alternative oil (and gas) supplies – as it is already doing in Central Asia, Africa, and South America. Such Chinese exploration would lead to tougher competition between Russia and China in Central Asia, which Russia seeks to avoid.

The financial crisis of autumn 2008 has put the $12.5 billion pipeline project under enormous strain, forcing Russian state companies Rosneft and Transneft to ask for a loan from China. After hard negotiations, in mid-February 2009 the two sides signed an intergovernmental agreement on the construction of the pipeline branch from Skovorodino to the Chinese border, and long-term Russian oil supplies of 110 million barrels of crude per year (15 million metric tons) from 2011 until 2030. In return, the Chinese Bank of Development will provide a $10 billion loan to Russia's oil pipeline operator Transneft and a $15 billion loan to state oil company Rosneft in order for them to strengthen their balance sheet, complete the ESPO project and to develop oil fields in East Siberia.[76] The deal clearly represents a shift in Russian policy which, before the economic crisis, was categorically against Chinese involvement in its eastern energy projects – as, for example, in 2002, when Russia rejected Chinese investment in its oil company Slavneft.[77]

Talks between China and Russia on the development of natural gas exports have focused on two main pipeline projects. The first project would link the gas fields of Western Siberia to China in the Xinjang–Uyghur region and then connect to the Chinese East–West main gas pipeline, which serves as the country's main gas artery; this is called the Altai project. The Altai pipeline would be connected to Russia's United Gas Supply System (UGSS) in Tomsk and then run through the border between Kazakhstan and Mongolia, thereby avoiding any transit countries. The pipeline would be 2,800 km long, and would supply 30 bcm of gas per year. In the long run, supply from the Yamal peninsula would also be delivered through this route.[78] The other project would connect East Siberian fields to China via the Pacific coast. Gazprom has, so far, given the Western project higher priority, essentially because it would connect China to the already producing fields of Nadym and Urengoi in West Siberia, while in East Siberia, the main field, Kovykta, is still in the development phase.

Many experts had from the start expressed doubts that the Altai project would ever be implemented, due to a number of difficulties. First, the chosen route goes through very difficult mountainous terrain, driving up the costs for a pipeline which is already priced at no less than $12 billion. Second, the Uyghur autonomous region of China is politically unstable, and some worry that insurgents may target infrastructure. Third, although as Gazprom officials point out, the pipeline length is shorter than some of the pipelines going to Europe, it is not entirely clear that a Chinese–Russian project could sustain the levels of investment necessary for even a shorter line. Finally, gas prices in China are controlled by the state at low levels, and Gazprom has expressed its desire that gas prices be linked to oil prices – a common practice when negotiating international gas contracts. China has so far shown unwillingness to agree to this point, offering a price about a third of what Russia received on the European market in 2006.

In fact, it came as little surprise when Russia's Energy Ministry excluded the Altai pipeline project from its blueprint for the gas sector, which it presented on 6 October 2008. Apart from the problems listed above, the blueprint took note of the fact that the Altai pipeline would not be competitive with the pipeline projects now under construction from Central Asia.[79] While the construction of a Russian oil pipeline to China looks like a realistic scenario for the near future, Russia's gas pipeline projects to China are unlikely to materialize any time soon.

Thus, even if Russia will indeed be able to increase oil exports to China via a new pipeline (it currently ships oil to China only via rail), China is unlikely to receive Russian gas from East Siberian fields any time soon. This also means that Russia will not be able to redirect gas destined for Europe from West Siberian fields eastwards to China, a fear frequently voiced by European observers.

China is clearly a logical partner for Russian energy, and Russia has now little choice but to accept Chinese financial involvement, but Russia's policy still seems to suffer from a psychological blockade fuelled by decades of mutual mistrust. Russia understands that it has to engage with China for economic reasons, but it feels uneasy about providing the fuel for China's modernization, which will inevitably accelerate the rise of a neighbour that could, from the Russian point of view, not only surpass Russia economically, but also pose a military threat in the future. Contrary to what is written in the Western media, the more pressing issue is, from Russia's perspective, not the balance of East against West, but the balance between the individual countries of East Asia and, in the case of Sakhalin, also the balance between Asia and the USA. Russia does not want to become over-dependent on China, and seeks to extend its energy relationships to Japan and Korea, as well as the USA and Southeast Asia. As things stand at the moment, however, China's dominant position among Asian–Pacific energy consumers means that the buyer is, in this instance at least, as influential as the seller.[80]

Trends in Russia's energy policy

Russia is not going to meet all its energy policy goals simultaneously, so the key question is how Russia will prioritize the various options. In the following section, we summarize the emerging key trends and make some projections into the future. We believe that in order to understand the trends in Russia's energy policy, we need to consider three major aspects: the impact of the global financial crisis on Russia, the urgency of attracting foreign capital and continuing the reform of the energy sector, and the need for Russia to remain focused on Europe as its main trading partner, despite some diversification of its energy exports to China.

The impact of the global financial crisis

The global financial crisis hit Russia particularly hard. Russian GDP grew for nine consecutive years at an average rate of about 7 per cent. This boom ended abruptly in autumn 2008, when the Russian Trading System Stock Exchange (RTS) index dropped by a staggering 70 per cent, making it one of the worst performing stock market indexes in the world. The reason for the financial slump was not only the fall of the oil price, from nearly $140 a barrel of Urals crude in July 2008 to about $45 a barrel in December, but also the fact that many investors withdrew from Russia, and credit sources for Russian companies dried up.[81]

The autumn crisis brought to light several negative characteristics which already featured in Russia's economy before the crisis actually broke. First, it clearly indicated how dependent Russia was on oil and gas exports, and showed the lack of diversification within the economy.

Second, it demonstrated that Russia's nationalization policy and the Kremlin's crack down on private business put severe strains on the economy, as it forced much needed foreign capital out of Russia. Foreign investors started to leave Russia earlier in 2008 when the Russian state signalled to the outside world that private business and investment were not safe, during the power struggle between the Russian and British owners of TNK–BP, and Putin's sharp public criticism of the privately-owned Mechel mining and metals company. Russia's invasion of Georgia in August 2008 and the cut-off of Russian gas to Ukraine and Europe in January 2009 did not do much to restore confidence in Russia. Yet the lack of foreign capital became most dire only when oil prices fell and rents from exports declined.

Third, Russia's steep and abrupt decline showed just how globalized its economy is. Russia is not only very dependent on access to international markets, and high prices for its energy, it is also dependent on access to credit. In fact, Russia's energy companies have borrowed heavily on the international market in order to finance their multiple projects. With smaller earnings from energy sales, these companies are now in a difficult financial position. This is also true for Gazprom. Shares in Gazprom, an enterprise worth an estimated $300 billion before the global financial crisis, fell by 76 per cent up to January 2009.[82]

Fourth, the crisis has also indicated the limits of the state's power to regulate the market, despite the fact that the state collected massive rents from energy exports over a period of five years. Russia had accumulated almost $600 billion in reserves derived from energy sales profits by August 2008, thanks to extensive exports. However, these resources started to dry up quickly, as the state injected billions to prevent its key businesses and banking system from collapsing. By 9

January 2009, Russia's reserves had shrunk to about $427 billion, according to official figures.[83] Thus, at the beginning of 2009, the outlook for Russia's economy was dire, though by the spring it had stabilized.

The need to attract foreign capital and continue reform

Clearly, Russia will have to supplement domestic funds by encouraging more foreign investment. Yet this would also mean that Russia needs to revise its legal framework and provide secure property rights for the assets of foreign companies operating in Russia. To encourage foreign investment, Russia needs to regain the confidence lost due to bad internal economic policies and a foreign policy which appeared increasingly assertive and even confrontational.

Russia will thus have to conduct its foreign energy policy as part of a broader international strategy, which requires an overall strengthening of foreign, political, and diplomatic ties. Russia is unlikely to forfeit what it considers key national interests, and will not shy away from applying harsh methods towards neighbours when it feels threatened. The Russia–Ukraine gas conflict of January 2009 indicated that Russia was ready to resort to extreme measures even at the potential cost of compromising its relations with its key European partners. At the same time, Russia has also shown more eagerness to repair diplomatic and political relations. In early 2009 it demonstrated increasing readiness to improve ties with Western countries and to cooperate more closely with Western security institutions, even including the possibility of working with NATO in addressing the Afghanistan crisis, though only after facilitating the closure of the US resupply base in Kyrgyzstan.[84]

Russia will need to improve its business climate considerably to attract foreign investors. Looking back at events surrounding the Sakhalin energy projects, for example, international energy companies have no guarantee that Russia will in the future respect contracts once projects start to become operational. Yet it is clear that the bargaining power of international institutions and companies vis-à-vis Russian companies has increased. While Transneft and Rosneft accepted a major loan from the Chinese Bank of Development in exchange for East Siberian pipeline oil in February 2009, Gazprom in autumn 2008 declared that it is considering the participation of a number of foreign companies, including US energy majors ExxonMobil and ConocoPhillips, in LNG projects in the Yamal region.[85] While the Russian state is unlikely to give up control in the energy sector, private Russian companies and foreign energy companies will be allowed to participate as minority stakeholders in larger projects, and the state and Russian state-controlled companies will probably seek to attract these companies to engage in the difficult terrain in East Siberia and offshore fields.

The future will probably see a further liberalization of the Russian energy market, the key element of which will be the liberalization of domestic gas prices. Once Russian consumers have to pay market prices, it will become more attractive for non-Gazprom companies to produce and sell gas to Russian costumers. An increase in the domestic gas price will hopefully also increase energy efficiency. Liberalization would not, however, include a break-up of Gazprom's and Transneft's monopoly on export pipelines, as control over pipelines is considered to be a main tool of leverage both vis-à-vis domestic Russian companies and foreign partners.

Europe remains Russia's key partner

How will Russia's energy policy play out vis-à-vis its various international markets? A key feature of Russia's foreign energy relations is to foster existing dependencies through downstream investment and the renegotiation of long-term contracts on energy deliveries. Russian companies seek to foster those dependencies, which are considered economically beneficial, but have disengaged from those which are burdensome. Accordingly, Russia's focus has been mostly on its traditional energy costumers in Europe, who pay high prices for the energy they consume. Russian oil and gas companies have made their largest investments in maintaining and expanding energy relations with their long-standing European clients, but they have also sought to expand into new European markets (such as the UK).

Russia's relationship to the Central Asian gas producers is largely a function of its relations with Europe. Russia needs the gas from Central Asia to free more of its own for export. In order to tie Central Asian gas to its market, Russia has offered these states much higher prices than it was willing to pay in the past, and access to markets outside Russia. At the same time, and again in order to foster relations with Europe, Russian companies have sought to reduce their dependency on transit states such as Ukraine and Belarus by starting to build new pipelines, and also by raising prices for Russian gas to these countries.

Diversification of energy sales to Asia is a central goal of Russian energy policy, both for geopolitical and economic reasons. At the same time, however, Russian companies have acted very cautiously when deciding on major investments. Russia and China are likely to see the construction of an oil pipeline in the near future, but plans to build a gas pipeline are currently on hold. There are multiple reasons why the long-discussed gas pipelines to China have not yet been built, but a major obstacle is the fact that the Chinese have been unwilling to pay a price which will guarantee the amortization of Russia's large up-front investments. Also, Russia doubts that a gas pipeline project is economically feasible now that the Central Asians have started to build their pipelines to China. Russia will continue to explore its options in Asia, but developments are unlikely to move forward quickly.

In this respect, Europe appears as a much more predictable and profitable business partner. Relations with Europe are, and will thus remain, the pillar of Russia's energy policy. Given the underlying tensions in Russia–Europe relations however, it is important that, besides intensifying their energy dialogue at the highest political levels, Europe and Russia look for areas of cooperation in the less politicized – but no less important – areas of their larger energy relationship. Among the many options, the one area of cooperation that has been largely neglected is the promotion of greater energy efficiency through the entire chain of production, transportation, and end use, as well as the development of renewable energy sources. These are largely unexplored areas of cooperation, which have, however, huge development potential, and are economically attractive for both sides. Moreover, the promotion of energy efficiency and renewables is in line with global efforts to reduce carbon dioxide emissions.[86]

The expansion of the European–Russian energy relationship to include technology sharing in the area of energy efficiency, and the development of renewables, is all the more important since Russia views the EU's energy policy, particularly its goals of reducing dependency on imported fossil fuels and diversifying imports, with some degree of suspicion. These moves make the traditional European oil and gas market look increasingly unstable for Russia, and expanding into other areas presents itself as a strategy which could smooth out eventual disruptions in Russian–European oil and gas relations.

Appendix: Oil and gas pipelines

5.1 Russian oil pipelines
5.2 Russian gas pipelines
5.3 Caspian oil pipelines
5.4 Caspian gas pipelines

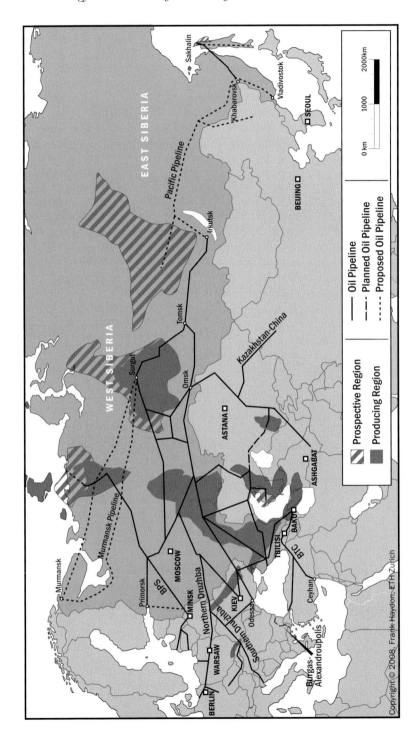

Map 5.1: Russian oil pipelines

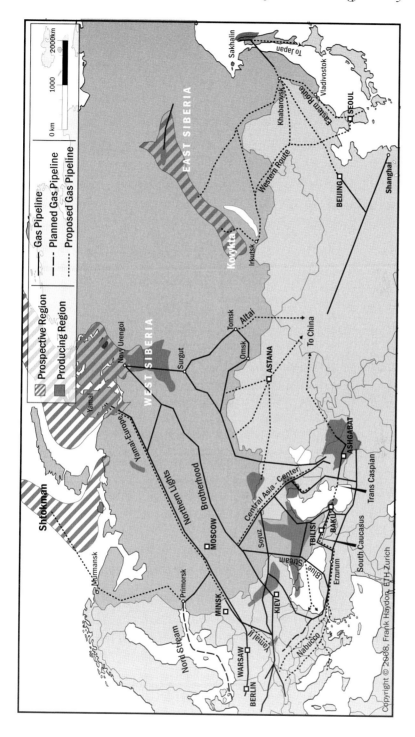

Map 5.2: Russian gas pipelines

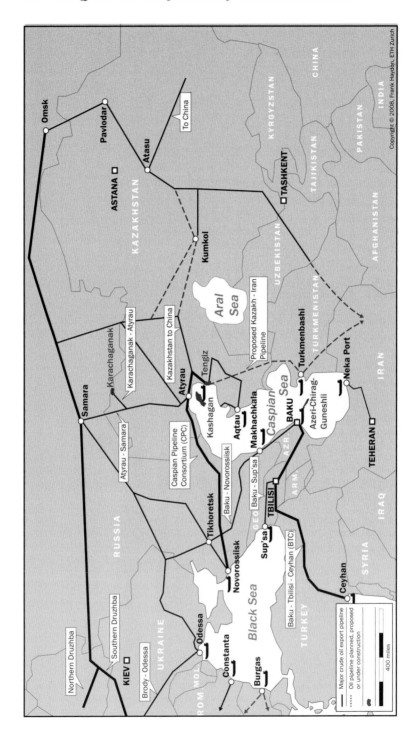

Map 5.3: Caspian oil pipelines

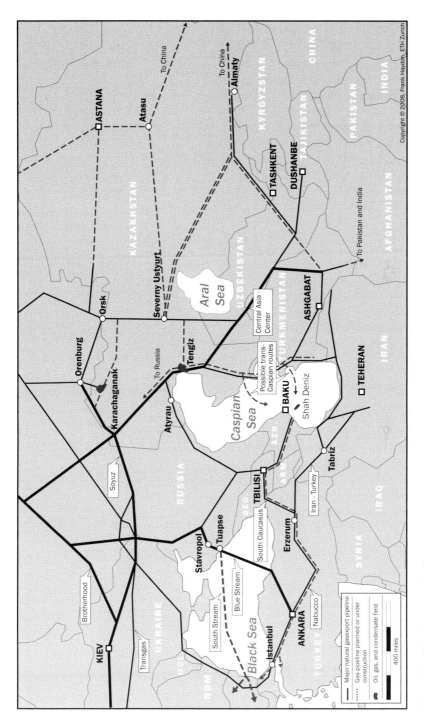

Map 5.4: Caspian gas pipelines

Notes

1   British Petroleum (BP), *Statistical Review of World Energy 2008*, British Petroleum, London, June 2008, 6 and 8.www.bp.com/productlanding.do?categoryId=6929&contentId=7044622

2   European Commission (EC), *The European Union and Russia: Close Neighbours, Global Players, Strategic Partners*, European Commission External Relations, Brussels October 2007, 13. http://ec.europa.eu/external_relations/russia/docs/russia_brochure07_en.pdf

3   'New Energy Source Comes Onstream at Sakhalin II: Russia's First LNG Plant Opened by President Medvedev', *Sakhalin Energy Media Centre Press Release*, 18 February 2009. www.sakhalinenergy.com/en/media.asp?p=media_page&itmID=259

4   Ministerstvo Promyshlennosti i Energetiki Rossiiskoi Federatsii (MPE RF), *Energeticheskaia strategiia Rossii na period do 2020 goda*, approved as decree no. 1234-r by the Russian government on 28 August 2003. www.minprom.gov.ru/docs/strateg/1/ In the meanwhile, MPE RF has commissioned work on a follow-up energy strategy until 2030. An early draft published in 2007 of the 2030 strategy is available at: www.energystrategy.ru/materials/koncepc.htm

5   For an overview, see Energy Information Administration (EIA), *Russia Energy Profile*, Department of Energy, Energy Information Administration, Washington, DC. http://tonto.eia.doe.gov/country/country_time_series.cfm?fips=RS

6   For background information: EIA, *Caspian Sea Country Analysis Brief*, Department of Energy, Energy Information Administration, Washington, DC, January 2007. www.eia.doe.gov/cabs/Caspian/Full.html

7   EIA, *China Country Analysis Brief*, Department of Energy, Energy Information Administration, Washington, DC, August 2006, 6.www.eia.doe.gov/emeu/cabs/China/pdf.pdf

8   The CPC ownership structure includes the Russian Federation (24 per cent), the Republic of Kazakhstan (19 per cent), the Sultanate of Oman (7 per cent), and a consortium of eight companies led by the Chevron Caspian Pipeline Consortium Company. Lukoil also participates in this project with a 12.5 per cent-share (through LukArco). For more information on the CPC, visit the project's official website at www.cpc.ru

9   For background information: EIA, *Caspian Sea Country Analysis Brief*.

10 Daniel Kimmage, 'Central Asia: Turkmenistan–China Pipeline Project Has Far-Reaching Implications', *RFE/RL*, 10 April 2006. www.rferl.org/featuresarticle/2006/4/55F9574D-407A-4777-9724-944E6C2ECD7B.html

11 'Kazakhstan Building Gas Pipeline to China', *CRI, Xinhua News Agency*, 10 July 2008. www.china.org.cn/environment/news/2008-07/10/content_15988108.htm; 'Uzbekistan, China Team up for Gas Pipeline Construction', 14 April 2008, *RIA Novosti*. http://en.rian.ru/world/20080414/104972866.html

12 See also Roland Götz, 'Zentralasiatische Energieexporte: Zwischen russi-
    scher Dominanz, Diversifizierungsplänen der EU und neuen Märkten in
    Asien', *Russlandanaylsen*, no. 137 (June 2007): 2–6. www.laender-analysen.
    de/russland/pdf/Russlandanalysen137.pdf

13 Vladimir Milov, Leonard Coburn, and Igor Danchenko, 'Russia's Energy
    Policy 1992–2005', *Eurasian Geography and Economics 47, No. 3* (2006), 305.

14 See the chapter by Jeronim Perovic in this book.

15 Putin quote from his interview with *The Times*, 4 June 2007. www.timesonline.
    co.uk/tol/news/world/europe/article1882140.ece

16 BP, *Statistical Review of World Energy 2008*, 8.

17 Data from Platts.

18 Heiko Pleines, 'Developing Russia's Oil and Gas Industry: What Role for the
    State?', in *Russian Energy Power and Foreign Relations: Implications for Conflict and
    Cooperation*, ed. Jeronim Perovic, Robert W. Orttung, and Andreas Wenger,
    Routledge, London and New York, 2009, 71–86, (here Page 75).

19 See Jeronim Perovic's chapter in this book.

20 Greg Walters, 'Russian Oil Companies Push East for New Growth', *Dow Jones
    Newswires*, 16 May 2007. www.rigzone.com/news/article.asp?a_id=45234

21 'Trutnev Tells Companies to Pump or Pay', *Upstreamonline.com*, 13 April
    2007. www.upstreamonline.com/incoming/article131252.ece

22 Sergei Blagov, 'Moscow Introduces New Economic Incentives for
    Oil Development in Eastern Siberia', *Eurasia Daily Monitor*, The
    Jamestown Foundation, 8 January 2007. www.jamestown.org/
    single/?no_cache=1&tx_ttnews%5Btt_news%5D=32364

23 'Gazprom Neft to Slash Investment Program, LUKOIL to Shelve Re-
    fining Projects', *Kommersant*, 29 October 2008. www.kommersant.
    com/p-13471/r_500/LUKOIL_Gazprom_Neft_shelve/

24 Michael Bradshaw, 'Striking a New Deal: Cooperation Remains Essential',
    Pacific Russia Oil & Gas Report, Summer 2007, 14.

25 MPE RF, *Energeticheskaia strategiia Rossii na period do 2020 goda*.

26 International Energy Agency (IEA), *Optimising Russian Natural Gas: Reform and
    Climate Policy*, IEA, Paris, 2006, 34; 'Board of Directors Examines Gazprom's
    Gas Production Strategy', *Gazprom News*, 26 February 2006. www.gazprom.
    com/eng/news/2006/02/18952.shtml

27 TNK–BP maintained the option to buy back a 25 per cent stake plus one
    share, for a price to be set in the future. 'Gazprom Gets Kovykta Gas Field
    on the Cheap', *The St. Petersburg Times*, 26 June 2007.

28 EC, Russian Federation: Country Strategy Paper 2007–2013, EC,
    Brussels, 2007, 36. http://ec.europa.eu/external_relations/russia/
    docs/2007-2013_en.pdf

29 Daniel Simmons and Isabel Murray, 'Russian Gas: Will There be Enough
    Investment?', *Russian Analytical Digest*, no. 27, September 2007, 2–5, (here
    Page 3). www.res.ethz.ch/analysis/rad/details.cfm?lng=en&id=39447

30 Gazprom regularly revises its investment plans, sometimes three times a
    year. The reason is that projects may get more expensive as prices for
    construction materials and services vary.

31 EIA, *Russia Country Analysis Briefs*, Department of Energy, Energy Information Administration, Washington DC, May 2008. www.eia.doe.gov/emeu/cabs/Russia/Full.html

32 'Gasprom erhöhte Investitionsprogramm um ein Drittel', *RIA Novosti*, 10 August 2008. http://de.rian.ru/business/20070810/70899038.html

33 'Gazprom Board Clears Record Investments for 2009', *Reuters*, 23 December 2008. www.reuters.com/article/rbssEnergyNews/idUSLN49629220081223

34 Vladimir Milov, 'Russian Energy Outlook – Implications for Strategic Investments', Presentation at the New York Energy Forum, New York City, 15 May 2008. www.milov.info/2008/05/rossijskij-energeticheskij-sektor-strategicheskie-perspektivy-dlya-investicij/

35 'Gazprom Sees State Co-Funding Bigger Investments', *Finanznachrichten. de*, 3 December 2008. www.finanznachrichten.de/nachrichten-2008-12/12538489-update-2-gazprom-sees-state-co-funding-bigger-investments-020.htm. See for more information on the 'Yamal megaproject' Gazprom's website at www.gazprom.ru/eng/articles/article32739.shtml

36 Milov, 'Russian Energy Outlook – Implications for Strategic Investments.'

37 For up to date developments around Shtokman: www.oil-and-gas.net/index. php?page_id=3630

38 'Gazprom Board Clears Record Investments for 2009', *Reuters*, 23 December 2008.

39 'Gazprom upal do $25 za barrel', *Kommersant*, 25 February 2009. www.kommersant.ru/doc.aspx?DocsID=1125617

40 Nina Poussenkova, 'Russia's Future Costumers: Asia and Beyond', in *Russian Energy Power and Foreign Relations: Implications for Conflict and Cooperation*, ed. Jeronim Perovic, Robert W. Orttung, and Andreas Wenger, Routledge, London and New York, 2009, 132–154.

41 Song Yen Ling, 'Market Eye: Chinese Oil Imports Inch Up', *International Oil Daily (Energy Intelligence Group)*, 26 October 2006. www.energyintel.com/

42 See A. Kontorovich, 'Going East: Hydrocarbon Resources of Eastern Siberia and Russia's Far East: Development Status and Prospects', *Oil of Russia*, No. 2 (2006). www.oilru.com/or/27/480.

43 See: IEA, *Optimising Russian Natural Gas*, 146–57.

44 Vyacheslav Kulagin, 'Energy Efficiency and Development of Renewables: Russia's Approach', *Russian Analytical Digest*, no. 46, September 2008, 2–8. www.res.ethz.ch/analysis/rad/details.cfm?lng=en&id=92055

45 *International Herald Tribune*, 30 November 2006. www.iht.com/articles/2006/11/30/business/rusgas.php.

46 Cited from interview with German Gref in: *RIA Novosti*, 1 May 2007; an English transcript can be viewed at: http://www.cdi.org/russia/johnson/2007-100-6.cfm.

47 See: Jonathan Stern, *The Future of Russian Gas and Gazprom*, Oxford University Press, Oxford, 2005, especially 50–9.

48 MPE RF, *Energeticheskaia strategiia Rossii na period do 2020 goda*; see also: Elena Duraeva, 'Erneuerbare Energien in Russland: Nutzung durch internationale Kooperation', *Osteuropa* 54, Heft 9–10, October 2004, 152–60.

49 Philip Hanson, 'The Sustainability of Russia's Energy Power: Implications for the Russian Economy', in *Russian Energy Power and Foreign Relations: Implications for Conflict and Cooperation*, ed. Jeronim Perovic, Robert W. Orttung, and Andreas Wenger, Routledge, London and New York, 2009, 23–50, (here page 27).

50 EC, *The European Union and Russia*, 13 and 26–31.

51 See John Robert's chapter in this book.

52 See the presentation by Nabuo Tanaka (IEA Executive Director), 'European Gas Demand in a Global Market', at the KVGN Symposium, The Netherlands, 30 September 2008.

53 IEA, *World Energy Outlook 2008*, IEA, Paris, 2008, figure 4.6, 120; also Roland Götz, 'Pipeline Popanz: Irrtümer der europäischen Energiedebatte', in *Blick in die Röhre: Europas Energiepolitik auf dem Prüfstand*, Osteuropa Energie Dossier 2009, Deutsche Gesellschaft für Osteuropakunde, Berlin, 2009, 5–20, (here page 10).

54 Stacy Closson, 'Russia's Key Costumer: Europe', in *Russian Energy Power and Foreign Relations: Implications for Conflict and Cooperation*, ed. Jeronim Perovic, Robert W. Orttung, and Andreas Wenger, Routledge, London and New York, 2009, 89–108, (here 96–99).

55 'Russia and EU Ignore Access Row', *Upstreamonline.com*, 16 October 2007. www.upstreamonline.com/live/article142431.ece

56 'Total Wins Share in Shtokman', *Kommersant*, 13 July 2007. www.kommersant.com/page.asp?id=782171

57 On the 2006 gas crisis: Jonathan Stern, *The Russia–Ukraine Gas Crisis of January 2006*, Oxford Institute for Energy Studies, 16 January 2006.www.oxfordenergy.org/pdfs/comment_0106.pdf

58 On the Russia–Ukrainian gas dispute of January 2009: Jeronim Perovic, 'Farce ums Gas: Russland, die Ukraine und die europäische Energiepolitik', in *Blick in die Röhre: Europas Energiepolitik auf dem Prüfstand*, Osteuropa Energie Dossier 2009, Deutsche Gesellschaft für Osteuropakunde, Berlin, 2009, 21–37.

59 See John Robert's chapter in this book.

60 Götz, 'Zentralasiatische Energieexporte', 2–6.

61 Jeronim Perovic, 'Russian Energy Companies in the Caspian and Central Eurasian Region: Expanding Southward', in *Russian Business Power: The Role of Russian Business in Foreign and Security Relations*, ed. Andreas Wenger, Jeronim Perovic, and Robert Orttung, Routledge, New York, 2006, 88–113, (here page 95).

62 'Turkmenistan, Uzbekistan, Kazakhstan to Raise Gas Prices to European Level in 2009', *Interfax*, 18 March 2008.

63 Oleg Mityayev, 'Outside View: Russia Hikes Gas to Ukraine', *UPI Energy-Analysis*, 3 December 2007. www.upi.com/International_Security/Energy/Analysis/2007/12/03/outside_view_russia_hikes_gas_to_ukraine/4986/; further reading: Julia Nanay, 'Russia's Role in the Eurasian Energy Market: Seeking Control in the Face of Growing Challenges', in *Russian Energy Power and Foreign Relations: Implications for Conflict and Cooperation*, ed. Jeronim

Perovic, Robert W. Orttung, and Andreas Wenger, Routledge, London and New York, 2009, 109–131.

64 'Gazprom Cuts Gas to Ukraine in Absence of New 2009 Price Deal; European Supplies Unaffected', *Global Insight*, 2 January 2009. www.globalinsight.com/SDA/SDADetail15486.htm

65 'Turkmenistan, China Seal Gas Export Deal', *The Moscow Times*, 18 July 2007.

66 Götz, 'Zentralasiatische Energieexporte', 2–6.

67 'Russia's Central Asia Energy Strategy Experiences a Few Setbacks', *Eurasianet.Org*, 11 May 2007.

68 Nanay, 'Russia's Role in the Eurasian Energy Market: Seeking Control in the Face of Growing Challenges', 128.

69 See: Alexei Mastepanov, 'Eastern Neighbours and Russia's Energy Policy' and Boris G. Saneev, 'Eastern Russian and Northeast Asia: Possible Directions for Energy Exports', *ERINA Report* 35, August 2000, 8–10 and 17–21, www.erina.or.jp/en/Publications/er/pdf/Er35.pdf

70 Greg Walters, 'Russian Oil Companies Push East for New Growth', *Dow Jones Newswires*, 16 May 2007. www.rigzone.com/news/article.asp?a_id=45234

71 For up to date information, visit the project's website at www.sakhalinenergy.com/en/. For background information on the Sakhalin oil and gas projects, see also: EIA, *Sakhalin Island Country Analysis Briefs*, Department of Energy, Energy Information Administration, Washington, DC, May 2008. www.eia.doe.gov/emeu/cabs/Sakhalin/Full.html

72 'Gazprom Puts a Cork in Sakhalin-1', *Kommersant*, 20 June 2007. www.kommersant.com/p775927/product_sharing_gas_exports/

73 For up to date information, visit the project's website at www.sakhalin1.com/en/

74 James Simms, 'China To Get Siberia Pipeline Oil First', *Dow Jones International News*, 23 June 2006. www.uofaweb.ualberta.ca/chinainstitute/nav03.cfm?nav03=47442&nav02=43661&nav01=43092

75 Ibid.

76 'Construction of ESPO Pipeline Leg Could Begin in April', *RIA Novosti*, 19 February 2009. http://en.rian.ru/russia/20090219/120228018.html; *China BOFIT Weekly*, 20 February 2009, www.bof.fi/bofit_en/seuranta/viikkokatsaus/index.htm

77 Gordon Feller, 'Pipelines Linking Russia, China not only Element of their Oil & Gas Relationship', *Pipeline & Gas Journal*, 1 January 2009. www.allbusiness.com/energy-utilities/utilities-industry-electric-power/11767304-1.html

78 See 'Altai Project' on Gazprom's website, www.gazprom.com/eng/articles/article22202.shtml

79 Sergei Blagov, 'Russia Sees Eastern Pipeline as a Major Victory', Eurasia Daily Monitor 5, no. 201, 22 October 2008. www.jamestown.org/single/?no_cache=1&tx_ttnews%5Btt_news%5D=34036

80 Bobo Lo, *Pacific Russia & Asia: An Edgy Engagement: Look at it This Way*, Asian Geopolitics Special Report, CLSA, September 2005, 16. www.chathamhouse.org.uk/files/6609_pacificrussia.pdf

81 Philip Hanson, 'Oil and the Economic Crisis in Russia', *Russian Analytical Digest*, no. 54, 3 February 2009, 2–4. www.res.ethz.ch/analysis/rad/details.cfm?lng=en&id=95992

82 'Behind the Russia–Ukraine Gas Conflict', *BusinessWeek*, 3 January 2009. www.businessweek.com/globalbiz/content/jan2009/gb2009013_045451.htm?campaign_id=rss_topEmailedStories

83 Hanson, 'Oil and the Economic Crisis in Russia', 3.

84 'Russia Open to Better Relations with NATO', *International Herald Tribune*, 11 February 2009. www.iht.com/articles/2009/02/11/europe/russia.php

85 'Gazprom Sees State Co-Funding Bigger Investments', *Finanznachrichten.de*, 3 December 2008.

86 On the potential for Russia–EU cooperation in the field of energy efficiency and renewables: Andreas Goldthau, 'Improving Russian Energy Efficiency: Next Steps', *Russian Analytical Digest*, no. 46, September 2008, 9–12. www.res.ethz.ch/analysis/rad/details.cfm?lng=en&id=92055

CHAPTER 6

AFRICA IN THE CONTEXT OF OIL SUPPLY GEOPOLITICS

Monica Enfield

Although Africa's reserves and production are much smaller than those of the Middle East or Russia, the continent nonetheless plays a strategic role in global energy markets. Africa matters because it is largely an energy producer, rather than an energy consumer. For the most part, the bulk of hydrocarbons produced on the continent are exported for consumption in key demand centres in North America, Europe, and, increasingly Asia. Very little of Africa's production is consumed domestically – lower levels of economic growth and industrialization hold back energy demand, and energy infrastructure remains undeveloped in most parts of the continent. Moreover, the preference of many oil-producing governments has been to secure immediate revenue flows through exports, rather than to utilize the domestic hydrocarbon resources as part of a strategic industrialization policy. As a result, Africa is largely open to foreign investment. This willingness to work with outsiders contrasts with the attitudes of other strategic energy producers in the Middle East and Eurasia, whose governments constrain foreign access to reserves. The result is a different type of producer–consumer framework from that outlined in other chapters, where producers are also consumers, and there are strategic energy security needs on both sides of the equation.

Africa's proven oil reserves stand at 117 billion barrels,[1] a potential supply that is much smaller than the more than 700 billion barrels of reserves in the Middle East (see Figure 6.1). The Gulf of Guinea producers – Nigeria, Angola, Congo Brazzaville, Gabon, Equatorial Guinea, and others – account for more than 45 billion barrels of proven and probable reserves, approximately 40 per cent of Africa's total (see Figure 6.2). However, 90 per cent of those reserves are held by two countries, Nigeria and Angola. Other large reserve holders on the continent include North African producers Libya and Algeria.

Africa's hydrocarbon producers can be grouped into three regions. The continent's overall production stands at 10 mb/d, trailing the Middle East (25 mb/d), Europe and Eurasia (18 mb/d), and North America (14 mb/d) (see Figure 6.1).[2] The North African producers, dominated

158

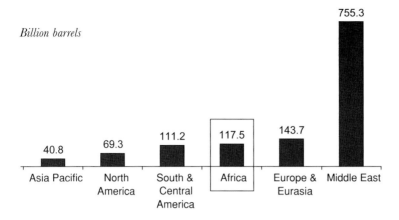

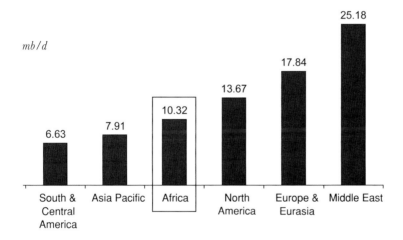

Source: BP's Statistical Review of World Energy, 2008

Figure 6.1: 2007 Proven oil reserves and 2007 crude oil production

by Libya and Algeria, produce nearly 4 mb/d and are hardwired into the Atlantic Basin. Their gas export pipelines, liquefied natural gas (LNG) trains and crude tankers are largely oriented to meet European and North American demand. The second group, which produces nearly 5 mb/d, includes the producers in the Gulf of Guinea in West Africa. The main producers in this group are Nigeria, Angola, Gabon, and Equatorial Guinea, with exports oriented towards North America, Europe, and Asia (See Figure 6.3). Mauritania and Sudan, part of the Sahel between North Africa and West Africa, produce about 1 mb/d

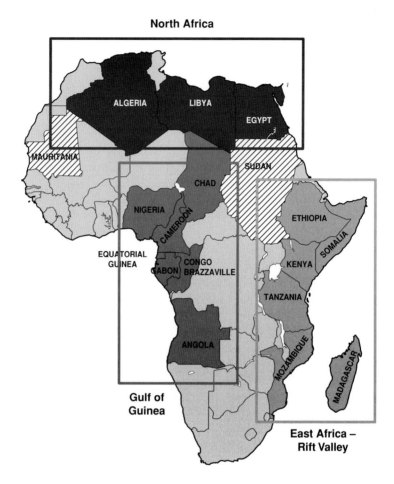

Figure 6.2: African hydrocarbon regions

and serve the same markets. The third group, East Africa, has production potential that will be determined by current exploration efforts, but is not yet producing in substantial quantities.

This chapter examines Africa in the context of hydrocarbon supply geopolitics. It first outlines the region's strategic role in supplying global energy markets by looking at the hydrocarbon potential, global flows, and key investment trends. It then examines how African countries define energy security, emerging trends, and the implications these will have on international security policies. The discussion here focuses on the West African producers, since the region accounts for the bulk of overall African production and investment.

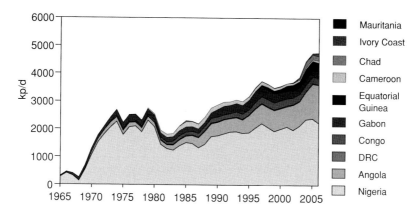

Source: PFC Energy

Figure 6.3: West African production growth

Africa's Energy Potential

This first section examines the energy resource potential in West Africa, including the role deepwater projects will play in the regional hydrocarbon production outlook, as well as the growing importance of natural gas and LNG. Additionally, the section outlines the destination of West Africa's hydrocarbon production exports, who the main consumers are and how that has changed in recent years. Finally, we discuss the main actors producing West Africa's hydrocarbons, including international supermajors, independent companies and, increasingly, Asian national oil companies.

African oil production growth

Africa is one of the last remaining regions that contain significant upside potential for exploration. Over the last 15 years, drillers working in West Africa found the second highest volume of cumulative oil reserves in non-OPEC countries.[3] Their success drew heavily on deepwater exploration in Angola and Nigeria. Expectations are high that deepwater triumphs will continue over the next several years.

Exploration activity in traditional areas (shallow water and onshore) in West Africa dropped steadily from the 1990s onwards, largely in response to significantly smaller mean discovery sizes in the region. At the same time, exploration activity in the deepwater sector (water depths greater than 1,000 feet) took off. As Figure 6.4 shows, explorers in 1970–1992 mainly drilled wells onshore and in shallow-water, but shifted to deepwater in 1995.[4] In 1999, exploration activities crashed in response to an oil price collapse in 1998. This pause in activity prompted companies to re-evaluate what they had spent in West Africa, and to reassess what they had found. This review showed most companies that the smaller discovery sizes and rising exploration costs required to make those discoveries meant that drilling on land and in shallow water no longer made financial sense.

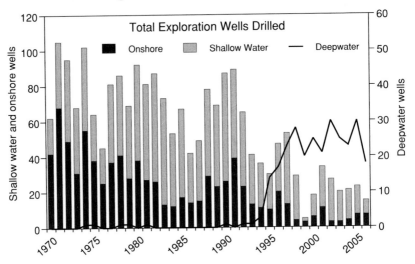

Note: Deepwater is defined as water depth of at least 1,000 feet

Source: PFC Energy

Figure 6.4: Growth of West African deepwater sector

Surprisingly, the increase in average oil prices after 2000 did not cause a noticeable resurgence in shallow water or onshore exploration activity. Instead, deepwater activity grew rapidly and stabilized at between 10 and 20 wells per year. A decade after deepwater hydrocarbon wells were first drilled, numerous projects across Nigeria, Angola, and Equatorial Guinea have come on-stream in the past few years. Many more projects are expected to begin production during 2008–2012, significantly pushing up West African output capacity.

Gas and LNG production growth

In addition to its crude oil output, Africa also produces and exports natural gas, although in smaller volumes, since many operators seek greater profit margins in crude oil sales. In cases where there are large volumes of associated natural gas, operators have monetized these resources through LNG or pipeline exports. In West Africa, where there has not been a large commercial market for natural gas, producers favour LNG exports. Nigeria leads the region in terms of LNG production and export, with numerous existing and planned projects. Equatorial Guinea became an LNG exporter in 2007, and Angola hopes to launch its own exports in the future.

African LNG serves the Atlantic Basin market, competing with European and South American producers to satisfy North American and European demand. African LNG is cost competitive and readily available, in comparison to other global LNG projects, because the gas is already being produced in associated oil fields, and there is typically no domestic demand competing for it.[5] However, the liquefaction costs in Africa are, on average, higher than in other regions. The main reason that LNG development in Africa is an attractive option is because the majority of deepwater fields that have been discovered in West Africa contain some portion of associated gas. Historically, operators flared this associated gas or reinjected it. However, neither approach is sustainable. Reinjection is only possible in the initial phases of a reservoir's exploitation. At the same time, host governments, global environment groups, and development agencies have exerted immense political pressure on operators to end flaring.

Africa and global export flows

Africa exports almost all of its hydrocarbon production rather than consuming it domestically. Gulf of Guinea hydrocarbon production primarily serves North American, European, and Asian demand centres (see Table 6.1).[6] Exports of West African crudes to global markets have soared since 2002, adding almost 700 kb/d between 2002 and 2005. Of these export volumes, Nigeria holds the lion's share in crude supply, with 54 per cent of West African exports to the global market. Angola is second, with a 27 per cent share. African exports are particularly important in Europe, where West African production is replacing the slumping output from the North Sea. As Figure 6.5 shows, North Sea fields have declined by over 400 kb/d year-on-year, while several projects across Nigeria, Angola, Chad, and Equatorial Guinea boosted production growth by over 400 kb/d year-on-year over the same period. This increase of high-quality crude in Africa replaces high-quality crude coming from the North Sea, which is refined in Europe into high-value products, such as gasoline.

Table 6.1: West African exports to selected markets

	Imports of West African Crude mb/d 2002	2005
China	150	560
Korea	80	80
India	260	360
Japan	120	50
USA	1150	1750
Europe	680	620

Notes: Europe includes OECD countries only
       Total balance completed by 'others'

Source: PFC Energy

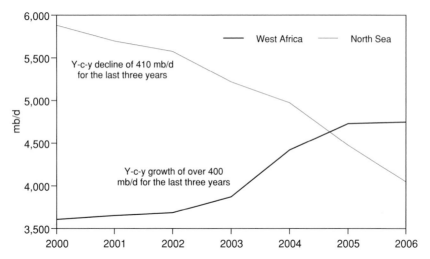

Source: PFC Energy

Figure 6.5: European crude supply by region

In general, West African exporters send their output to the USA, where imports from more than 10 key countries comprise the US crude slate.[7] Canada is the top exporter of crude to the USA, followed by Saudi Arabia, Mexico, Venezuela, and Nigeria, in fifth place. Angola and other West African producers also export to the USA, but in far smaller volumes. Even though West Africa is not the largest exporter to the USA, the US government views the region as a strategic component of its energy security policies, and expects to increase its imports from the region to 25 per cent by 2015, according to the National

Intelligence Council.[8] Following 9/11, US policymakers emphasized the need to diversify the country's energy sources away from the perceived dominance of the volatile Middle East.

West African crude is considered high quality, with low sulphur content, making it easy to refine into superior products. The US refinery system is diversified, and can handle a variety of crudes, meaning that it does not have to rely on only one type of crude. Nevertheless, Nigeria's Bonny Light is an important emergency crude in the US refinery system. After Hurricane Katrina had damaged key refineries, unaffected, but less complex, refineries increased imports of Nigerian Bonny Light, so they could make up for the production drop at the damaged refineries.[9]

Increasing Asian energy demand over the past decade has caused a general shift in global energy flows beyond North America and Europe. Middle East exports satisfied this demand for some time through dedicated supply contracts. However, in recent years, Asia has sought out more West African barrels. African crude is highly attractive to China, for example, where less complex refineries dominate, and simple types of crude are preferred to meet internal product demand. Although the Middle East remains the key player in global exports due to its long-term relationships and supply contracts, the increase in global energy flows from West Africa to Asia is worth noting.

In China, energy demand is outpacing supply, forcing the country's leaders to address energy security needs. According to BP's Statistical Review of World Energy, in 2006 China produced 3.684 mb/d of oil, but consumed double that amount at 7.445 mb/d. Additionally, India produced 807 kb/d of oil, but consumed 2.575 mb/d.[10] For Asian countries that consume more resources than are domestically available, energy security is a choice between: a.) increasing domestic energy production; b.) reducing consumption; c.) increasing imports from the global energy market; or d.) increasing equity barrels through international investments. Africa plays a role in these options – it both provides direct exports to the region and offers investment opportunities that allow for equity barrels to be sent home.

Africa has been a significant part of Asian energy security for some time. China, Japan, Korea, India, and others have been buying small quantities of West African barrels for years. These numbers grew as West African production expanded (largely due to offshore Nigeria and Angolan projects coming on-stream) and Asian demand rose. As noted in Table 6.1, changes in exports from 2002 to 2005 were substantial. Indian imports of West African crude grew by about 100 kb/d year-on-year. China's imports from the region rose by an average of 350 kb/d year-on-year.[11] While China imports crude from more than 40 countries, 10 of these account for more than 80 per cent of all imports, with the Middle East followed by Russia and Angola as top suppliers.[12] Angola made headlines in 2006 when it surpassed Saudi Arabia in monthly export figures, but in general the two countries are about the same in terms of exports on an annual basis.[13] Along with Congo Brazzaville, Equatorial Guinea, and Sudan, Angola accounts for more than a quarter of all Chinese crude imports (Figure 6.6).

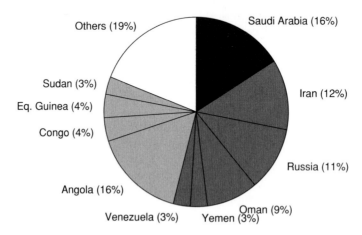

Source: PFC Energy

Figure 6.6: Chinese crude imports, 2006

Africa open for business

Beyond Africa's contribution to the global energy architecture through its production and exports, the region is significant because it is generally open to foreign investment. As shown in Figure 6.7, more than 75 per cent of global hydrocarbon reserves and production are locked up by governments and their national oil companies (NOCs).[14] Russian companies, which currently constrain foreign investment, hold a further 6 per cent. NOCs that allow limited access to foreign investment control 11 per cent, while foreign investors have full open access to only 6 per cent. Many African countries fall into the fully-open category and allow energy companies to 'book' assets for reserve replacement and equity production as part of their overall company value.

From the 1950s to the present day, foreign companies have largely had access to West African reserves, with the main exception being

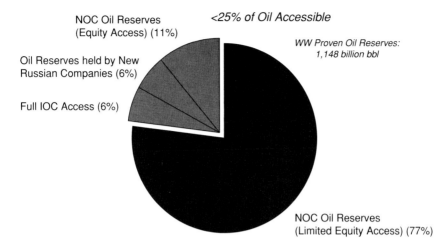

NOC Oil Reserves
(Equity Access) (11%)

<25% of Oil Accessible

Oil Reserves held by New
Russian Companies (6%)

WW Proven Oil Reserves:
1,148 billion bbl

Full IOC Access (6%)

NOC Oil Reserves
(Limited Equity Access) (77%)

Source: PFC Energy

Figure 6.7: Access to world oil reserves

the partial privatization of Nigerian assets in the 1970s. The largest
foreign investors in the region are supermajors, including France's
Total, Netherlands' Shell, Italy's Eni, and the USA's ExxonMobil and
Chevron. These Western companies enjoyed first mover advantage into
the region in the 1950s, through assistance from their home governments and colonial linkages. Shell, for example, established a strong
position in the onshore Niger Delta, while Chevron, working through
its Gulf Oil subsidiary, developed a strong asset position in Angola's
Cabinda province for more than 30 years. For decades, the supermajors
explored onshore acreage throughout the Gulf of Guinea, and across
the continent, taking advantage of tax and royalty concessions.

    In the 1990s, the supermajors pushed the Gulf of Guinea's hydro-
carbon potential even further by investing in deepwater regions (at
the time considered to be a region deeper than 1,000 feet). This new
frontier required extensive capital and technology, and a new risk-
sharing contract, prompting a number of governments to implement
production-sharing agreements (PSAs) that allowed more upside potential to operators concerned about recouping large upfront expenditures
in risky conditions. As outlined above, deepwater production makes up
a large component of West Africa's future growth potential. For foreign
companies that have invested billions of dollars in new technology and
production programmes over the past decade, the deepwater assets
constitute a critical portion of their global portfolios. Total's sub-
Saharan African assets comprise over 25 per cent of its overall holdings;

similarly, sub-Saharan African resources represent nearly 15 per cent of ExxonMobil's and Chevron's overall global portfolio. Even with heavily diversified assets around the world, sub-Saharan Africa will remain a critical component of these supermajors' portfolios moving forward.[15]

However, supermajors are not the only actors in Africa. Smaller independent companies are intensively engaged on the continent, particularly in so-called 'frontier' countries, where there has been little past exploration activity. These smaller players are important because they usually have much higher risk tolerance than supermajors, and are more willing to undertake exploration activities than the larger companies. Moreover, because these companies are smaller, they are willing to develop smaller hydrocarbon deposits because they do not need the large profit margins of the bigger companies. The smaller companies are particularly active in Gabon and Cameroon, which have an overall declining production outlook, but still remain attractive to smaller, niche hydrocarbon companies. Some key examples of independent companies are US-based Vanco, Vaalco, and Noble Energy, or the French company Maurel & Prom, which have strong asset positions in West Africa alongside the supermajors (in relative portfolio share).[16]

Asian national oil companies

More recent investors in the West African region are the Asian national oil companies. In just the past 10 years, China, India, Malaysia, Taiwan, Korea, and Japan have put their flag on the African continent through numerous exploration and production asset investments, as seen in Figure 6.8. Driven by a mandate from their governments to go abroad, these companies have invested in Africa for a variety of reasons. First is the need to secure equity barrels of oil – the more direct the ownership of equity barrels from a producing asset, the more energy security for a country. Second, the need to improve the companies' skill set is driving the move abroad – international activities force national oil companies to acquire new skills and to improve efficiency. A third driver is the economic linkages formed through international expansion, particularly in such high value-added areas as LNG production and petrochemicals, as well as opportunities for related oilfield service companies to gain entry into new markets. Finally, international expansion meets social objectives. For China in particular, overseas investments offer a way to address labour surpluses at home by moving large numbers of workers to overseas exploration and production sites.

National oil companies, such as China's CNOOC, CNPC, and Sinopec, together with India's ONGC and Malaysia's Petronas, have

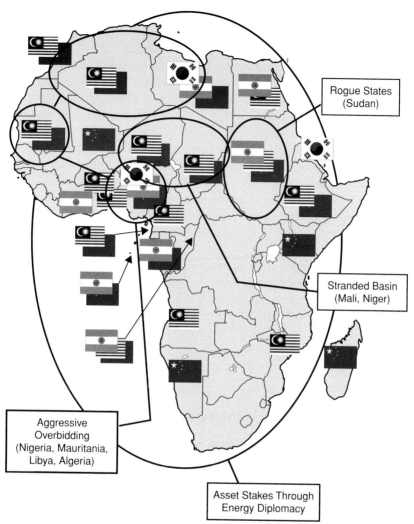

Source: PFC Energy

Figure 6.8: Asian upstream Exploration and Production investments in Africa

heeded that mandate, and their strategies for African investments have evolved accordingly. As shown in Figure 6.8, Asian national oil companies first invested in countries where Western international oil companies could not. Sudan was a natural entry point, and all of the companies listed above now have substantial asset positions there. Sudan offered attractive terms because the host government was eager to secure investments in the face of US sanctions and the growing risk to corporate reputation that forced Canadian and European companies to exit the country. As a second move, Asian national oil companies entered stranded basins – those countries without a natural export outlet. Traditional international oil companies (IOCs) decided that it did not make economic sense to work in countries such as Niger and Mali because there was no way to bring the crude output to market without building expensive, and risky, export infrastructure. By 2004, Asian national oil companies bid on key relinquished acreage from the mid-1990s deepwater boom. All bidding companies were flush with cash, due to sustained high global oil prices, but the Asian national oil companies had more money to offer signature bonuses, and won out on key bid rounds in Nigeria, Libya, and other countries. Africa is now at a point where Asian governments are willing to use the full range of diplomatic tools to help their national oil companies secure investments.

In summary, West Africa has considerable energy potential, which adds to overall global energy security. Deepwater project development, along with growing natural gas production, led by a variety of Western and Asian investors, will add to West Africa's positive production outlook. Exports to key demand centres in the USA, Europe, and increasingly Asia, help offset declining production in mature basins, such as the North Sea, to meet global demand.

Emerging African trends impacting oil supply geopolitics

Foreign companies and the global energy market have played the predominant role in shaping West Africa's hydrocarbon development. Outside forces prevail because, unfortunately, West African countries have largely positioned their economies and governments to act as rent seekers, rather than as active managers of their natural resource base. As noted above, nearly 100 per cent of West African hydrocarbon production is exported, rather than consumed or put to economic use at home. Traditionally, there has not been a strong sense of energy security within the region or individual countries, beyond a basic strategy of expanding production and investment levels to extract greater rents. The situation is evolving at an uneven pace across the continent as national leaders face various socio-political demands. So far, West African leaders have not prepared thoroughly-defined energy security policies; rather they are beginning to address key emerging trends that are likely to have an impact on global energy security and geopolitics in the future.

Resource curse

The global recession, with the concomitant uncertainty in the price of oil, is likely to have a strong impact on Africa because the continent's oil producers cannot quickly diversify away from their reliance on energy production. Most African leaders are currently not using oil wealth to restructure their economies. Looking forward, the recession will probably create additional obstacles which will prevent these countries from using their wealth for development purposes.

Even before the crisis began, Africa lagged behind the rest of the world in both economic and political development. Years of political strife, economic mismanagement, and colonial legacies have had an impact on the 50 or so countries on the African continent in a variety of ways. Compared to other regions of the world, sub-Saharan Africa as a region ranks last on the United Nations' Human Development Index (HDI).[17] The HDI is a composite ranking of socio-economic indicators, such as infant mortality, literacy, access to health care, and GDP per capita. The average sub-Saharan African HDI value is 0.472 out of a possible score of 1.000. Above Africa are South Asia, with an HDI value of 0.599, the Arab States at 0.680, and the OECD region at the top (0.923), as outlined in Figure 6.9.

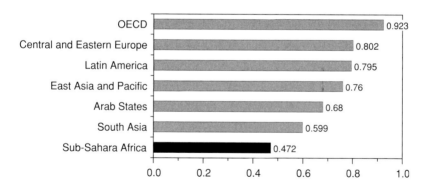

Figure 6.9: United Nations' Human Development Index

Within the Gulf of Guinea, the main hydrocarbon producing countries do not far outpace the sub-Saharan average, despite their tremendous hydrocarbon resources (Figure 6.10). In fact, Nigeria and Angola, with the largest hydrocarbon resources, actually have a lower HDI value than the sub-Saharan average. Only Equatorial Guinea and Gabon buck the regional trend, but this 'success' is entirely due to oil revenues, since their small population size helps these countries achieve

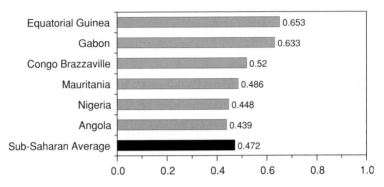

Figure 6.10: United Nations' Human Development Index in sub-Saharan Africa

high GDP per capita levels. Other socio-economic indicators are poor, indicating that the governments are unable to distribute oil wealth and to provide basic human and health services. Indeed, this same story holds true for the other Gulf of Guinea countries – an incapacity to distribute government services deflates HDI values.

These countries clearly suffer from the 'resource curse'. Numerous studies, including those by economist Jeffery Sachs, demonstrate that countries with abundant natural resources have slower economic growth than countries without natural resources.[18] Countries afflicted with the resource curse also suffer from low levels of democracy, weak institutional capacity, poor human resource development, higher levels of conflict, revenue volatility, excessive borrowing during economic crises, and rampant corruption. All these characteristics can be found in the Gulf of Guinea. Throughout the 1980s and 1990s, lower oil prices devastated the economies of these countries, resulting in debilitating levels of debt, despite large hydrocarbon resources. International financial institutions imposed financial orthodoxy, but such structural reforms were implemented haltingly, because the systems relied heavily on political patronage to gain access to resources and to control revenue distribution. With rising oil prices after 2003, the governments found themselves with windfall profits, and gained an opportunity to reorient their economic policies to address the 'resource curse', but under their terms, not those imposed by international financial institutions.

Nigeria took a key step forward in addressing the resource curse when the Olusegun Obasanjo administration concluded a deal with the Paris Club in 2005 that allowed it to cancel part of its foreign debt. The deal was both a political and economic victory for Africa, and this achievement came with the backing of international NGOs that had long advocated debt relief for Africa. Nigeria's tremendous debt burden, acquired through massive corruption under previous military regimes, had become a key example of the obstacles to overcoming the resource curse. Led by then-Finance Minister Ngozi Okonjo-Iweala, Nigeria crafted an articulate message to Washington, London, and other Paris Club lenders that its debt burden should be eased in order to free up government funds to use towards structural economic reform plans. Later that year, the Paris Club agreed in principle to write off $18 billion of Nigeria's debt after Abuja agreed to pay back the remainder of its $30 billion in bilateral debt to member countries from excess oil revenues.[19]

Elsewhere in the region, African countries are working to define their own economic growth policies. Angola has combined quasi-socialist state-controlled resource distribution with heavy non-oil sector investment by Asian and Western companies.[20] Gabon is relying on Western international financial institutions to build institutional capacity to prepare for a future without oil, while Sao Tome hopes the same institutions will help it use hoped-for prospective oil resources wisely. Despite the different approaches, West African polities are now aware of the resource curse, and are consciously seeking ways to address the challenge of using their natural resource wealth wisely.

Resource nationalism

Along with the resource curse, the region has witnessed a rise in re-source nationalism, a belief among Africa's elite that states should own and manage the natural resources on their territory. The consequence of this nationalism over the past several decades has been higher oil prices, resulting from the nationalization of assets, restrictions on foreign investment into the hydrocarbon sector, new regulatory mandates, the growth of NOCs, and stricter contract terms for investors. The end result is that resource-owning states now take a larger share of oil revenues, leaving less for foreign investors. Within Africa, resource nationalism has not meant a re-nationalization of assets, but an attempt to gain a greater share of the profits from natural resource development through a combination of new regulatory structures, more favourable fiscal terms, and a greater role for NOCs.

Rather than simply exporting their natural resources, the leaders of key countries such as Nigeria and Angola have recently begun to insist that local resources be utilized in other productive sectors of the economy. In practical terms, they are implementing this policy by requiring greater local content, amending contract terms in the government's favour, and tying access to resources to investments in the non-oil sector. Local content requirements are a mechanism for a country to capture higher value-added from the hydrocarbon sector by mandating that local companies perform the attendant services to the industry. Such services vary from catering, to the fabrication of drilling rigs. Norway, Malaysia, and even Brazil have been models of energy-producing countries which have utilized strict local-content regulations to transform the economy.[21] Within Africa, Nigeria has made some initial moves, mandating that 75 per cent of the industry be 'indigenous' by 2010. Although it remains to be seen if those high levels will be achieved, statutes and policies promoted by the Nigerian national oil company, NNPC, have been introduced in recent PSAs to mandate local content. For foreign operators, these mandates are likely to have a large impact on project planning, as there is a lack of qualified Nigerian companies to complete some of the highly technical engineering work at present. Nevertheless, local content has become a buzzword in Africa, as governments are keen to develop the indigenous sector and to train local workers in high-value skills. Angola and, to a lesser extent, Equatorial Guinea have also pushed local-content requirements as a way of bolstering their domestic economies. Moving forward, such policies may impose an investment risk on projects in these African countries, if the infrastructure, educational system, and governance oversight are not put in place to support such local-content mandates.

In line with many other producers around the globe, many African governments revised elements of their model contracts in their favour, to take advantage of higher oil prices and restricted access to global resources in 2007 and 2008. Nigeria, Angola, and Equatorial Guinea rewrote certain portions of their PSAs to better protect the government, by raising its share during periods of higher oil prices, while making symmetrical adjustments during low-price cycles. Additionally, to counter similarly rising production costs, governments have introduced stricter cost-recovery periods, placing caps on how long operators can recover costs (known as cost oil) before sharing profit oil with the government.[22]

West African governments have also begun to seek backward economic linkages from their hydrocarbon resources. Nigeria and Angola have been most prominent in this regard, simply because they have the most leverage to do so. Both countries have stressed an explicit link between access to upstream hydrocarbon resources, and commitments to invest in other sectors of the economy. Nigeria started this trend in 2005 by offering 'rights of first refusal' to companies that promised to invest in Nigeria's decaying downstream sector. Although the initial bid round resulted in confused block awards, it set the trend for another two bid rounds where onshore and offshore acreage was only awarded to those companies pledging investment in infrastructure, as well as in the natural gas, power, and refining sectors.[23] The current Umaru Musa Yar'Adua administration remains committed to this policy, although the execution of the non-oil projects has been slow, and blocks awarded in 2005 have been revoked due to inactivity by the investors. Angola followed suit in 2006, when it held a licensing round for relinquished deepwater acreage, but made the foreign company's willingness to invest in a second refinery in the south of the country a condition of access to one block.[24] China's Sinopec won the block, but the strategic deal to invest in the Lobito refinery has failed to materialize. Although the success of Nigeria's and Angola's bid round strategies is questionable, both governments remain committed to channelling investment into strategic non-oil sectors, even in the post-2008 lower oil price environment.

Community activism

Another key trend worth highlighting is the increase in community activism among the citizens of hydrocarbon-producing countries. In contemporary Africa, there is a new set of stakeholders with views on governance that are sharply critical of past practices, and they are having an impact on the way in which governments and foreign investors manage national resources. West African governments have long been defined as 'rentier states', where revenues are distributed based on a system of acquiescence and patronage, giving extensive authority and discretion to elite decision makers. In a country such as Nigeria, with an extremely large population, a wide variety of groups place demands on the state for revenue sharing and resource redistribution. An increasingly vocal set of non-elite groups want a say in the way resources are managed.

The clearest example of this new community activism is in the Niger Delta, which has both violent and non-violent elements. At the heart of the unrest is the poor distribution of wealth and resources.[25] Ethnic groups in the oil-producing Niger Delta have long claimed discrimination and unfair distribution of oil wealth, which is extracted from their area and which contributes over 80 per cent of the country's GDP.

The federal government's response to the unrest had simply been to create more federal states, rather than to implement sustainable, responsible economic development policies. By creating additional states, ethnic groups were put in control of federally-allocated revenues, which gave them a vested interest in the federal system. More often than not, it created another layer of tribal-based patronage and corruption, rather than effective institutions.

No longer content with merely a new political space carved out for the Niger Delta groups, the communities now want a visible role in the political system, decentralization of decision-making powers, and the ability to control hydrocarbon resources directly. Niger Delta groups, frustrated by the lack of social and economic mobility, have resorted to illicit activities and violence in order to advance their cause. Other groups, including some working under the banner of an organized militia, have a legitimate agenda, and seek dialogue with the government to address the structural deficiencies of the federal state system.

The result has been that operators have taken more than 500 thousand b/d of production offline, due to violence and insecurity in the Delta since 2006. Massive attacks, beginning in January 2006, have damaged numerous hydrocarbon fields, pipeline infrastructure, and export infrastructure, and this output remains shutdown nearly 36 months later (at the time of writing), costing the Nigerian state millions of dollars in potential export revenues. The Yar'Adua administration is attempting to negotiate with Niger Delta groups as part of its comprehensive master plan for the region, but has so far not managed to put together a permanent, structural solution to the violence.

Civil society groups working toward improving transparency and governance represent a less violent, but equally important example of the emerging new stakeholders. Although led in part by Western institutions and NGOs, indigenous African groups are increasingly holding governments accountable for releasing information on where hydrocarbon revenues come from and how they are spent. In Gabon, Congo Brazzaville, Nigeria, and Sao Tome, the governments have signed on to the Extractive Industries Transparency Initiative (EITI).[26] Initiated in 2002 by UK Prime Minister Tony Blair and the UK Department for International Development, EITI is a voluntary programme for governments to increase the transparency of their income and expenditures from oil, gas, and mining activities. Participants in the initiative subscribe to a set of principles that include revenue disclosure. In exchange, EITI offers monetary assistance to any developing country willing to start the programme through capacity building, diplomatic outreach, and technical assistance. A key milestone for EITI participants is the establishment of a multi-stakeholder committee that creates a legitimate political space for civil society to engage the government on transparency and governance issues. Within West Africa, the success of EITI can be debated, but the opening of this civil society space is a step in the right direction.

Overall, there are three key emerging trends which may alter the established producer–consumer framework that has prevailed in West Africa. The 'resource curse' has led to slow economic development and a wide variety of governance issues, but leaders are now at least aware of the problems, and may be able to address them. As resource nationalism spreads, West African states are taking a larger share of the profits from the sector. While these policies do not constrict access to resources, they may slow the pace of foreign-led development, having an impact on overall regional production-growth outlook. Additionally, growing community activism is creating a political space for civil society to demand better oversight and distribution of hydrocarbon revenues.

Implications for International Relations

The emerging trends for West Africa's hydrocarbon production outlook outlined above have a number of implications for international relations. First, instability in Africa has the potential to have an impact on the flow of supplies from West Africa to consuming regions. Second, resource nationalism and the diversifying geopolitical realignment toward Asia have the potential to make an impact on the producer–consumer relationship that has existed between the West and Africa for decades. Finally, the international political system, where the USA and China compete for influence, is being tested in Africa, potentially affecting global oil supply geopolitics.

Stability in Africa

The poor governance, resource nationalism, and community activism shaping Gulf of Guinea producers will have a number of implications for the global energy community. Potential political or social instability in the producing countries has the most immediate impact on global energy markets. Nigeria is the primary example of unmanageable community unrest having an impact on global energy flows, particularly as key export volumes remain shut-in. As discussed previously, the level of poverty within the Niger Delta, and the government's inability to distribute hydrocarbon wealth equitably, has fostered an environment where disaffected community groups and armed militias have the ability to disrupt oil and natural gas production, which in turn has an impact on export flows to consuming countries.

Although Nigeria is an extreme example of political, social, and economic unrest, instability can also afflict other West African producers.

To address such concerns, recent regional initiatives have focused on integrating maritime security and political/economic cooperation policies. Examples include the long-standing Economic Community of West African States (ECOWAS), and the 1999 Gulf of Guinea Commission,[27] which was intended as a self-initiated regional grouping of states to settle maritime conflicts, but has since been overshadowed by the US military's creation of an African command, that includes a mandate to facilitate or lead various African security initiatives.[28] Cooperation at this regional level has moved slowly for a variety of reasons, not least of which is the individual states' reluctance to cede control of their internal security to outsiders. While countries must address the possibility of an external threat, instability in West Africa is more likely to come from within. Even though a number of West African producers – such as Gabon, Equatorial Guinea, and Angola – have relatively stable political leadership and have benefitted economically from higher energy prices and increasing output in the first part of the twenty-first century, many outside the ruling elite resent the unequal distribution of oil wealth. Competition for control of hydrocarbon wealth is likely to remain a key source of political and social instability in these countries. This instability affects the above-ground risk environment for hydrocarbon sector investors and operators. For the USA, Europe, and Asia, with their direct reliance on African crude exports, potential production and export disruptions have an impact on energy security and economic activity.

Producer–consumer relations

Beyond physical flows, African resource nationalism may have implications for producer–consumer relations over the medium- and long-term. It is unlikely that individual African governments would dramatically nationalize their assets – as was the case elsewhere in the 1970s, or even more recently in Bolivia and Venezuela – simply because the African governments and their NOCs lack the skills and capital to fully manage and operate the sector on their own at present. The reliance on foreign companies to deliver immediate revenues to the government is high, further mitigating the possibility that the major resource holders in West Africa would completely constrict access to resources. However, tightening fiscal terms and stricter local content requirements will have an impact on the timing and pace of new project developments executed by foreign operators, which add to overall global oil production. In Nigeria for example, higher service sector costs, combined with government mandates to source services and construction from local firms, are affecting overall project economics and forcing companies to rationalize their exploration and production plans in the region. Combined with existing political instability, these developments could lead to delays in planned exploration and production, and in turn temper the bullish production outlook desired by the consuming regions. Moreover, the current oil price environment and global financial crisis may mean constrained capital budgets for some operators, further extending production timetables.

Additionally, resource nationalism comes into play with regard to the long-term expectations host governments have in managing the life of the hydrocarbon reserves. Two West African countries, Nigeria and Angola, are members of OPEC, with Angola having joined the organization in January 2007. While Nigeria has been a member of OPEC since 1971, Angola's recent entry reflects the state's desire to manage the long-term potential of its resources by closely monitoring how quickly new source projects are developed before hitting peak production. As members of the cartel, the countries are expected to co-ordinate production output in order to manage global oil markets. Such coordination also implies that member states limit production capacity growth, and cap production when exceeding organization quotas. As of January 2009, Angola's quota was 1.52 mb/d, while Nigeria's was 1.67 mb/d.[29] Both Nigeria and Angola have the potential to increase production capacity, given the slate of deepwater discoveries planned for development by foreign companies. However, with OPEC actively managing markets to support prices, the two countries have been tasked by the organization to cut production. Although full compliance from all member states is rare, flows from the West African region are constrained by OPEC membership.

International political system

Finally, African hydrocarbons are in the middle of potential tensions between China and the USA over access to resources and global influence. Chinese NOCs have several perceived advantages over the traditional Western oil and gas companies in terms of securing hydrocarbon sector investments. First, Chinese NOCs can bundle asset negotiations with diplomatic linkages, developmental aid, and financial, military, and commercial assistance. The November 2006 China Africa Cooperation Forum – where almost every African head of state was present, and China signed $1.9 billion in trade deals and pledged more than $5 billion in grants and aid – demonstrates this advantage.[30] Secondly, because the strategic interests of Chinese NOCs differ from those of Western companies, the way they approach bid rounds and project economics are different – they can essentially eliminate the competition through huge signature bonuses and equity participation commitments that would be financially unattractive to Western companies. This advantage helped secure some block awards in recent bid rounds in Libya, Nigeria, and Angola. The NOCs also have different policies towards transparency and corporate governance that give them an advantage in the region over Western companies, which are bound, at home, by financial market stakeholders, and legislation concerning foreign corrupt practices. Finally, the Chinese companies offer African governments an opportunity to diversify to new markets. All this has contributed to the increased presence of Chinese NOCs, oilfield service companies, and other state-owned companies in Africa as Chinese energy demand continues to rise.

The USA responded to China's foray into Africa coolly, prompting Congress and think-tanks to thoroughly study the implications for US energy and foreign policy.[31] Beyond direct competition for resources, there is a growing awareness that Chinese and other Asian investment offers a new strategic relationship, which often comes without conditionality, such as that mandated by the IMF, World Bank, US development agencies, and other stakeholders. With guaranteed assistance from China, India, and others, African governments are able to reduce the amount of leverage held by the West. American policy makers are increasingly concerned that China's increasing influence over the continent is reducing the USA's ability to encourage economic reform, political liberalization, transparency, good governance, and attention to human rights. Moreover, France's recent policy shift away from 'francafrique' limits Paris' engagement with regional leaders, and confines European engagement in Africa largely to multilateral forums, rather than the direct leader-to-leader deals that had defined French policy for decades.[32] If such trends continue unabated, a bleak picture emerges in which African resources become closed to Western interests, with energy flows directed entirely towards Asia. However, such fears are exaggerated, as African oil remains a global commodity, with both the USA and China buying it from an international energy market.

Even in the face of this competition, there are areas of mutual cooperation which have an impact on Africa, and help ensure global energy security. The USA and China have the opportunity to jointly engage Africa on peacekeeping issues, trade flows, and health and education development, as outlined in a 2007 report by the Center for Strategic and International Studies. Additionally, the countries can lead in multilateral engagement around issues such as debt relief, development assistance, and poverty reduction.[33] At the same time, the USA continues to retain naval pre-eminence with regard to securing maritime security for tankers transporting oil and LNG from producing to consuming states, West Africa in particular. US efforts to secure the shipping lanes help the Chinese as well.

Conclusions

Africa will continue to play a strategic role in global energy geopolitics. Although smaller in reserves and production than other producing regions such as the Middle East, West African production is significant because it is almost entirely exported rather than consumed domestically, and goes towards meeting demand in key consuming regions of North America, Europe, and Asia. Moreover, West Africa remains open to investment, allowing foreign companies to explore and produce hydrocarbons for export. In terms of overall energy security, geopolitics in the Middle East and Russia capture far more of the world's attention, with West Africa playing a small, but strategic role in meeting energy demand. This producer–consumer relationship has proved resilient over the years, in part because African leadership has remained primarily motivated to extract rent from the hydrocarbon sector.

However, there are some emerging trends on the continent that will alter the producer–consumer framework. The 'resource curse' and the poor distribution of energy wealth contribute to instability in West Africa, with Nigeria as an example of community unrest affecting the global energy market. Some half a mb/d remains shut-in by operators due to violence, depriving the market of barrels of light, sweet crude. Additionally, requirements for local content, altered fiscal terms, and increased leverage against Western international financial institutions to execute 'home grown' economic development policies make the environment more difficult for investors. Overall, these trends will not drive away foreign operators who are bringing new volumes of oil and gas on-stream in the region, but the pace of development for new projects could be delayed, affecting the available energy resources in the market.

Africa is having an impact on the larger producer–consumer relationship because it is making available new supplies that are enabling consumers in the West and Asia to diversify their sources of energy. African sources help consumers like the USA, Europe, and China to diversify away from difficult suppliers. In particular, North Africa provides oil to Europe, and helps it reduce its dependence on Russia. West Africa is becoming an increasingly important energy supplier to the USA, though it is also building new links to China. The continent likewise offers opportunities to newcomers like India, but such emerging importers will have to learn to compete effectively with the already established players.

Naturally, the growing competition creates a potential for conflict. Potentially, two consuming countries could clash over access to the same oil. Additionally, to some extent, the growth of African production presents a threat to other global producers, like the Middle East and Russia. The rise of Africa could adversely affect their security of demand for energy sources. However, since Africa's reserves are relatively small, the world's traditional energy producers have little to fear from the continent.

While the West and China might come into conflict as they seek to gain control over African assets, the African continent presents a much greater array of opportunities for cooperation. China is seeking to build long-term relationships with African energy suppliers, and will probably continue its policy of not interfering in the domestic political situation of its partners. Its expansion is driven by its search for energy, rather than any anti-Western intentions. Accordingly, market-based competition will be the main determinant in shaping development opportunities.

Notes

1   British Petroleum, 'Statistical Review of World Energy 2008'. www.bp.com/productlanding.do?categoryId=6848&contentId=7033471
2   Ibid.
3   PFC Energy, Upstream Consulting Practice, proprietary analysis.
4   Ibid.
5   PFC Energy, Global Gas Consulting Practice, proprietary analysis.
6   PFC Energy, Markets and Country Strategies Consulting Practice, proprietary analysis.
7   United States Department of Energy, Energy Information Administration, 'U.S. Imports by Country of Origin'. http://tonto.eia.doe.gov/dnav/pet/pet_move_impcus_a2_nus_ep00_im0_mbblpd_a.htm
8   National Intelligence Council, 'Global Trends 2015: A Dialogue about the Future with Nongovernment Experts', National Foreign Intelligence Board, December 2000. www.dni.gov/nic/NIC_globaltrend2015.html#link8c
9   PFC Energy, Markets and Country Strategies Consulting Practice.
10 BP, 'Statistical Review of World Energy 2007'.
11 PFC Energy, Markets and Country Strategies Consulting Practice.
12 Ibid.
13 Winnie Lee, 'Angola remains China's major crude source in June', *Platts*

Oilgram News, 7 August 2006.

14 PFC Energy, Upstream Consulting Practice.
15 Ibid.
16 Ibid.
17 United Nations Development Program, 'Human Development Report, 2006' online statistics. http://hdr.undp.org/hdr2006/pdfs/report/HDR06-complete.pdf
18 Key works on the 'resource curse' include Jeffrey D. Sachs and Andrew M. Warner, 'Natural Resource Abundance and Economic Growth', *National Bureau of Economic Research Working Paper*, No. 5398, 1995; Macartan Humphreys, Jeffrey D. Sachs, and Joseph E. Stiglitz, eds., *Escaping the Resource Curse*, Colombia University Press, New York, 2007; and Terry Lynn Karl, 'Paradox of Plenty: Oil Booms and Petro-States', *Studies in International Political Economy*, 26,1997.
19 'Nigeria Receives $18 Billion in Debt Relief From Paris Club', *Bloomberg*, 20 October 2005.
20 'A plan from the centre – how to win friends and influence voters', *Africa Confidential*, 1 December 2006.
21 Willy H. Olsen, 'Oil and Gas in Africa: Local content issues', speech to the Corporate Council on Africa, U.S.–Africa Business Summit, 22 July 2005.
22 PFC Energy, Upstream Consulting Practice.
23 'Nigeria targets $500 mm in 2006 bid round', *Alexander's Gas & Oil Connections*, 9 November 2006.
24 Steven Swindells, 'Upstream Link Spurs Angola Refinery Plan', *Platts Oilgram News*, 9 December 2005.
25 'The Swamps of Insurgency: Nigeria's Delta Unrest', *International Crisis Group, Africa Report No. 115*, 3 August 2006.
26 Extractive Industries Transparency Initiative, 'Implementing Countries'. www.eitransparency.org/implementingcountries
27 'Angola to host Gulf of Guinea Commission Headquarters', AngolaPress, 23 August 2007. www.angolapress-angop.ao/noticia-e.asp?ID=467201
28 Walter Pincus, 'U.S. Africa Command Brings New Concerns', *Washington Post*, 28 May 2007.
29 PFC Energy, Markets and Country Strategies Consulting Practice.
30 Winnie Lee, 'China seals trade partnership with Africa', *Platts Oilgram News*, 8 November 2006.
31 Key reports on the implication of Chinese investment in Africa for US policy include, Bates Gill, Chin-hao Huang and J. Stephen Morrison, 'China's Expanding Role in Africa: Implications for the United States', Center for Strategic and International Studies, February 2007 and Carla A. Hills and Dennis C. Blair, 'U.S.–China Relations: An Affirmative Agenda, A Responsible Course', Council on Foreign Relations, New York, April 2007.
32 Henri Astier, 'Sarkozy's Africa policy shift', *BBC News*, 26 September 2007.
33 Gill et al, 'China's Expanding Role…'.

CHAPTER 7

ENERGY SECURITY IN LATIN AMERICA

Roger Tissot

Latin America is a mid-level energy producer that supplies a significant portion of the key US market. The continent's ties with the USA and the international energy companies have defined the overall producer–consumer relationship in the region. Although the major oil companies played an early role in developing the region's resources, the individual states on the continent ultimately established much greater control over local oil and gas supplies by creating national oil companies (NOCs) and imposing greater restrictions on the operations of international oil companies (IOCs). How these countries and their NOCs are dealing with the challenges of globalization is determining their level of success in the marketplace, with Brazil apparently finding an effective balance of market forces and support for a state-owned oil company.

The key energy producers on the continent face enormous challenges as the global economic crisis that started in the second half of 2008 exacerbates problems and trends that already existed. In Venezuela, against a backdrop of plummeting energy prices, the populist government of Hugo Chavez must find money to pay for his expensive social policies, while also spurring new production. In Mexico, the government must address the problem of encouraging new investment to replace depleted reserves, while also overcoming a policy of resource nationalism that has blocked foreign investors.

This chapter will examine the role of Latin America in the larger global system of consumers and producers. First, it provides an overview of the energy potential that the region currently represents. Second, it lays out the key trends that define the energy situation in the region. These are declining reserves, growing resource nationalism, increasingly assertive indigenous movements, and a rising interconnectedness among states' energy security in the region. Third, the chapter examines how these trends affect regional producer–consumer relations. Most important here are the rise of the NOCs, the reaction of the different countries to the processes of globalization, the growing challenges to the USA's traditional dominance in the region, and the need for incentives to spur investment. Finally, the conclusion ties together the analysis, examining the implications of the long-term trends and the global economic crisis for the region's development.

Latin America's Energy Potential

Latin America[1] is a mid-level energy power with 16 per cent of the world's installed hydroelectric capacity, 4 per cent of its oil reserves, and 4 per cent of its gas reserves. The region's oil reserves (approximately 116 billion barrels) are larger than Eurasia's (78 billion barrels), but slightly lower than Africa's and far behind those of the Middle East (743 billion). Extra-heavy crude oil reserves in Venezuela's Orinoco belt (approximately 200 to 235 billion barrels)[2] significantly increase Latin American total oil reserves, potentially making it the largest source of oil after the Middle East. The region also holds approximately 267 thousand cubic feet (tcf) in gas reserves. Hydrocarbon reserves in Latin American are unevenly distributed, with Venezuela holding nearly 70 per cent of the region's oil reserves (not including heavy oil), followed by Mexico at 11 per cent, and Brazil with 9 per cent[3] (see Figure 7.1). Venezuela also accounts for nearly 60 per cent of Latin American natural gas reserves, but almost 90 per cent of those reserves are in the form of associated gas. Trinidad and Tobago, Bolivia, Argentina, Mexico, and Peru also have important gas reserves (see Figure 7.2). Mexico, Venezuela, Brazil, Argentina, Ecuador, and Colombia are the key oil producers in Latin America (see Figure 7.3). Latin American

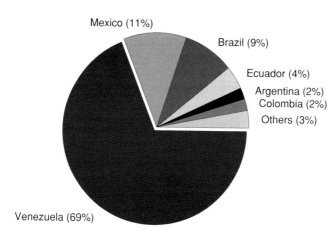

Source: BP Statistical Review of World Energy 2007

Figure 7.1: Latin American oil reserves in 2006

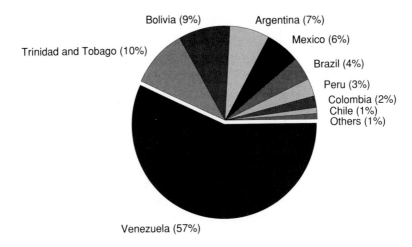

Source: BP Statistical Review of World Energy 2007

Figure 7.2: Latin American natural gas reserves in 2006

oil output has remained relatively constant in the last 15 years, with Brazil's production increase offsetting a decline in all other Latin American producers. Brazil's production will continue to expand due to a series of successful discoveries. In November 2007, the Brazilian state oil company Petrobras announced the mega-discovery of Tupi, which could have as much as 8 billion barrels of oil equivalent (boe), representing nearly 40 per cent of Brazil's petroleum reserves.[4] Tupi appears to be the beginning of more discoveries, since in January 2008 Petrobras announced the discovery of Jupiter, a mostly gas field expected to be of similar size to Tupi.[5] The Sugar Loaf area, near Tupi, could be five times as big as Tupi and, according to Petrobras, will be easy to explore.[6] Outside Brazil, Latin American countries face rapidly depleting reserves and declining production, with Mexico being the most pressing case.

Evolving Trends

While each of the countries in Latin America has a unique history and energy policy, several trends are defining the evolution of the region's energy situation. First, two of the key producers, Mexico and Colombia, are facing depleted reserves and must find a way to address this situation. Second, the late 1990s and the first part of the new century have witnessed a resurgence of resource nationalism in several

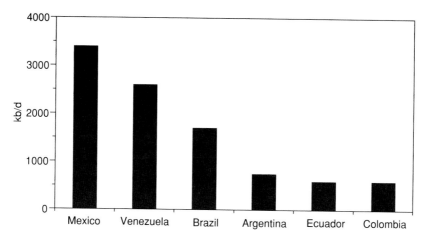

Source: BP Statistical Review of World Energy 2007

Figure 7.3: Latin American oil production in 2005

countries in the region, particularly in Venezuela. While Mexico and Brazil have also faced resource nationalism, they have dealt with these pressures in ways strikingly different from Venezuela. Third, indigenous movements seeking to gain greater control over energy resources have grown increasingly vocal, most notably in Bolivia and Ecuador, but also in Peru and elsewhere.

These trends combine to demonstrate the interconnectedness of energy security across the countries of Latin America, and taken together they are defining the way in which the continent interacts with the outside world. While there are now opportunities for international investment to develop new resources, there are also clear limits on how far this investment can go.

Depletion of oil supplies

Several of the countries in Latin America are suffering from the exhaustion of their oil resources, with Mexico and Colombia among the prominent examples. Despite the common problem, however, the two countries have chosen dramatically different responses. Mexico has sought to develop its resources on its own, while Colombia has opened itself to foreign investment.

Mexico's current oil reserves are a fraction of what they were just 20 years ago (see Figure 7.4). The depleted supplies are a legacy of Mexico's nationalistic petroleum strategy and short-term rent-driven fiscal policies. In fact, for many decades, Mexico relied heavily on

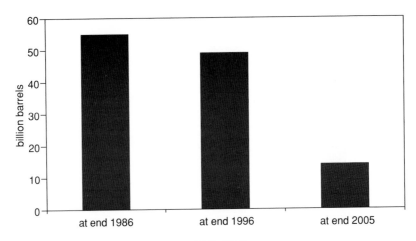

Source: 2007 BP Statistical Review of World Energy

Figure 7.4: Mexico's proven oil reserves

profits from its oil exports to subsidize the rest of its economy. The country faces wrenching policy choices in order to address its current challenges, but has yet to demonstrate a willingness to implement extensive changes to past policies.

According to a 2007 study published by Mexico's Secretary of Energy (SENER), Mexico's oil future is uncertain.[7] Indeed, in the pessimistic scenario, production will drop from 3.2 million barrels per day (mb/d) in 2006 to less than 2.3 mb/d by 2016, resulting in a decline of oil exports to less than 0.3 mb/d. In 2006, Mexico exported approximately 1.8 mb/d, with 80 per cent of those exports going to the USA.

To avoid this dramatic decline in output, Mexico requires an aggressive oil exploration programme. The challenge is to shift from what has been Mexico's main petroleum policy to a new one.

Mexico nationalized its oil industry in the 1930s in a bitter dispute with American and British firms. The assertion of local ownership became a source of national pride. However, Mexico's politicians did not always make the best use of the resources. In the 1970's, following the discovery of large fields,[8] which coincided with a surge in oil prices, Mexico became a rentier state financed by its NOC.

Large oil rents allowed Mexico to postpone economic reforms and to maintain its inward-looking import-substitution economic development model until its economy collapsed in the early 1980s under the pressure of declining oil prices and rising debt. Mexico's economic collapse triggered Latin America's 'lost decade' and forced the country to shift to an export-oriented economic model, culminating in Mexico's entry into the North American Free Trade Agreement (NAFTA). Mexico's new development model transformed it into a supplier of manufactured goods and tied economic growth to the USA, its largest customer. To succeed, the strategy assumed the presence of cheap labour, low energy costs, and low taxes.

Unfortunately, the new strategy did not work out as well as had been hoped. Although NAFTA has contributed to Mexico's economic development, China's rapid export-oriented economic growth has severely challenged Mexico's manufacturing sector. The government kept most industrial taxes low by over-taxing the state-owned oil company, Petróleos Mexicanos (Pemex), leaving the NOC with insufficient capital to finance new exploration. As Pemex focused almost exclusively on oil production, Mexico became a net importer of gas, despite expectations that the country held large gas reserves itself. The ultimate consequence of these policies has been that Mexico's oil reserves have declined rapidly in the last 20 years.

Pemex will not have sufficient resources to invest in developing new production until the government is able to reduce its reliance on oil revenues. To encourage more exploration activity, government energy policy was reformed, recognizing that it must allow Pemex to retain a greater share of its profits to invest in exploratory work. Mexico's 2007 fiscal reform modestly raised taxes on non-oil activities while simultaneously lowering them on Pemex, allowing the company to retain nearly US$7bn for investments.[9]

Despite mid-course corrections, the energy reform fell short of initial objectives, which were to improve private access to the upstream sector and to reduce the need for extensive petroleum product imports by increasing domestic refining capacity through private–public partnerships. Although the reform represented a positive first step, it was not sufficient to overcome the financial and technical challenges required to unlock the oil reserves lying in the Gulf of Mexico's deepwater. To improve the chances of future success, the government should consider a more radical policy shift aimed at opening the upstream sector to private investment in hydrocarbon exploration and production. Without greater exploration by Pemex and/or outside companies, Mexico will cease exporting oil and become increasingly dependent on imported natural gas.

Colombia faces a situation similar to that of Mexico, but it has responded differently – by offering market-friendly mechanisms. Petroleum makes a relatively small contribution to Colombia's GDP (less than 8 per cent), but oil is the main source of government revenues. If the current production decline continues as expected, Colombia could be forced to stop exporting oil and become a net importer in the next decade[10] (see Figure 7.5). Such an output decline would deliver a double blow to the economy: the government would lose its main source of income, and the country would have to use hard currency earned from other exports to import oil. Colombia's energy policy has therefore focused on postponing that eventuality.

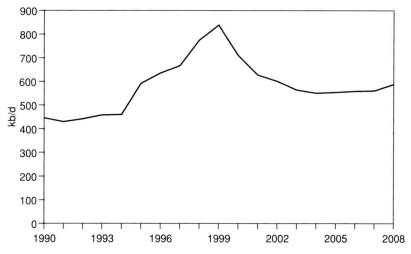

Source: BP Statistical Review of World Energy 2007

Figure 7.5: Colombia's oil production

The Colombian government has adopted a series of market-friendly regulations aimed at increasing private investment in oil exploration. It first terminated the exclusive exploration rights of Ecopetrol, the NOC, and forced it to compete as an equal with other companies for exploration acreage. The government then created a new regulator in charge of granting and managing oil concessions, the Agencia Nacional de Hidrocarburos. The new agency drastically reduced royalties and taxes, and streamlined the permission processes.[11]

The combination of improving security conditions in Colombia, higher oil prices, and a deteriorating business environment for IOCs in other countries brought an increase in exploration and production (E&P) investments in the middle of the decade. Initially, companies venturing into the country were small players focusing on niche opportunities, but large IOCs have increased their investments, particularly on Colombia's Caribbean coast. However, the announcement of a dry well by the Exxon, Petrobras, and Ecopetrol consortium exploring the Tayrona block in the Caribbean Coast is cooling the country's expectations for large discoveries of oil and/or natural gas.[12] The government is now focusing on the heavy crude oil projects in the Llanos basin where Ecopetrol's production in three fields (Rubiales, Nare, and Castilla) has increased from 35 kb/d in 2002 to 96 kb/d in 2007. Ecopetrol believes production of heavy crude oil could rise as high as 200 to 300 kb/d.[13]

Since more than 90 per cent of Colombia's oil fields are defined as small or marginal,[14] Colombia's oil production could benefit from increasing investments by junior oil companies. These companies are content to discover and work with medium- to small-size pools. Although such activity is unlikely to transform Colombia into a large oil producer, the sum of the smaller oil companies' investments could have a significant impact on the local economy. Each of these companies is a consumer of diverse services, from engineering to financial and legal advice. A successful outcome could result in the development of a dynamic domestic capital market financing oil and gas projects. In the best case, Colombia could emulate what has happened in other mature basins, such as Alberta, Canada, a province with transparent regulations and a stable political environment. To achieve such an end, however, Colombia needs to continue developing its capital market and improving its security situation.

Resource nationalism

Many of the Latin American countries have pursued a policy of resource nationalism. Typically, they have set up a state-owned company to control their hydrocarbon resources and then severely restricted access to foreign companies that seek to invest in extracting the country's resources. In several cases, one consequence of these policies is that the local companies do not have enough capital to invest in increasing the production of oil and gas, while at the same time they block investment from IOCs.

While resource nationalism is present throughout Latin America, it has manifested itself in different forms across countries. Mexico has done poorly with these policies. As mentioned before, its NOC does not have the resources to develop local oil and gas supplies, and the country's politicians have not been willing to open up to outside companies. Venezuela has dramatically cut relations with the major IOCs and is banking on its ability to work with the NOCs of countries with which it has friendly relations. Brazil, on the other hand, has been willing to force its NOC to compete in a limited way

Mexico nationalized its energy industry in the 1930s, as noted above.

Pemex, its NOC, does not, by itself, have sufficient resources to carry out the required exploratory activities to find new sources of oil and gas in Mexico to replace production at its depleted fields. To address this problem effectively, Mexico will have to lift its ban which blocks foreign oil companies from participating in the development of its upstream sector. Unfortunately, there is no political will in the country to remove Pemex's monopoly control. In fact, both of the key political parties, the Institutional Revolutionary Party (PRI) and the Party of the Democratic Revolution (PRD), have opted for the status quo.[15] The Senate Energy Committee has agreed to maintain Article 27 of the Constitution, which basically guarantees Pemex's monopoly control over all upstream activities, closing the door to potential deals with IOCs and foreign NOCs in the deepwater Gulf of Mexico. There is no clarity regarding a further opening of Mexico's downstream sector to foreign involvement. In addition, PRI Secretary Jesus Murillo announced in January 2008 that the party will continue to oppose any privatization of Pemex, although it is open to other ideas, such as allowing strategic alliances between Pemex and foreign companies to develop offshore projects located at the border between Mexico and the USA.

Venezuela has also long relied on a policy of resource nationalism, which has had dramatic effects on its ability to produce energy and its relations with other countries. Since the 1970s, Venezuela's oil production has vacillated with the political changes in the country (see Figure 7.6). Soon after Venezuela began to export oil in 1917,[16] the

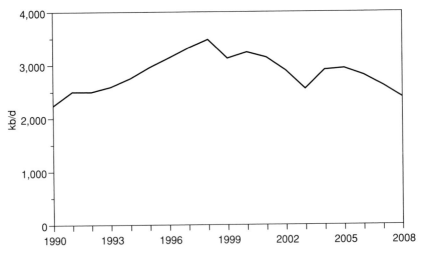

Source: BP Statistical Review of World Energy 2007

Figure 7.6: Venezuela's oil production

competition over petroleum rents between IOCs and the government defined the country's political and economic development. Ultimately, the government opted to capture all the rent when it nationalized the industry in 1976. Since then, Venezuela's production profile has been influenced by political volatility and varying degrees of adherence to quotas set by OPEC, of which Venezuela was a founding member.

Since nationalization, Venezuela has had considerable difficulty in managing its oil sector. Soon after the state took over oil production, output declined because the state sought to adhere more strictly to OPEC quotas, and because IOCs had cut back their investments in the local industry even prior to nationalization. In an effort to ensure the source of revenue that supported their ability to rule, the political elite tried to minimize the transition from a sector dominated by foreign companies to one completely controlled by the government. Venezuelan staff who previously worked for the IOCs became employees of the new NOC Petroleos de Venezuela S.A. (PDVSA).[17] Initially, there was tension between the state and the new company, as PDVSA managers were concerned about the politicians' populist tendencies. Accordingly, the company soon developed a technocratic elite that aimed to protect it from government interference. Over time, the politicians and company managers learned to respect each other, since they shared the same priorities: the maintenance of a democratic regime favouring the local elites and urban middle classes.

During the 1990s, when oil prices were low, Venezuela paid less attention to OPEC quotas, and opened the oil sector to foreign investment. The government sought to compensate for declining oil prices by ramping up output and securing a larger market share in the USA. During those years, PDVSA also opened the industry to private investors; inviting IOCs to participate in a variety of projects. The most important joint venture was the development of the heavy crude oil reserves of the Orinoco Belt. While these reserves are vast, they are technically complex to bring to market.

This accord between the state, oil company, and population fell apart when oil prices declined in the late 1990s, and Venezuela had to curtail its traditionally generous state spending policies. The population reacted negatively to the loss of its previous benefits, eroding support for the political elite and the party system that had been in place since the early 1950s. Hugo Chavez rode this discontent to win election as president in 1998, and quickly reversed the energy policies of his predecessors upon taking office. He forced his country to return to strict respect for the OPEC quota system, resulting in a decline in production. In 2003, production declined further, when union workers and managers at **PDVSA** went on strike, protesting at what they perceived as Chavez's political interference in the oil sector. In the aftermath of the strike, Chavez dismissed almost 20,000 employees, including a large number of senior and highly experienced technical staff. PDVSA's strike allowed Chavez to break the implicit pact between technocrats and politicians, ending the technocratic rule and putting the resources of the oil company at the disposal of his political agenda. Since then, the company has struggled to recuperate its operating efficiency and production levels.

In 2006, strengthened by a convincing re-election that gave him another five-year term, Chavez began to pursue ever more radical leftist policies. He nationalized electric utilities and telecommunications, and re-negotiated arrangements with the private companies operating the heavy crude oil projects in the Orinoco Belt, making the state-owned PDVSA a majority shareholder and producer in these projects. Despite its technical limitations, the 'new PDVSA' has been a successful tool for Chavez's radical left political strategy, which emphasizes expensive populist social programmes, such as the Bolivarian missions (a variety of anti-poverty and literary campaigns), increasing state control over key aspects of the economy, and using oil to gain international influence.

Ironically, the benefits of the oil price rise materialized during Chavez's administration, cushioning Venezuela's drop in output. In fact, by the end of the 1990s, Venezuela produced approximately 3 mb/d, all from PDVSA. Large investments from the IOCs resulted in an increase in output of nearly 1 mb/d 10 years later. Chavez's 'true-nationalization'[18] removed IOCs from one of the last bastions of their dominance – the Orinoco Belt – to the benefit of PDVSA and NOCs from geopolitically strategic regimes allied with Chavez. However, Chavez' profligate social spending is forcing PDVSA to invest in non-oil activities. According to Ramon Espinaza, a former PDVSA executive, the company's debt increased to US$16.7 bn in 2007 against a background of falling oil production.[19] A significant component of that debt was to pay for the nationalization programmes.

Future oil production will depend on Venezuela's ability to expand production from the Orinoco belt. The government has ambitious plans, suggesting an increase in output from 680,000 barrels per day in 2008 to more than 1.2 mb/d by 2012. However, doubling production from the Orinoco belt will not be an easy task. IOCs have reduced their activities in the country to a minimum, and two companies, ExxonMobil and ConocoPhillips, have left Venezuela. Moreover, faced with increasing cash flow difficulties as oil prices collapsed toward the end of 2008, PDVSA officials are looking at cutting back expenditures and investments. The future appears to lie with the NOCs that Chavez has invited to operate in his country.[20] Although some of these are Latin American or Asian firms with no capital or expertise, others such as CNPC, Petrobras, ONGC, or Gazprom, have the will, financial resources, and probably the technical expertise to develop Venezuela's heavy crude oil potential. However, as economic pressures mount, one should not be surprised to see Venezuela offering partnership opportunities with PDVSA to IOCs, either through technical transfers or as minority participants in NOC–NOC deals. Assuming that there is no complete ban on private investment, the lure of Venezuelan oil riches will continue to be a powerful force for IOCs.[21]

Brazil represents a more successful contrast to both Mexico and Venezuela. After years of importing oil, Brazil attained effective self-sufficiency in petroleum production in 2006 (see Figure 7.7).[22] Ending dependence on outside sources marked the realization of a long-held goal for the Brazilians.

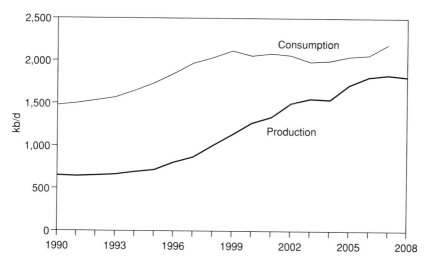

Source: BP Statistical Review of World Energy 2007

Figure 7.7: Brazil's oil production and consumption

When the IOCs made clear that they were not interested in the country due to its high exploration risks, the Brazilian government set up its own NOC, Petrobras, in the mid-1950s. Initially, the company focused on downstream activities. Efforts to find substantial oil deposits were not successful, causing political controversy, because Brazilians believed their country was blessed with an abundance of natural resources, including oil.[23] By the early 1960s, at the government's direction, the company gave up efforts to explore in Brazil and instead opted to search out resources abroad. Technocrats from Petrobras felt the government was admitting defeat in its goal of attaining petroleum self-sufficiency. However, in 1974, Petrobras discovered the large Campos basin oil deposit, demonstrating that Brazil was indeed blessed with oil, although it was not enough to achieve self-sufficiency. Brazil continued to be a net oil importer during the petroleum crisis of 1982, contributing to the country's huge fiscal deficits and hyperinflation. Depressed oil prices and a restrictive investment environment eroded exploration activity in Brazil until 1995, when a new regulatory framework was adopted.

The Cardoso administration (1995–2003) implemented reforms aimed at liberalizing Brazil's economy, including the energy sector. Petrobras lost the exclusive rights to control all upstream and most downstream activities. To give the former monopolist greater competition, the government created a new entity, the Agencia Nacional do Petroleo (ANP), and assigned it the task of transferring development rights to private companies and Petrobras through concessions.

Despite the reforms, Petrobras remains in a dominant position. ANP launched a series of bidding rounds that initially attracted significant interest from the private sector. However, after 10 rounds, it became obvious that the IOCs' best chance of success was by partnering with Petrobras. Years of previous exploration activity helped Petrobras accumulate a large amount of data on the Brazilian basins, allowing the company to make more attractive bids than the IOCs were prepared to offer, since they tended to be more risk averse.[24] The Brazilian company also enjoys a dominant market position in the downstream sector, controlling the transportation infrastructure and 98 per cent of the refining market. The result is a virtual monopoly of the oil sector in Brazil, despite local boasts claiming a flexible and de-regulated market environment.

Brazil has been lucky to find significant new fields in recent years, and these have strengthened Petrobras' position. Discovery of the major Tupi field in 2006 prompted President Luiz Inácio Lula da Silva (2002–2011), known as Lula, to say that 'God must be Brazilian'[25] since the discovery seemed to ensure the country oil, and perhaps natural gas, self-sufficiency, and even the possibility of Brazil becoming an important oil exporter. Some have even discussed the idea of Brazil joining OPEC. However, Tupi will probably not produce oil before 2013, according to Wood Mackenzie, an energy consultancy firm. [26] Since it faces a 10 per cent decline rate, Brazil must make a significant effort to replace reserves. Bidding delays and declining interest from IOCs, disappointed by the government's decision to remove some areas from bids after Tupi's discovery, will increase Petrobras' role as the main source of future oil production.

Brazil now stands at a crossroads and must choose between becoming a rentier economy dependent on its NOC, or instead focusing on strengthening the country's competitiveness by securing access to reliable and low-cost energy sources through competitive market mechanisms. Brazil's role in the region's energy security is not limited to oil. In fact, today Brazil is emerging as a global leader in the production of sugar cane biofuels. An idea that was developed as a response to the first energy crisis, and which the government maintained despite its high costs during the subsequent decades of lower oil prices, is paying off. Ultimately, the choice will influence how much oil Brazil can produce, contributing to the country's and to the region's energy security.

Increasingly Active Indigenous Movements

In recent years, the poor, indigenous populations of Latin America have exerted themselves more forcefully, in a manner similar to the community activism in Africa described by Monica Enfield in her contribution to this volume. The indigenous movements have protested against what they see as an unfair distribution of the profits made from the development of their country's natural resource wealth. They seek to replace past policies with access for a much wider part of the population to cheap energy through subsidies, and for a renewed sense of national pride. In countries such as Bolivia, the indigenous populations have come to power and have gained control of the natural resources themselves. This rise in their political power has had tremendous consequences for the political elites in their country and for the IOCs with which they did business.

Bolivia's development of its resources ultimately led to a backlash from a deeply dissatisfied indigenous population. Bolivia's full hydrocarbon potential came into play only after 1985, when President Paz Estenssoro adopted a radical shift toward market capitalism. He privatized Bolivia's NOC Yacimientos Petroliferos Fiscales Bolivianos (YPFB) and opened the economy to foreign investments. The subsequent administrations of Jaime Paz Zamora (1989–1993) and Gonzales Sanchez de Lozada (1993–1997) continued Estenssoro's policies. During that period, energy sector investments transformed Bolivia into a regional natural gas power. The country even expected to become a South American gas hub, with pipelines exporting gas to Brazil and Argentina, and potential exports of liquefied natural gas (LNG) to Mexico through Chile.

While the government was making plans for a glorious future fed by massive natural gas exports, an increasingly dissatisfied indigenous population protested against the privatizations. Eventually, street protests forced out the administration of Sanchez de Lozada and, after the politically-weak interim administration of Carlos Mesa, Bolivians opted for a shift toward populism. They elected Evo Morales president in 2006 with massive support, on a platform that included re-nationalization of the hydrocarbon industry, increasing the price of gas exports, and refusing to export gas to Chile as long as Bolivia's demands for access to the Pacific coast were not addressed.

Ecuador has also seen the rise of indigenous groups, and their new political clout has had an impact on the country's energy policies. In 2006 the election of Rafael Correa as president by a large margin marked the arrival of the first legitimate national leader in Ecuador's troubled political environment in a decade. In office, Correa has to balance a variety of competing demands as he works to expand oil production while meeting the concerns of the indigenous population. Prior to his victory, Ecuador suffered from a dysfunctional political system, with weak presidents and a Congress controlled by political parties that were unable or unwilling to compromise, acting mostly as a series of private lobbies. Correa benefited from the support of indigenous groups, centre-left nationalists, and populist parties. Since his election, he has boosted his popularity with a series of crowd-pleasing measures, such as food subsidies and charging IOCs higher royalties. He also vowed to improve Ecuador's NOC, PetroEcuador, allocating a larger budget for exploration activities.

Despite his popularity, Correa faces a political challenge in balancing his pro-development, nationalist strategy with the expectations of indigenous and environmental organizations. Pro-development nationalists support additional oil production in the Amazon, including the exploitation of the large Ishipungo, Tambococha, Tiputini (ITT) oil project, located near the Yasuni National Park. They want development to be carried out by Ecuador's NOC, either alone or in partnership with foreign NOCs. Indigenous leaders oppose any additional oil development, and are more likely to support the creative suggestion of former Energy Minister Alberto Acosta, who asked the international financial and environmental community to finance the 'non-development' of the ITT project.

The main priority is to halt the decline in production caused by a lack of investment from PetroEcuador and the IOCs (see Figure 7.8). However, Correa's decision to raise taxes on extraordinary profits from 50 per cent to 99 per cent when the oil price rises above a threshold of US$42/b, and to convert current agreements to service contracts,

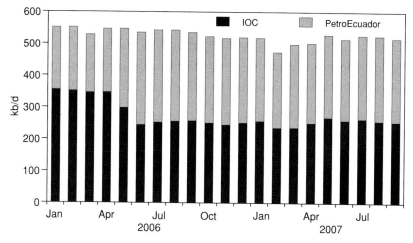

Source: Asociacion de la Industria Hidrocarburifera del Ecuador AIHE Ecuador 2007; Central Bank Ecuador (2007 data)

Figure 7.8: Ecuador's oil production

is unlikely to foster more investments from IOCs. On the other hand, the government has hinted its willingness to find a negotiated solution with the IOCs. Given the still attractive oil potential in Ecuador, an under-utilized infrastructure able to transport oil from the jungle to the Pacific coast, and high oil prices, the IOCs will probably welcome a negotiated solution which would allow them to continue investing in Ecuador, if the government can guarantee fiscal and contractual stability.

However, with Correa's preference for resource nationalism, Ecuador's oil future appears to rely most heavily on the president's ability to transform PetroEcuador into a high performing corporation,[27] which would be no small feat. In fact, observers describe the dysfunctional PetroEcuador as a bastion of corruption that does not even use performance indicators.[28] To turn the company around, Correa appointed senior members from the Naval Force as managers of the company, and approved a larger budget for capital expenditures. It is still too early to say if these efforts will produce the expected results, but at least Ecuador has a legitimate government with a strong mandate, which is willing to address the numerous inefficiencies of PetroEcuador.

With the collapse of oil prices, however, Ecuador's oil and economic future turned bleak. The government defaulted for a third time on its external debt obligations, and PetroEcuador has been unable to improve its performance. Correa's controversial decision to rejoin OPEC only complicated matters. As a marginal producer, there was no clear gain for Ecuador in becoming a member, other than perhaps having access to the expertise of the cartel members. Still the government has been forced to comply with the organization's production cuts of approximately 4.2 million barrels.[29] The cuts have been imposed on private producers, further eroding foreign companies' confidence in any future oil activities in the country.

In striking contrast to Bolivia and, to a lesser extent, Ecuador, Peru's government has favoured pro-development strategies, but these are at risk due to the rise of increasingly assertive indigenous movements. Since his election in 2006, President Alan Garcia of Peru has maintained the pro-business hydrocarbon policies adopted by previous administrations. The government's main priority is to secure the development of large gas reserves, and to increase oil exploration in northern Peru, where the government and IOCs hope new crude oil reserves can be found. The most important project is Camisea, an 8 tcf gas project in the Peruvian jungle. Camisea's LNG exports will reduce Peru's energy dependency. The government is also considering the development of a petrochemical industry to add value to its gas output.

Peru has not been immune from resource nationalism, but has limited it mostly to the mining sector, where political leaders have echoed popular sentiment in favour of higher royalties. Although Peru has avoided a shift to political populism, maintaining a pragmatic approach, the government has suggested the re-entry of Petroperu, the local NOC, into the upstream business, in partnership with other Latin American NOCs.[30]

However, support for pro-business policies is fragile, particularly in the mineral-rich highlands and hydrocarbon-rich jungles. Indigenous communities and NGOs have held an increasing number of protests denouncing social and environmental degradation, while low income and middle class residents of Lima question the fairness of gas pricing policies that penalize domestic users in favour of exports.[31] In order to meet both the needs of the consortium developing the Camisea LNG project and the government objective of gas-based industrialization, more exploration will be required, increasing IOC encroachment into the Peruvian jungle, and creating the potential for heightened confrontation with indigenous communities.

Interconnectedness of Latin American Energy Security

While the depletion of energy resources, rising resource nationalism, and growth of assertive indigenous movements have affected each of the individual Latin American countries to a greater or lesser extent, these trends have had an impact across the continent, making apparent the fact that Latin America's energy security is tightly interconnected within the regional market. The cascading consequences of the rise of indigenous movements in Bolivia and the resulting resource nationalism illustrate this impact most clearly. Contrary to other recent nationalist initiatives in Latin America, Bolivia's resource nationalism has had a profound impact on the region's energy security, having the greatest affect on Brazil, Argentina, and Chile, each of which has responded differently.

Brazil opted to rely on its own hydrocarbon potential, while also diversifying sources of supply in the short term. Soon after the nationalization of the gas sector by president Evo Morales in 2006, Brazil halted its plans to increase investments in Bolivia. These plans had aimed at encouraging greater exports, but Brazil opted instead to expand exploration efforts of its own offshore resources. Even though these efforts have proven successful, Brazil is still vulnerable to energy supply shortages, since the newly discovered domestic sources will not start producing for many years. As a short-term solution, Brazil is also considering LNG imports.

In Argentina, President Nestor Kirchner confronted the economic meltdown of 2001 by adopting a series of policies aimed at minimizing the social cost of the crisis and kick-starting the economy. He increased government revenues by imposing a tax on hydrocarbon exports. He also implemented a cap on energy prices in order to reduce inflationary pressures and shelter the urban and industrial sectors from the effects of rising global hydrocarbon prices. Kirchner's policies were successful in bringing the Argentinean economy back from deep recession, but at a significant cost. Private oil companies reduced their investments in exploration, preferring to maximize production. With a growing economy and subsidized energy prices, domestic demand boomed while supply declined, resulting in growing energy shortages and eventually an energy crisis.

The Argentinean government's response to the crisis was to disown its export obligations to Chile, while accepting higher import prices for Bolivian gas. Argentina is also engaged in the construction of an additional gas pipeline (Bolivia Northeast Argentina, BNEA) which will import up to 20 million cubic metres of gas per day from Bolivia.[32] However, due to lack of exploration activity by IOCs and the uncertainty surrounding YPFB, Bolivia's ability to meet its export obligations to Brazil and Argentina are in doubt.[33]

For the Chilean government and business class, the loss of Argentinean gas was traumatic. Chile's booming economy had become increasingly dependent on imports of natural gas from Argentina, which had promised to treat Chile 'as a domestic client', and the Chileans had no viable short-term substitutes. Chilean businesses had to invest large sums of money over a very short period in the re-conversion of gas-fired electric generation plants to fuel oil or diesel, and in some cases back to coal.

Chileans realized that, although they were surrounded by energy-rich neighbours, energy security would not be achieved through market-driven regional integration. As long as resource nationalism and populism prevailed, Chile's energy security would be at risk from shifting political preferences in exporting countries (Argentina, Bolivia, and Peru). Chile's energy security policy therefore focuses on achieving greater diversity of supply (albeit at greater cost), importing LNG, and increasing the use of fuel oil, diesel, and coal. The government is also promoting exploration of hydrocarbons in the Southern Cone, additional hydroelectric developments, and the possibility of developing nuclear energy.

Implications for International Relations

The issues of resource depletion, growing resource nationalism, and increasingly assertive indigenous movements will have strong implications for the international relations of Latin America. The rise of the NOCs in the region has made it difficult for the IOCs to operate in many of the countries. The differing responses of each of the countries to the challenges of globalization have also had an impact on the way in which they interact with the outside world. All of these changes pose particular challenges for the USA, which is seeking to maintain its predominant influence in the region. Finally, each of the countries has to address the question of stimulating sufficient levels of investment in local production capacity. This section will examine each of these issues in turn.

Rise of Latin American NOCs and relations with IOCs

In past decades, Latin American countries have turned to NOCs to manage their energy resources, and they have assumed even greater power on the back of rising resource nationalism and protest movements among the indigenous poor. The rise of the NOCs has complicated working conditions for IOCs, but has not made it impossible for them to work in the region.

IOCs initially played a large role in developing Latin American resources, but they eventually ran into resistance from increasingly powerful domestic groups in the countries where they were working. In the early years of the industry, Latin American markets were relatively small and unable to benefit from economies of scale, resulting in quasi-monopolistic market structures controlled by foreign companies. Initially, 'major oil companies saw the region as a backwater, where high tariffs and poor communications inhibited sales', according to one authoritative analysis.[34] By the 1920s, investments from IOCs grew significantly, playing a major role in the local economies of Venezuela, Colombia, and Argentina.[35] Dependence on oil products from private suppliers often created political tensions when prices increased. Governments also disliked the fact that foreign companies controlled their energy resources, and often appealed to concepts of national security to justify the creation of a national oil company.[36] By the mid-twentieth century, most of the region had established NOCs whose main priority was to improve the supply of oil products to the domestic market.

The new NOCs played different roles, depending on whether their country was an energy producer or a consumer. Following the ideas of import substitution promoted by the United Nations Economic Commission for Latin America and the Caribbean (ECLAC), resource-rich countries used NOCs as a mechanism to promote industrialization and income distribution objectives as well as security of supply, even at the cost of lower energy rent income for the government. For energy-dependent countries, the chief priority was access to reliable and low-cost resources, while avoiding dependence on private monopolies. Energy dependent countries fostered energy diversification and endorsed the creation of NOCs to carry out high-risk investments that the private sector was unwilling to make. However, typically for NOCs working in energy-consuming countries, the main priority was control of the downstream sector, allowing the NOC to capture monopolistic rents from the domestic market.

The rise of NOCs affected IOCs' activities, as governments adopted more restrictive contractual conditions. During the 1980s, Mexico, Venezuela, and Brazil banned IOC activities. In other countries, IOCs had to form partnerships with the local NOC to continue their operations.

State corporatism continued in the energy sector during the 1990s, even as most of Latin America followed the USA's efforts to spur globalization. The states in Latin America created a transnational economic architecture aimed at supporting capitalism, international trade, and, to a lesser extent, democratic regimes. With the collapse of the Soviet empire, globalization thrived as never before during the 1990s.

Either directly or through the international institutions it created, the USA managed to persuade a growing number of countries to adopt a set of policies aimed at strengthening market reforms. Many countries were willing to follow these reforms rather than see their investment risk increase, and suffer a decline in foreign direct investment.

Pressured by a debt crisis and the low commodity prices of the 1990s, Latin America adopted a series of policy measures known as the 'Washington Consensus.'[37] In the hydrocarbon sector, this meant a regulatory 'race to the bottom' as the countries opened to the outside world by eliminating as many rules as possible. Countries changed their nationalistic policies, opened exploration activities to private companies, ended NOC monopolies, reduced royalties and taxes, and, in some cases, sold their NOCs. Low commodity prices reduced fiscal and trade imbalances from importing countries, while oil exporters' main concern was to secure enough investment to keep production up.

After a short-lived economic recovery, the region's economy stagnated in the late 1990s. The population became disillusioned by the growing social inequalities caused by the 'Washington Consensus' policies. When the countries abandoned their currency boards and inflation reappeared, the cost of maintaining expected rates of return for private investors supplying the domestic market became unacceptably high.

As Latin America began to reject economic orthodoxy and market-friendly reforms, it was ready for a shift in political direction. In 1998, Brazil elected Luis Ignacio 'Lula' da Silva, the leader of the leftist Workers' Party. In 2000, Venezuela's political collapse brought radical populist Hugo Chavez to power. By 2006, Latin America's political map had changed significantly, and neo-populist regimes were in power in several countries.

Differing responses to globalization

With the rise of NOCs, what Latin Americans were choosing was not so much a shift to the left as an alternative to the inevitability of globalization. However, not all the countries followed the same policies or ideology, and the current post-globalization political map of Latin America could be described as consisting of three types of countries: anti-, soft-, and pro-globalizers.

Anti-globalization countries oppose the kind of globalization that emerged under US leadership and the unilateralism of President George W. Bush's foreign policy. President Hugo Chavez of Venezuela is the best-known representative of this group. Anti-globalization countries tend to favour economic policies that make the state the main driving force of economic growth. They use price controls to limit inflation, while fuelling consumption and investment through massive government spending. These countries seek economic and political independence from the USA by promoting regional integration and new political partnerships with emerging powers such as China, India, and Russia. These policies have led to a major change in the way that countries like Venezuela deal with IOCs.

For the anti-globalization countries, the rise of neo-populism and resource nationalism brought a change to the established relationships of the 1990s, particularly concerning the control of natural resources. Encouraged by the major shifts taking place in natural resource markets at the turn of the century, such as the rapid increases in commodity prices, growing global competition for resources from industrializing countries such as China and India, and the depletion of easily accessible oil supplies, anti-globalization countries opted to pursue an energy policy centred on maximizing government rents, re-establishing government control over hydrocarbon policy, and using energy revenues to promote social and economic development.

Venezuela was the first country to force IOCs to renegotiate their contracts so that they would pay more to the state, but Bolivia and Ecuador followed suit. These actions brought massive popular support to leaders who often talked of 're-nationalizing' the hydrocarbon industry. Unlike earlier nationalizations that were led by enlightened elites,[38] recent resource nationalism has been an affair of the poor. Nevertheless, despite the political rhetoric, the 're-nationalizations' in Venezuela and Bolivia have not been as radical as earlier nationalizations. Private companies are still allowed to invest, although fiscal terms have changed in favour of governments, and there is increasing political interference through direct participation by NOCs, local content quotas, and requirements to invest in broader economic development.

Soft globalization countries, such as Brazil, are not directly opposed to globalization. In fact, their administrations have kept many of the gains achieved during the 1990s, particularly in the area of orthodox economic policies. For example, they have maintained fiscal surpluses, paid their debts, and built strong foreign reserves. However, they are also seeking more equitable international trade relations, and questioning the USA's NAFTA initiative. Finally, they are increasingly attentive to income distribution and social development issues.

The more moderate soft globalization countries are following policies driven less by ideology than pragmatism. Brazil has benefited from the successful reforms adopted by the administration of President Cardoso, which ended Petrobras' monopoly and attracted large investments into the country. Petrobras has proven to be a shrewd competitor, capturing the best fields in the country, and rapidly expanding production. IOCs have opted to form partnerships with Petrobras as the safest entry strategy for Brazil, allowing Petrobras to benefit from their technical, strategic, and management expertise. Since the election of President Lula, however, Petrobras has been subject to increasing political interference. It has been used as a national champion to promote Brazil's regional influence, and as a tool for energy security and domestic industrialization. Compared to other regional NOCs, however, Petrobras' strategic and operating capabilities remain very strong.

Pro-globalization countries include Mexico, the countries of Central America, Chile, Peru, and Colombia. Pro-globalization countries tend to prioritize economic integration with the USA, with which they have strong economic and/or political linkages. These countries have essentially maintained a pro-business strategy, improving regulations in order to attract foreign investors. However, the situation is not so clearly straightforward. Mexico is trying to follow a more difficult path, reflecting the political contradictions of a country committed to free trade and market-oriented policies, while blocking access to its energy sector. Nevertheless, Mexico's energy policy, like that of Colombia, is driven by the pressure to reverse rapidly declining reserves. However Mexico, because of its legacy of strict nationalization which forbids any private role in the petroleum industry, has fewer options than Colombia.

Central American and Caribbean countries have flirted with the petroleum generosity of Hugo Chavez while being cautious of the diplomatic impact of close ties with Venezuela, particularly vis-à-vis their most important trading partner, the USA.[39] Some Central American countries, with the support of Mexico, are pursuing an ambitious energy integration strategy that includes electricity, gas pipelines, and the oil market. This initiative, which is strongly supported by the Inter-American Development Bank,[40] Central American countries, and Colombia, is sometimes seen as Washington's response to the growing influence in the region of Chavez' petroleum diplomacy.

Increasing Challenges to the USA in the Region

The USA now faces many difficulties in maintaining its traditional dominance in Latin America. Venezuela's Chavez openly challenges Washington's role in the region. At the same time, growing energy consumers like China and India are looking for new sources of energy. Simultaneously, Russia, an energy producer and traditional rival of the USA, is seeking out opportunities for its NOCs to work in the region and compete with the USA on political grounds.

High oil prices have allowed Chavez to finance a booming economy through vast government spending, and to promote his leftist agenda in Latin America and abroad. Chavez' petroleum diplomacy uses Venezuela's petroleum wealth to foster Latin American regional integration and to oppose US influence in the region. For example, Chavez has eased Cuba's energy crisis by exporting nearly 100,000 b/d of oil, in exchange for the services of Cuban doctors and social workers who now provide medical aid and other forms of assistance in poor areas of Venezuela. The deal reduces the financial burden of Cuba's hydrocarbon imports, while allowing Chavez to provide popular social programmes independently of Venezuela's largely hostile professional class.

Energy-dependent countries in the Caribbean and Central America have also benefited from Chavez's petroleum generosity through PetroCaribe, a programme that sells oil at discounted rates. The deal has strings attached: the oil can only be handled by NOCs, and recipient countries may be expected to support Venezuela's positions in international affairs. This political aspect of the policy was apparent in Chavez's unsuccessful attempt to gain the Security Council's rotating Latin American seat in autumn 2006.

Venezuela has also cultivated stronger ties with perceived global competitors of the USA, particularly China, Russia, and adversaries like Iran. Although Venezuela's oil product exports to China are still modest (around 170 kb/d) they have grown significantly at a time when exports to the USA have declined. PDVSA and CNPC, the Chinese NOC, have begun a series of large-scale development projects to increase the extraction, upgrading, transportation, and refining of heavy crude oil from the Orinoco belt. China is also assisting Venezuela with various industrialization projects, including the local construction of drilling rigs.[41]

China's quest for resources has not gone unnoticed in the region, or in Washington. A 'Latin American invasion', is how well-known commentator Saul Landau put it.[42] However, despite the increasing investments of Chinese NOCs in Latin America, it would be fair to assume that 'There is no strong correlation between Chinese economic or political movements in the region and a calculated agenda of anti-Americanism.'[43] In fact, Venezuela's oil exports to the USA still dwarf those to China, while Brazil is already planning a growing presence in the USA by investing in refineries there.[44] Moreover, China's investments in Latin America will ease the investment gap in the oil sector in Latin America, resulting in a growing global supply of oil.

Iran and Venezuela have engaged in numerous industrial exchange programmes, and Russia has become an important supplier of military equipment to Venezuela. Moreover, Russian gas giant Gazprom signed a series of energy cooperation agreements with Chavez and Minister of Energy and PDVSA President Rafael Ramirez. Gazprom investments in Venezuela cover a large array of strategic sectors, including offshore natural gas exploration and development of Orinoco belt reserves with other Russian companies. Gazprom is also extending its reach in partnership with PDVSA into Bolivia and Ecuador, focusing on potential oil exploration activities.

In addition, with the drop in oil prices in autumn 2008, Venezuela worked closely with OPEC to try to bring prices back up. However, these efforts were not initially effective, and the price of oil was well below $50 a barrel by the end of the year as the global economic recession resulted in the reduction of petroleum demand by 200 kb/d. Oil demand had not contracted since 1983, and IEA forecasts expected it to remain weak for 200.

For the USA, the main impact of the recent period of rising resource nationalism is a declining supply of oil and increasing diplomatic tensions with countries – for example Venezuela and Ecuador – attacking the interests of US oil companies. However, Mexico's oil nationalism is likely to have a much greater impact since Mexico is the second largest supplier of oil to the USA, after Canada (see Figure 7.9). The USA will have to find a balance between the strongly held views of resource nationalism in Mexico, encouraging petroleum sector policies that are more open to private investments, while also being willing to offer a more realistic solution to illegal immigration and strengthening the NAFTA agreement, for example, by allowing Mexican truck drivers to transport merchandise into US territory. Failure to do so will result in nationalistic retrenchment in both countries, with declining levels of investment and oil production and, of course, increasing pressure on legal and illegal immigration at the US borders.

Despite these growing challenges, the global economic downturn will weaken the USA's rivals. Venezuela, under increasing economic pressure caused by a mismanaged economy, is expected to lose some of its regional influence. Chavez, emerging from his first electoral defeat in December 2007, in which he unsuccessfully tried to win public support to amend the constitution to allow him to stay in office for additional terms, had to shore up his domestic support to finally win

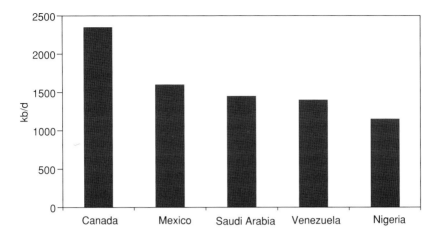

Source: US Department of Energy

Figure 7.9: US oil imports by country

a referendum on this issue in February 2009. Declining production will increase the cost of Venezuelan petroleum diplomacy, probably forcing the country to reduce its generous handouts, while building up resource-producing relations with NOCs, and even IOCs, willing to help PDVSA increase output.

Bolivia, losing some of the economic support it has received from Venezuela, is expected to tone down its nationalistic rhetoric, focusing instead on meeting its gas export obligations to Brazil and Argentina, and in the process entering into new agreements with NOCs and IOCs currently operating in the country. Already, Petrobras and the Bolivian government have agreed to resume some investment programmes in Bolivia.[45] The Argentine oil company YPF has also expressed interest in increasing investments in Bolivia, to export gas to Argentina.[46]

Incentives needed for investments

Producer–consumer relations in Latin America will be driven by the need for investments, in order to reverse production declines. In fact, according to ECLAC, developing the Latin America energy sector requires approximately US$55bn per year from now until 2030.[47] With hydrocarbon production declining and private investors reluctant to invest, due to regulatory and political uncertainty, populist administrations will have to rely on investments from their own NOCs, either alone or in partnership with foreign NOCs from resource-seeking nations and perhaps Russia. Governments will be under pressure to allocate resources to high-risk exploration activities, while at the same time domestic political pressures push them to increase public spending on populist projects such as energy subsidies, increasing employment by expanding local bureaucracies, and building domestic infrastructure projects.

Complicating the task is the USA, and global economic downturn, forcing populist regimes to adjust to a less favourable economic environment while maintaining high levels of popular support. If they adopt expansionary policies, ignoring inflationary pressures and fiscal prudence, they risk repeating past errors. On the other hand, reducing demand growth by cutting government spending will erode popular support.

The global economic crisis will have profound impacts on Latin America's energy sector. First, faced with the difficult choice of stimulating the economy and addressing pressing social needs, or increasing high risk investments in exploration activities, governments – populist and otherwise – will focus on the first. NOCs' access to funding will be severely limited. The shortage of funds will inevitably affect investments and future production. The most vulnerable countries are those that have restricted participation from private companies. For their part, private companies, facing difficulties in accessing capital to finance their activities, are likely to postpone new investments or to delay development programmes, when possible.

Governments will be forced to revise their petroleum policies. If the global economy recovers relatively quickly, pressure for improving contracts and adopting a more pro-business strategy will diminish. However, if the global economic recovery is modest and prices remain low (in the vicinity of $40/b or lower) countries will be required to revise some of their policies and strategies, perhaps by reducing royalties and taxes, or by improving access to private companies.

In the short- to medium-term one can expect a decline in production, investments, and reserves. Some countries – particularly Peru and Brazil – should be in a good position to avoid this trend. The rest of the region, however, will probably not be so lucky.

Conclusions

For most of the twentieth century, the history of oil in Latin America has been about the host governments' struggles to control their resources. In the early years, before 1928, Latin American countries welcomed IOCs because they drove growth, even if they occasionally

engaged in barbarous acts and had little sympathy for the local population.[48] As global output increased following the Great Depression,
companies were willing to cooperate to protect market prices. As prices
increased, producing countries started to erode the dominant role of
IOCs. Concerns about military matters and the dominant position of
foreign companies in their domestic markets drove these actions.

Nationalistic sentiments in countries such as Brazil resulted in the
preference for a secure national supplier of oil. Brazil's leaders feared
that in case of a future military conflict with, for example, Argentina,
foreign companies would be unwilling to supply the armed forces
with oil, or would try to take advantage of the situation by increasing
prices. From the upstream perspective, many consider the military to
be the most credible custodian of the country's vast oil-rent wealth.
Local elites were viewed as vulnerable to the unhealthy influence of
foreign companies. This is, for example, part of the heritage from the
Gran Chaco war fought between Bolivia and Paraguay to control land
which was (incorrectly) thought to be rich in oil. Different oil companies
backed the two sides in the conflict.

After World War II, following import-substitution industrialization
strategies, most countries in the region encouraged the creation of
NOCs and forced the IOCs to pay the government a greater share
of their profits. Despite the region's alignment with the USA (except
Cuba), Latin America's energy sector was driven by state corporatism
with various degrees of openness. However, the debt crisis of the 1980s
brought with it a paradigm shift in the region's economic model and
its energy policies. Privatization, deregulation, and market competition
dominated the language of energy policy makers, resulting in massive
investments from IOCs, particularly in Venezuela, Brazil, and, to a
lesser extent, Bolivia and Argentina.

However, as Latin America entered the new millennium, the region
moved away from market solutions, instead preferring options that
stressed populism and resource nationalism. Encouraged by global
trends which strengthened NOCs,[49] populist governments adopted a
tougher attitude toward IOCs, seeking to rebalance what they perceived
as tax and royalty policies that were too biased in favour of the IOCs as
the price of oil continued to increase. Although these policies resulted
in increased government revenues, they have also caused drastic declines
in investments.

The rise of resource nationalism has had a dramatic impact on
producer–consumer relations. The Washington Consensus had been
geared toward the idea that everyone would work together. When one
country stopped trading with its partners, it had a significant negative

impact on the countries that depended on foreign sources of energy. After the supply shutoffs of recent years, it will be difficult to rebuild producer–consumer relations at the regional level. Local problems also have an impact at the global level. The loss of access to Latin American supplies naturally has a negative impact on the USA, but may provide new opportunities for China and other new consumers. Likewise, while Western IOCs will have trouble working in Latin America, state-controlled companies from countries like China and Russia will find extensive new opportunities to produce and sell energy products.

As the global economy feels the effects of the USA's recession, it is expected that Latin America's resource nationalism will face increasing pressures. Governments will continue to demand more revenues to maintain popular programmes, while inflation will increase pressure on governments to adopt stricter monetary policies. Declining production will force NOCs to increase productivity. However, the economic crisis will not force a return to the 1990s, with countries competing to open up their hydrocarbon sectors.

The situation is not nearly as dire as it seems for either local NOCs or IOCs that want to work in the region. Local NOCs now have a much wider set of options. First, most of the regional governments have built strong foreign reserve 'war chests' and the financial situations of local NOCs have been strengthened. In contrast to the past, international oil service companies are willing partners who can help NOCs overcome some of their technical limitations. Moreover, NOCs from resource-seeking countries, such as China and India, are also eager partners willing to negotiate with local NOCs without extensive concern for political stability.

Likewise, despite the perception of a growing threat from NOCs, the picture for IOCs is 'not as bad as it seems'.[50] IOCs take the lead in production in frontier areas, and the exploitation of non-conventional oil resources. Moreover, they lead the LNG and gas-to-liquid business, making the development of new energy sources possible, and dominate the refining, logistics, and retailing sectors. Moreover, IOCs are adapting to the new realities of a world with restricted access to petroleum reserves and tougher terms, by highlighting their technical expertise at producing oil in the face of challenging conditions, such as ultra-deepwater or extra-heavy crudes. Finally, after years of international scrutiny, IOCs, particularly large supermajors, have improved their environmental and social corporate responsibility practices, and are more sensitive to local issues. As economic pressure forces local governments to address the investment gap, Latin American governments will be forced once again to turn to IOCs in a search for capital.

Notes

1   Latin America includes Mexico for the purposes of the current discussion.
2   PDVSA webpage: www.pdvsa.com
3   Excludes recent discoveries made by Petrobras.
4   'Oil Discovery Rocks Brazil', CNN, 9 November 2007. http://edition.cnn. com/2007/WORLD/americas/11/08/brazil.oil.ap/
5   *Argus LatAm Energy*, 23 January 2008, 5.
6   *Business News Americas*, 25 January 2008. www.bnamericas.com/
7   Secretaria de Energia de Mexico (Sener), *Prospectiva del mercado de petroleo crudo 2007-2016: Direccion General de Planeacion Energetica*, 2007. www.sener.gob. mx/webSener/res/PE_y_DT/pub/Prospectiva%20Petroleo%20Crudo%20 Finas.pdf
8   Cantarell was discovered in 1971 by a fisherman, Rudecindo Cantarell, who informed the authorities of an oil stain on the waters of the Campeche Sea. Eight years latter Cantarell became the largest oil producing well in Mexico, according to Pemex (www.pemex.com).
9   Confirman cambios en Pemex, www.reforma.com, 14 September 2007.
10 Hugo Serrano, 'Colombia a importar petroleo', *Revista Javeriana*, no. 702, 2004.
11 A. Fioritti Campos, M. Tiomno Tolmasquin, and C. Alveal, 'Restructuring the oil segment in South America. Public policy, private capital', *Oil & Gas Science and Technology, Rev. IFP*, 61, 3, 2006, 422.
12 'El primer pozo del bloque Tayrona resultó seco', *El Tiempo*, 9 January 2008.
13 Presentation by Ecopetrol's Mauricio Salgado, 'Proyecto de Crudos Pesados en Colombia', II Colombian Oil & Gas Investment Conference, Cartagena, Colombia, 2006.
14 Carlos Molina, *El Boom de los pequenos petroleros, America Economia edicion* 353, April 2007.
15 'Senate Committee Reaches Consensus on Energy Reforms', *BusinessAmerica*, 11 January, 2008.
16 Bernard Mommer, *Petroleo Global y Estado Nacional*, Ediciones Comala.com, Caracas, Venezuela, 2003, 129.
17 Antonio Perez Marquez, *Implosion Corporativa Lecciones de una cultura organizacional*, INVERMARK Ediciones, Caracas, 2005, 31.
18 'Autentica Nacionalizacion', www.pdvsa.com/. The 'true-nationalization' refers to the government changes in contracts signed with IOCs, resulting in higher royalties, taxes and PDVSA securing a majority shareholding position and becoming the operator of all petroleum projects in the country.
19 Ramon Espinaza, *Preocupa que Pdvsa se endeude no para aumentar la producción sino los gastos*, 25 January 2008. www.unionradio.com.ve/
20 A component of PDVSA energy integration is to form partnerships with Latin American NOCs for the production and development of the Orinoco belt. In addition, PDVDSA has signed agreements with NOCs from

214 Energy and the Transformation of International Relations

geopolitically strategic countries, aimed at strengthening a multi-polar world. See PDVSA website: www.pdvsa.com

21 Total, Statoil and Shell signed several agreements with PDVSA. See various issues of *Business News Americas*, January 2008. www.bnamericas.com

22 Georges D. Landau, 'Brazil', in *Energy Cooperation in the Western Hemisphere Benefits and Impediments*, Sidney Weintraub, ed., Center for Strategic and International Studies, Washington DC, 2007, 246.

23 George Philip, *Oil and Politics in Latin America. Nationalist Movements and State Companies*, Cambridge University Press, Cambridge, 2006, 373.

24 Landau, p. 268.

25 Andres Oppenheimer, 'Brazil's oil: new wealth or petropopulism?' *Miami Herald*, 25 November 2007.

26 Dave Cohen. 'God is Brazilian?', *ASPO/USA Energy Bulletin*, 5 December 2007. www.energybulletin.net/node/38218

27 PetroEcuador production increased in 2006 as a result of the take over of Occidental's 15th block. However, shortly after PetroEcudor took control of the project, production declined from 90 kb/d average to 80 kb/d.

28 'Ecuador nunca tuvo un sistema de control de calida', www.ecuadorinmediato.com/ediciones/, 28 January 2008.

29 OPEC press release. www.opec.org/opecna/Press%20Releases/2008/pr172008.htm

30 'Tres gigantes se unen para explorar la Amazonia en busca de oro negro', 22 November 2007. http://perupetro.com.pe/desarrollo/intranetpp/intranetpp.nsf

31 Humberto Campodonico's webpage: Cristal de Mira, 'No se debe exportar ni una molecula de gas del lote *88*', http://cristaldemira.com/, 16 January 2008.

32 'Bolivia–Argentina pipeline project moving forward', *Argus LatAm Energy*, 6 February 2008.

33 Ibid

34 Philip, p. 9.

35 Ibid, p. 10.

36 Nicolas Gadano, *Urgency and Betrayal, three attempts to foster private investments in Argentina's oil industry*, Centro de Implementacion Politicas Publicas para la Equidad y el Crecimiento (CIPPEC), 3.

37 The 'Washington Consensus' was a term suggested at a conference in Washington in November 1989 by economist John Williamson from the International Economic Institute presenting what were the main reforms that were widely agreed in Washington to be needed to restore Latin American economic growth. Pedro Pablo Kuczynski and John Williamson, *After the Washington Consensus. Restarting Growth and Reform in Latin America*, Peter G. Petersen Institute for International Economics, Washington DC, 2003, 24.

38 Philip, p. 315.

39 Rickey Singh, 'Worrying signals in Caricom', *Trinidad Express*, January 30, 2008, posted with authorization at Petroleumword.com (www.petroleumworld.com/).

40 Luis Alberto Moreno, 'Viewpoint Optimism on Energy', Comments made at the Western Hemisphere Energy Security Forum, Washington DC, 24 October 2006. Available at InterAmerican Development Bank website: www.iadb.org/

41 Agencia Bolivariana de Noticias, 'Venezuela y China firman 11 acuerdos en materia energetica, financiera y tecnologica', 6 November2007. See ABN website: www.abn.info.ve

42 Saul Landau, 'Chinese influence on the rise in Latin America', *Foreign Policy in Focus*, June 2005.

43 Wenran Jiang, 'China and India come to Latin America for Energy', in Weintraub, ed., *Energy Cooperation in the Western Hemisphere*, 489.

44 'Petrobras eyes refineries in US, Japan and Europe'. See Business News Americas website : http://bnamericas.com/, 30 August 2007.

45 'Petrobras to invest US$1bn in neighbor Bolivia'. See Business News Americas website: http://bnamericas.com/. 17 December 2007.

46 'Repsol YPF eyes Argentina's gas export market', See Business News Americas website: http://bnamericas.com/. 5 October 2007.

47 Jeremy Martin and Roger Tissot, 'An analysis on Latin America Energy Security', See PetroleumWorld website: www.Petroleumworld.com.

48 Philip, p. 494.

49 According to PFC Energy (www.pfcenergy.com), NOCs hold more than 75 per cent of world oil reserves.

50 Milton Costa Filho and Pedro Martinez Lara, 'A new role for NOCs in a challenging energy sector', *Fundamentals of the global oil and gas industry: 2007 World Petroleum Council Yearbook*, p. 37.

PART III

CONSUMERS

CHAPTER 8

THE USA: THE KEY GLOBAL DRIVER

Michael E. Webber

The USA is by far the largest overall energy consumer in the world, and the largest per capita energy user among the populous, industrialized nations. Accordingly, US energy consumption remains one of the main drivers affecting US and world energy security. However, because the USA is historically a dominant energy producer (and today remains one of the world's largest producers) and a leader in technological innovation, it also has an opportunity to lead the transition towards a globalized and decarbonized energy system that solves multiple problems – energy security, ecological impacts, and climate change – simultaneously. Thus, the USA is part of the problem (through high consumption) and part of the solution (through high production and the development of advanced energy technologies).

It is not clear whether the USA will continue on its path of unsustainably-rising demand for energy, or whether it will lead the world towards a greener route in the name of energy security and environmental protection. As the USA is presently witnessing rapid shifts in popular and political opinion about energy, the environment, and climate change, an opportunity exists to shift onto a path of energy consumption and production that is more sustainable, economically efficient, and beneficial for global energy security. Whether the USA makes this shift remains to be seen.

This chapter will present the main contours of the current US energy policy debate, and challenges to its energy future, both at home and abroad. The chapter begins with an overview of the energy situation in the USA today, in terms of consumption, domestic production, and energy imports. Next is an explanation of shifting attitudes towards energy in the USA, and evolving concepts about the definition of energy security. Then a quick summary of US energy policies sets out the context for considering the main challenges to a secure energy future in the USA. These three primary energy challenges are: bridging the gap between energy consumption and domestic production; reducing greenhouse gas emissions from energy consumption; and avoiding calls for energy isolationism. The chapter subsequently examines US plans for securing current and future energy supplies, and whether that search will bring it into conflict, or potentially stimulate cooperation, with other countries also seeking energy resources. As the USA has such high energy consumption, it is fair to argue that if the USA solves its own energy problem, it will have gone a long way towards solving the world's energy problem.

Energy in the USA

As a mega-consumer, the USA is both part of the problem and, as a mega-producer and technological innovator, potentially part of the solution when addressing the world's energy problems. The USA's energy situation presents an extremely complicated picture. The USA is by far the world's largest energy consumer, having approximately 5 per cent of the world's population it is responsible for approximately 23 per cent of global annual energy consumption. Though other energy-rich countries such as Dubai consume more energy per capita, their overall population is very small. Of the large, industrialized nations, the USA consumes far more per capita.

The US Energy Situation

Total energy consumption in the USA in 2005 was approximately 100 quadrillion British thermal units (BTU), or 100 quads.[1] Worldwide, consumption in 2004 was about 445 quads.[2] Overall, these figures have not changed substantially between 2005 and 2009. Energy consumption in the USA, shown in Table 8.1, was mixed across a variety of sources, with approximately 85 per cent coming from fossil fuels. Though the USA is often criticized for the amount of petroleum and other fossil fuels it uses, the relative energy mix is similar to the rest of the world. The primary difference is that the rest of the planet uses slightly less oil (35 per cent instead of 41 per cent) and instead uses more biomass (10 per cent instead of 2 per cent). A fifth of the global tally of biomass sources (i.e. 2 per cent, the same value as that given for the USA) represents a similar use of biomass to that of the USA (e.g. for electricity or liquid fuels), with the remaining four-fifths (8 per cent) in the form of traditional biomass, such as wood and dung in stoves for heat and cooking.[3]

The similarity between the fuel mixes for the USA and the global average is important, because it presumably means that the interests of the USA and the rest of the world will be aligned for securing energy supplies. That is, the USA and the rest of the world should have plenty

Table 8.1: The percentage contribution from a variety of sources for US and global energy consumption in 2005 (USA) and 2004 (global)

Energy Source	US Consumption	Global Consumption
Liquid fuels and other petroleum	41%	35%
Natural gas	23%	20%
Coal	23%	25%
Nuclear Power	8%	6%
Hydropower	3%	2%
Biomass	2%	10%
Other Renewable Energy	1%	1%

Source: USDOE, *Annual Energy Outlook 2007: With Projections to 2030*, U.S. Department of Energy, Energy Information Administration, Washington, 2007 and J. Goldemberg, 'Ethanol for a Sustainable Energy Future', *Science*, 2007, 315.

of incentive to cooperate on energy use and development issues, because their top-level aggregate energy consumption is so similar; what is bad for the USA in terms of energy security is also bad for the world, and vice versa.

What sets the USA apart from Europe and other countries for whom energy security is a pressing topic, is that it is both a large energy producer and a large energy consumer. Other large energy consumers, such as Japan or Germany, do not produce much energy. Other large energy producers, such as Iran or Saudi Arabia, are not large energy consumers. Table 8.2 lists the top five producers and consumers of oil, gas, and coal. Only the USA and Russia are in the top five of all the

Table 8.2: The world's top five producers and consumers for oil, gas, and coal

	Top World Oil Producers	Consumers	Top World Gas Producers	Consumers	Top World Coal Producers	Consumers
Rank	[2006]	[2006]	[2006]	[2006]	[2005]	[2005]
1	Saudi Arabia	**USA**	Russia	**USA**	China	China
2	Russia	China	**USA**	Russia	**USA**	**USA**
3	**USA**	Japan	Canada	Iran	India	India
4	Iran	Russia	Iran	Germany	Australia	Germany
5	China	Germany	Norway	Canada	Russia	Russia

Source: USDOE, International Energy Annual 2005 and 2006, U.S. Department of Energy, Energy Information Administration, Washington, 2005 and 2006, and USDOE, International Petroleum Monthly 2005 and 2006, U.S. Department of Energy, Energy Information Administration, Washington 2005, 2006.

categories listed in the table. Consequently, it is reasonable to conclude that the behaviour of these two countries will be the key drivers for the world's energy systems. However, because Russia is a net exporter of both oil and gas, and the USA is a net importer of both, their roles on the world stage are different.

The USA uses nearly 21 million barrels of crude oil and oil products per day, importing just over 12 million barrels or approximately 60 per cent.[4] Similarly, the USA uses nearly 22 trillion cubic feet of natural gas annually, of which 18.5 trillion cubic feet is produced domestically, with the balance (about 15 per cent of total gas consumption) supplied by imports.[5] The USA is self-sufficient in coal[6] and sits on the largest reserves in the world.[7]

Renewable energy production and consumption in the USA is growing rapidly, as a consequence of new legislative targets for renewable fuel consumption in transportation[8] and renewable portfolio standards (RPS), which require a certain percentage of power generation from non-hydroelectric renewable sources, such as wind and solar power, and are currently in place in approximately half the states. Though these sources of energy are growing rapidly in the USA, projections show consumption of traditional sources essentially growing at the same pace, meaning that the total relative contributions to the mix are not projected to change much.[9] Whether energy consumption will level off or continue to grow is not clear, and consequently projections by different analysts come to different conclusions. Energy consumption might increase because of population and economic growth, or it might level off or decrease because of economic contraction and/or aggressive market penetration of conservation and efficiency measures.

The primary way in which the USA engages with the world's energy systems is through oil markets; its gas interactions are very small beyond Canada, and its coal purchases and sales are approximately zero. This situation is in contrast with Europe, which actively engages in both the world's oil and gas markets, and thus feels a different sense of energy vulnerability. Potential gas shortages in Europe would have an impact on heating and electricity, to which people are very sensitive, as evidenced by the tense negotiations between Russia and Ukraine, and subsequent supply cutoffs in 2006 and 2009. As the USA is self-sufficient in coal and either produces most of its own gas or imports it from Canada, which has no history of making threats or taking action to cut off supplies, Americans feel very little sense of vulnerability regarding fuels for their electricity system. However, many Americans feel that oil supplies are vulnerable.[10] As we discuss in much greater detail below, because the USA buys from the world market, that sense of vulnerability is generally ill-founded, as supplies are likely to be available to meet US demand in the event of major disruptions to the oil supply system, though presumably at much higher prices.

In the future, the USA faces steadily increasing energy consumption up to 2030, assuming continuing economic growth and an increasing population, according to an analysis by the Energy Information Administration (EIA), an independent arm of the US Department of Energy (DOE) that collects and analyses energy statistics. Figure 8.1 shows that US energy consumption is projected to grow for each major fuel category between 2005 and 2030, while total US energy consumption is projected to grow from 100 quads in 2005 to approximately 120 quads in 2030. According to these projections, a growing portion of the energy to meet US demand will be satisfied by imports. As many factors, such as regulatory changes which could affect energy use and production, are not included in these projections, they should not be considered predictions for the future, but rather projections based on business-as-usual approaches. Working with these assumptions, both energy consumption and the gap between production and consumption continue to grow in unfettered fashion, revealing the increasing challenge of solving the energy problem. How the USA seeks to bridge the gap between projections for consumption and for production will be of serious consequence for the world's efforts to address energy security.

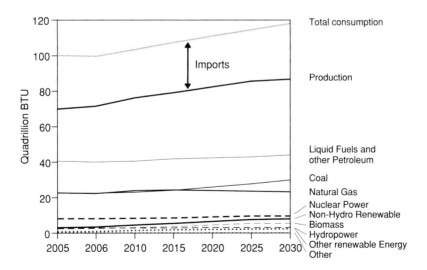

Source: US Energy Information Administration, Annual Energy Outlook, 2008

Figure 8.1: Energy consumption by fuel, total consumption, and total production in the USA 1980–2030

Defining Energy Security

The definition of energy security in the USA has evolved over time. In the aftermath of the 1970s oil embargoes, the traditional view of energy security in the USA was primarily concerned with the security of supply. Energy security meant ensuring that a reliable and affordable stream of energy resources would be available to consumers. In the face of the Arab oil boycott in 1973, the US response to energy security concerns emphasized conservation, and efforts to reduce oil consumption in the transportation and power sectors. In the aftermath of the crisis, American consumers were able to save considerable amounts of energy by changing their habits, and as a result of requirements for more fuel-efficient vehicles. Unfortunately, however, the return of cheap oil in the 1980s brought an end to these conservation practices and automotive fuel-efficiency levelled-off partway through the decade.

Since that time, the concept of energy security in the USA has evolved to include the interconnection of American energy consumption with terrorism, national security, and foreign policy. This shift in the definition of energy security is partly because of a growing awareness that a majority of US oil (nearly two-thirds) and a significant fraction of US energy resources overall (about one-third) are imported from oil-producing countries, some of which are hostile to US interests. That awareness, combined with a heightened sense of vulnerability as a consequence of the terrorist attacks in 2001, has helped push the evolution of energy security concepts. Today, an increasing number of Americans are concluding that, in some way, America's enemies are enriched by their purchases of petroleum-based fuels. For example, a majority of Americans believe that 'money spent on Middle Eastern oil eventually finds its way to funding terrorist activities', according to Rasmussen Reports.[11] These fears of a terrorist connection to energy purchases are in addition to traditional concerns about gasoline prices and availability.[12]

This shift in mindset is a driving force for modern discussions of energy policy, with emphases on 'security' and 'independence' instead of 'conservation' or 'reliability'. Though some of the challenges are the same as those in the 1970s, the solutions appear to be different, because the concept of energy security has broadened from reliability to national security, in parallel with changes in the political climate, as described below in greater detail.

US Energy Policies

The USA does not have a single robust energy policy that can be used to address the challenges it faces in achieving energy security. Much of the problem is institutional, because in the USA there is no single person or agency in charge of energy policy. This section lays out the various players in the US energy policy-making process. The way in which the executive branch carries out its research and development (R&D) work is then examined, since this research work defines US energy policies in practice. The clear conclusion is that the USA is much more focused on finding new supplies of energy than on reducing its consumption.

The process of making energy policy in the USA is extremely complicated because there are numerous players involved, including the president, Congress, big energy companies, manufacturers, lobbyists, unions, and environmental groups. Each presidential administration pushes its priorities via the federal agencies through the allocation of R&D budgets, and whether it actively enforces environmental regulations. For example, President George W. Bush emphasized nuclear technologies and hydrogen by providing these areas with extra research funding. During most of his administration, he downplayed concerns about global warming in his rhetoric, and by weakening Environmental Protection Agency (EPA) enforcement of key environmental regulations. President Barack Obama has emphasized investments in green infrastructure to enable greater market penetration of renewable sources, along with an approximately tenfold increase in R&D for a wide range of energy-related fields.

Congress is a critical player, and periodically passes updated energy legislation, such as the Energy Policy Act of 2005 (EPACT 2005)[13] and the Energy Independence and Security Act (EISA 2007 adopted on 19 December 2007). Business lobbies and environmental groups actively work to shape the funding priorities of the administration and the context of the legislation approved by Congress. Beyond the federal government, states and localities also make decisions that have an important impact on the shape of the country's energy policy.

The consequence of this complicated patchwork of federal, state, and local entities that have varying and overlapping responsibilities and differing impacts on various pieces of the energy problem is that it is difficult to create a comprehensive, robust, and forward-looking energy policy. By comparison, smaller, more homogenous countries such as Denmark, where policies originate from fewer stakeholders, have been able to successfully create and implement comprehensive energy policies.

As the most relevant part of the executive branch, the DOE oversees most energy-related R&D expenditures through its national labs and research contracts; it operates many energy efficiency programmes, and periodically invests in large-scale production programmes.[14] The DOE is active in energy research, but does not intervene in the markets to set energy price, production, or consumption in the way many other countries' governments do. Furthermore, because it is responsible for managing nuclear weapons, its mission is not singularly focused on energy issues.

The DOE is not the only federal agency actively addressing the impacts, use, or production of energy. The US Department of Agriculture has a very ambitious bioenergy programme for creating new energy supplies from agricultural crops, waste, or other biofeedstocks. The EPA is involved with the impacts of energy production and use, manages the Energy Star rating programme for household appliances, and is responsible for testing automotive vehicles to certify their fuel economy. The US Geological Survey is responsible for questions regarding access to federal lands for production of energy resources. The Department of Defense, which is the single largest governmental energy consumer in the USA (about 2 per cent of total energy consumption) has pledged to become energy self-sufficient, and is involved with peacekeeping and nation-building efforts in energy resource-rich regions of the world. Furthermore, the burden of maintaining shipping lanes, or of quickly restoring order to energy-producing allies in the event of unrest, falls on the military. In addition to all these federal stakeholders, state and local governments have their own standalone energy or environmental agencies.

Though the USA has invested over $100 billion in cumulative energy-related R&D since 1978 (in constant 2000 dollars)[15] with significant positive benefits,[16] total public and private energy R&D has declined steeply over time.[17] Public energy-related research investments have fallen from a peak of $8 billion (in constant 2002 dollars) in 1979 to less than $4 billion in 2005. During that period, combined public and private energy-related R&D dropped from 10 per cent of all R&D in 1980 in the USA to 2 per cent of total R&D in 2005. As noted by Kammen and Nemet, some individual pharmaceutical companies today invest more R&D dollars by themselves than all private R&D in energy combined,[18] perhaps offering a signal about the relative importance Americans attribute to solving the energy problem versus the value of Viagra. Though R&D budgets for energy have increased in the last few federal budgets, the levels are still near historic lows.

Typically, R&D expenditures focus on developing new sources of energy supply, such as alternative fuels, oil shale, advanced nuclear power, and so forth.[19] Historically, only 10–20 per cent of total R&D

expenditures at the DOE have been invested in efforts to reduce energy consumption through conservation or greater efficiency. While the total amount of energy R&D that has been invested by the USA is an indicator that it is doing its part in terms of sharing the research burden for solving the energy problem, these investment trends reveal a shortcoming in the R&D, in that they reflect a generalized attitude in the USA that there is nothing wrong with the amount of energy Americans consume, and that any negative environmental or national security impacts resulting from that consumption should be addressed through technological solutions that produce improved sources of supply. A public poll, which concluded that '71 per cent say developing new energy sources is more important than conserving energy (21 per cent).' supported this notion.[20]

It is also important to note that the relative allocation of this research between energy conservation and new sources of supply is bipartisan and decades-long, though the priorities shift back and forth under different presidential administrations. Under the administration of President George W. Bush, the R&D budgets at the DOE have increased from those at the end of the Clinton Administration, but included a shift in priorities even further away from conservation research. The DOE's R&D budgets for conservation and efficiency were cut by a third between 2001 and 2007. Instead, Bush gave heavy emphasis to fission and fusion nuclear energy.[21]

Also, strikingly, many policies in other parts of the federal domain actually require increased energy consumption. For example, in vehicles, many requirements over the last few decades for increased levels of safety equipment (crumple-zones, airbags, anti-lock brakes, and so forth) or for technologies which minimize emissions, have indeed improved safety and environmental impact, but have also added to the weight of vehicles, which has affected efforts to improve fuel economy.[22] Furthermore, the requirement for television stations to broadcast in digital format, and subsequently for manufacturers to shift production of televisions entirely to digital format in 2009, represents an increase in overall energy consumption, because digital televisions consume more electricity for their operation than older versions.[23]

Historically, the greatest activity related to energy policy in the USA was in the 1970s, when the USA responded to the oil embargoes by reducing oil consumption in the power and transportation sectors. For the electricity sector, emphasis switched instead to gas, coal, nuclear, and other forms of energy that were primarily domestically-produced and considered to be more reliable. Oil was the source for 12–17 per cent of the US electricity mix in the 1970s, and today it is less than

2 per cent of the total electricity mix.[24] Other responses included establishing the DOE, calling for conservation, and creating corporate average fuel economy (CAFE) standards to reduce the role of oil in transportation. While efforts to reduce the portion of oil contributing to electricity generation were widely successful, oil remains the dominant transportation fuel of choice, comprising more than 96 per cent of the energy for transportation needs. Thus, despite an average fuel economy that is much higher today than 30 years ago, the absolute amount of oil that is used for transportation has grown steadily to about 14 mb/d in 2006, as the overall population has grown and total vehicle miles travelled has increased. Furthermore, efforts to improve fuel economy stagnated in the mid-1980s, staying flat between 1986 and today.

Under the Bush administration, solutions differed from those adopted after the 1973 energy crisis, and the political leadership devoted little serious attention to conservation.[25] In contrast to the 1970s, when CAFE standards were quickly brought into place, more than six years passed between the 2001 terrorist attacks and the passage of EISA 2007, which legislated stricter automobile fuel economy standards in the coming decades by requiring a CAFE of 35 miles per gallon (mpg) by 2020. Notably, EISA includes the words 'security' and 'independence' in its title. Combined with the fuel economy standards are mandates for the inclusion into the fuel mix of 36 billion gallons per year of domestically-produced biofuels by 2022 (this amount, though, is only a small fraction of overall use: in 2006, the USA consumed 180 billion gallons combined of petroleum-derived gasoline and diesel).

While we are at the beginning of a new flurry of energy policy activity in the USA, it is not clear in which direction it will go, or how long this attention will last. However, with the election of President Barack Obama, energy policy is likely to take a sudden shift in the direction of renewable sources and low-carbon fuels and technologies. Strikingly, a centrepiece of President Obama's early actions include massive investments in energy R&D, with proposals to raise the R&D budget from approximately $1.5 billion annually, to $15 billion, a ten-fold increase. This R&D boost is similar to previous historical episodes for challenges identified as national missions (for example, the Manhattan Project, the Apollo program, Project Independence in the 1970s, the defence build-up of the 1980s, and health spending in the 1990s and early 2000s). The appointment of technical leaders such as Dr. Stephen Chu (a Nobel prize winner) as Secretary of Energy and Dr. John Holdren (an outspoken activist on energy and climate) as Assistant to the President for Science and Technology and director of the Office of Science and Technology Policy, signal the return of scientific research as a prominent solution to the energy problem. Biofuel mandates are likely to increase, through with perhaps more of an emphasis on second-generation fuels from algae or cellulosic sources rather than soy or corn. In addition, observers anticipate that the government will fund large-scale demonstration projects of carbon capture, solar thermal power, and other promising technologies. In parallel, the government will probably sponsor infrastructure investments, such as transmission capacity for wind power, to enable broader integration of renewable sources into the grid.

Three Energy Challenges for the USA

Several important fault lines of debate about energy policy in the USA have emerged in the last few decades. These debates revolve around three energy challenges. The first focuses on making sure that the USA does not consume any more energy than it produces, making the country energy independent. The second emphasizes the reduction of greenhouse gas emissions to protect the global environment. The third relates to ensuring that the USA stays engaged in the global energy system, avoiding calls for energy isolationism. This section addresses each of these issues in turn.

Bridging the Gap between Energy Consumption and Domestic Production

The primary challenge for America's energy future is the impending requirement to bridge the gap between energy consumption and domestic production. The complicated and overlapping mix of policy actors who have a stake and role in setting US energy policy, and the bias towards using policy instruments that emphasize new sources of supply instead of reducing demand, suggests that projections foreseeing increased demand for energy are well founded. Consequently, in line with historical tradition, we can expect that US energy policies will be tuned towards meeting the increasing demand for energy with new supplies, rather than working to reduce that demand. Over the last 30 years, the USA has met its growing energy demand by increasing imports. The USA imported approximately 30 per cent of its energy in 2005, and the EIA now uses this reliance on imports in making its baseline projections.[26]

Energy consumption in the USA has historically grown year-on-year, due to population and economic growth, with most projections showing this increased consumption continuing unabated. However, projections are often wrong, and shifts in economic or environmental conditions can drastically affect energy demand. As the USA is relatively large (having a population of roughly 300 million people) with a per capita energy use larger than other industrialized nations (twice as high as in France or the UK), if energy consumption continues at its previous pace, the USA will remain the dominant energy consumer on the world stage for many years, despite the rapidly expanding economies and much larger populations in China and India.

However, while Americans continue to consume more imported energy, this option is becoming increasingly less popular. For example, a proposal to build a terminal to receive liquefied natural gas (LNG) in Long Beach, California, met very stiff local opposition from people who did not want the facility in their neighbourhood. It is a telling sign that all of the presidential candidates for both major political parties in the 2008 presidential elections pledged to make the USA independent of imported oil, with almost all of them proposing new biofuels sources – predominantly corn-based ethanol – as the solution. Notably, despite the emphasis on cutting imports, there is little discussion of ratcheting back per capita energy consumption.

If the USA does seek to reduce its imports, one question that emerges is how the country will tackle its growing energy consumption. Will it try to reduce its per capita energy use, bringing it more in line with what other highly industrialized nations consume, in order to avoid competition for resources, or will the USA seek to fulfil its need for energy from increased production of domestic supplies? While environmental groups have pushed for decades to reduce energy consumption, the current prevailing political sentiment indicates that conservation is not a top priority for the country.[27] More specifically, concerns have been voiced that conservation will become a drag on the economy. Consequently, the answer to this debate has remained for decades that new supplies will be bought, rather than demand lowered. However, as with any other market, expectations can change quickly due to prevailing economic conditions. For example, the economic downturn in 2008 and 2009 led to a decline in demand in a way that was not foreseen by most analysts. That is, even if society does not emphasize conservation through its policies, a depressed economy might effectively introduce conservation anyway.

However, the debate has now probably reached a turning point, as more groups are embracing conservation as the best option for the economy. For example, an analysis by the McKinsey Global Institute concluded that investments in energy efficiency and conservation would have significant economic benefits.[28] Also, some municipally-owned utilities, which do not have a financial incentive to increase consumption, have noted that the amount of money they need to invest to reduce energy consumption is significantly less than the amount of money that is needed to build new capacity.[29] Furthermore, these utilities are demonstrating that they are effective partners in assisting their customers to become more energy-efficient, illustrating one of the policy solutions under consideration nationwide: pursuing a process of 'decoupling' so that utilities no longer profit from excessive energy use by their customers.

Additionally, many Americans are becoming aware of the effects of climate change. Accordingly, they are pushing for energy solutions that will take into account environmental factors. For example, cities such as Austin and Portland are creating action plans to deal with resource depletion and the effects of climate change. Municipalities are creating green building programmes, states are establishing renewable portfolio standards (RPS), companies such as HP, General Motors, General Electric, and others, are actively touting their green credentials. Current or former elected officials, such as former Vice President Al Gore, Governor Arnold Schwarzenegger, and Mayor Michael Bloomberg, have seen their public approval ratings increase when discussing and pushing for stronger energy and environmental initiatives. Simultaneously, universities are creating energy research centres and degree programmes. All these factors combine to raise the overall exposure of Americans to energy issues, and are indicative of the growing attention to 'green' energy.

Consequently, the first obstacle to bridging the gap between domestic production and US energy consumption is public opinion, which is turning away from energy imports. Under current conditions, it seems more likely than ever that the USA will seek to reduce its per capita energy consumption. However, even if the resistance to imported energy continues and the USA chooses to turn away from energy imports, it will be difficult to increase domestic production sufficiently to make up the gap.

In the sphere of public opinion, a related problem is that, generally speaking, Americans do not know where their energy comes from, how large US reserves of oil and gas are, or which mix of fuels is used for electricity. For example, according to a 2007 survey conducted by Harris Interactive on behalf of the American Petroleum Institute, Americans do not have even basic knowledge about who the USA's main oil suppliers are.[30] A poll for the Consumer Federation of America showed that 'Most Americans are sorely misled when it comes to how much oil America controls.'[31] The consequence of this ignorance is that since many Americans believe that US oil reserves are larger than has been proved, they are likely to believe that the USA can meet its needs simply through increased production of conventional petroleum. Furthermore, because many Americans fail to recognize that the electricity grid and US petroleum consumption are mostly uncoupled from each other, they might wrongly believe that the USA can simply quit importing oil by building new nuclear power plants. This lack of awareness is an important impediment to change, and makes it difficult for the USA to implement a coherent energy policy.

A second obstacle is the restricted opportunity for increased oil and gas exploration and production in the USA, particularly in the outer continental shelf in the Gulf of Mexico. For example, despite recent policy manoeuvres by Congress and states, the future of off-shore drilling and exploration is unclear. Also, the Alaskan National Wildlife Refuge (ANWR) has not been opened for drilling, thereby demonstrating political resistance to increased domestic energy production. There are also constraints on ramping up domestic electricity production (through increased nuclear and renewable power generation, such as wind, solar, and geothermal) because of infrastructure constraints (e.g. the lack of transmission lines and suitable large-scale energy storage). In addition, liquid fuels such as coal-to-liquids, unconventional petroleum (e.g. oil shale), and biofuels (ethanol, biodiesel) all face resource or environmental constraints. While most of these possibilities are receiving increased budgets for R&D, some, such as geothermal energy research, had their R&D budgets zeroed out under the Bush administration. The others, while popular in the press and a hot topic among researchers, face serious political, environmental, or infrastructure constraints.

It is worth examining the situation in several specific cases. Installed nuclear capacity has been roughly level since the last power plant came online in 1995, but in 2008, while energy prices were high and before the economic crisis began, several companies took the first steps to file for permits to build new power plants in the USA, heralding what many have billed a 'nuclear renaissance'. Notably, some of the environmental resistance to nuclear power has subsided because of the realization that it is one way to decarbonize the energy mix in the USA. However, waste disposal, public safety, and proliferation concerns remain. Advanced generation III/III+ reactor designs are in process, but the most proliferation-resistant generation IV designs are still decades away from construction. Since the nuclear-trained workforce is aging, some consider that construction of new nuclear capacity is a critical step for reinvigorating this skilled labour pool. Also, since nuclear inspections worldwide require trained experts, the USA will need this labour pool in order to contribute to these international nuclear threat-reduction efforts. Within the security community, the issue of whether increased domestic nuclear power is, on balance, good for energy security – because it would displace imported LNG which would otherwise be required, is essentially carbon free, and would lead to a new generation of nuclear experts who could conduct nuclear inspections – or bad – because it would cause a cascading effect of increased nuclear energy worldwide, which has its own national security implications, is still being debated. Consequently, the concerns about nuclear power have not completely subsided, and it is not clear at this time whether the recent flurry of initial siting and permitting steps for nuclear power will lead to bringing new capacity online.

Renewable power is also receiving considerable attention as a possible solution. Installed renewable power capacity is increasing rapidly year-on-year, but since many renewable resources, such as solar and wind, are very land-intensive and located far from demand centres, their growth is limited by lack of suitable infrastructure, most notably of transmission capacity. This limitation is particularly relevant in Texas, which already has more wind power installed than any other state in the nation, at about 5,000 MW (and growing). Project developers would like to install another 15,000 to 20,000 MW of wind capacity, but are restricted by their inability to deliver this power to customers. Though the state of Texas is addressing this shortcoming, and has set up competitive renewable energy zones (CREZ) for building new transmission capacity, it will be several years before all that potential wind power can be brought on line. Unfortunately, this type of infrastructure limitation is duplicated throughout the USA. In addition, environmental constraints are slowing down the market penetration of some renewables. In other parts of the country, such as off the coast of Massachusetts, popular protests are holding back wind power installations because neighbours are concerned that the giant propellers will spoil the natural landscape.

For increased domestic liquid fuels production, several pathways are available. While coal-to-liquids (CTL) and oil shale have attracted much more scientific and industrial interest in recent years, the EIA projects that the penetration of CTL into the market is likely to be less than 6 billion gallons per year in 2030, with even less from shale.[32] The US Department of Defense is also pushing for increased CTL production for its aviation fuel needs, which might push production of this fuel beyond projections. The more appealing and popular route at this time is for ramped up biofuels production, which has been identified as a public policy priority by the US DOE because of the opportunity they provide to displace petroleum, and potentially reduce greenhouse gas emissions.[33] Biofuels production targets included in EISA 2007 are 36 billion gallons per year by 2022. For comparison, in 2007 the USA produced about 7.5 billion gallons of ethanol, and in 2005 the country consumed approximately 140 billion gallons of reformulated gasoline and 40 billion gallons of diesel.

Despite the optimism of these targets, several constraints can significantly delay or restrict biofuels production. The first is environmental, with limits on available land, water, and agricultural productivity to produce the corn currently used in making ethanol. The DOE estimates that the production of ethanol from corn through standard pathways is limited to approximately 13–18 billion gallons per year in the USA,[34] consequently the production of liquid or gaseous fuels using feedstocks other than starches will be necessary to avoid falling short of the targets noted above. Smartly, EISA 2007 reflects that limitation, capping the amount of allowable ethanol from corn at 15 billion gallons per year. However, alternative pathways are not yet economical under the existing market regimes, and significant work remains to be done. Additional restraints include a lack of infrastructure for large-scale biofuels production, distribution, and use, specifically for ethanol. As ethanol has about 30 per cent less energy content per volume than gasoline, larger amounts of liquid fuels will have to be produced and distributed than before unless fleetwide fuel economy improves. However, since ethanol cannot be shipped through existing standard pipelines, an entire dedicated distribution system will need to be built, at a cost of many tens of billions of dollars. In the meantime, distribution will continue by truck and rail, thereby limiting overall production, and in the process consuming diesel from traditional petroleum sources. These infrastructure and environmental constraints remain as a critical limitation to America's ability to reshape its energy future in a way that emphasizes domestic energy supplies.

Reducing greenhouse gas emissions from energy consumption

One of the biggest questions that has a widespread impact on the world's energy systems is whether the USA will make explicit efforts to reduce greenhouse gas emissions. Even though public opinion in the USA clearly believes that mankind is a significant contributor to global warming,[35] throughout most of President George W. Bush's administration, the USA resisted any efforts to reduce greenhouse gas emissions. As a result of Bush administration policies, the National Resource Defense Council (NRDC) sued the EPA for its failure to include controls of CO_2 emissions within its authority. Ultimately, the Supreme Court ruled against the EPA in April 2007. President Bush himself made many public statements that called into question the science behind claims that climate change is at least partly induced by mankind, but towards the end of his administration his position shifted to an approach more in line with scientific findings. Public statements in September 2007 included recognition that climate change is real, serious, and partly caused by anthropogenic activities. Though these acknowledgements represented a great rhetorical shift in President Bush's political position on climate change, he did nothing to act on his sentiments through the end of his term. Shortly after taking office, President Obama pledged to take swift and serious action on climate change, promising significant reductions in national emissions compared with 1990 levels. In particular, he supported a cap-and-trade scheme, similar to what was used to tackle acid rain in the 1990s.

As the USA has such significant coal reserves, it could address many energy security and price issues simply by ramping up electricity production from coal, and either coupling transportation systems to the grid (for example, through plug-in hybrid electric vehicles) or by creating a CTL programme for liquid fuels production. However, concerns about greenhouse gas emissions have largely removed the increased use of coal from consideration. In early 2007, citizens' groups, citing fears about damage to local air quality and additional global warming, blocked the proposed construction of more than a dozen coal plants designed to meet projected electricity needs in Texas. These environmental concerns will make it harder to build new coal facilities across the USA. In the end, efforts to reduce carbon output will probably push the USA towards the use of oil and gas, both of which are less carbon-intensive than coal, or towards widespread implementation of carbon-capture systems for coal plants. However, by increasing its demand for oil and gas, the USA will only be exacerbating the energy security issues that are already associated with those fuels. Solving the coal vs. oil vs. gas questions will be a key challenge for the USA to overcome.

Avoiding calls for energy isolationism

As the popular connection between energy and national security becomes more widespread, there is a risk that the USA will consider becoming an energy isolationist. This isolationism could take several forms, but essentially amounts to the USA embarking on a crash programme to increase domestic production of liquid fuels through biofuels, CTL, or oil shale. Potentially compounding this issue is the growing attention to climate change, which further emphasizes biofuels, whose carbon intake during feedstock photosynthesis reduces the overall carbon impact of fuel production. Politicians are responding to both of these sentiments with widespread pledges to 'get off foreign oil' and to increase production of corn-based ethanol. It is worth noting that every single president since Richard Nixon has pledged to reduce US reliance on foreign oil, only to see oil imports steadily grow year-on-year. Following on in this tradition, today's leaders also pledge to get off foreign oil, calling for ramped-up production of 'domestic' or 'home-grown' fuels such as corn-based ethanol. These calls are made partly to garner support from America's agricultural industry, which will benefit from these new policies, but also partly to play on the notion that buying oil enriches terrorists, whereas buying ethanol enriches middle-America's farmers. Leaders' rhetoric about the need to achieve energy independence, combined with political pandering to the Midwest in support of corn-based ethanol, has an air of energy isolationism, despite the fact that a great portion of US energy is imported from the USA's neighbours Canada and Mexico, neither of whom is classically described as a nation which is hostile to US interests.

The rise of energy isolationism would have consequences for the world, because it would signal even further estrangement from the international community. Also, more practically, US ingenuity is desired to increase oil and gas production in challenging fields, where more sophisticated techniques are required. Consequently, if the USA pulls back from engaging with the world on energy supply issues, it could potentially affect world energy production rates, and therefore affect energy supply reliability and prices.

The USA currently pursues some policies that promote isolationism. One prominent example is the 54 cents a gallon tariff on imported Brazilian ethanol designed to protect domestic ethanol production.

The USA in a Global Context

As this discussion has made clear, efforts to reduce per capita consumption and increase domestic production are not likely to meet future US energy needs. Consequently, the search for energy supplies will bring America into further interaction with the world. How will US efforts to meet its energy needs affect international politics? Much will depend on whether the USA decides to work on the supply or demand side of the problem. If the USA seeks to purchase more energy on international markets, it will probably come into conflict with other traditional consumers, such as the European Union and Japan, and new consumers like China and India who are also looking to increase their imports. On the other hand, if the USA focuses attention on reducing its enormous energy demand, it will probably create more opportunities for cooperation, as it can work with other countries in developing technologies that make such cooperation possible. Most likely, because of its enormous energy needs, the USA will make significant efforts on both the demand and supply sides. Accordingly, future US action will have cascading global consequences.

Energy supplies are likely to remain tight around the world, and it will be difficult for the USA to find new sources that do not create some kind of tension, as a variety of buyers jockey for advantage. Participating in the international energy system has historically served US interests well, providing sufficient energy supplies at acceptable prices. Buying energy on international markets in the future will not necessary reduce US energy security, and could even enhance it by building up a system of mutual interdependence, but the country faces a number of challenges. A survey of potential suppliers shows the range of these issues.

Canada is currently the top crude exporter to the USA. If it develops its oil sands reserves, it could potentially provide extensive new sources of energy to its southern neighbour. However, developing these sources will be an extremely dirty process, and environmental concerns may make it unmanageable.[36] US efforts to increase supplies from Latin America are also not straightforward. Mexico has been a major US supplier in the past, but its supplies are rapidly depleting. Another key supplier has been Venezuela, but Hugo Chavez has made life difficult for foreign companies working there, forcing them to hand over majority stakes in their projects to the NOC. In early 2008, the US company ExxonMobil won a judgment against Venezuela in a suit seeking to be compensated for two projects that had been nationalized.[37] Chavez has developed plans to increase output, but his country's production has in fact declined 25 per cent since he took office in 1999. Production is unlikely to increase while he continues to siphon money from Venezuela's state energy company to fund a variety of social projects at home and abroad. In order to increase energy imports from Brazil, the USA will have to remove its current tariff on Brazilian ethanol.

Russia is currently not a major energy supplier to the USA, but it has expressed interest in supplying the USA with LNG as part of its plans to expand production and to diversify its customer base, which is currently primarily focused on Europe. Russia could potentially supply the USA with LNG from its production sites on Sakhalin Island and the Shtokman field in the far north. Both of these projects will require extensive investment before they are developed sufficiently to provide substantial amounts of gas to the USA. In buying Russian energy, the USA would potentially strain its relations with Europe, which is deeply concerned about whether Russia will have enough energy to supply it.[38] In the case of Sakhalin, the USA would be competing with China and Japan, which are already actively seeking Russian energy sources and are in a tense standoff.

The USA also might be able to increase its supplies from the Middle East. According to IEA estimates, most of the increased energy output to 2030 will come from OPEC countries.[39] Growing US dependence on Middle Eastern energy supplies would be extremely unpopular at home, given popular perceptions that the region is politically unstable and reliant on vulnerable supply routes. In this context, Africa may prove to be a possible alternative. The USA already imports a substantial amount of energy produced in Nigeria and other African countries, and set up a military command for Africa on 6 February 2007 (currently based in Germany).[40] By 2015, the USA expects to increase its imports from the region to 25 per cent.[41] However, because China and India are also actively seeking energy supplies on the continent (China is particularly interested in West African crude because its high quality would make it easy for China's refineries to handle), many expect that increased US purchases there could provoke conflict or undesired competition that might bleed over into the diplomatic sphere. However, concerns of conflict are probably exaggerated, because African energy is going onto the world market, where it is available to both the USA and China.

Clearly, US efforts to increase its energy supplies will face enormous challenges. However, the more the USA focuses on reducing energy demand, the more opportunities there will be for stimulating international cooperation. The USA has a variety of possibilities in weighing its energy options. Among the most likely to increase US energy security and to address climate change problems are improving the efficiency of the US automobile fleet and of energy use in buildings, while developing alternative forms of energy, such as cellulosic ethanol, wind power, and solar.[42]

The USA can help itself and work with other countries by promoting technological change.[43] The USA is a leader in innovation, drawing on its strength as the world's largest market. Public policy interventions will be required to create the incentives to develop clean energy technology and to prepare public opinion to accept it. The US National Academy of Engineering is working on problems for the twenty-first century, and has identified 'making solar energy economical' one of the key problems that needs to be addressed.[44] To have the greatest impact, these technologies need to be used as widely as possible. Therefore the USA can work with developing countries like China to ensure that proven technologies are used in poorer countries as well as in the rich ones.[45] One way to make sure that this transfer takes place is to have a cooperative element in the technology development from the start.

Although they often see themselves as competitors, as the world's largest consuming countries, China and the USA have a common interest in collaborating in the development of new energy efficiency technologies and alternative sources. Lower energy prices in China make it possible for the country to continue producing and exporting relatively inexpensive products to the USA and Europe. Additionally, energy saved in China reduces the amount of pollution the country produces, some of which is already reaching the US west coast, and relieves pressure on the global demand for oil.[46] So far, US–Chinese cooperation is more of a hoped-for outcome than a practical reality. The relationship suffered a serious setback when the China National Offshore Oil Cooperation (CNOOC) tried to purchase the US oil company Unocal, but was rebuffed by US lawmakers on national security grounds. However, there is considerable hope among analysts on both sides that mutually beneficial efforts will move forward.[47] For example, there may be many opportunities for US businesses to work with Chinese companies to generate energy efficiency technology for use by Chinese firms in China. Much of the USA's extensive technological know-how can be put to use in China's rapidly evolving industry, which is hungry for innovative new ways to produce alternative sources of energy in an efficient and sustainable way. Likewise, the two countries are both major consumers of coal, and need to find ways to limit the impact of this fuel on the global environment.

While the USA proactively takes steps to improve the world's supply of energy, during the Bush administration it dragged its feet on addressing climate change and conservation. The environmental impact of US energy usage, particularly greenhouse gas emissions, has brought the USA into conflict with the rest of the world. The USA refused to ratify the Kyoto accord, refusing to accept limits on its greenhouse gas production, fearing that such constraints would hurt the US business community, and the Bush administration did not play a constructive role at subsequent international climate change meetings. In contrast to the European Union, the USA has not imposed tough environmental and energy standards on itself. Barack Obama has promised that his administration will devote more effort to these issues.

With the recent trend in the USA towards tackling the climate crisis, and new leadership in the White House, an opportunity exists for international cooperation to address critical technological barriers blocking reductions in greenhouse gas emissions. These opportunities include research for carbon capture and sequestration, large-scale energy storage capability for the integration of intermittent sources such as wind and solar into the grid, energy efficiency technologies, and breakthrough scientific research on materials and other enabling disciplines. While it is not clear whether the USA will pursue this path, doing so could produce significant economic benefits from the proliferation of technologies that are suited to improving energy security and to addressing the environmental impacts of energy. There is a variety of ways in which the USA can engage in international cooperation in this arena. At the governmental level, countries can exchange information on best practices and policies toward stimulating greater efficiency. At the corporate level, firms that have developed effective efficiency techniques should be encouraged to spread these techniques as widely, and as rapidly, as possible.

Conclusion

As the world's largest overall energy consumer, and one of the largest energy producers, the USA is a key player for determining the evolution of producer–consumer relations and global energy security in the coming years. In the past, the USA has sought to find new sources of energy supplies to meet its voracious and rapidly increasing demand. Now the USA is at a potential turning point, when it could adopt a new energy strategy focused on reducing its overall energy demand and increasing its energy efficiency. If this change happens, the USA would probably emerge as a powerful partner and potential leader of the transition to a new energy era.

The chances for such a change taking place will depend on the political balance favouring and opposing such a development. There are now strong pressures for a new energy policy and practices in the USA. With relatively high energy prices, concerns about national security and terrorism, a growing awareness of the problems caused by climate change, and expanding interest in taking ameliorative action, public opinion increasingly supports newer, cleaner energy sources and technologies. As a result, prominent politicians are boldly pledging changes in US energy policies.

At the same time, there are obstacles to implementing such changes. Reducing US dependence on fossil fuels and switching to new sources of energy will require extensive investment. Many powerful vested interests have a stake in maintaining the old system. The USA also boasts the world's largest coal reserves, and many would like to see further use of this resource. While there are numerous promising technologies on the horizon, none is close to presenting a realistic alternative to petroleum. Entrepreneurs and innovators still have a long way to go before they can make serious inroads into US energy use patterns. It will take years before new energy sources and energy technologies will be widely integrated.

How the USA defines its energy policy moving forward will ultimately depend on the confluence of political, economic, environmental, and technological factors and how they are manipulated by politicians, entrepreneurs, corporate lobbyists, and the general public, particularly in the way that it consumes energy. Energy policies are made over the long term, and it is impossible for decision-makers today to know what the conditions in the future will be when defining their policies. For example, there are enormous uncertainties about the future price of oil. Likewise, the rate of technological innovation is unpredictable, and unanticipated discoveries could quickly change the viability of alternative energy and efficiency technologies. Similarly, there is no certainty in the pace of climate change. Growing evidence that climate change is speeding up could greatly affect the way decisions are made. The US population appears to be in the middle of an attitude shift, with growing support for reducing energy demand. That shift will probably be the biggest driver of new policies.

If the USA makes a serious effort to reduce its use of energy in the future, its shrinking need for energy imports will have a powerful impact on producer–consumer relations. The USA will largely benefit from decreased reliance on outside suppliers. However, less US consumption will undermine the producers' security of demand. While producers will probably be able to find new customers for their fossil fuel exports in Asia to replace lost sales in the USA, they will eventually need to find ways of diversifying their economies away from a heavy reliance on energy sales. Accordingly, they will have a strong interest in expanding technological cooperation with the USA and Europe, and in finding new ways to engage with the international trading system.

Notes

1   USDOE, *Annual Energy Outlook 2007: With Projections to 2030*, U.S. Department of Energy, Energy Information Administration, Washington, 2007.

2   J. Goldemberg, 'Ethanol for a Sustainable Energy Future', *Science*, 2007, 315.

3   J. Goldemberg, 'Ethanol for a Sustainable Energy Future', *Science*, 2007, 315.

4   USDOE, *August 2007 International Petroleum Monthly*, U.S. Department of Energy, Energy Information Administration, Washington, 2007.

5   USDOE, *International Energy Annual 2006*, U.S. Department of Energy, Energy Information Administration, Washington, 2006.

6   USDOE, *International Energy Annual 2005*, U.S. Department of Energy, Energy Information Administration, Washington, 2005.

7   British Petroleum, *BP Statistical Review of World Energy*, 2007.

8   *Energy Policy Act of 2005*, One Hundred Ninth Congress of the United States of America, 2005 and *Energy Independence and Security Act of 2007, Public Law 110–140*, 19 December 2007.

9   USDOE, *Annual Energy Outlook 2007: With Projections to 2030*, U.S. Department of Energy, Energy Information Administration, Washington, 2007.

10 Consumer Federation of America (CFA), *Americans Alarmed About Dependence on Oil Imports and Resulting High Gas Prices and Funding of Terrorism,*: Consumer Federation of America, Washington, 2007, and '71% Say Finding New Energy Sources More Important than Conservation', *Rasmussen Reports*, 2006.

11 '71% Say Finding New Energy Sources More Important than Conservation', *Rasmussen Reports*, 2006.

12 Consumer Federation of America (CFA), *Americans Alarmed About Dependence on Oil Imports and Resulting High Gas Prices and Funding of Terrorism*, Consumer Federation of America, Washington, 2007.

13 EPACT 2005 was mostly a series of authorizations for expenditures and tax incentives for various forms of energy production and alternative supplies, and did not directly tackle questions of robustness in the energy infrastructure, environmental impacts, or greenhouse gas emissions.

14 Examples include the Synfuels Corporation in the early 1980s, and the more recent FutureGen efforts for hydrogen and power production from coal using integrated gasification combined-cycle (IGCC) along with carbon sequestration.

15 According to the report on energy R&D by the National Academies 2001, federal R&D for energy exceeded $90 billion from 1978 to 1999 (in constant 2000 dollars). Combining that total with approximately $2 billion in annual R&D investments by the DOE since then through 2007 creates a total in excess of $100 billion.

16 Committee on Benefits of DOE R&D on Energy Efficiency and Fossil Energy, Board on Energy and Environmental Systems, Division on Engineering and Physical Sciences, National Research Council, *Energy Research at DOE: Was It Worth It? Energy Efficiency and Fossil Energy Research 1978 to 2000*, National Academy Press, Washington DC, 2001.

17 D. M. Kammen and G.F. Nemet, 'Reversing the Incredible Shrinking Energy R&D Budget', *Issues in Science and Technology*, Fall 2005.

18 D. M. Kammen and G.F. Nemet, 'Reversing the Incredible Shrinking Energy R&D Budget', *Issues in Science and Technology*, Fall 2005.

19 Committee on Benefits of DOE R&D on Energy Efficiency and Fossil Energy, Board on Energy and Environmental Systems, Division on Engineering and Physical Sciences, National Research Council, *Energy Research at DOE: Was It Worth It? Energy Efficiency and Fossil Energy Research 1978 to 2000*, National Academy Press, Washington DC, 2001 and comments by K. S. Gallagher, Director, Energy Technology Innovation Project, Belfer Center for Science and International Affairs, Cambridge, MA, 2007.

20 '71% Say Finding New Energy Sources More Important than Conservation', *Rasmussen Reports*, 2006.

21 Comments by K. S. Gallagher, Director, Energy Technology Innovation Project, Belfer Center for Science and International Affairs, Cambridge, MA, 2007.

22 M. Tarbet, *Cost and Weight Added by the Federal Motor Vehicle Safety Standards for Model years 1968–2001 in Passenger Cars and Light Trucks*, National Highway Traffic Safety Administration, Washington, December 2004.

23 P. Ostendorp, S. Foster, and C. Calwell, *Televisions: Active Mode Energy Use and Opportunities for Energy Savings*, National Resources Defense Council, Washington, 2005.

24 USDOE, *Annual Energy Outlook 2007: With Projections to 2030*, U.S. Department of Energy, Energy Information Administration, Washington, 2007, and EIA, *Monthly Energy Review: September 2007*, EIA, Washington, 2007.

25 Press Briefing by Ari Fleischer, Office of the Press Secretary for President George W. Bush, 7 May 2001 and M. Kettle, 'Cheney promises big US nuclear power expansion', *The Guardian*, 2 May 2001.

26 USDOE, *Annual Energy Outlook 2007: With Projections to 2030*, U.S. Department of Energy, Energy Information Administration, Washington, 2007.

27 Press Briefing by Ari Fleischer, Office of the Press Secretary for President George W. Bush, 7 May 2001 and M. Kettle, 'Cheney promises big US nuclear power expansion', *The Guardian*, 2 May 2001.

28 F. Bressand et al., *Wasted Energy: How the US Can Reach its Energy Productivity Potential*, McKinsey Global Institute, 2007.

29 AustinEnergy, *Energy Plus: Austin-Energy Customer News, December 2007*, Austin, Texas, 2007.

30 *Energy IQ Survey*, Harris Interactive, Reston, VA, 2007.

31 Consumer Federation of America (CFA), *Americans Alarmed About Dependence on Oil Imports and Resulting High Gas Prices and Funding of Terrorism*, Consumer Federation of America, Washington, 2007 and '71% Say Finding New Energy Sources More Important than Conservation', *Rasmussen Reports*, 2006.

32 USDOE, *Annual Energy Outlook 2007: With Projections to 2030*, U.S. Department of Energy, Energy Information Administration, Washington, 2007.

33 USDOE, *Biomass as Feedstock for a Bioenergy and Bioproducts Industry: The Technical Feasibility of a Billion-Ton Annual Supply*, Department of Energy and Department of Agriculture, Washington, 2005 and USDOE, *Multi-Year*

Program Plan--Biomass and Biorefinery Systems R&D: 2007–2012, Department of Energy, Washington, 2005.

34 USDOE, *Annual Energy Outlook 2007: With Projections to 2030*, U.S. Department of Energy, Energy Information Administration, Washington, 2007; USDOE, *Multi-Year Program Plan--Biomass and Biorefinery Systems R&D: 2007–2012*, Department of Energy, Washington, 2005; National Corn Growers' Association, *How Much Ethanol Can Come From Corn?*, National Corn Growers' Association, Washington, 2007; and K. Morgan 'Ethanol demand prompts corn growers', *The Tribune*, Greeley, CO., 29 April 2007.

35 BBC, *All Countries Need to Take Major Steps on Climate Change: Global Poll*, BBC World Service Poll, London 2007.

36 Elizabeth Kolbert, 'Unconventional Crude', *The New Yorker*, 12 November 2007.

37 Peter Wilson, 'Venezuela Bites Back at ExxonMobil', *Business Week*, 8 February, 2008.

38 Philip Hanson, 'The Sustainability of Russia's Energy Power: Implications for the Russian Economy', in Jeronim Perovic, Robert Orttung, and Andreas Wenger, eds, *Dealing with an Assertive Russia: Power, Perceptions, and the Role of Energy*, Routledge, London, 2009.

39 International Energy Agency, *World Energy Outlook 2007*, IEA, Paris 2007, 43.

40 http://www.africom.mil/AboutAFRICOM.asp

41 See chapter on Africa in this volume by Monica Enfield.

42 Jeffrey Logan and John Venezia, 'Weighing U.S. Energy Options: The WRI Bubble Chart', *WRI Policy Note*, July 2007. http://pdf.wri.org/weighing_energy_options.pdf

43 See the discussion in David Sandalow, *Freedom from Oil: How the Next President Can End the United States' Oil Addiction*, McGraw Hill, New York, 2008, 169.

44 'Make Solar Energy Economical'. www.engineeringchallenges.org/cms/8996/9082.aspx

45 Jeffrey Sachs, 'Technological Cooperation', Policy Innovations: The Central Address for a Fairer Globalization, 4 March 2008. www.policyinnovations.org/ideas/commentary/data/000041

46 Zha Daojiong and Hu Weixing, 'Promoting Energy Partnership in Beijing and Washington', *The Washington Quarterly*, 30:4, 112–3.

47 Hongtu Zhao, 'Some Thoughts on Sino–U.S. Energy Cooperation', in Greg Austin and Marie-Ange Schellekens-Gaiffe, eds., *Energy and Conflict Prevention*, Gidlunds Forlag, Hedemora, 2007, 88–107.

CHAPTER 9

ENERGY CHALLENGES FOR EUROPE

John Roberts

The 27 countries that collectively make up the European Union (EU) are the third largest energy consumer in the world, following the USA and China. Although energy demand in Europe is shrinking, the continent's limited natural resource reserves are disappearing even more quickly. As a result, Europeans face a future in which they will increasingly have to rely on energy imports. The security of European energy supplies is now at the top of the continent's policy agenda.

The key energy concern for European consumers is natural gas, and that means Russia is a focus of attention. Russia supplies a significant part of European gas needs through pipelines that connect the continent to Siberian sources. While fears that Russia may try to use its energy resources as a weapon have haunted some Europeans, a greater concern is that Russia will not make sufficient investments in developing new fields, making it unable to meet Europe's growing demand for imported gas.

At the same time, the EU has ambitious goals for protecting the global environment, increasing its own energy efficiency, and developing alternative sources of energy. Scientific studies have demonstrated that increased use of fossil fuels, including such 'clean' sources as natural gas, is having a strongly negative impact on the environment. Therefore Europe has committed itself to dramatically reducing its use of fossil fuel energy resources, and developing alternative supplies, preferably those that can be generated domestically.

However, while a transition away from fossil fuels may ultimately ensure Europe's energy security, such a move would have a deleterious impact on producers such as Russia. If Europe slowly weaned itself off Russian energy resources over the long term, Russia would lose much of the considerable income it now derives from energy sales to the West. Ultimately, while Europe is worried about its security of supplies, Russia is concerned about security of demand.

This chapter proceeds by first presenting the energy situation in the EU. It then examines the key issues facing Europe on the supply side. Ensuring security of supply means building relationships with Russia,

Europe's most important provider, as well as diversifying away from Russia to find other sources. The chapter then looks at the challenges on the demand side. Europe needs to coordinate its policies so that it can effectively increase energy efficiency and develop new sources of energy, such as solar and wind power, to reduce demand for oil, gas, and coal. Next, the implications for Europe's foreign energy policy of meeting these challenges are presented, particularly the options for building the relationship with Russia. The chapter concludes by looking at efforts to balance supply security with Russia's need for demand security.

Europe's Energy Situation

The EU is one of the world's largest energy consumers. It was responsible for 15.7 per cent of the world's primary energy consumption in 2007.[1] By comparison, the USA consumed 21.3 per cent and China consumed 16.8 per cent. The next largest energy users were Japan and India, which consumed 4.7 per cent and 3.6 per cent respectively. Even though Europe is more energy-efficient than either the USA or China, its high standard of living absorbs a large share of the world's energy output.

Within each of the specific types of energy, Europe also ranks highly. In 2007 Europe made up 17.8 per cent of global oil consumption, trailing only the USA, which used 23.9 per cent, but using much more than China (9.3). Europe accounted for 16.4 per cent of global natural gas usage (22.6 for the USA and 2.3 for China) and burned 10.0 per cent of coal (18.1 for the USA and 41.3 for China). Europe is the global leader in the nuclear field, consuming 34.0 per cent of global production, compared with 30.9 per cent in the USA, 10.1 per cent in Japan, and 5.8 per cent in Russia.

Fossil fuels still make up the overwhelming majority in Europe's energy mix. In 2006, oil dominated European energy consumption, comprising 37 per cent of overall energy use. This figure is just above the global average of 36 per cent, but below the USA's 40 per cent and Japan's 48 per cent. Natural gas makes up 24 per cent of European energy consumption, exactly the global average. With its heavy reliance on oil and gas, Europe consumes less coal than other parts of the world. Solid fuels, including coal and biomass, comprise 18 per cent of overall consumption, at a time when the world relied on coal for about 28 per cent of its energy. Thanks to large investments since the 1970s, Europe has an extensive nuclear energy infrastructure, which makes up 14 per cent of overall energy consumption, compared to

6 per cent globally. Renewables comprised just 7 per cent of energy consumption in 2006.[2]

Europe is working hard to make its energy mix even more environmentally friendly. In comparison to the 1990s, the consumption of oil dropped by 1 per cent in the overall mix, while the share of gas and nuclear increased by 6 and 2 points respectively. The use of natural gas is growing rapidly as the continent moves away from coal. Accordingly, the share of solid fuels, which tend to have a strongly negative impact on the environment, shrank considerably, dropping by 10 points. Nevertheless, the share of renewables remains small (7 per cent) although it has grown 3 points since 2000. The EU has set an ambitious goal of bringing this figure up to 20 per cent by 2020. The individual countries within the EU have different energy usage mixes, depending on their local resources and past choices about whether to build nuclear plants.

Despite its comparatively high consumption rate, the EU is making efforts to reduce its overall need for energy. Energy consumption in the EU declined by 2.2 per cent in 2007, while it increased by 1.7 per cent in the USA, 7.7 per cent in China, 6.8 per cent in India, although it dropped by 0.9 per cent in Japan. Europe's oil consumption fell by 2.6 per cent and its natural gas consumption by 1.6 per cent in 2007. This shrinking energy use both reflects the improving energy intensity of the European economy as EU members use energy more efficiently, and the relatively slow growth of the economy. Long term projections (to 2020) of energy use depend on how effectively Europe is able to implement its plans to increase efficiency and expand the use of renewable energy sources. According to baseline assumptions, Europe's energy needs would grow 5 to 9 per cent by 2020, depending on oil prices. If the EU is able to implement its current plans, energy consumption in 2020 could be 6–8 per cent less than current consumption.[3]

Despite its declining energy consumption, Europe's need for imports is expected to grow. The continent has very few fossil fuel deposits of its own, and those are dwindling quickly. The EU member states possess only 0.6 of the world's proven oil reserves and 2.0 per cent of natural gas reserves.[4] The EU imported 54 per cent of its energy in 2006.[5] Since indigenous fossil fuel production is shrinking, the EU expects to import more energy moving forward. The *European Energy Outlook to 2020* predicted that Europe would import two-thirds of its energy by 2020, including up to 75 per cent of its natural gas.

Oil makes up the vast majority of EU energy imports, totalling 60 per cent of overall imports. Gas (26%) and solid fuels (13%) follow, with electricity and renewable energy making up less than 1 per cent.

The EU produces less than one-fifth of the oil that it consumes. Oil imports come from OPEC countries (38%), Russia (33%), Norway (16%), and Kazakhstan (5%). Europe currently faces a slightly better situation with natural gas, because it is able to produce two-fifths of what it needs. The imports come from Russia (42%), Norway (24%), Algeria (18%), and Nigeria (5%).

Key Challenges on the Supply Side

While the EU's overall energy use is shrinking, the rapid decline in its domestic production of fossil fuels means it is increasingly dependent on imported supplies. As the continent moves to cleaner fuels, it is increasingly relying on natural gas. Accordingly, the main concern for Europe's energy supplies is Russia, the largest supplier of natural gas. The following section describes the nature of these concerns.

Europe's indigenous production of oil and gas is dropping much faster than its energy consumption. The EU's production of natural gas declined by 6.4 per cent in 2007, even as global gas production rose by 2.4 per cent. The EU's gas production has been declining since 2001. Similarly, oil production dropped by 0.9 per cent in 2007 and has been declining since 1999. Over the long term, the EU is expecting an increasing reliance on outside sources of energy.

Most experts expect that Europe will face more difficulty in securing reliable supplies of natural gas than oil. That is because oil is an essentially fungible commodity that is widely available from a variety of sources on the international market. Gas, particularly pipeline gas, is still largely a bilateral issue in which long-term agreements and non-interruptability of supply are crucial. (If oil from one source is reduced or halted for any reason, the impact is much less significant than if a similar amount of gas were to be cut off for all sorts of reasons, including multiplicity of supply, storage, flexibility of delivery mechanisms, and flexibility of usage.) Gas is thus an issue that concerns both the terms and conditions of actual supply arrangements, and the terms and conditions of third country transit for some current or prospective suppliers to the EU.

Since Russia is Europe's key supplier of natural gas, Europe faces a number of concerns in assuring reliable supplies from its eastern neighbour. Establishing a productive dialogue with Russia is the toughest element of the European Council's Energy Policy for Europe. The EU wants – and needs – to develop a partnership with Russia concerning energy supplies. The underlying logic is – or should be – undeniable.

The EU is the world's biggest gas importer, and Russia is the world's biggest gas exporter. In practice, developing a stable relationship has been difficult. Russia's decision to shut off gas supplies to Ukraine, the transit country responsible for moving 80 per cent of Russian gas shipments to Europe, at the beginning of 2006 and again in 2009 raised serious concerns in European minds about Russia's reliability.

Dealing with Russia

The problem of how to develop a partnership between the EU and Russia relates to the current asymmetrical relationship between the two sides. This asymmetry goes to the heart of the problem, both in terms of Russia's own energy supplies to the EU, and in terms of its role as a transit country for Central Asian energy producers. The most obvious asymmetry is that while the EU is endeavouring to create a single open-access market in energy, Russia can scarcely be said to operate any kind of internal market. At least four key factors differentiate Russia from the EU in this regard:

- Integration of state and company.
- Different attitudes to prices.
- Different attitudes to investment.
- Transparency.

Integration of state and company.

In dealing with Gazprom, EU companies, are, in effect, dealing with the Russian state. Gazprom CEO Aleksei Miller reportedly saw President Putin three times a week at times during Putin's second term. Accordingly, there is a fundamental asymmetry in terms of negotiating powers, since most negotiations over both gas purchases and investment opportunities have, on the one side, individual EU member states or companies and, on the other, an integrated state-owned and state-backed giant called Gazprom.[6]

This situation raises the question of whether the EU needs to speak with a single voice when its companies engage in commercial negotiations with Gazprom for deliveries of Russian gas, or for access to investment opportunities in upstream Russian hydrocarbons development. Does the EU, in sum, need to confront a state-controlled monopoly with a state-backed monopsony?

In addressing this question, the EU Council on 23–24 March 2006 urged 'developing a common voice in support of energy policy objectives when addressing third countries fostering a more cooperative approach regarding access to energy resources, stability in transit and producer countries, and energy security'.[7] Likewise, the EU's Green Paper called for EU member states to speak 'with a single voice'.[8] This raises the question of whether speaking with a single voice is sufficient, or whether such negotiations, to prove effective (and to avoid individual EU member states or companies being picked off one-by-one) require a single EU negotiating team. Also, if a single EU negotiating team is considered appropriate, does this then mean that it should consist of representatives from both the private and public sectors, in order to match Russia's merging of state and corporate activities? In this regard, perhaps the EU should recall that its member states operate neither total capitalist nor total state-run economies but actually run – and favour – the mixed economy. For the EU, in dealing with an integrated Russian state–Gazprom team, the response may have to include an integrated public–private negotiating team. Putting together such a team would be difficult, but perhaps essential if the EU is truly to speak with a single voice.

The EU is unlikely to develop a coherent policy on obtaining secure energy supplies any time soon. Europe has a difficult time in defining a coherent, common energy policy because the energy situations of the individual member countries vary considerably. Denmark is the only country that is self-sufficient in terms of energy supplies, while Poland and the United Kingdom import only around 20 per cent of their energy. In contrast, Ireland, Italy, Portugal, and Spain must import approximately 80 per cent of their energy. The situation also varies in terms of dependence on one supplier for specific types of fuel. Estonia, Latvia, Lithuania, Bulgaria, Slovakia, Ireland, Sweden, and Finland all rely on Russia for 100 per cent of their natural gas supplies, while Greece, Hungary, and Austria are more than 80 per cent dependent on the same supplier.[9] Some of the EU countries farther west purchase little Russian gas and therefore are not vulnerable to Kremlin pressure in the same way. While it is desirable for European countries to work together in their relations with Russia, there are many reasons why they do not do that.

Different Attitudes on Prices.
As Russia continues to provide price subsidies for its domestic customers, it has less gas to export. Russia has said that it understands the need to introduce market principles into domestic gas pricing, but these are likely to take a long time to implement. Following decisions taken between 2003 and 2004, the Russian Government is committed to raising domestic gas prices to $125/tcm by 2011. When Russia committed itself to almost tripling domestic prices, from levels around

of $40–50, increases on such a scale appeared very significant indeed. Since 2003, gas prices have risen considerably, and they remain highly volatile. There is little evidence that price increases to date have had an impact on domestic demand. The increase in Russian consumption between 2003 and 2008 has far exceeded the increase in production in percentage terms, and has almost kept pace with it in terms of absolute volumes. The result is that Russia has scarcely any more gas available for export in 2008 than it had in 2003. Meanwhile, prices paid by mainstream European importers for Russian gas rose to more than $350/tcm in 2008, and then began to drop in the face of the global crisis. It does not look likely that, once reached in 2011, a price level of $125/tcm will have a significant impact on Russian domestic demand. Judging by highly preliminary indications from price increases in Ukraine in 2007–8, an increase to closer to $200/tcm may be required for price elasticity to start reining in consumption.

To the outsider, reared on conventional market economics, high external prices constitute an excellent reason why Russian domestic prices should be steadily liberalized, since this would rationalize Russian consumption, thus boosting export availabilities. To the Russian government, working on a more immediate political rationale, the conclusion might be somewhat different. Subsidies in general, and low domestic gas prices in particular, may seem to the Government to be the easiest way of proving to the Russian people that their government cares about them: 'Look how high prices are abroad – and look how little it costs you!'

Different Attitudes Towards Investment.
During the period 2000–8, President Putin essentially presided over an economy which placed immediate benefits over long-term income maximization. The goal was reaping the spoils, not developing the common wealth, with lack of sufficient investment in gas production not seeming to worry the Kremlin overmuch. During the Putin era, it was reasonable to infer that Russia was seeking to regard European attitudes to gas in much the same way as many OPEC producers regard European attitudes to oil: the customers may grumble about higher prices and protest that investment in production capacity is failing to keep pace with demand, but the bottom line is that they will continue to pay higher prices. Thus, the producer countries win, in the sense that their investments are restricted, yet their revenues grow.

This model is quite capable of lasting for several years, but when it breaks, the fall out will be substantial. The question that Europe has to ask itself is whether it wishes to prevent this approach from becoming the standard model for gas – in effect, by reaching some kind of grand agreement with Russia that provides for extensive external investment in Russian gas production – or whether it will have to prepare itself for a world of low gas investment by Russia, persistently high prices for gas, and thus a need to enforce greater efficiency in the use of energy in general and gas in particular. Given the current global energy balance, in oil as in gas, it would be prudent for the EU to adopt the latter course by increasing efficiency.

A key issue in this regard is that Russia does not appear to understand its own investment requirements. Russia's current energy taxation structure ensures that there is little reason for Russian energy companies to invest in their own industry, other than under compulsion from the state. In 2002, the International Energy Agency (IEA) estimated that Russia's gas industry required investment of some \$161 bn–\$171 bn in the 18-year period to 2020, and that oil investment requirements would fall between \$157 bn and \$197 bn during the same period. On the assumption that both oil and gas require investment rates of around \$9 bn–\$10 bn a year, this means they each require around 1.5 per cent of GDP in fresh investment.[10] Russia's own national energy strategy likewise postulates an investment requirement of between \$170 bn and \$200 bn for the period 2003 to 2020, with specific investment levels ranging from \$9.4 bn to \$11.1 bn a year. In contrast, the EU considers that Russia's overall energy investment needs to be much greater than this. Between 2003 and 2030, the EU has estimated that Russia will need to invest no less than \$735 bn, an average of \$27.2 bn a year. Yet Russia's entire GDP in 2004 stood at just \$598 bn. By comparison, the EU's totalled \$11,650 bn.

Unfortunately, as noted in the chapter on Russia in this volume, Gazprom has devoted a considerable share of its investment to purchasing distribution pipelines rather than in increasing actual production. Thus by 2006, when Gazprom was spending as much as €6 bn (\$9 bn) a year on purchasing assets outside the gas sector[11], the IEA was in a far more pessimistic frame of mind, anticipating actual declines in Russian output of as much as 20 bcm a year.[12]

In light of EU estimates of Russia's overall energy investment requirements, and because of the implications that an attack of Dutch disease might have on the Russian economy, further studies are necessary in this regard. One problem in EU–Russian relations is that words may have different meanings in different locations, and this might well apply to terms concerning investment. Overall, most external analysts continue to believe that Russia faces serious internal energy investment problems, despite high oil and gas prices.

The EU's approach to the investment issue is commonly associated with the concept of reciprocity, with openings that would enable EU energy companies to invest in Russia's upstream balanced by openings for Russian companies in European downstream, distribution, and sales. However, genuine reciprocity will be difficult to secure, given the current asymmetry between the EU and Russia. Moreover, there are serious issues concerning how the two sides view reciprocity. Thus Katinka Barysch argues:

> The trouble is that Europeans and Russians mean completely different things when they talk about reciprocity. The EU wants a mutually-agreed legal framework to facilitate two-way investment. The Kremlin wants asset swaps. Europe wants openness, Russia wants control.[13]

From this perspective, the danger is that instead of liberalizing Russian markets, the EU might find itself rendering its own liberalized markets more vulnerable to external monopolistic predators. However, this issue is now being addressed by the EU, and may be on the way to resolution. In 2007, the EU Commission drew up plans to force companies to separate energy production, transmission, and distribution. Although aimed at European monopolies, such as E.ON Ruhrgas and Wintershall in Germany, Gaz de France, and Eni of Italy, the plans would severely limit Gazprom's ability to operate within Europe. The European energy companies have fiercely opposed this idea, and Brussels has not been able to move forward.

Overall, resolving the issue of how EU companies can secure – or maintain – investment positions in major Russian energy projects will require close cooperation between the EU, member state governments, and EU companies. In terms of EU corporate investment in Russia, EU-based companies, at the very least, might need to know that, they can count on EU and/or EU member government support for their activities in Russia. True reciprocity would allow EU companies operating in Russia to offer real competition to current monopolies. It would also enable companies such as TNK–BP to augment their existing right to develop hydrocarbon resources in Russia with rights to develop export systems of their own to get the oil and gas they produce to market, or else to be able to access, particularly in the case of gas, the Gazprom network to effect exports to China – or anywhere else. Whether this is feasible is far from certain and will clearly depend on how much Russia's president, former Gazprom Vice-Chairman Dmitri Medvedev, is his own man. One of the defining energy acts of the last year of the Putin administration was, after all, the double assault on TNK–BP, first of all preventing it from developing the giant Kovytka gas deposit, and then renewing assaults on its officials for alleged visa irregularities and back taxes.

Transparency

Gas deals generally require long-term take-or-pay agreements, which often include greater or lesser degrees of government-to-government commitments. With regard to Russian gas sales to some EU purchasers, these deals have not always been fully transparent. There may be requirements for payments to be made to third parties as part of the conditions of sale, raising serious questions concerning corruption. Gazprom's opaque relations with such ventures as Itera, EuralTransGas, and RosUkrEnergo are particularly worrisome in this context. Indeed the Moscow-based Hermitage Capital Management has argued that both Gazprom and Transneft, the Russian oil pipeline monopoly, are essentially corrupt organizations.[14] The role played by intermediaries was a significant factor in Russia's decision to shut off gas supplies to Ukraine in both 2006 and 2009. The resolution of the 2009 crisis seems at least to have reduced the role of RosUkrEnergo in the bilateral energy relationship.[15]

Diversifying Supplies away from Russia

Since dealing with Russia is fraught with uncertainty, Europe would like to hedge its bets by developing alternative sources. In order to diversify supplies of natural gas away from Russia, the European Council has recommended that 'New gas supply routes should be opened up in particular from the Caspian region and North Africa.'[16] If Iran is able to address the issues surrounding its desire to build a nuclear power plant to the West's satisfaction, it could also serve as a supplier to Europe.

North Africa:

With regard to North Africa, little needs to be said, or, at least by the EU and its executive arms, done. Three lines – two from Algeria and one from Libya – have already been built; two more are under construction, and a line from Egypt to Syria and Lebanon, and for which the Turkish authorities are currently negotiating an extension to southern Turkey, has already reached the central Syrian city of Homs. There may be a need for further lines, including a possible overland pipe from Nigeria to Algeria, but these are not immediate priorities, since normal commercial expansions should prove sufficient to bolster supplies of North African energy for the next decade or so. The bottom line here is that the EU is not required to broker new agreements, as is the case with Russia or Central Asia; it need only voice continuing support for expansion of lines from North Africa. Development of new lines to and through North Africa, such as the proposed Nigeria–Algeria line, might require EU support, not least in terms of ensuring that they aid the development of transit countries and, indeed, of communities in both producer and transit countries affected by the pipeline. This, of course, is part of the much larger question of the attitude shown by corporations towards development issues in host nations and host communities.

Caspian:

All the Caspian countries – Azerbaijan, Kazakhstan, Iran, Russia, Turkmenistan, and nearby double-landlocked Uzbekistan – contain significant gas reserves. Russian gas reserves reach the EU directly; Iranian gas is already exported to Turkey by direct pipeline and, from December 2006 onwards, Azerbaijani gas began reaching Turkey by means of the South Caucasus Pipeline (SCP).

The issue of augmenting gas supplies from the Caspian essentially falls into four parts.

- Physical interconnectors between Turkey and the EU, combined with expansion of Turkey's main East–West gas trunkline.
- Suppliers for EU diversification routes.
- New connections from Central Asian producers to existing pipelines or pipeline corridors reaching Turkey or other Black Sea states with onward pipeline connections to the EU.
- Resolution of the Iranian issue.

Physical interconnectors between Turkey and the EU

For both Azerbaijan and Iran, onward connections to EU markets are very much in prospect, with physical construction of a pipeline from Turkey to Greece under way (the first stage of a planned Turkey–Greece–Italy interconnector) and advanced preparations for a gasline from Turkey to Austria (the Nabucco project).

The EU has long backed the Turkey–Greece interconnector (TGI), and little more needs to be done in terms of either moral or financial support. The line from Turkey to Greece has already been built and is operational, whilst the onward connection from Greece to Italy is on the verge of physical construction. Development of both projects may also be facilitated by implementation of the EU–World Bank plans for a West Balkans gas ring, which would connect a cluster of Balkan countries in the south to gas entering Europe via Greece, and in the north, via Croatia, to a European gas hub in Austria.

It is the Nabucco project, however, which probably holds the key towards major EU diversification from specific dependence on Russian supply. In essence, Nabucco is a project which can carry up to 31 bcm/y of gas from a multiplicity of prospective or potential suppliers via Turkey to core EU markets by means of a terminal at Baumgarten in Austria.

There are two main customers in mind – and a third is a logical prospect. The first customers are the countries through which the line passes: Turkey, Bulgaria, Romania, and Hungary. Supplies by Nabucco would, initially, not so much replace Russian deliveries as take care of prospective demand increases. However, if Russia were to prove unable to increase its gas exports to Europe in absolute terms, then Nabucco would, in practice, serve to reduce Russia's share of this market. The second group of customers are commercial offtakers at Baumgarten. Current plans in this regard are focused on smaller gas consumers but, as the line develops, major purchasers can be expected to join the bidding. The third logical customer is Ukraine (and Moldova). A spur from Romania to Ukraine, possibly involving little more than a reversal of current Ukraine–Romania gas connections, would provide Ukraine with its best – and cheapest (in terms of development cost) – option to end its reliance on Russia's supply monopoly.

One great advantage of the Nabucco project is that it can be developed in two clear stages. The first relies essentially on existing capacity through the Turkish pipeline system, and thus reduces initial expenditures to construction of the line from Turkish Thrace to Austria. A second phase will involve expansion of Turkey's East–West trunkline, in effect, the laying of a new parallel pipe, and expansion of the Turkey–Austria sections by means of new pressure stations. Nabucco is already far advanced in terms of detailed planning and feasibility studies. However, strong EU support in terms of financing – the European Investment Bank might be an appropriate vehicle – would clearly help.

This chapter is not concerned with the issue of whether Russia is seeking to develop its proposed South Stream pipeline under the Black Sea to Bulgaria, Serbia, central Europe, and Italy as a possible spoiler for Nabucco. Suffice it to say that, as far as can be ascertained in mid-2008, South Stream does not appear to bring on line any new gas production; it only serves to re-route existing Russian gas supplies to hard cash European customers. In contrast, the Nabucco project, although it is structured as a transit pipeline, serves to access a variety of piped gas supplies that Europe would not otherwise be able to access.

Suppliers for EU diversification routes
Both TGI and Nabucco are essentially predicated on the same combination of supply sources. The most important of these is Azerbaijan. Deliveries from the first stage of the giant Shah Deniz field to Turkey were, in 2008, close to their projected plateau of 6.6 bcm/y, and are projected to stay at that level until around 2023. From 2013 or thereabouts, deliveries from the now projected 15–16 bcm/y second stage of Shah Deniz should come on stream. These are expected to yield an additional 10–12 bcm/y for onward delivery to Georgia, Turkey, and beyond via the SCP.[17]

New connections from Central Asian producers.
Three Central Asian countries – Kazakhstan, Turkmenistan, and Uzbekistan – produce gas, and all are looking to secure new export routes. At present only Turkmenistan has an alternative to Russia, in that it is able to export some 6 bcm/y to Iran by means of a gas pipeline along its Caspian coast which connects to Iran's main East–West Caspian system. Turkmenistan is the key to potential gas connections to Europe that bypass Russia (and which can also bypass Iran). That is because any pipeline designed to avoid both Russia and Iran would have to enter Europe via Azerbaijan – and by far the easiest crossing of the Caspian is to be found between Turkmenistan and Azerbaijan. Although Kazakhstan and Azerbaijan share a common maritime seabed boundary, thus making a trans-Caspian pipeline (TCP) politically feasible, the route is both much deeper and more beset by mud volcanoes and difficult geological conditions. In 1999, Turkmenistan signed an agreement to supply 30 bcm of gas to Turkey – with 16 bcm going to Turkey itself and 14 bcm for onward throughput to Europe – via a trans-Caspian pipeline that would have then crossed Azerbaijan and Georgia before entering Turkey. The agreement is only due to take effect as and when Turkmenistan is in a position to deliver gas to the Turkish border. Turkmenistan rejected detailed proposals for such a plan from the project's promoters, which included Royal Dutch Shell, in 2000–1.

Revival of this project is now favoured by a broad array of external parties, notably the USA and the EU, with the new Turkmenistan government of President Gurbanguly Berdymukhammedov specifically expressing interest in it. Azerbaijan's Industry and Energy Minister Natiq Aliev has said a trans-Caspian gas pipeline would be able to carry gas from both Turkmenistan and Kazakhstan via Azerbaijan and Georgia to European markets. Aliev has urged Turkmenistan and Kazakhstan to back the project, declaring that opposition to the pipeline was political, not technical, and that a revived TCP 'would ensure Europe's energy security and protect it from Russian monopolism'. On 8 May 2007, Azeri deputy Foreign Minister Araz Azimov said 'if the project is implemented, Azerbaijan will take part with great pleasure'.[18] Turkey specifically endorses the concept of a revived trans-Caspian gasline from Turkmenistan, arguing that it is the only factor that can ensure Nabucco gets off the ground on schedule.[19]

On 13 April 2008, EU External Relations Commissioner Benita Ferrero-Waldner said she had received assurances from Berdymuk-hammedov that his country would set aside 10 bcm/y for delivery to Europe, and that new gasfields would also be made available for tendering. However, there was no indication as to how or when these supplies would be delivered to Europe.[20]

Iranian gas and Iranian nuclear issues
With declining supplies from Russia, Europeans will probably need Iranian gas in the future. Bringing these new supplies to Europe will only be possible as part of a larger package addressing Iran's apparent attempts to build a nuclear bomb. At the United Nations in April 2006, the United Kingdom was reported to have proposed that efforts to resolve the Iranian nuclear issue should include positive incentives. Gas is the most obvious such incentive. Iran was to have been (with Azerbaijan) one of the two original sources of gas for the Nabucco project, but in June 2005, Nabucco's CEO told the author of this chapter that the controversy over whether Iran was developing nuclear weapons effectively meant that, until this issue was resolved, Nabucco would not be able to look to Iran as a supplier.

During the Khatami era, Iran clearly believed there was a direct link between gas exports and the nuclear issue. In November 2004, when Iran and the EU were about to open talks on the nuclear issue, Iranian Mining Minister Eshaq Jahangiri told the author that 'even before this agreement (to open the nuclear talks) we had started serious discussions with Europe on the export of gas'. He added: 'We expect the EU to stick to its end of the bargain and expedite trade relations with Iran'. Asked whether he specifically had gas in mind when he spoke of expediting trade relations, Jahangiri replied: 'This is the most important argument in our view of our relations with the EU – the export of Iranian gas to the EU. It's the basic component.'[21]

If the EU is to offer an incentive to Iran, then one obvious option would be for the EU to revive the concept of such a link; to offer access to the European market as part of a resolution of the nuclear issue. This would have profound repercussions for Iran, in terms of both direct income from exports to the EU, and the indirect advantages to be gained from resolving a dispute which is also likely to limit, if not end, EU corporate investment in major Iranian gas programmes, notably the LNG plants planned for Assaluyah, and the giant $7.1 bn pipeline projected to carry Iranian gas to Pakistan and India. In 2004, the IEA's Chief Economist, Fatih Birol, estimated that the EU might be importing as much as 157 bcm/y from the Middle East by 2030. Although he did not specifically say so, a good proportion of this would presumably come from Iran. Indeed, it is not unreasonable to suppose that, all things being equal, Iran might ultimately supply the EU with as much as 60–80 bcm/y of gas. Moreover, were Iran to operate in a sanctions-free environment, EU companies would be expected to invest heavily in Iranian LNG. In contrast, if the nuclear issue is not defused, Iran may find it hard to develop its LNG facilities without major inputs of both western investment and western technology. Almost certainly this would result in a substantial decrease in the size of Iranian LNG projects – both individually and collectively – thus considerably increasing the unit cost of LNG production. At the same time, in order to sell its LNG in a potentially sanctions-ridden environment, Iran might have to discount its exports heavily.

One further point might perhaps be made at this stage. Iran does not understand Western international concerns. Iranian officials simply cannot understand why their own protestations that they are not seeking to develop nuclear weapons does not end the matter. In other words, they simply do not understand the level of concern in Europe. Resolving the nuclear issue peacefully may therefore require what amounts to a long programme of education for both Iranian officials and the Iranian people regarding Europe's nuclear concerns.

Summary

This section has shown that Russia is Europe's most difficult energy supplier. While the EU is seeking to build a stable relationship with Russia, it is also trying to find other sources of natural gas supply. Simultaneously, Europe is trying to address energy security by reducing its overall demand for gas by encouraging greater efficiency and alternative sources of energy. That is the focus of the next section.

Key Challenges on the Demand side

The EU is making a big investment in reducing its demand for energy, and is pushing itself harder than other regions of the world to increase energy efficiency and the use of alternative sources of energy. Europe hopes to achieve two goals with this policy. First, it seeks to reduce the amount of energy that it will have to import. Second, it is trying to address the profound environmental concerns arising from global warming caused by an extensive reliance on fossil fuels. As one of the largest energy consumers in the world, the EU is a major contributor to the problem.

The leaders of the EU member states stuck with their 20-20-20 climate change plan at a meeting held in December 2008. This plan calls for reducing greenhouse gas emissions by 20 per cent from their 1990 levels, making renewables 20 per cent of final energy consumption, and implementing a 20 per cent saving in future energy demand by 2020. The EU Commission argued that 'Cleaner, more diverse and more efficient energy would improve Europe's energy supply and economy and create a more stable, consistent and transparent environment for new energy investments.'[22] In adopting the plan, however, EU leaders made concessions to some of the east European countries most reliant on coal, with some of the most polluting industries.[23]

While it may be difficult to achieve greenhouse gas reductions in a depressed economy, and alternative energy development is dependent on technology advances, a major – and very toughly implemented programme – of energy conservation offers several short-, medium-, and long-term advantages. To begin with, it immediately helps offset rising energy import costs. Moreover, it has the potential to have an impact on energy balances quite quickly, within a year or two. This compares well with the development of new power sources such as gas-fired power plants, and brilliantly by comparison with the development of nuclear plants.

In the medium-term, it means that there is an accumulation of savings, and the start of a steady drip of pressure on producers, as conservation measures take effect. In the long run, it either prompts energy producers into a complete reassessment of the need for interdependence between producers and consumers, or else it forces a price collapse by creating space for renewables, new technologies and, in some instances, nuclear, either to curb prospective increased gas (and oil) deliveries or to pre-empt them altogether. In fact, the overall energy intensity of the European economy has improved significantly over the last 10 years.[24]

Developing alternative sources is a key part of Europe's strategy of reducing its dependence on Russian gas. At the end of 2008, renewable energy accounted for 9 per cent of EU energy consumption, up from 7 per cent in 2006, and is the most likely source of greater indigenous energy production to replace declining fossil fuel supplies.[25] Even though this figure has been rising rapidly in recent years, it will be difficult for the EU to lift it up to 20 per cent by 2020, as planned.[26] However, in contrast to the USA, where there are low taxes on gasoline, Europe has imposed substantial taxes, so the prices remain relatively high even when the price of oil falls. Typically, falling prices would reduce the incentive for increasing energy efficiency.

Europe is a leader in alternative energy production, and has made a major investment in solar and wind power. Germany is the world's leading producer of photovoltaic panels, and dominates the market for wind turbines.[27] European countries such as Spain, Germany, and Denmark, have used feed-in tariffs (FIT), a government programme that forces utilities to purchase renewable energy at above-market rates, to encourage the production of solar and wind power. Even though the USA initiated many of these policies and technologies, it is the Europeans who have actually put them to work.

International implications: What can the EU offer Russia – and what must the EU secure?

Despite difficulties, the opportunity to develop an energy partnership between Russia and the EU, based on the common pursuit of a clear programme of specific energy projects intended to boost both Russian and EU energy security, is an attainable goal. The logic of the core concept of long-term commitments for EU investment in Russian energy, in exchange for long-term Russian commitments to supply energy to the EU, remains unassailable. However, it may be worth setting out some elements of what the EU can offer Russia, whilst also setting out key commitments that the EU must secure from Russia.

What can the EU offer Russia?

Firstly, it can stress the sheer wealth of the EU, its member states and, above all, its companies. These possess the funds required to transform Russia, not just in energy but in other economic spheres as well. Moreover, unlike the USA, the EU, with its much greater belief in the mixed economy, can stress to Russia that it is not seeking to impose unbridled capitalism, but that it genuinely wants a partnership. That could include agreements that cover EU upstream investments in Russia in exchange for Russian downstream investments in the EU.

Secondly, it can recognize that Russia has its own energy concerns, including one which the EU needs to address more fully. Just as consumers naturally crave security of supply, so do producers desire security of demand. The EU Council did say on 24 March 2006 that 'subject to competition requirements, the contribution of long-term contracts should be acknowledged from both the demand and supply side'.[28]

If there is to be a formal partnership with Russia, its core would almost certainly need to consist of a welter of long-term agreements covering sale-and-purchase of Russian gas supplies, development of new and expanded pipeline systems, development of price mechanisms to ensure that long-term contracts reflected prevailing market conditions, and long-term agreement on both the investment regimes applicable in both Russia and the EU and the amounts of investment that can be expected, particularly in terms of EU investments in Russia. Such a set of agreements – which would no doubt be interlinked – would effectively require close cooperation between public and private bodies within the EU. It might be a useful time to remember that the EU and its member states all live in a mixed economy, rather than a purely market economy.

Thirdly, the relatively energy-efficient EU can intensify its offer to assist a woefully energy-inefficient Russia to develop an internal energy market that reduces the amount of oil, and particularly gas, that is wasted as a result of de facto subsidies to domestic consumers. In 2006, Russia produced 612.1 bcm of gas, but it actually consumed 432.1 bcm, almost as much as total EU-25 consumption of 467.4 bcm. In per capita terms, Russians consume three times as much gas as do the citizens of the EU – and different climates do not wholly account for the gap! Russia's domestic energy saving potential could well total as much as 150 bcm/y, roughly equivalent to current Russian exports to Western Europe. Helping Russia in this regard would improve the finances of both Gazprom and the central Russian government, thus freeing up cash for major energy sector investment. This should appeal to the nationalist streak in the Russian government, since greater cash in Russian hands means a reduced requirement for foreign direct investment (FDI) and, at present, Russia seems to have a somewhat ambivalent attitude to energy-sector FDI.

In much the same way that Russia has helped propel Ukraine towards free market pricing of its core energy imports – a process which involves substantial short- and medium-term pain, but which should in the long run prove extremely helpful – so the EU can also help Russia become a more competitive supplier, not least by encouraging a more rapid expansion of gas imports from non-Russian suppliers.

The very existence of new projects such as the Nabucco pipeline from Turkey to Austria, or the interconnector linking Turkey, Greece, and Italy will have an impact on the price and terms under which Russian gas is exported to the EU. For the EU itself, such pipelines need to be considered as strategic pipelines, almost regardless of the volumes of gas they may bring into Europe from new suppliers, simply because they have the potential not only to alleviate EU dependence on Russian gas supplies, but, by allowing other suppliers to access the EU market, they promote competition, and thus serve either to help reduce outright the prices paid by European importers for Russian gas or, more probably, to ensure such prices do not rise as fast as they would otherwise do. However, in considering how private companies may view the development of strategic projects, the EU should perhaps bear in mind that the consumers who stand to gain from paying less for Russian gas are unlikely to be the same people or groups as those who might be called upon to finance alternative pipelines. The Commission might wish to investigate ways of squaring this circle, since it is quite feasible, particularly in an era of comparatively high energy prices, that the cost-savings on long-term gas imports in general, and on Russian gas imports in particular, might well exceed the costs associated with constructing or expanding infrastructure to serve non-Russian suppliers.

What must the EU secure from Russia?

In considering how to negotiate with Russia, the EU and its member states might wish to recall that EU dependence on Russian gas imports is a two-way street; Russia is correspondingly dependent on the EU market. Thus the EU's dependence on Russian gas – which constitutes nearly half of all gas imports and a quarter of all gas supplies – is more than matched by the fact that Russian energy supplies – oil, gas, and electricity – to the EU account for well over half of all Russia's export earnings. In contrast, Russian energy imports to the EU constitute only 2.5 per cent of overall EU imports.

Moreover, while both the EU and Russia can talk of diversification – with the EU stressing the availability of new suppliers and Russia concentrating on new customers – the EU's financial muscle makes it likely that diversified supply pipelines serving the EU will precede the construction of new export pipelines from Russia to China and/or Japan. Finance and geography both aid the EU in this regard.

The development of new export pipelines from Central Asia – regardless of whether they go to Europe, South Asia or, more likely, China, also strengthen the EU's position. As Turkmenistan, Uzbekistan, and Kazakhstan secure access to an alternative major market, such as

China, Russian purchases will have to be made in an atmosphere of at least modest competition. Anything which prompts Russia to understand it is entering an era in which competition for gas – whether from Russia or Central Asia – is increasingly commonplace, should improve the long-term development of an EU–Russian energy partnership. That is because it should encourage energy reform within Russia, and a Russia committed to domestic energy reform, with all its energy operations essentially placed on a commercial basis, becomes a better partner for the EU than a Russia which bases much of its energy policy, and not a little of its political relations, with its neighbours on its ability to exercise monopoly powers in terms of both energy purchases and transit.

Although there are obvious opportunities for EU investment in upstream Russian energy projects, particularly in terms of the development of Russian gas reserves in the Yamal peninsula and other Arctic regions, there is still a concern that pouring investment into a country which is still so wasteful of its own energy use, and which uses its powers to restrict other countries' access to global markets, may not prove to be the best use of EU investment resources. In seeking to develop a meaningful partnership, it therefore seems logical to argue that the EU will need to push for further economic reform in Russia to encourage foreign direct investment, particularly in the energy industry. Foreign investments in Russia have been falling off in recent years as business conditions inside the country worsen. In this regard, the EU can particularly stress the availability of European investment funds, so long as the investment climate is suitable.

In seeking to develop an energy partnership with Russia, the EU will obviously want to ensure that it means what it says when it rules out destination clauses in energy contracts. Once Russian gas enters the common market that is the EU, the future disposition of that gas is an internal EU matter. This will not please Russia, since it will reduce Gazprom's negotiating power, but it is a core principle that needs to be upheld. It will also show that the EU means business.

Getting Russia to sign the Energy Charter Transit Protocol and to ratify the Energy Charter Treaty ought to be a *sine qua non* for any partnership. The only exception would be if, simply in order to save face, Russia were formally to sign up to exactly the same principles and requirements, but in an alternative but equally legally-binding format, such as a Russia–EU energy treaty. These actions are essential if a level playing field is to be secured, to enable Central Asian producers to secure open access to hard cash markets in Europe via Russia. In this regard, the EU should also insist on a Central Asian element in its bilateral dialogue with Russia.

Conclusion

All the challenges in the European–Russian relationship put pressure on the producer–consumer framework. These problems are obvious in the political overtones shaping the relationship – disruptions in the supply through Ukraine such as occurred in 2006 and 2009, and a variety of other problems. In order to improve the relationship moving forward, the EU and Russia need to recalibrate this regional producer–consumer framework.

Europe faces major challenges as it works to secure its energy supplies. As its domestic energy sources dry up, it is becoming increasingly reliant on Russian provisions of natural gas. However, Russia's domestic political situation presents a number of challenges, and it is not clear that it will be able to meet European needs. The Europeans are definitely right to be concerned about dwindling supplies from Russia.

Seeking to reduce its dependence on Russia, while also addressing growing concerns about the environment, Europe has focused on a policy of increasing energy efficiency and of accelerating the development of alternative energy sources. Unfortunately, Europe's efforts to ensure security of supply undermine Russia's attempts to guarantee security of demand. To avoid upsetting their Russian suppliers, the Europeans must show, transparently, that their adoption of alternative sources will necessarily be a slow change over time that will not have a major impact on the Russians in the near future, allowing them plenty of time to make adjustments.

Europe has also sought to increase energy imports from Africa, the Caspian, and Central Asia. Such projects require the construction of new pipelines. While the links from Africa to Europe do not require European political intervention, building pipelines from the Caspian to Europe is straining European–Russian relations.

There is a way for the EU and Russia to work together to achieve their common energy interests. A big part of this effort can be in jointly developing energy efficiencies. Putting such projects in place, however, will take a considerable amount of political will and acumen on both sides. Europeans should not fall into the trap of trying to be completely energy independent, rather they need to put their policies into the larger framework of environmental protection and mutual economic growth through developing efficiency and alternative energy supplies, in order to balance Europe's and Russia's energy securities. Despite the numerous difficulties that lie ahead, there is reason for optimism; even though there is tension in the relationship, both sides will realize that they are stuck with each other and must work together to calibrate the demand–supply picture.

Notes

1 BP Statistical Review of World Energy 2008, June 2008. www.bp.com/productlanding.do?categoryId=6929&contentId=7044622
2 Commission of the European Communities, *Second Strategic Energy Review*, Brussels, 13 November 2008, 8. http://ec.europa.eu/energy/strategies/2008/doc/2008_11_ser2/strategic_energy_review_wd_future_position2.pdf
3 European Commission Directorate-General for Energy and Transport, *Europe's Energy Position: present and future*, European Communities, Luxembourg, November 2008, 12. http://ec.europa.eu/energy/publications/doc/2008_moe_maquette.pdf
4 Energy Information Administration, 'Country Analysis Briefs: European Union', January 2006, 2. www.eia.doe.gov/emeu/cabs/European_Union/pdf.pdf
5 European Commission, 'Securing your energy future: Commission presents energy security, solidarity and efficiency proposals', Rapid Press Release, 13 November, 2008. http://europa.eu/rapid/pressReleasesAction.do?reference=IP/08/1696&format=HTML&aged=0&language=EN&guiLanguage=en
6 As William F. Browder, Chairman of Moscow's Hermitage Capital Management, said in late 2005: 'If you own Gazprom stock, you accept that it is a political arm of the Russian government'. (Andrew W. Kramer, 'Gazprom Becomes the Bear of Russia', *New York Times*, 27 December, 2005.)
7 European Communities, *Key Institutional Decisions in the Field of External Energy Policy, 2006-2007*, Brussels, 2007, 33, http://ec.europa.eu/external_relations/energy/docs/key_institutional_decisions_06-07_en.pdf
8 Commission of the European Communities, *Green Paper: A European Strategy for Sustainable, Competitive, and Secure Energy*, Brussels, 8 March, 2006. http://europa.eu/documents/comm/green_papers/pdf/com2006_105_en.pdf
9 Commission of the European Communities, *Second Strategic Energy Review*, Brussels, 13 November 2008, 9. http://ec.europa.eu/energy/strategies/2008/doc/2008_11_ser2/strategic_energy_review_wd_future_position2.pdf
10 In 2004, Russia's GDP totalled $584.5bn, calculated on the IMF basis of production-based GDP totaling 16,752bn roubles and an average exchange rate of 28.66 roubles to the dollar.
11 Alan Riley and Frank Umbach, 'Out of Gas: Looming Russian gas deficits demand readjustment of European energy policy', *IP*, Spring 2007, 83–89.
12 International Energy Agency, *Optimising Russian Natural Gas: Reform and Climate Policy*, IEA, Paris, 2006, 34.

13 Katinka Barysch, 'Reciprocity will not secure Europe's energy', *CER Bulletin*, Issue 55, Centre for European Reform, London, August/September 2007.

14 No author, 'Good News about Bad Press: For Corporate Governance, Humiliation Pays Off', Knowledge@Wharton, June 27, 2007, http://knowledge.wharton.upenn.edu/article.cfm?articleid=1762

15 Simon Pirani, Jonathan Stern, and Katja Yafimava, *The Russo-Ukrainian Gas Dispute of January 2009: a comprehensive assessment*, Oxford Institute for Energy Studies, February 2009. www.oxfordenergy.org/pdfs/NG27.pdf

16 European Communities, *Key Institutional Decisions in the Field of External Energy Policy, 2006-2007*, Brussels, 2007, 32. http://ec.europa.eu/external_relations/energy/docs/key_institutional_decisions_06-07_en.pdf

17 Until 2007, there was a strong perception that Turkey's excess imports might constitute a significant input for Nabucco, TGI, the Trans-Adriatic Pipeline via Albania, and any other lines seeking to carry gas to European markets via Turkey. The assumption was that Turkey's contracted import volumes would continue to exceed actual or projected consumption, as they did for the opening years of the decade. Current assessments are that Turkey itself will need to step up imports on its own account from many of the sources, notably Azerbaijan, on which Nabucco, TGI, and TAP are relying for at least their start-up input. Moreover, Turkish transit has become problematic in another way, with Ankara seeking to assess whether its role as an energy hub can extend from serving as a centre where diverse sources of energy can converge and then disperse, and as a prime location for value-added projects in refining and petrochemicals, to a trading centre where gas is purchased from the suppliers before being sold on to eventual purchasers in other European countries. As of mid-2008, this last issue was still alive, although its principal proponent was no longer in charge of administering Turkish energy policy. The issue of Turkish re-exports, of course, goes to the heart of EU concepts of a single integrated market and the extension of the Energy Community in South East Europe to include Turkey.

18 'Azerbaijan will join the Trans-Caspian gas pipeline if it is built – official', Interfax, Moscow, 8 May, 2007.

19 Kart Celalettin, Director-General, Turkish Foreign Ministry, particularly stressed this point at a seminar in Berlin on 8 May 2007. Author's notes.

20 'Turkmenistan to cut EU dependence on Russian gas', *EU Observer*, 14 April 2008.

21 Interview conducted at the 'Fueling Economic Growth in Iran Conference' at the DTI Conference Centre in London on 17 November 2004.

22 European Commission, 'Securing your energy future: Commission presents energy security, solidarity and efficiency proposals', Rapid Press Release, November 13, 2008. http://europa.eu/rapid/pressReleasesAction.do?reference=IP/08/1696&format=HTML&aged=0&language=EN&guiLanguage=en

23 James Kanter and Stephen Castle, 'EU Strikes Agreement on Global Warming', *International Herald Tribune*, 13–14 December 2008.

24 Commission of the European Communities, *Second Strategic Energy Review*,

Brussels, 13 November, 2008, 7. http://ec.europa.eu/energy/strategies/2008/doc/2008_11_ser2/strategic_energy_review_wd_future_position2.pdf

25 Commission of the European Communities, *Second Strategic Energy Review*, Brussels, 13 November 2008, 4. http://ec.europa.eu/energy/strategies/2008/doc/2008_11_ser2/strategic_energy_review_wd_future_position2.pdf

26 See the progress toward targets at the energy.eu website (http://energy.eu/).

27 Warren Wilczewski, 'Germany Moves from Atoms to Photons', Policy Innovations, 10 December 2008. www.policyinnovations.org/ideas/briefings/data/000094

28 European Communities, *Key Institutional Decisions in the Field of External Energy Policy, 2006-2007*, Brussels, 2007, 33, http://ec.europa.eu/external_relations/energy/docs/key_institutional_decisions_06-07_en.pdf

CHAPTER 10

FUELLING THE DRAGON: CHINA'S ENERGY PROSPECTS AND INTERNATIONAL IMPLICATIONS

Mikkal Herberg

China's extraordinary long-term economic growth has resulted in a truly unprecedented period of escalation in energy demand. While China accounted for 16 per cent of total world energy demand in 2007 – second only to the USA and about equal to the entire energy consumption of the European Union-25 – China is expected to account for 38 per cent of the total growth in global energy demand over the next 25 years.[1] China's expanding energy footprint has enormous global energy, economic, environmental, and strategic significance. China is destined to become a major force in global energy and oil geopolitics and energy security dynamics, and its future energy consumption is likely to transform global oil markets and, potentially, global natural gas, coal, and renewable energy technology markets. China also seems destined to become the source of a virtual *tsunami* of carbon emissions and energy-related pollution, with profound implications for future climate change negotiations and the geopolitics of carbon emissions.

However, the path forward is shrouded in uncertainty due to mounting problems and challenges in China's longer-term energy outlook. Put simply, energy demand since 2001 has been outrunning China's ability to mobilize energy supplies, and to finance and build the energy infrastructure to fuel the economy growing at its current pace. Moreover, mushrooming domestic and regional environmental problems related to energy use, particularly coal, make the current trajectory of consumption appear fundamentally unsustainable. It seems likely that China's leadership will be forced over the next 5–10 years to adopt a fundamentally new energy model based on much stronger demand management, radically improved energy efficiency, and a much cleaner energy mix.

In their rhetoric and in a number of recent energy policy initiatives, China's leaders are demonstrating a new commitment to addressing the energy demand and environmental issues that will shape the country's future. The main question is whether this shift is occurring rapidly enough to allow for a gradual transition over a manageable period of time toward an increasingly effective and robust energy policy framework and implementation of reforms, or whether truly fundamental reforms will be postponed, leading ultimately to a much more abrupt, disruptive, and economically and politically costly series of major changes forced on China's leaders by converging environmental and supply–demand crises. The path that China chooses has enormous implications for global energy markets, energy geopolitics, and global energy–environment questions.

This chapter will analyse China's energy situation, its growing energy challenges, prospects for change and reform, and the global implications. It will begin with a survey of energy conditions, long-term supply and demand trends across key fuels, and a review of the current direction of energy policy and the role of key energy policy institutions. It will then consider the key political, economic, environmental, and energy policy challenges China faces in moving towards a more manageable and sustainable energy future, including ensuring energy security, sustaining rapid economic growth, and coming to grips with worsening energy/environmental outcomes. Finally, the chapter will consider the implications for international relations, global energy markets and geopolitics, and global environmental outcomes.

China's Overall Energy Situation

Coal dominates China's primary energy mix, making up almost 70 per cent of total commercial energy consumption (See Figure 10.1). Comparatively, coal accounts for about 29 per cent of energy use globally.[2] Oil accounted for roughly 20 per cent of energy use in China in 2007 compared to a global average of 36 per cent (40 per cent in the USA and 48 per cent in Japan). Natural gas, which accounts for roughly 24 per cent of energy use globally, comparable to coal's share, comprises just 3 per cent of China's energy mix. Hydroelectric makes up roughly 6 per cent of energy use, comparable to international averages, and nuclear energy accounts for just 1 per cent compared to 6 per cent globally. All other renewables account for less than 1 per cent.

Despite a long period of very rapid economic growth, China's energy demand grew at relatively modest rates over the last two decades of the twentieth century. Between 1980 and 2000, energy demand grew at less than half the rate of economic growth, meaning that overall demand grew at roughly 4 per cent per year relative to 9–10 per cent long-term economic growth rates. This relationship between economic growth and energy demand was remarkably low compared to most

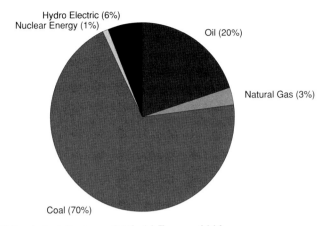

Hydro Electric (6%)
Nuclear Energy (1%)

Oil (20%)

Natural Gas (3%)

Coal (70%)

Source: BP Statistical Review of World Energy 2008

Figure 10.1: China's energy supply (2007)

other developing countries, especially those in Asia, which have generally experienced an elasticity of at least 1.0, meaning energy demand
grew at the same rate as economic growth or usually somewhat higher
(often 1.3–1.5 times economic growth rates). In effect energy demand
was largely de-coupled from economic growth between 1980 and 2000,
which resulted in a doubling of energy demand in this period, while
the economy increased in size six-fold.[3]

Assuming that this favourable experience would continue, China's
energy policymakers predicated their 2000–2020 energy plans on a
similar quadrupling of the economy and a doubling of energy demand.[4]
However, since 2001 energy demand has shifted sharply upward, and
has been growing at an average of 1.5 times the economic growth rate.
The result has been an astonishing 86 per cent rise in total energy
demand in just the five years to 2007. By 2007 total energy demand in
China was nearly *60 per cent higher* than planned. Several factors appear
to be behind the rising energy demand growth rate.[5] First, the 10–11
per cent economic growth rate spurred a rapid expansion in per capita
incomes, and the country's swift urbanization only boosted the wealth
expansion. China's consumers now need more energy to fuel their new
purchases. Moreover, industry in China accounts for an unusually high
70 per cent of commercial energy demand, so accelerating industrial
growth since 2000 translated into strong energy demand growth. The
additional explosive factor appears to have been the extraordinary rise
in investment in heavy, energy-intensive industries since 2000, which
led to a burst of energy demand from the steel, aluminium, cement,
paper, glass, and petrochemical sector.

This surge in energy consumption is truly unprecedented. For ex-ample, between 2003 and 2007 China's energy demand grew by an amount that *exceeded Japan's total energy use in 2007*, the fourth largest energy market in the world.[6] The high rate of overall energy demand growth has consequences across the spectrum of fuels, but manifests itself in different ways depending on the particular fuel's supply and demand situation, and the range of trade-offs among different fuel choices. Accordingly, the rapid growth has created a range of energy policy dilemmas. Before discussing these, however, it is necessary to review the basic supply and demand situation in each key energy sector, and the challenges China faces in meeting its future energy needs in the context of its current trajectory.

China's Oil Sector

Oil demand in China has grown rapidly since the mid-1980s, as eco-nomic growth accelerated. Industry, which accounts for 60 per cent of oil demand, largely drove this increase. Transportation needs consume only 35 per cent of China's oil supply, compared to 68 per cent in the USA.[7] Oil demand has roughly doubled each decade since the mid-1980s, from 1.7 mb/d in 1984 to 3.4 mb/d in 1995 to 7.0 mb/d in 2006.[8] China's oil reserves are modest, with total proven reserves of 15.5 billion barrels accounting for just 1.3 per cent of global oil reserves. China has been the largest oil producer in Asia since the 1960's, producing 3.7 mb/d in 2007, but output has flattened out over the past decade as China's large oil fields in the north-east of the country mature and decline, and new discoveries in the west and offshore just manage to replace declining current production capacity. With rising demand and relatively flat oil production, China became a net importer in 1993, and by 2007 imported roughly 50 per cent of its total oil needs. In 2003 China surpassed Japan as the second largest oil consumer behind the USA.

China's rising oil demand and imports are already having major international ramifications, which are likely to grow over time. China's booming oil demand has become a major factor in global oil markets and prices. In 2007 China accounted for just 9 per cent of total world oil demand, but its annual increases have accounted for one-third of the rise in global demand over the past decade. Demand has been growing at roughly 5–6 per cent per year and now translates into a 400,000 b/d average annual increase, a larger growth increment than any other country, including the USA, whose total base consumption is three times China's.

The International Energy Agency (IEA) forecasts that China's oil demand will rise from 7.5 mb/d in 2007 to 16.6 mb/d by 2030, driven both by continuing industrial and economic growth, and by the rapidly growing use of motor vehicles in China.[9] Transportation uses will increasingly have an impact on oil demand over the next two decades. The IEA forecasts that the light-duty vehicle fleet in China will grow from 28 million vehicles on the road in 2005 to 230 million vehicles by 2030, representing nearly one-third of the global light-duty vehicle fleet growth.[10] China is already the second largest vehicle market in the world by annual sales, behind the USA, having recently surpassed Japan.

At the same time, oil production in China is expected to largely plateau around current levels. As a result, by 2030 China is likely to be importing 75 per cent of its total oil needs.[11] As is the case for the other major oil importing countries of the world, most of this future imported oil will need to come from the Persian Gulf, along with new supplies from Russia and Central Asia, Africa, and Latin America. It will also increasingly be transported along the long and precarious maritime routes to Asia.

China's rising oil import dependence has made the issue of energy security a powerful strategic concern for its leadership, who fear that potential future global oil supply shortages and disruptions, along with high and volatile oil prices, could undermine economic growth, weaken job creation, and chip away at social stability. China's leaders have responded with a number of policies, mainly focused on supply-side efforts.[12] First, they have continued efforts to re-shape China's domestic oil industry, to boost domestic oil production and improve the investment efficiency and operating effectiveness of China's state oil companies. Over the past decade, three major national oil companies (NOC) have been created out of the previous energy ministries: China National Petroleum Corporation (CNPC), Sinopec, and China National Offshore Oil Corporation (CNOOC). They have won progressively greater freedom to compete both within China, and internationally, along cross-cutting business lines of oil, natural gas, refining, and distribution. New exploration areas in Xinjiang and offshore have been opened to foreign oil companies to spur exploration and development of new domestic oil supplies. Plans are being developed to make major investments in converting coal into liquid fuels (CTL) given China's enormous domestic supplies of coal. However, such plans will have to overcome major obstacles due to the limitations in water availability for such developments, and the severe carbon-emission problems associated with CTL technology.

Internationally, the government has promoted a 'go out' strategy for China's NOCs to support efforts to secure control over, and access to, oil supplies globally. This strategy includes Beijing's energy diplomacy in support of its investment efforts abroad, along with direct state financial support. China's NOCs have now become major investors in global oil and gas development in all the key energy-exporting regions.[13] China and its NOCs also are working to develop overland oil pipeline projects to bring oil from Central Asia and Russia, and to diversify their oil import slate to increase oil imports that would not have to transit various seaborne bottlenecks, most importantly the Malacca Straits.[14] In response to its growing dependence on maritime flows of oil, China has accelerated naval development, in order to eventually gain greater influence over the key sea lanes (SLOCs) of South East Asia[15] and the Indian Ocean, routes which the US Navy presently controls. Finally, China has begun to incorporate multilateral, regional, and bilateral cooperation into its pursuit of energy security. China recently completed four Strategic Petroleum Reserve (SPR) storage sites to set aside crude oil supplies for use during international supply disruptions, and has begun a dialogue with the IEA about potential cooperation with the agency in the use of its SPR oil.[16] China has stepped up bilateral cooperation with the USA and Japan, and is seeking to introduce energy cooperation and coordination efforts into the Shanghai Cooperation Organization (SCO) framework.[17]

Until 2007, most policy efforts addressed the supply side of the oil security dilemma. However, since then, the leadership has also begun to develop more complex, and politically sensitive, demand-side policies which are needed to reduce the rate of long-term demand growth. The evolution of the supply-side vs. demand-side policy debate reflects China's evolving approach to, and definition of, energy security. In a political system that has traditionally been centralized, focused philosophically on energy self-sufficiency, and committed to increasing energy availability as being central to economic growth, rising standards of living, and social peace, energy security has been approached from a strategic, rather than a market, perspective. China's leaders understand energy security in the traditional terms of securing adequate and reliable energy supplies at reasonable prices. However, the leadership is deeply suspicious that the unstable and volatile global oil markets of the past decade cannot deliver reliable supplies at reasonable prices. Therefore, a strategic, state-centric focus on supply insecurity has predominated over a willingness to rely on markets, as most of the other major industrial countries largely do.[18] Only over the past few years has the realization grown, first among energy policymakers and, more recently, among the senior political leadership, that supply-side efforts will not suffice to meet China's energy security needs, and that steps must be taken to reduce demand growth at the same time. Hence, there is a new focus on demand measures in the oil sector. Examples include major taxes imposed on new vehicles with larger engine displacement, and new stringent requirements on the vehicle industry to produce more fuel efficient vehicle engines, standards that approach European vehicle efficiency standards and exceed US standards. Nevertheless, energy security policy regarding China's future oil needs remains strongly influenced by supply-side thinking.[19]

Natural Gas

As discussed earlier, natural gas presently accounts for a tiny share, just 3 per cent, of China's overall energy consumption. Domestic production meets virtually all of China's modest gas needs, although imports will grow significantly post-2010. As in the case of oil, industrial demand makes up most gas use, accounting for 50 per cent of consumption, with commercial and residential use each taking a roughly 25 per cent share.

Current energy policy efforts seek to rapidly boost natural gas use by reducing the reliance on coal for electricity generation, diversifying overall energy supplies and flexibility, and providing cleaner-burning fuel for environmental reasons. Current plans call for double-digit annual growth rates in gas use, and for gas to make up 8 per cent of energy demand by 2020. Consumption is slated to rise substantially at a rate of nearly 6 per cent annually, from 58 billion cubic metres (bcm) in 2006 to 221 bcm by 2030.[20]

In order to boost gas use, Beijing is accelerating domestic gas exploration and development, and expanding the national gas pipeline system to transport more gas from fields in north, central, and western China to the major cities along the east coast. In the wake of recent new large gas exploration and development in Xinjiang in western China, a major West–East 2,500 mile pipeline has been built to move significant gas supplies from the sparsely populated Xinjiang Uyghur Autonomous Region to Shanghai. A second large trunkline for gas is now being planned to branch off from the West–East line to take gas south to Guangzhou and the southeastern coastal region. Gas development has been accelerated in Sichuan Province and the Ordos Basin, along with new pipelines to link up to east China's dynamic cities.[21] Gas exploration is also being encouraged in China's offshore waters, which can feed demand in the fast-growing coastal cities. The government is also working to develop gas demand and markets by creating more effective regulatory structures, increasing flexibility in gas pricing and transport, and promoting more gas use in electricity generation. However, market development has been slow due to the delayed preparation of market policies on gas pricing and transportation, along with the low price of competing coal supplies.[22]

China's natural gas growth is also likely to have significant international energy market and geopolitical ramifications. Beyond 2010, gas demand is likely to begin significantly outrunning domestic production, and a growing share of gas needs will have to be met with imports, both as Liquefied Natural Gas (LNG) and by long-distance pipeline. The US Department of Energy (DOE) and Lawrence Berkeley National Laboratory forecast that imports are likely to account for 40 per cent of China's total gas needs by 2020, and the IEA forecasts that imports will reach 48 per cent of consumption by 2030.[23] Most of this gas will be needed along the east coast, where economic and industrial growth is dynamic.

Unlike the case of oil, in which future imported supplies will come largely from outside Asia, significant LNG and pipeline gas imports will be available from within the Asia–Pacific region. South East Asia is home to a number of major LNG producers, including Australia, Indonesia, Malaysia, and, in the future, East Timor. China completed its first LNG receiving terminal in Guangdong Province; this began receiving gas in mid-2006, and a second terminal in Fujian began receiving LNG in April 2008. Two more LNG terminals are under construction or planned in Shanghai and Shandong Province. At least eight other LNG receiving facilities have been proposed for the east coast markets. Pipeline gas supplies are also likely to be available from South East Asia over the longer-term, as China moves forward with plans to build a major gas pipeline through Myanmar to move its offshore gas north to southern China.[24] In North East Asia, both LNG and pipeline gas will be available. Russia's huge Sakhalin-2 project, led by Shell and now majority-owned by Gazprom, began shipments of LNG to Japan and South Korea in 2009. Gas from the Sakhalin-1 project, run by ExxonMobil and Rosneft, but with Gazprom likely to become a new partner, now seems likely to feed into the LNG stream at Sakhalin-2. In recent state visits to Beijing, Russia's Prime Minister Vladimir Putin has promised to build two large pipelines to bring gas from West and East Siberia to China, to link up with the West–East trunk line to move gas to China's east coast. Unfortunately, the Kremlin has been very slow to follow-through on these promises, and negotiations over gas pricing have been going very slowly. For example, a plan to build a major gas pipeline from East Siberia's enormous Kovykta gas field to north-eastern China and on to Korea has been delayed for years by Kremlin politics and re-organization and re-centralization of Russia's oil and gas industry. In Central Asia, China is now building a new long-distance 30 bcm/year gas pipeline from Turkmenistan to western China to link up to the West–East trunkline, and Beijing is also discussing the possibility of bringing Kazakhstan gas to western China in the future.[25]

While significant amounts of gas will be available from the Asia–Pacific region and Eurasian sources, LNG supplies are also likely to be needed from major Persian Gulf producers. CNPC recently signed a new three million ton per year LNG contract with Qatar's Qatargas consortium for deliveries to a planned Dalian terminal, to commence in 2012.[26] China's Sinopec has signed a preliminary memorandum of understanding (MOU) for a major LNG project in Iran from the massive offshore South Pars gas field, which would provide long-term LNG supplies to China. Most recently, CNOOC has signed an MOU for another potentially large LNG project tapping the North Pars gas field.[27] However, both companies are moving slowly on these Iranian proposals in the face of strong US opposition against energy investment in Iran, and political uncertainty about a potential USA–Iran conflict.

Given plans for rapidly expanding gas use in China, combined with the growing supply of LNG being developed in Asia and globally, China is expected to be a major force in Asian and global natural gas and LNG markets in the future. The Asian LNG market is by far the largest regional LNG market in the world, and China could become the second largest incremental buyer of LNG in Asia over the next 10–15 years, behind only South Korea. LNG is therefore likely to loom relatively large in China's energy future, although there is a substantial range of uncertainty over volumes.

Coal

As suggested earlier, coal is king in China, accounting for two-thirds of total energy consumption and 80 per cent of electricity generation. Coal's future in China is inextricably bound up in expectations about future electricity demand, and a challenging set of alternatives available to China to meet its future electricity needs. Moreover, much depends on China's future evolving policy toward managing electricity demand. As China's current coal use accounts for 41 per cent of total world coal consumption, its future policy choices will have major implications for global coal markets and prices. Finally, the global environmental implications of China's rising coal consumption are difficult to overstate.

China has the third largest coal reserves in the world behind the USA and Russia, and has traditionally met all of its coal needs from abundant domestic coal resources. It is by far the largest consumer, annually using more than twice as much coal as the USA, the second largest coal consumer. As with overall energy demand, between 1985 and 1996, coal demand grew at roughly half the rate of economic growth, around 4 per cent annually. Between 1997 and 2000 coal consumption declined as a proportion of the total, officially due to the closure of tens of thousands of small mines. However, coal demand accelerated sharply after 2001, rising at an average of 15 per cent per year through 2007, reflecting the underlying upward shift in the elasticity of demand to nearly 1.5 times GDP growth rates. In just five years between 2002 and 2007, Chinese coal demand *increased* by an amount equal to *total US consumption in 2007*.[28] Figure 10.2 shows the growing importance of coal in China's economy.

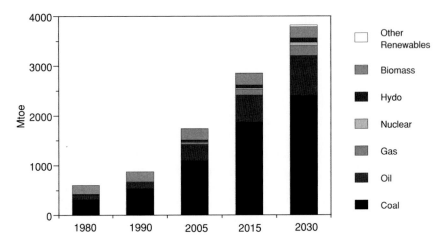

Source: IEA World Energy Outlook 2007, page 289

Figure 10.2: China's primary energy demand in the IEA's reference scenario

Industrial use and power generation dominate coal consumption. Both accelerating industrial and electricity demand explain the sharp shift upward in demand growth after 2001. Between 2001 and 2006, electricity demand doubled, growing at over 15 per cent per year.[29] Surging electricity demand triggered widespread power shortages across China between 2003 and 2006. In response, China built 102 Gigawatts (GW) of power generation, equivalent in one year to the combined generation capacity of the UK and Thailand, 90 GW of which was coal-fired.[30] In 2006 China built on average the equivalent of a large 250 megawatt (MW) coal-fired power plant every day, and in that year China accounted for 72 per cent of the entire global increase in coal consumption. Coal consumption in China is likely to more than double by 2030, and China alone is likely to account for two-thirds of the entire global increase of coal consumption during that period.[31]

It appears that China became a net coal importer for the first time in 2007, and then began to have a significant impact on world coal prices with its growing imports.[32] Longer-term, the IEA forecasts that China is likely to become a net importer of 88 million tons per year by 2030.[33]

Electricity

Rising demand for electricity has historically shaped the consumption mix of key fuels, most importantly coal. Electricity demand growth will also shape the future of other generation sources such as nuclear, hydroelectric, natural gas, and renewables. China has the second largest electricity market in the world behind the USA, with an installed capacity of roughly 700 GW by the end of 2007. Currently coal accounts for 78 per cent of generation, hydroelectric meets roughly 16 per cent, while nuclear and oil meet about 2 per cent each, with natural gas about 1 per cent.[34]

Electricity demand is expected to triple between 2005 and 2030, creating enormous challenges in building generating capacity to meet rising requirements.[35] Given the limitations on supplies of other, cleaner fuels and the abundance and low cost of domestic coal, the IEA forecasts that 70 per cent of the increased generation capacity will be coal-fired.[36] This means a doubling of coal use in China over this period. Hydroelectric is expected to make up another 15 per cent of capacity additions. China is already the world's largest producer of hydroelectric power, and the government plans to build the equivalent of a new Three Gorges dam capacity every 30 months over the next 25 years. Even with such rapid hydroelectric growth, however, its share of electricity generation is forecast to decline from 16 to 12 per cent by 2030, as power demand outstrips capacity development. Natural gas should make up another 7 per cent of the growth in generation capacity, assuming the continued domestic gas supply growth and gas imports discussed earlier. However, even so, at the end of the period, gas will account for only 4 per cent of capacity. Nuclear, which accounted for 2 per cent of generation in 2006, is planned to make up 2 per cent of capacity additions as China embarks on the largest nuclear generation building programme in the world. China plans to add an ambitious 32 GW of nuclear capacity over the next 15 years when, by 2020, nuclear will still meet just 4 per cent of electricity needs.

Renewables

The main role of non-hydro renewables in China will be in the electricity generation area in the form of wind and solar power. Other minor components will appear in the transport sector in the development of biofuels for motor transport, mainly ethanol.

In electricity generation, renewables currently make up less than 1 per cent of generation capacity, mainly from wind power. The IEA forecasts that renewables will make up 6 per cent of generation capacity growth to 2030, at which point renewables would make up roughly 3 per cent of total generation capacity. China's wind power capacity was 1.3 GW in 2005 (roughly 0.25 per cent of capacity) and this doubled in 2006. The government aims to raise wind power capacity to 30 GW by 2020, but the IEA forecast capacity will reach 29 GW by 2030, meeting 1.5 per cent of total electricity needs. China is already the world's largest consumer of solar energy and the largest producer of solar photovoltaic thermal systems. Roughly 70 MW is online currently, mainly in remote applications for locations far off the national grid. China plans to have 1.8 GW of solar capacity by 2020, and the IEA forecasts a rise to 8 GW of solar capacity by 2030, equal to roughly 0.5 per cent of generation capacity.

Production of biofuels, in the form of corn and other agricultural products being turned into ethanol liquid fuels for use in transportation, is already substantial in China, but it trails both the USA and Brazil by large amounts. China has made development of biofuels a priority, giving substantial subsidies to promote development. China has established two ethanol production centres, with a combined production capacity of about 1 million tons per year, or about 20,000 barrels of liquid fuels per day, equivalent to about one-quarter of 1 per cent of China's oil demand. The ambitious target for liquid biofuels is 2 million tons per year by 2010 and 10 million tons per year by 2020, which would be equal to about 200,000 barrels per day of liquids, at that point accounting for about 1.5 per cent of total oil demand. This target will be difficult to reach since there is already a growing debate about the impact of diverting corn production away from human consumption to the production of fuels, and the impact on corn supplies and food prices. In fact the government suspended the use of edible grains for fuel production at the end of 2006 over concerns about livestock feed prices and food security. Corn prices have already risen sharply due to the diversion.

Energy Policy

The Chinese government maintains a significant degree of central control over the energy sector, although over the past 15 years there has been a gradual transition towards greater reliance on market mechanisms and pricing. Responsibility for policymaking and implementation has evolved substantially among a changing group of official agencies. Prior to March 2008, the top energy policy body was the National Energy Leading Group, an agency of the State Council, established in 2005 to respond to the need for greater coordination in energy policymaking among ministries and other government agencies. The Office of the National Energy Leading Group (ONELG) provided advice by undertaking a broad set of studies to support the development of a long-term energy strategy. The National Development and Reform Commission (NDRC), the main economic ministry, also played a key role in energy policy. The NDRC's Energy Bureau had key regulatory and policy functions, such as major energy project approvals. The Energy Research Institute (ERI), another unit within the NDRC, served as the energy think tank for the NDRC, and did research on energy efficiency, pricing, and regulation. A variety of other government agencies have important roles, which makes energy policymaking highly complicated. Moreover, in March 2008, the government approved the creation of two new agencies to coordinate policy. The National Energy Commission (NEC) replaced the ONELG and seeks to strengthen energy decision-making and coordination. Additionally, a new National Energy Administration (NEA) is to absorb the Energy Bureau and handle the day-to-day work of the NEC. The NDRC retained the ERI and its energy pricing authority.[37]

The national government's five-year economic plans are the main reference point for policy discussions on energy and for energy industry planning. The 11th Five Year Plan covering 2006–2010 sets out key supply infrastructure projects, as well as goals for energy efficiency, environmental protection, and research and development. The NDRC and other ministries and agencies issue periodic policy statements, advisories, and circulars focusing on specific issues. In response to rapid change in the energy situation, the government is preparing a new comprehensive Energy Law to set out principles and responsibilities of various government agencies regarding energy.

The 11th Five Year Plan stresses the goals of saving energy and of expanding domestic supplies. The central goal is to reduce primary energy intensity by 20 per cent in 2010 compared to 2005. China did not meet its goal in 2006, having achieved only a very small reduction in energy intensity, although this performance did reverse the upward trend of the previous five years. Other objectives are to diversify energy resources, protect the environment, enhance international energy cooperation, and to ensure a stable supply of affordable and clean energy to support social development. The plan sets specific goals for each major fuel and identifies ways to expand supply.

The Energy Policy Debate: Supply-side vs. Demand-side Solutions

The core energy policy debate in China has traditionally been focused around how to mobilize energy supplies quickly enough to meet booming demand. China's leadership is deeply fearful that shortages of energy could derail economic growth, slow the job-creation machine, and potentially fuel social instability, seeing energy as a major potential Achilles heel for the economy. This fear, combined with the traditional instincts for self-sufficiency and for central direction of the economy, has historically reinforced a powerful tendency to pursue supply-side solutions to meet energy security and economic needs. Therefore, until recently, the debate has revolved around how to mobilize energy and infrastructure investment sufficiently rapidly to keep up with energy demand. In this context, the key influential actors have been the major state energy companies with vested interests in growing energy demand and investment, the various ministries tied closely to each industry, other industries (such as the rapidly growing vehicle sector, which the leadership sees as a huge potential future employer, as well as a key future export industry), and the top economic and political leadership intent on keeping supplies available and energy costs low in order to continue fuelling extremely high economic growth. Also important are provincial and local officials, whose incentive systems are largely driven by economic and industrial growth, rather than efficiency. Taken together, these groups constitute what might be called the '*Growth Coalition*', which has driven energy policy until recently.

However, at least three critical factors have intervened to change this energy and political balance in recent years, shifting the debate toward a growing emphasis on energy efficiency and demand-side solutions. First, the enormous surge in energy demand since 2001 has increasingly convinced many in the leadership and in economic ministries that an exclusive focus on increasing energy supplies is no longer practical, and increasingly risks leading to the very shortages and price spikes that they hope to avoid. The severe shortages of coal, rail capacity, and electricity between 2003 and 2006, and the winter 2008 coal and electricity crisis, were critical turning points on this score. Second, the global surge in energy prices, particularly for oil but also for natural gas, along with worsening global oil market instability and geopolitical uncertainty about future oil supplies, have also forced a reconsideration of whether the acceleration of domestic supply development combined with the 'go-out' strategy to acquire international oil supplies will suffice to meet China's needs. China is starting to realize that it must face up to the demand growth problem domestically. Third, accelerating domestic energy-related environmental air and water pollution problems, and growing political sensitivity about China's rapidly rising carbon emissions and coal consumption are forcing the leadership to re-consider a whole new range of energy efficiency and pollution-reducing strategies.

These new pressures have gradually raised the influence, and increased the power of, the pro-efficiency, demand-oriented groups in the energy policy debate, including the NDRC's Energy Research Institute and the State Environmental Protection Agency (SEPA). As part of the March 2008 energy policy changes, SEPA gained ministry status, signifying the growing recognition of the importance of energy–environmental matters. These trends have also increased the influence of those among the top leadership arguing for a more coherent and balanced energy policymaking system, which accounts partly for the recent creation of the new NEC and NEA. As a result, energy policy has begun to focus more intently on improving demand-reducing measures to meet China's growing energy constraints.[38] For example, in late 2007 the State Council published a key *White Paper on Energy*, which included a strong focus on energy conservation, efficiency, and promoting market mechanisms and prices in its recommendations for future energy policy.[39]

Key Energy Policy Challenges and Uncertainties

China faces enormous challenges in its rapidly evolving efforts to reduce the rate of energy demand growth and to increase energy supply and infrastructure, while maintaining rapid economic growth and rising standards of living. The underlying structural challenge is that the high rate of energy demand growth is closely linked to the structure of the economy and to the heavy industry, energy-intensive nature of Chinese economic growth. Although the leadership recognizes the need to reduce energy intensity in the economy and industry, the economy has been resistant to change, and efforts to shift this mix will take a long time to mature. There is a frank recognition among many Chinese energy experts that the industrial structural impact of China's economic growth is overwhelming its efforts to boost energy efficiency. At the same time, rapid urbanization and rising consumption are accelerating the pace of consumer-driven energy demand for the future. Finally, politically, there is little appetite in Beijing among the leadership to risk doing anything that might slow down the economic and job growth machine.

Energy Security

Achieving a stronger base for energy security will remain a major challenge of energy policy. Fundamentally, China has no reasonable alternative to substantial dependence on global oil markets for its future oil supplies. In the longer run, China is also likely to depend heavily on regional and global natural gas and LNG supplies if it wants to rapidly increase the use of cleaner natural gas in industry and power generation. Policies pursued recently to address these concerns include accelerating domestic oil and gas supply development, encouraging national oil companies to 'go out' to invest in oil development globally, developing a Strategic Petroleum Reserve to be available in case of a major oil supply disruption, and constructing the infrastructure for importing LNG on a large scale.

The challenge for Beijing going forward will be two-fold. First, China's leadership needs to expand the country's oil and gas integration into global energy markets to ensure *access* to crude oil supplies and natural gas, rather than continue to focus much more narrowly on a strategy of trying to gain physical control of oil and gas supplies through national company equity investments. The real issue is access rather than ownership, and as Beijing gradually evolves toward this more market-oriented solution to the supply situation, the more successful it will be in securing reliable supplies. Adopting a market approach also means joining in multilateral efforts to ensure oil market stability through cooperation with the IEA and other international energy organizations. China has recently engaged much more actively with the IEA on managing emergency oil stocks, as it has begun building its own strategic stockpile.

Second, and more importantly, Beijing needs to strengthen its demand-side efforts regarding oil use, which means addressing the prospective enormous rise in vehicle use and manufacturing that will increasingly drive oil demand. New, more aggressive efforts to promote efficient use of oil in transportation will be needed. The leadership has begun to move in this direction with new taxes on large vehicle engines, new mileage requirements on new vehicles, rapid promotion of mass transit in the big cities, and efforts such as converting bus fleets in major cities to compressed natural gas. However, these efforts will have to be greatly expanded in the future, and China needs to consider how it can fundamentally alter its trajectory on transportation-driven oil consumption. Doing so also means taking on sensitive issues such as raising transportation fuel prices to international levels and imposing much higher fuel taxes, in order to encourage more efficiency in transportation. In a major new shift, in December 2008 subsidies for transportation fuels were eliminated as world crude prices dropped, providing a window of opportunity.[40]

The Energy–Environment Nexus

China's heavy reliance on coal, the high rate of electricity demand growth, and the growing role of oil for transportation use is intensifying an environmental crisis in terms of air pollution in the cities, severe water and soil contamination, deforestation, and a huge rise in carbon emissions with global implications. The IEA estimates that in 2007, China surpassed the USA as the largest emitter of carbon, and is on a trajectory to account for 49 per cent, nearly half, of the world's future carbon emissions to 2030.[41] Coal and electricity are central to progress on this issue, and China is making many new efforts in this regard. Beijing has begun to set standards for emissions from power plants and industrial sources, called for environmental impact assessments for some large projects, begun switching to natural gas generation where possible, and accelerated nuclear and hydroelectric development plans. The latest five-year plan sets strong targets for curbing energy use and pollution, including the 20 per cent energy intensity reduction and a 10 per cent reduction in sulphur dioxide (SO_2) emissions. In 2007, a new Climate Change Leadership Group was established, which led to the first national plan to address climate change.[42] The leadership has begun to promote the idea of 'Green GDP' in order to begin shifting economic development in a cleaner direction, energy being a key element of that effort.[43] However, the rapid pace of energy demand growth is outrunning these efforts, and the lack of effective regulatory and enforcement mechanisms further undermines achieving even these limited goals. As in the case of energy security, the leadership will need to move much more quickly and forcefully if it is to make serious headway on curbing the environmental problems that China's energy use is causing.

Energy Efficiency and Market Reforms

As suggested earlier, the energy policy debate has been shifting gradually towards a stronger focus on efficiency, and reducing the rate of energy demand growth across the fuel spectrum. There is a growing political will behind these measures. For example, one of the key new initiatives is the Top-1,000 Energy-Consuming Enterprises programme, under which contracts and targets have been drawn up with the 1,000 largest companies in terms of energy consumption. The overall goal is to achieve savings of 100 Metric tons carbon equivalent (Mtce) compared to the expected 2010 energy consumption of these businesses. In addition to end uses, efficiency in energy production and transformation are also top priorities. Efficiency potential is greatest in the largest energy-intensive sectors – industry and power generation. Among these, steel, building materials (cement, brick and tile, flat glass, ceramics), chemicals, and nonferrous metals are particularly important. In addition, in June 2007 the NDRC published the *Comprehensive Action Plan for Energy Saving and Emissions Reduction*, which aims to ensure implementation at all levels of government. The government is also promoting efforts to boost the role of renewable sources of solar and wind power electricity.

However, the announced measures are essentially top-down ones at a time when China needs more bottom-up and market-based instruments to achieve its energy efficiency goals. Moreover, the level of investment in energy efficiency efforts needs to be boosted drastically. A 2005 study by Lawrence Berkeley National Laboratory suggested that investments in energy efficiency were only 10 per cent of the level needed to achieve the reduction in energy intensity called for in the latest energy plan.[44] Efficiency improvements take years to develop, and also depend on enforcing new standards on the construction of new building, new factories, and new power plants. Also, efficiency gains put a heavy premium of effective regulation and implementation, which remain a challenge.

Other elements that will be critical for China in achieving the efficiency gains are market reform and market pricing for energy. Price-setting remains a sensitive issue, and subsidies continue to be widespread and significant in energy pricing. Coal prices are now set largely by market forces, but electricity prices remain under tight government control, particularly for residential use.[45] Oil product subsidies have also been significant. During the recent world oil price surge domestic fuel prices fell substantially behind world price levels. Rising crude prices, combined with controlled product prices, led to large losses among refiners, particularly Sinopec, and contributed to major product shortages in southeastern coastal China in 2005, 2006, and 2007. The government compensated by providing large direct payments to cover losses. As mentioned earlier, the government finally moved to end fuel subsidies in late 2008, taking advantage of sharply lower crude prices. Nevertheless, energy pricing and taxation will require substantial new reforms in the future and these will test the government's commitment to vital demand-side reforms.

Administrative Reform and Political Constraints

Two other key areas remain as major challenges for future energy policy. First, energy policy-making remains fragmented and diffused, and lacking in a central and strategic focus. Despite the creation of the new National Energy Commission and National Energy Administration, authority remains divided between the NEA and the NDRC, and is further diffused among as many as 12 ministries. Horizontal coordination across ministries remains extremely difficult, and policy-making tends to be strongly stove-piped. Efficiency efforts, in particular, require much stronger coordination across issue areas. At the same time there is no Energy Ministry to pursue a more coherent package of reforms. There was extensive discussion in the run-up to the March 2008 National People's Congress meeting that an Energy Ministry would be created to overcome fragmentation in energy policy, but bureaucratic and large state energy company opposition to the creation of a new ministry eventually killed the proposal.[46]

Related to this problem is the continued political resistance to demand-side reforms. This opposition comes from vested interests among the state and large non-state energy enterprises as well as provincial and local officials, the *growth coalition*, who resist necessary changes. Finally, the top leadership also remains reticent in facing up to the more controversial requirements of reform, such as reducing electricity subsidies, raising the cost of energy, and loosening its control over the energy industry, for fear that higher costs and market price volatility will slow job creation and risk provoking social and political unrest.

Looking forward, energy imbalances and Beijing's slow pace of energy market reform have the potential to cause major political and social problems. Beijing remains caught between two very unpalatable choices. One is essentially maintaining the current mix of policies, institutional arrangements, and long-term energy trajectory with only the modest, incremental, and piecemeal steps toward energy reform we see today. This approach has the virtue of maintaining short-term stability, avoiding many of the painful social and political consequences of moving much more rapidly toward rigorous energy market reforms. It would postpone the pain of increasing energy prices and taxes, removing popular energy subsidies, imposing stronger regulatory restrictions on industry and consumers, and pushing for major structural changes to improve energy efficiency through altering the shape of the industrial economy and the autonomy of the major state energy companies. However, this path raises the risks over the longer term of increasingly chronic energy shortages and bottlenecks, rising social tensions over energy availability, potential greater damage to long-term economic growth and job creation, and an unprecedented deterioration in environmental outcomes as the economy consumes ever greater quantities of coal and oil. The risks entailed in this choice are visible in the proliferation of recent episodes of oil product, electricity, and coal shortages experienced across China.[47]

The alternative choice is to move much more aggressively towards efficiency and energy reform, which would require the leadership to take on the tough political challenges of vested economic and energy industry interests, imposing strong new government institutional reforms and overcoming consumer resistance to higher energy prices and taxes in the very near-term, rather than postponing needed change. This approach would increase the risks of near-term political and social turmoil over energy costs and availability, but would promise to lead China to a much more manageable and environmentally-sustainable long-term energy trajectory. Given how central energy is to China's economic outlook, it is also very likely that accelerating energy reform would also require a much faster pace of broader economic and even political reform to be effective.

Neither choice is an easy one for the leadership; each path has powerful implications for China's future domestic political, economic, and social stability. However, the longer the leadership postpones these difficult decisions, the more it risks facing a long-term future of growing energy shortages, chronic disruptions, and damage to economic growth and job creation that it so deeply wishes to avoid.

International Implications of China's Energy Trajectory

China's energy choices over the next two decades also have enormous implications for its place within the global community. Internationally, it is difficult to overstate the impact China is likely to have on global energy markets and geopolitics over the next two decades. China's entrance into the world's energy markets is much more like the emergence of another continent, not simply another country. For example, between 2002 and 2007 China added to global primary energy demand the equivalent of another Latin America, from Mexico to Argentina.[48]

Nevertheless, China's global energy market impact is likely to vary significantly across energy sectors. The greatest impact will be felt in the global oil market and in the oil industry. In its *World Energy Outlook 2008*, the IEA forecasted that if current expectations hold firm, China is likely to account for one-third of global oil demand growth over the next 25 years.[49] If China's economic growth rate averages 7.5 per cent over the next 25 years, rather than the 6 per cent assumed in the IEA's Reference Case, China's oil demand could rise to 21 mb/d by 2030 and account for over 40 per cent of global oil demand growth.[50] Therefore, Beijing's decisions about transportation, vehicle fuel technologies, and oil use generally will have profound implications for global oil prices and the energy security of other oil importers. China will depend on imported oil for virtually all of this increasing demand. In the course of less than a decade, China's three national oil companies have become significant new players on the global oil industry scene, with increasing investment stakes in the Middle East, Central Asia and Russia, Africa, and the western hemisphere.[51]

China's rising oil consumption and imports, the growing investments of its oil companies, its commercial diplomacy in support of those companies, and Beijing's intensifying concerns about oil supply security, are forging China's emergence as a key player in global energy geopolitics. Beijing has made energy security an important reference point for its global diplomacy and economic and trade ties. While China has a broad range of strategic interests in a growing number of regions around the world, energy relationships are a major contributing factor to the emergence of China as an important player in the Persian Gulf, Central Asia and Russia, and Africa. This new role has important long-term implications for major power cooperation or rivalry, for influence in these key regions.

As China emerges as a major force in both world energy markets and geopolitics, it is creating important new challenges as well as opportunities in its relations with other major energy players, most importantly the USA, Japan, and Russia. A drift toward an atmosphere of competition for access to, and control over, oil and gas supplies has in some cases aggravated broader strategic relations among China, the importers of North East Asia, and the USA. Also, China's frustrations in its efforts to access Russian energy supplies have added to underlying strategic tensions between Beijing and Moscow. However, China and the other consumers, as well as Russia, can all benefit if they can overcome their suspicions and take advantage of their shared interests in energy and environmental issues. Energy cooperation has the potential to be an important source of greater strategic cooperation and trust among these countries, if they can muster the leadership to act together on their common interests.

Of particular importance is the impact of China's energy emergence globally, on US strategic and energy interests, and the potential impact on USA–China relations. The USA–China relationship is arguably the single most important bilateral relationship for the world over the next three decades. During the past several years, China's growing energy reach has led to new tensions in USA–China relations regarding China's energy involvement in Iran and Sudan, and over US perceptions that China's energy investments are part of a mercantilist strategy to gain control over global oil supplies and potentially undermine US energy security. The 2005 episode in which China's CNOOC attempted to acquire Unocal, and the political firestorm this created in Washington DC epitomizes the mirror-image prism of strategic suspicion through which each side views the other's global energy intentions and influence. However, since that debacle, there have been new efforts by both Beijing and Washington to avoid this negative dynamic, with new efforts to promote energy cooperation between the USA and China.[52] China and the USA have established a new bilateral energy dialogue, have begun to work together on energy efficiency and clean coal technology, and have both deliberately toned down the nationalistic rhetoric about energy security. Energy cooperation has been a key agenda item for the USA–China Strategic Economic Dialogue (SED) launched in 2007. China and the USA ultimately have strong common interests in stabilizing global oil markets and prices, preventing major oil transportation disruptions in the Malacca Straits, and, as the two largest coal-consuming countries in the world, forging cooperation for a more environmentally-sustainable energy mix. However, it will take continued leadership in both Beijing and Washington to strengthen these early, tentative efforts at cooperation. Much will depend on the policies of the new Obama administration, and whether it continues the energy cooperation efforts established through the SED during the latter part of the Bush administration. Although progress is being made on energy efficiency and clean coal cooperation, the more strategic issues have continued to vex USA–China relations. Among these are the implications of China's global energy investments, and the two countries' common interests in improving maritime security in the Malacca Straits.

A similar struggle between the impulses toward energy competition or cooperation has been occurring in Asia. China's expanding energy footprint has combined with growing energy security fears among Japan, South Korea, and India, increasing the perception of regional competition to control oil and gas supplies. These fears are feeding and, at the same time, are fed by the broader strategic rivalry over future relations in the region among the key powers. In particular, concern over energy has aggravated an already tense Sino–Japanese relationship. However, the situation is also changing gradually, as recent efforts by Japan and China to negotiate a new agreement over disputed natural gas fields in the East China Sea have made progress. Not coincidentally, this forward momentum has coincided with improved Sino–Japanese strategic relations, following the deep freeze in relations under the Koizumi government in Japan. Japan and China have also begun a new bilateral energy dialogue, focused on assisting China's energy efficiency efforts, and new energy efficiency technology development.[53] Energy competition has also become a significant irritant in Sino–Indian relations. Nevertheless, China and India have also begun to make new efforts to avoid direct competition among their national oil companies bidding for acquisitions of major oil production assets globally.

As China has reached out to diversify its growing oil and gas imports, it has turned to Russia as an enormous potential supplier that could help China limit its future dependence on seaborne imports of oil and LNG. Many analysts expected rising energy trade to be a major source of stronger strategic relations between China and Russia in view of the profound complementarity of their oil and gas resource and demand patterns.[54] However, the results have been mixed and, if anything, energy become more a source of mistrust than of closer ties.[55] Since the late 1990s, Russia has been shipping roughly 250 kb/d of oil exports via rail to north-east China. By 2000, China and Russia were discussing major deals to build new pipelines for oil and gas supplies to China from East Siberia's Kovykta gas fields and Angarsk oil fields. However, despite repeated promises from Moscow, most of these plans have stalled as the result of Russia's reorganization and recentralization of the energy industry under Vladimir Putin. Moreover, there is evidence of reticence among Russia's leadership to provide energy on a large scale to fuel China's powerful economic rise, which exerts a concomitant economic gravitational force on Russia's Far East. After much indecision, Russia is now building the long-promised 600 kb/d East Siberia–Pacific Ocean pipeline (ESPO) to move oil to a point near China's border at Skovorodino that would presumably connect with a pipeline planned by China from Daqing. In February 2009, China provided Russia with large loans to move this project forward. However, Russia's promises to build gas pipelines to China look likely to be pushed much further out into the future, due to Gazprom's preoccupation with supplying European gas markets, and lack of needed investment in East Siberian gas development. Moreover, China has resisted agreeing to pay full market prices for Russian imported gas, which has further complicated negotiations over gas pipeline imports. At present, China remains quite frustrated with the slow progress in expanding imports of Russian oil and gas, and energy has become a source of suspicion in relations between the two, rather than supporting stronger strategic ties.

In part because of frustration with slow Russian developments, China has turned enthusiastically towards accessing Central Asian oil and gas supplies, and energy has been a source of growing cooperation, especially between China and Kazakhstan. China built an oil export pipeline from Kazakhstan carrying 200 kb/d, which is being expanded to 400 kb/d, and its NOCs have major investments in the Kazakh oil and gas industry. China also recently signed a major gas pipeline deal with Turkmenistan and has begun construction, bringing into sharp relief the contradiction of China sponsoring a 6,000 mile pipeline to utilize gas from Turkmenistan while it is unable to gain access to huge Russian gas supplies within 2,000 miles at Kovykta.

China's long-term impact on other global and regional energy markets and geopolitics are likely to be more muted than for oil. As China seeks to expand the role of domestic gas use, imports are expected to rise toward 40 per cent of demand by 2020. Recent forecasts suggest China could be importing as much as 50 million tons per year of LNG by 2020, mainly from South East Asia (Australia, Malaysia, Indonesia) and the Persian Gulf (Qatar, Iran) along with the equivalent of another 50 million tons by pipeline (roughly 70 bcm) from Russia and Central Asia. China is likely to become the second largest importer of new incremental supplies of LNG in the Pacific Basin behind South Korea, and could easily be the largest if it approaches the 50 MT range by 2020. Geopolitically, LNG imports are likely to enhance China's relationships and influence in South East Asia, pulling China into closer economic and diplomatic relationships with Australia and Indonesia.[56]

China's rising future coal consumption will have great importance globally, beyond its impact on the global coal market and coal prices, due to the global, national, and regional environmental and CO_2 emission implications. Oil also is central to these dynamics. By 2030 China is still likely to rely on coal and oil for 85 per cent of its primary energy mix, due to limits on the practical pace of substituting natural gas, nuclear, hydro and renewable sources of energy. This inability to move away from oil and coal implies an enormous increase of CO_2 emissions from China. China's carbon intensity (carbon emitted per dollar unit of GDP output) is 50 per cent higher than the OECD average. The power sector accounts for 50 per cent of China's CO_2 emissions due to the fact that 80 per cent of power generation is coal-fired.

Looking forward, on the current trajectory, CO_2 emissions from China are still likely to more than double between 2005 and 2030, rising from 5.1 to 11.4 billion tons per year, increasing China's global share of annual emissions from 19 per cent in 2005 to 27 per cent by 2030.[57] China's incremental increase in CO_2 emissions to 2030 would be nearly three times the increase of the entire OECD. By 2030 China's total stock of carbon emissions since 1900 would reach 16 per cent of the entire global stock of CO_2 emissions, compared to 25 per cent for the USA and 18 per cent for the EU. China alone would account for 49 per cent of global incremental CO_2 emissions to 2030, compared to 37 per cent for rest of world, excluding India at 14 per cent.

These estimates suggest that China's energy usage will become one of the central issues in the global debate over carbon emissions, and that China will inevitably come under increasing international pressure to alter its current coal- and oil-centric energy trajectory.[58] For the Chinese leadership, this will be an increasingly difficult balance to keep. On the one hand, China legitimately points out that its emissions per capita are only one-third of those of the OECD and one-fifth of those of the USA. Even by 2030, per capita emissions would still be less than one-half of those in the USA. Moreover, China currently accounts for just 8 per cent of cumulative emissions, compared to 27 per cent for the USA and 24 per cent for the EU. Nevertheless, the scale of China's looming CO_2 impact will make it difficult for China to avoid considering a new approach in the global negotiations over carbon and climate change. As a result, the leadership has recently become increasingly pro-active in staking out its position in upcoming climate negotiations. In late 2008 Beijing released a new policy paper laying out its position on climate change negotiations, stating that while China was moving rapidly on domestic measures to slow the growth of its carbon emissions, it was ultimately the responsibility of the rich countries to solve the carbon problem caused by their 150 years of industrialization and growing wealth.

Conclusion

China's current trajectory for energy consumption bears with it the seeds of fundamental long-term changes that are just beginning to come into view. Profound movement toward a fundamentally new, less energy-intensive development model will be needed to avoid a series of looming problems: the domestic political risks of more frequent and economically damaging energy-driven shortages with accompanying social dislocations and tensions, rising strategic competition and rivalry for energy supplies globally that undermines key strategic relationships, and an unsustainable environmental outcome both in terms of domestic air pollution and international environmental and climate change consequences. China's leadership can either choose to begin addressing the difficult but manageable transition towards a changed energy–economic model, or put off making the fundamental decisions and risk much larger, long-term political, economic, and environmental problems.

Notes

1 International Energy Agency, *World Energy Outlook 2008*, International Energy Agency, Paris, 2007, 81.
2 All data for this paragraph come from the *BP Statistical Review of World Energy 2008*, BP, London, 2008. www.bp.com/productlanding.do?category Id=6929&contentId=7044622
3 For a good discussion of this evolution, see International Energy Agency, *World Energy Outlook 2007: China and India Insights*, International Energy Agency, Paris, 2007, 263–4; also Rosen, D.H. and T. Houser, *China Energy, A Guide for the Perplexed*, Center for Strategic and International Studies and Peterson Institute for International Economics, Washington DC, 2007, 6–9.
4 Jonathan E. Sinton, et.al., *Evaluation of China's Energy Strategy Options*, Lawrence Berkeley National Laboratory, May 2005, 1–4.
5 IEA, 2007, 264–5; Rosen and Houser, *China Energy*, 7–10.
6 BP Statistical Review of World Energy 2008.
7 David Fridley, 'China's Energy and Economy: Paths to 2020', presentation, Lawrence Berkeley National Laboratory, San Francisco, 2 March 2007.
8 All demand, production, and reserve figures in this paragraph from BP Statistical Review, 2008.
9 IEA, 2008, 93.
10 IEA, 2008, 99–100.
11 IEA, 2008, 105.
12 This section is based on a growing literature on China's energy security concerns, for example Phillip Andrews-Speed, et.al., *The Strategic Implications*

of China's Energy Needs, Adelphi Papers #346, The International Institute for Strategic Studies, Oxford University Press, UK, 2002; David Zweig and Bi Jianhai, 'China's Global Hunt for Energy: The Foreign Policy of a Resource Hungry State', *Foreign Affairs*, September/October 2005; Xuecheng Liu, *China's Energy Security and its Grand Strategy*, The Stanley Foundation, US, September 2006; Erica Downs, *China*, The Brookings Foreign Policy Studies Energy Security Series, Washington, DC, 2006; Roland Dannreuther, 'Asian security and China's energy needs', *International Relations of the Asia–Pacific*, Oxford University Press, Oxford and the Japan Association of International Relations, 2003, 197–219; Zha Daojiong, 'China's Energy Security: Domestic and International Issues', *Survival*, 48:1, Spring 2006.

13 Mikkal E, Herberg, *The Rise of Asia's National Oil Companies*, Energy Security Survey No. 14, National Bureau of Asian Research, Seattle, 2007; John Mitchell and Glada Lahn, *Oil for Asia*, Chatham House, Royal Institute of International Affairs, London, 2007; *The Changing Role of National Oil Companies in International Energy Markets*, Baker Institute Policy Report No. 35, The James A. Baker III Institute for Public Policy, Houston, 2006.

14 Stephen Blank, 'China, Kazakh Energy, and Russia: An Unlikely Menage a Trois', *The China and Eurasia Forum Quarterly*, 3:3, November 2005, 99–109; Rajan Menon, 'The New Great Game in Central Asia', *Survival*, 45:2, January 2003, 187–204; Stephen Blank, 'China's Emerging Energy Nexus with Central Asia', *Jamestown Foundation China Brief*, VI: 15, 19 July 2006.

15 For example, Zhang Wenmu, 'Sea Power and China's Strategic Choices', *China Security*, Summer 2006, 17–31.

16 Gabriel Collins, 'China fills first SPR site, faces oil and pipeline issues', *Oil and Gas Journal*, 20 August 2007, 20–29.

17 Stephen Blank, 'China Makes Policy Shift, Aiming to Widen Access to Central Asia Energy', *Eurasianet.org*, 13 March 2006.

18 Kenneth Lieberthal and Mikkal Herberg, *China's Search for Energy Security: Implications for US Policy*, NBR Analysis 17:1, April 2006, 13–19.

19 See Mikkal E. Herberg, 'China's Approach to Energy Security', Testimony, US–China Economic and Security Review Commission, 14 June 2007, Washington, DC.

20 2020 estimates from Fridley, 'China's Energy and Economy', 2030 demand estimates from IEA, 2008, 110–112.

21 Martin Clark, 'Natural Gas: Reality Bites', *Petroleum Economist*, December 2004, 1.

22 For a discussion of LNG, see Mikkal E. Herberg, 'The Geopolitics of China's LNG Development', in Gabriel B. Collins, et.al., *China's Energy Strategy: The Impact on Beijing's Maritime Policies*, Naval Institute Press, Annapolis, 2008, 61–80.

23 IEA, 2008 118; David Fridley suggests imports reaching 40 per cent of demand by 2020, Fridley, 'China's Energy and Economy'.

24 'Myanmar's Pipeline Politics', *The Economist*, 23 May 2007.

25 Blank, 'China's Emerging Energy Nexus with Central Asia'.

26 'PetroChina Reaches LNG Agreement with Qatar', *China Economic Review*,

14 February 2008.

27 Sally Jones, 'Iran and China's CNOOC Sign $16 Billion Gas Deal', *Dow Jones Newswire*, 20 December 2006; 'Iran: Looking East with Multimillion Dollar MOUs', *Petroleum Economist*, December 2004.

28 BP Statistical Review 2008.

29 BP Statistical Review 2008.

30 For an excellent discussion of China's electricity, see IEA, *China's Power Sector Reforms: Where to Next?*, IEA, Paris, 2006, particularly 56–60.

31 IEA, 2008, 125.

32 Shai Oster and Ann Davis, 'China Spurs Coal Price Surge', *Wall Street Journal*, 12 February 2008, A1; David Winning, 'China Scours Asia for Coal', *Wall Street Journal*, 22 March 2007.

33 IEA, 2008, 132.

34 IEA, 2007, 343–8.

35 IEA, 2008, 140.

36 All forecasts in this paragraph from IEA 2007, 344–8.

37 For an excellent discussion of the new bureaucratic arrangements, see Erica S. Downs, 'China's "New" Energy Administration', *China Business Review*, November–December 2008, 42–5.

38 'China Proposes Market-Based Energy Pricing in Draft Energy Law', Interfax-China, 5 December 2007.

39 *White Paper on Energy*, The State Council Information Office, Beijing, 26 December 2007.

40 Geoff Dyer, 'China Moves to Overhaul Retail Fuel Prices', *Financial Times*, 5 December 2008, 4.

41 IEA, 2008, 385–6.

42 See Joanna Lewis, 'China's Climate Change Strategy', *Jamestown Foundation China Brief* 7: 13, 27 June 2007; also Joanna I. Lewis, 'China's Strategic Priorities in International Climate Negotiations', *The Washington Quarterly*, Winter 2007–08, 155–74.

43 Wenran Jiang, 'China Debates Green GDP and its Future Development Model', *Jamestown Foundation China Brief* 7: 16, 8 August 2007.

44 Sinton, et.al., *Evaluation of China's Energy Strategy Options*.

45 See, for example, Richard McGregor, 'Coal Price Debate at Root of Power Shortage', *Financial Times*, 29 January 2008; also McGregor, 'Coal Shortages Put Pressure on Beijing', *Financial Times*, 28 January 2008.

46 'Draft Energy Law Suggests the Establishment of a Ministry of Energy', *Interfax-China*, 10 October 2007; but also Richard McGregor, 'Hopes for New China Energy Ministry Fade', *Financial Times*, 25 February 2008.

47 For example, the summer electricity shortages of 2003–6, the annual summer oil product shortages in south-eastern China in recent years, and the coal and electricity emergency of the February 2008 snow storms.

48 BP Statistical Review 2008.

49 IEA WEO 2008, 93.

50 IEA WEO 2007, 166.

51 Geoff Dyer and Sundeep Tucker, 'In Search of Illumination: Chinese

Companies Expand Overseas', *Financial Times*, 3 December 2007.

52 Lieberthal and Herberg, *China's Search for Energy Security*; also Daojiong Zha & Hu Weixing, 'Promoting Energy Partnership in Beijing and Washington', *The Washington Quarterly* 30: 4, Fall 2007 105–15.

53 For an excellent discussion of growing Sino–Japan energy cooperation, see Shoichi Itoh, 'China's Surging Energy Demand: Trigger for Cooperation or Conflict with Japan', *East Asia: An International Quarterly*, Spring 2008.

54 See for example, Flynt Leverett and Pierre Noel, 'The New Axis of Oil', *The National Interest*, July 2006.

55 See Shoichi Itoh, 'Russia's Energy Diplomacy toward the Asia–Pacific: Is Moscow's Ambition Dashed?', *Slavic Eurasian Studies*, Spring 2008.

56 On LNG and South East Asia, see Mikkal E. Herberg, 'China's search for energy security: The implications for South East Asia', in *The United States and South East Asia: Contending Perspectives on Economics, Politics, and Security*, Evelyn Goh and Sheldon Simon, eds, Routledge, London 2007.

57 All figures in the next two paragraphs come from the Reference Case, IEA WEO 2008.

58 Nathaniel T. Aden and Jonathan E. Sinton, 'Environmental Implications of Energy Policy in China', *Environmental Politics*, 15:2, 1 April 2006, 248–70.

CHAPTER 11

INDIA'S QUEST FOR ENERGY

Tanvi Madan

By 2030, India is expected to overtake Japan and Russia to become the third largest global consumer of energy. As India's appetite for energy grows, concern about where this energy is going to come from has been increasing in the country as well. Though a few analysts dismiss energy security as an over-hyped concern, overall there is alarm that without 'clean, convenient, and reliable energy', India will not be able to sustain a high growth rate across all sectors of its economy.[1] Thus energy security is an oft-mentioned term in India these days – in the speeches of senior leaders; in the deliberations of government committees; at various government and non-governmental conferences; and in numerous reports generated by the government, think tanks, consulting companies, and the media.

The reasons for heightened concern go beyond the need to satisfy India's 'growth compulsions'.[2] The apprehension has political, socio-economic, and strategic dimensions as well. India's leaders have learned that the benefits and drivers of growth, including access to energy, must be more widely distributed, not just for overall economic growth and development, but also to maintain social stability and their own political position. In addition, there is some concern that an energy-insecure India will be unable to take what its decision-makers believe is its rightful place as a great power on the global stage.

Despite the common concern, 'energy security' means different things to different people – security of oil and natural gas supply; protection against price volatility;[3] affordability; independence from imports; or going beyond the country's requirements as a whole and looking at the needs of individuals.[4] While the term itself is used extensively without definition, the Planning Commission of India has come closest to providing a comprehensive official definition of energy security, stating

> We are energy secure when we can supply lifeline energy to all our citizens irrespective of their ability to pay for it as well as meet their effective demand for safe and convenient energy to satisfy their various needs at competitive prices, at all times and with a prescribed confidence level considering shocks and disruptions that can be reasonably expected.[5]

This definition highlights the magnitude of the problem, as well as the country's objectives. Read carefully, it also reflects the connection of energy security with India's foreign policy, and its leadership's domestic political, fiscal, and socio-economic concerns. With India's policymakers increasingly looking abroad to help deal with the extensive and imminent energy challenges the country faces, the implications of its policies will have a crucial impact not just on India's economic growth, and its internal political and social stability, but also on its international relations. This outward focus has made India's energy policies the subject of much attention, not just at home, but, increasingly, abroad. This chapter considers these policies, situating them within the larger context of India's overall domestic and international concerns. Furthermore, it explores the impact of India's quest for reliable, affordable energy on the country's behaviour beyond its borders.

The first section examines the energy situation India faces by presenting the overall energy demand–supply picture in the country, the reasons for its leaders' concern, as well as the key elements of the debate within the country about optimal policy. The second section considers the challenges policymakers confront when determining energy policies, including the need to assess the political, environmental, socio-economic, and geopolitical impacts of these policies. It also provides an overview of India's supply-side policies, including the activities of both the country and its companies abroad, and its demand-side management efforts. Finally, the third section examines the international political implications of India's search for energy. The conclusion previews the road ahead, and also briefly explains how India influences the evolving producer–consumer framework.

The Energy Situation and Debate in India

Together, China and India will account for almost half of increased global demand between 2005 and 2030.[6] With a primary energy mix of coal (51 per cent of total usage), oil (32 per cent), natural gas (9 per cent), hydroelectricity (7 per cent), and nuclear power (1 per cent), India is the fifth largest energy consumer in the world, accounting for 3.6 per cent of the world's consumption.[7] This mix does not include the 158 million tons of oil equivalent (Mtoe) of traditional energy sources used in two-thirds of India's households.[8] Taking into account that consumption, India's total energy demand in 2005 of 537 Mtoe is expected to more than double by 2030 to 1,299 Mtoe.[9] Per capita primary energy consumption, however, remains fairly low in the country

– less than a third of the world average – with large disparities in energy consumption patterns across economic strata.[10]

With domestic supply increasingly unable to keep up with demand, today India is importing some portion of each of its three major sources of energy – oil, natural gas, and coal (see Figure 11.1). The country has abundant reserves of coal, its primary source of energy, but mines this coal inefficiently, and, if consumption follows the current trajectory, the country is projected to run out of coal in 40–45 years.[11] India's domestic reserves of oil and gas are not extensive, and its dependence on imported oil, which is already greater than that of the USA and China, is expected to increase even further. While the oil comes from more than two dozen countries, almost three quarters of it is imported from six countries, all located in regions that are considered fairly unstable. The Middle East alone was the source of 67 per cent of India's foreign oil purchases.[12]

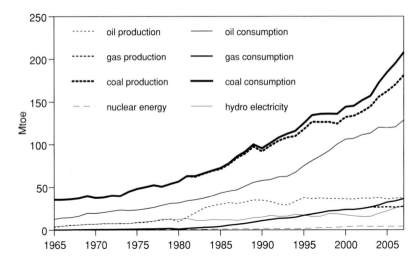

Source: BP Statistical Review of World Energy 2007.

Figure 11.1: India's primary commercial energy consumption and production, 1965–2006

India must deal with the same international energy prices as other countries, and watched oil and gas prices rise inexorably until the middle of 2008, and then drop. In the medium- to long-term Indian policymakers expect these prices to rise substantially again. Furthermore, trouble has beset India's plans to import natural gas through pipelines and in the form of liquefied natural gas (LNG). Continuing geopolitical uncertainty has stoked fears of natural gas and oil supply disruptions abroad, and/or price volatility. The potential for domestic disruption due to the vulnerability of onshore and offshore facilities (by accident, attack, or natural disaster), union strikes, and exposed rail and pipeline links has added to the concern. Furthermore, there currently seem to be few viable energy alternatives (especially, but not exclusively, in the transport sector) – progress in India's nuclear programme has regularly fallen behind schedule, though policymakers hope that nuclear energy will contribute more to the mix with the possible entry of new players in the sector; large-scale development of hydroelectricity generation facilities has been stymied by financial, social, and environmental concerns; and non-conventional sources, such as solar and wind power, are not yet considered affordable or reliable for widespread use.

India's energy predicament is of long-standing. For years, however, its decision-makers' concerns were tempered by the fact that India had abundant coal reserves, and its energy requirements were not as substantial as they are today, and projected to be in the future. Currently, the debate about the best solutions involves a broad range, and a large number of participants, with the popular press and strategic community joining what were once arcane dialogues among a few experts. Most sets of proposed policy prescriptions revolve around similar themes, but are stressed to highlight varying measures, and with different emphases. Advocates frequently call attention to solutions that reflect organizational or sectoral affiliation, tending to prove the axiom 'where one stands depends on where one sits'.

There are some solutions on which there tends to be broad agreement, including the need to improve energy conservation and efficiency, procure enhanced technology, and access better information and analysis. Other subjects have been more contentious. For example, experts calling for altering the energy mix disagree about which fuel could potentially represent the 'silver bullet'. Some emphasize the use of hydrocarbons, others recommend a decrease in dependence on fossil fuels, and yet others offer up geographically-differentiated sourcing plans. Other experts point out that there is no silver bullet, and efforts need to be made to enhance the supply of all fuels.

Another source of debate involves the issue of where these fuels are going to come from. For those concerned that India's economic growth 'stands hostage' to imported energy,[13] the solution lies, at least rhetorically, in self-sufficiency, which has been a key theme in political discourse in India since it gained independence.[14] Critics of this perspective – and there are many – argue that imported energy is going to be a fact of life in India; they assert that energy independence will be impossible to achieve, barring a major breakthrough in exploiting solar or nuclear energy, which itself would probably require, or stem from, foreign assistance or participation.[15] Other participants in the debate contend that the government and its companies should take more initiative abroad in acquiring energy assets. Some experts and decision-makers believe that instead of all-out competition for assets abroad, the focus should be on cooperation and coordination, especially with other major consumers. They argue that, in an interdependent world, no country can formulate an effective energy policy without considering the concerns and actions of others.

Another major debate involves the role of government. Champions of continued government involvement contend that the state should maintain a fairly high degree of control, ensuring the dominance of state-owned companies in the energy sector. Others, including some within government, argue that the country has run fiscal deficits for a number of years and, increasingly, there is a limit to how much the state can spend (and spend efficiently). They believe that the government should restructure and liberalize the sector, ceasing preferential treatment for state-owned companies, providing incentives for private investment, and clarifying policy frameworks (in terms of energy pricing, market structure, cross-border investments, and import and export of energy products). In addition they support the introduction of independent regulatory mechanisms,[16] and tax and price reform. These proponents of reform further contend that the government should reduce its stake and/or control of the state-owned energy companies, which need better access to the latest exploration technology, better management, and the ability to attract better talent, make better alliances, and meet global benchmarks for efficiency.[17] Another group of experts go further and call for privatization – of everything from public sector companies to ports and pipelines – in order to bring in much-needed capital, technology, and skills.

Clearly, there is no lack of perspectives or solutions being put forward, and given the magnitude of the problem, India's response has been decidedly, if not ironically, Churchillian. Churchill's views on oil – 'on no one quality, on no one process, on no one country, on no one route and on no one field must we be dependent. Safety and certainty in oil lie in variety and variety alone' – are representative of Indian decision-makers' broad thinking on energy.[18] With the complex challenges they are facing and the distributed decision-making structure involved in energy policymaking, their approach reflects the concept: 'on no one solution must we be dependent'.

Energy Policies and Challenges

While private participation in the country's energy sector has been increasing steadily, the government still looms large over the sector, through legislation, regulation, and policies, as well as through its state-owned companies. Its policies are numerous and disparate, but they reflect a theme: diversification – of fuels, suppliers, pricing, and technologies – which India's key decision-makers believe gives the country more options and insulation, to a certain extent, from area-specific shocks.[19] Moreover, the policy diversity is considered not just a question of choice, but of necessity, with decision-makers admitting that growing energy demand makes it imperative that India explores every option possible.

In the absence of an overarching interconnected strategy, however, a key hurdle to meeting India's energy needs has been the lack of strategic planning and prioritization. Successive governments continue to lay out their overarching vision and priorities in five-year plans, but critics assert that actual policymaking can be 'directionless', 'fractious', and 'ineffective', with 'dismal implementation'.[20] While the Planning Commission of India has worked toward generating an integrated strategy, it has no implementation authority. As a former state-owned company executive pointed out, what India seems to need is a 'Doing Commission'.[21] This is especially the case on the demand side, which has tended to be more the subject of rhetoric, rather than an arena for concerted action.

The plethora of policies and lack of implementation are partly a result of the scale and complexity of the problem, and partly a consequence of the number of government agencies involved in energy policymaking. These include the Department of Atomic Energy, the Ministry of Coal, the Ministry of Petroleum and Natural Gas (MPNG), the Ministry of New and Renewable Energy, the Ministry of Power, and the Planning Commission, as well as the state governments. With a stove-piped decision-making structure, even an energy strategy on paper is unlikely to have the required impact on practice. There are some, in fact, who contend that, given the complexities of energy issues, such a strategy may not be desirable or necessary.[22]

In the absence of a strategy with backing from the Prime Minister's Office, at the very least, there needs to be better integration of, and coordination on, the various policies.[23] The Energy Coordination Committee, formed in 2005, is a step in the right direction in bringing various stakeholders together, but coordination needs to be given higher priority; it also needs to be both broader in terms of the stakeholders it includes, as well as deeper in terms of the levels at which it operates.[24] To achieve results on the ground, it especially needs to bring in the state governments as and when their interests and jurisdictions are involved.

Since the various energy issues are interrelated, such coordination and integration is imperative, to ensure that policies are efficient and cost-effective, not overlapping and redundant or contradictory. Given that decisions on, and implementation of, energy policies have to be weighed against other policy considerations – strategic, political, fiscal, socio-economic, and environmental – that often trump the quest for energy, this interaction would also help policymakers operating in the different energy-related areas come to terms with the broader framework and limits under which they are operating.

On the strategic dimension, Indian companies and the government are not engaging in energy-related projects and partnerships abroad in a vacuum. These activities are occurring in the context of India's developing strategic relationships with a number of countries, some of whom view a few of these 'energy relationships' with concern. For example, while India wants to build a strategic partnership with the USA, its interests have clashed with the USA's over the Iran–Pakistan–India pipeline project, as well as over its engagement with energy-producers such as Myanmar, Sudan, and Venezuela. In each instance, therefore, before acting on its energy security imperatives, India's decision-makers have to consider other strategic interests, and the trade-offs. In fact the foreign ministry, realizing the potential for clashes, and wanting to assert its role as the lead agency for international activities, has set up a division to consider energy security issues.

India's political leadership will also judge any energy solution, no matter how desirable or necessary, by its probable electoral consequences. The case of price adjustments is instructional. There always seems to be an election around the corner in India, with national elections, and assembly elections for India's 29 states and six union territories held every five years in batches (or more often if a government falls). India's politicians are sensitive to the prospect of being punished at the polls (or by their coalition partners) for high energy prices. Thus there is always a great deal of hand-wringing before any government approves an energy price hike, even if it is clearly required. Price increases, when implemented, are small and timed extremely carefully – often after elections. In addition, subsidies are a commonly-used policy tool. Despite a shortfall, politicians regularly promise subsidized (or even free) electricity to their constituents, even though it skews the demand picture. Even the price of liquid petroleum gas (LPG), used mostly by the middle and upper economic classes, has been subsidized – when asked why, a former minister responded that while it makes 'little economic sense, it does make abundant political sense'.[25]

While the political considerations make one doubt that 'affordability' is simply an altruistic goal, the reality is that with 28–35 per cent of India's population still living below the poverty line,[26] for most policymakers any strategy needs to enhance the availability of energy at reasonable prices, especially for the poor in rural areas.[27] Thus, while there is acknowledgement that subsidization in its current form cannot be continued indefinitely, there is widespread concern about the political, economic, and social effects of removing subsidies completely.[28]

However, policies designed to address these concerns require trade-offs on other fronts. The political and socio-economic imperatives to maintain the status quo on issues like pricing, for example, are increasingly running up against fiscal concerns. As an observer noted, if governments continue to resist price rationalization, 'the price of today's procrastination will…be paid by future generations'.[29] Though governments have reduced expenditure on subsidies over the years, central government subsidies on petroleum products alone were still equivalent to 2.5 per cent of the government's fiscal deficit. In 2005–06, MPNG estimated that the national oil and gas companies (NOGCs) subsidized customers by \$8.7 billion in petroleum products.[30] Government-issued oil bonds (given to the companies to help them offset these costs) were equivalent to almost 4 per cent of the fiscal deficit. These figures vary with oil prices but, with both upstream and downstream companies bearing part of the burden, these costs have an impact on balance sheets in times of either low or high oil prices. India's energy expenditures are also affecting its trade balance. In 2006–07 India spent \$57 billion to import crude oil, up from \$43.4 billion the previous year. This amount comprised almost a third of India's total import bill, and contributed significantly to India's persisting trade deficit, which stood at \$64.2 billion.[31]

Even if fiscal concerns are addressed through policies such as targeted subsidization, other trade-offs will need to be assessed and made. Since a large number of Indians still live off the land, a particular problem that will need to be tackled is the food versus fuel dilemma.[32] Some of India's coal reserves, for example, are located under heavily forested or agricultural areas. The development of almost all non-conventional energy sources requires land, which is limited in India. Thus, discussions about increasing exploitation of these various energy sources has given rise to food security concerns, as well as reservations on environmental grounds.[33] People living in rural areas have been considering (and have been at the receiving end of) these trade-offs for years. Increasingly, though, the environmental impact of energy policies has also become the subject of attention in urban areas, amid visible signs of increasing pollution in many Indian cities, growing numbers of cases of respiratory illnesses, shrinking forest cover, and reports that India's carbon dioxide emissions have been rising 'alarmingly'.[34] Also, a significant source of these emissions has been coal, which is likely to continue to be the largest single contributor to India's energy mix.

Supply-Side Policies

Like the USA and China, India has focused considerable attention on increasing the supply of energy. Coal dominates India's energy mix, accounting for more than half of consumption.[35] With the fourth largest coal reserves in the world, the International Energy Agency (IEA) expects coal to continue this dominance (see Figure 11.2). Despite its abundance of coal, however, India has recently had to start importing this fuel, because of the quality of the coal, as well as the fact that production has struggled to keep up with consumption.[36] The domestic coal shortage is expected to persist for another few years, with India likely to spend $6 billion a year importing coal until 2015.[37] The shortage resulted partly from the slow pace of reform in this sector, and from the continued monopoly of state-owned Coal India Limited (CIL). The company is considered inefficient, with overstaffing, under- and misdirected funding, and low productivity.

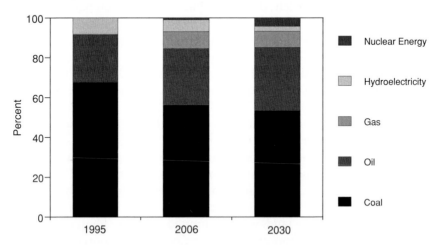

Source: *BP Statistical Review* 2007 and International Energy Agency, *World Energy Outlook 2006* (OECD, Paris, 2006)

Figure 11.2: India's changing energy mix, 1965–2006–2030

In addition, it lacks the technical capacity to mine efficiently, and access coal in deeper areas.

Continued resistance in parliament to amending legislation to allow private investment in coal mining has led the government to focus on changes that can be implemented through executive action. Central government has expanded the ability of end-users, such as steel and power generation companies, to mine coal for their own use (a process called captive mining), and has permitted state government-owned companies to undertake mining as well. In addition, it has allowed foreign investment in captive mining in the power sector and, to avoid delays, decided that the Coal Ministry, instead of an interagency committee, would allocate blocks for captive mining through a competitive process.[38] To facilitate imports, the government has reduced the customs duty on imported coal, and is exploring the acquisition of equity coal. Finally, state-owned companies are working on coal gasification and coal-bed methane gas projects, with the government encouraging them to seek technology abroad. Furthermore, private companies have been allowed to take part in the bidding process for coal-bed methane gas blocks.

Problems persist, however. Strong unions and the political parties they support have stymied attempts to reform CIL. Surplus coal produced by captive mining is not allowed to be sold on the open market; some potential captive mining operators have yet to develop the blocks they were allocated. There continues to be little transparency in CIL's price determination process, and a lack of independent regulation of the coal sector. Earlier attempts to allow private participation in the sector have stalled. Given current availability of technology, and its costs, the viability of coal gasification projects is under review. Adding to the mix is the problem of inadequate transport infrastructure – both to support increased imports and to transport domestic coal.

Moving beyond coal, India's consumption of the other major fossil fuels – oil and natural gas – is also growing considerably. As Figure 11.2 indicates, they are expected to account for a greater amount of the country's consumption in the future. While global oil demand is expected to increase at an annual average rate of 1.3 per cent, India's demand for oil is expected to increase at 3.8 per cent annually from 2005 to 2030 – when it is expected to become the world's third largest consumer of oil.[39] However, India's oil production has increasingly been unable to keep up with consumption (see Figure 11.1). More than two-thirds of India's oil comes from beyond its borders, whether through spot purchases, or short-term or long-term contracts (see Figure 11.3 for suppliers). By 2030, India is expected to import 92 per cent of its oil needs.[40]

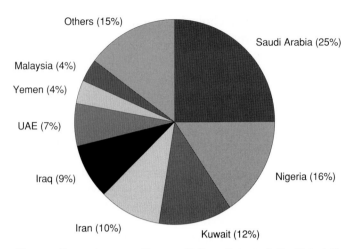

Source: Expert Committee on Energy Policy, *Report of the Expert Committee on Integrated Energy Policy*, Planning Commission, New Delhi, 2006, 59.

Figure 11.3: Sources of India's oil imports (2004–05)

India's demand for natural gas is estimated to grow even faster over the next quarter of a century, at 4.8 per cent a year.[41] About 80 per cent of natural gas consumed annually in India is sourced domestically. While India only started importing natural gas in 2004, with only 0.6 per cent of the world's proven gas reserves, the portion of natural gas consumption being imported is expected to increase to more than half.[42]

One reason for India's increasing dependence on imported oil and gas is the relatively poor exploration and production (E&P) track record of the state-owned Oil and Natural Gas Corporation (ONGC), which produces three-quarters of India's domestic crude output and two-thirds of its gas output, and controls more than half of India's hydrocarbon acreage.[43] The government has tried to improve domestic E&P by encouraging greater investment – both public and private – in the sector and by pushing for improved performance at its NOGCs, which many consider relatively inefficient, uncompetitive, and lacking sufficient technological or financial resources.[44] The government is using its role in allocating funds and setting production targets to push its companies to improve recovery from existing fields. It is also considering policies to stem the attrition of talented personnel from these companies, and has given the companies greater (though not complete) autonomy. Furthermore, to bring in much-needed technology, skills, and capital to the sector, the government instituted the New Exploration Licensing Policy in 1997–98. This policy, which fast-tracked the government's allocation of oil and gas exploration licenses, has achieved only mixed success.

Even with increased domestic production, however, India is unlikely to find all the oil and gas it needs at home. The Indian government has thus been facilitating the acquisition, by state-owned and private sector Indian companies, of energy assets abroad, considering participation in gas pipeline projects, upgrading infrastructure, and conducting aggressive 'energy diplomacy'.

At the forefront of India's energy-related efforts abroad has been the purchase by Indian companies of stakes in overseas E&P companies, and equity in oil and gas blocks. Over the last six years, ONGC subsidiary ONGC Videsh Limited (OVL) has alone spent over $5 billion to undertake projects in 16 countries (including Australia, Angola, Iran, Iraq, Libya, Myanmar, Nigeria, Russia, Sudan, Syria, Venezuela, and Vietnam). OVL's planned expenditure allocation will increase from $3.2 billion in the Tenth Five Year Plan (2002–2007) to over $13 billion in the eleventh (2007–2012); ONGC expects OVL to produce 20 million tons (MT) per year of oil and oil equivalent gas by 2020, up from the 4.73 MT of oil and 1.71 Mtoe of gas its assets produced in 2005–06.[45]

Indian companies have taken steps to be more competitive abroad, forming subsidiaries or divisions to focus on acquiring and developing overseas assets, and establishing partnerships to operate internationally with other domestic and foreign companies. ONGC joined with Mittal Investment, for example, to pursue oil and gas projects in Central Asia and Africa.[46] As part of a larger set of cooperative energy agreements between their governments, Chinese and Indian companies agreed to jointly bid for assets as well. Indian companies are also learning to make their bids more attractive, by including the undertaking of related projects in host countries – OVL, for example, undertook refinery upgrades and pipeline projects in Sudan, and private company Reliance decided to take a 30 per cent stake in a refinery construction project in Yemen.[47]

However, it has not been all smooth sailing for the companies. Some partnerships (like that of ONGC–Mittal) have run into trouble.[48] OVL has drilled dry wells in Australia, Libya, and Cote d'Ivoire. It has also lost bids to other companies (especially Chinese ones), in Angola, Kazakhstan, Nigeria, and Russia. NOGC officials often point to the approval process they have to go through as being responsible for their unsuccessful bids. Any overseas projects they propose which require investment above a certain amount have to win government authorization. This process is not simply a formality – in 2004, for example, the government did not allow OVL to raise its bid for a producing asset in Ecuador; a year later it blocked OVL from acquiring a stake in Nigeria's Akpo field on security grounds.

While the companies express unhappiness about having to go through the approval process, and the speed of official decision-making, the government argues that its fiscal and security concerns are real, and that, left to their own devices, company officials would overbid or invest in unviable projects. They also point out that Indian companies are not yet as competitive as their counterparts, lacking networks and presence in producing countries. They contend that government involvement, in fact, aids the NOGCs in establishing contacts in these countries – a benefit that the companies acknowledge – and that when NOGCs tend to charge ahead on deals without coordinating with them, the companies often return to request help when they realize that they need the diplomatic resources of the government.

Critics of the companies outside the government are even more forceful, and say that India's late start in the acquisitions game has been compounded by the fact that both the government and its companies have 'lousy game plans, obsolete strategies, and a parsimonious mindset'.[49] They argue that while the companies have experienced and trained professionals to run the projects, both the NOGCs and the government need specialized teams of technical and business-savvy professionals to plan and undertake bids on projects. These observers had also been critical of India's lack of ability and willingness to offer more direct and indirect incentives, stating that a number of Indian NOGC bids had been submitted without offers of aid or investment, or with offers that paled into insignificance in comparison with those from other countries. In Angola, for example, in conjunction with the bids of one of its companies, China had reportedly promised development assistance totalling $2 billion, whereas India had offered to undertake a $200 million rail project.[50]

Other analysts criticize the lack of rigorous guidelines surrounding acquisitions and reviews of existing investments. Some question whether these overseas investments actually enhance energy security, or are merely a way for the companies to get better returns. Even within the government there are occasional murmurs of concern that overseas acquisitions are causing NOGCs to divert their resources and attention away from their domestic operations, where they need to improve their performance.

Moving beyond the acquisitions of overseas assets, the possibility that supply disruptions could prevent oil imports has caused the government to consider building strategic reserves. The country has stored oil for some time now. Indian oil companies, for example, are required to maintain crude oil and petroleum product reserves. As a precautionary measure, in anticipation of a crisis or a substantial price hike, they sometimes also buy up additional oil supplies. However, in addition, to hedge against short-term supply disruption, India intends to establish a strategic petroleum reserve (SPR). The government has also recently considered proposals to build a 15-day strategic gas reserve.[51] The SPR had been considered for a decade, with the government only finalizing a decision to proceed in 2003, when the Iraq war had created a renewed sense of urgency. However, the construction of the reserve, which will hold 5 million metric tons, or 15 days of the country's oil imports, has since been delayed by a few years.

In terms of increasing imports of natural gas, there is a debate among decision-makers about whether LNG contracts or pipeline projects should be the preferred method of import. The government has considered three major gas pipeline projects, but none has actually materialized. Pipelines along the Turkmenistan–Afghanistan–Pakistan–India and Myanmar–Bangladesh–India routes have been considered, but have not got off the ground for technical, financial, and strategic reasons. An Iran–Pakistan–India pipeline, discussed for over a decade and a half, continues to be the subject of negotiations. While the route through Pakistan is considered the most economically viable method of transporting gas from Iran to India, many in the Indian strategic community consider such a project to have serious security obstacles, believing Pakistan could potentially disrupt (or at least threaten) India's natural gas supply. Proponents of the pipeline suggested ways of mitigating security risks, and when there was a more positive political climate (due to the India–Pakistan Composite Dialogue) and willing leadership on all sides, serious negotiations were conducted. The three countries, however, remain divided on issues such as transit fees. Furthermore, the tense situation between India and Pakistan following the 2008 terrorist attacks in Mumbai has also made evident the fragility of the relationship between those two countries.

While the pipeline projects have stalled, LNG imports have continued through purchases on the spot market, and a long-term contract with Qatar. To aid these efforts and to encourage others, there have been plans to improve existing infrastructure and to build additional receiving capacity.

LNG proponents consider its import to be more cost-effective and less likely to be affected by geopolitical problems than pipeline gas.[52] One notes that 'pipelines do not buy diversity' – because of the enormous investment required in pipelines, the consumer is locked into that option.[53] Indeed, a former minister who was a strong proponent of pipelines admitted that conventionally-shipped LNG could be a better option when importing gas from countries like Bangladesh and

Myanmar, especially because they had the potential to become 'impossibly difficult.'[54]

Those who prefer pipelines assert that they offer greater supply security than either equity oil or LNG, because the supplier and transit countries also have a stake in the pipeline, having made infrastructure investments. Pipeline proponents argue that international guarantees could provide a remedy to any potential problems. They point to the Indus Water Treaty, which has been in place between India and Pakistan for years, as proof that a dispute resolution mechanism can be worked out. Pipeline supporters further argue that economic interests can outweigh security concerns, and that pipelines are more economical over short distances. They assert that LNG requires additional transport and storage costs, as well as the need to factor in losses in the liquefaction process; furthermore, the price of LNG is linked to oil pricing in some long-term contracts (India's deal with Qatar, for example, links the cost of LNG to a predetermined basket of crude). Such arrangements can mean that LNG's price tends to be volatile, while the price of pipeline gas can be fixed for a longer term, and determined by negotiations.[55]

Indeed, LNG proponents received a setback when Iran reneged on a deal to supply India with 7.5 MT of LNG by 2015 because market prices had changed while the deal was being negotiated.[56] However, there was also a crisis of confidence in pipelines, when Russia cut off gas supply to Ukraine in 2006, with pipeline opponents taking the chance to contend that pipelines could become a tool for blackmail, and that international guarantees could merely reduce, but not eliminate, the chances of a supply cutoff.[57]

Regardless of the debate, with diversification in mind, the government is pursuing both options. Some experts have also suggested a third option that would involve constructing gas-fired power plants in the producer or transit countries, with power, rather than gas, being transmitted over high-voltage direct current lines.[58] This option, of course, could also be susceptible to a cut-off in case of tensions between or within any of the countries involved.

Beyond fossil fuels, the government is focusing on hydroelectricity and nuclear energy, which account for 6 per cent and 1 per cent of India's energy mix respectively. The government is providing financial support to develop some hydroelectricity generation projects, to offset high initial set-up costs and risks, and trying to attract more private sector investment (currently at just 3 per cent) by providing investment incentives. It is also considering a proposal that would put state-owned companies in charge of projects in the gestation stage; after the government approves these projects, they would be transferred to private companies, or operated through a joint venture. The government is also trying to rationalize tariffs, to assess completion costs accurately, and, if the political climate allows, to consider investments in hydroelectric projects in Nepal,[59] hoping to replicate its successful projects in Bhutan.

On the nuclear energy front, which has been receiving a lot of attention in the media and the corporate sector, the state-owned Nuclear Power Corporation of India Limited has thus far had a monopoly on civilian projects. The government is moving ahead with various plans to increase the country's production capacity. Eight nuclear reactors (pressurized heavy water and light water) are under construction, and another eight reactors have been cleared for construction. Furthermore, as part of the second stage of India's nuclear programme, a company has been established to construct a prototype 500 MW fast-breeder reactor (FBR).[60] The programme's third stage involves development of FBRs that would use thorium, of which India has large reserves (unlike uranium).

India is also looking to the Indo–US nuclear agreement that, if implemented, would allow sale or transfer of nuclear technology, equipment, and materials for India's civilian nuclear programme. Both countries made the case that the deal will enhance India's energy security. To broaden and garner support for the agreement, India aggressively courted members of the Nuclear Suppliers' Group (NSG), who could supply India with much-needed uranium as well as technology, to grant India a waiver.[61] The agreement and NSG waiver, which was granted in September 2008, could open the door for companies from a number of countries to participate in the sector, which led to considerable support in the nuclear industry for the agreement – with the country aiming for 25–28 more reactors, official estimates over the next decade and a half indicate that the nuclear reactor business in India could be worth up to $40 billion.[62] While the government has yet to announce the guidelines for participation in the sector, a French company and Russia have signed preliminary deals to sell India up to 10 reactors.[63] Recently, Russia also agreed to supply India with uranium.[64]

It is important to keep in mind that in the past India has fallen short of its own, mostly rhetorical, nuclear energy targets. Government officials acknowledge that it is going to take a while for nuclear energy to make a significant impact, and it needs to be viewed as a medium-term, if not long-term, source.[65] Thorium exploitation technology is not yet available for commercial use, and is probably decades away. Finally, nuclear energy projects involve a number of waste disposal and safety issues – issues that could lead to delays and resistance to the projects in local communities – which do not seem to have been fully thought through yet.

Alternative renewable energy sources are also receiving increasing attention (though not necessarily resources), since they are considered to be cleaner and more viable in the long run than fossil fuels.[66] It is estimated that India has 50 million hectares of wasteland and 34 million hectares of protected forest areas that could be used to cultivate crops for biofuels. Some planners talk of producing about 100,000 MW of power from the cultivation of 40 million hectares.[67] The government has supported the establishment of a technology centre for jatropha – a plant used for biodiesel production – as well a $10 million biodiesel production facility, which is aiming to produce 10 million litres a year. There is also a government proposal to cultivate 11 million hectares to aid the production of biodiesel.[68] One state government has even announced its intention to become biofuel self-reliant by 2015, and is encouraging the cultivation of the jatropha plant in all districts.

With estimates that India has about 300 clear sunny days annually, solar energy is also considered to have vast potential. The country has one of the largest decentralized solar energy programmes in the world, under which hundreds of thousands of home lighting and cooking systems are being used in some rural parts of the country.[69] Funded by a loan from the United Nations Environment Programme, over the last four years the programme has increased access to solar power systems in additional areas as well.[70]

By 2004, India ranked fifth in wind energy production;[71] three years later the total installed production capacity almost doubled, topping 7,000 MW.[72] The private sector, aided by government tax breaks, dominates this business. Encouraged by estimates indicating that India has the potential for grid-connected wind capacity of around 20,000 MW and with the promise of extensive tax write-offs, even some non-energy companies are setting up wind energy farms.[73]

Tides, clean biomass, and hydrogen are also being explored as energy sources by the government. To exploit all these possibilities, the government is actively seeking technological assistance from abroad, without which these sources are unlikely to become technically or financially feasible. However, India requires a 'more visionary plan' if it hopes that non-conventional sources will make more than a modest contribution to the country's energy mix.[74] There are significant problems to overcome. While some of these renewable sources do not have the kind of externalities that fossil fuels have, their use will require some trade-offs. Biodiesel and biomass projects divert much-needed water from other uses (as well as fertilizer, the production of which in turn requires natural gas). Solar energy remains expensive. As for wind energy, capacity utilization is sub-optimal, and there is a limited number of regions in the country where wind speeds allow effective harnessing of this resource. Finally, the ministry in charge of exploring and encouraging the development of these sources has not had the resources or the clout to be truly effective.

Thus, on the supply side, the government has been trying to address challenges on a number of fronts, with mixed results, overall. The management of challenges on the demand side, however, has suffered from a lack of attention, despite the fact that it should be an integral and important part of any energy strategy.

Demand-Side Management

Demand-side management has taken a backseat to supply-side management – in terms of official attention, resources, and even media coverage. However, the government has formulated some policies related to price and tax reform, fuel substitution, and conservation and efficiency.

Price reform has been the toughest nut to crack because it runs up against a number of other political and socio-economic imperatives. For these reasons, the price of petroleum products, for example, has continued to be kept artificially low – between 7 September 2002 and 7 September 2005, the price of Dubai crude rose almost 111 per cent. The retail price of regular gasoline in the USA, during the same period, increased 124 per cent; in India, the retail price of gasoline rose only 49 per cent.[75] Indian coal prices do not vary according to calorific value. Power prices are distorted as well. State governments effectively subsidize electricity for some consumers, especially in the agricultural sector. Meanwhile industrial and commercial consumers are charged a higher price to recover costs.

Controlled pricing has led to a heavy subsidy bill for the government and its companies, discouraged new private sector entrants (domestic and foreign), and skewed consumer behaviour. The government recognizes the need to pursue a 'rational pricing policy', and there have also been suggestions of removing subsidies altogether.[76] However, most officials feel that a more realistic solution would be to implement a targeted and transparent subsidy system.[77]

The government has taken small steps toward price reform, encouraged by various committees and by rising market prices. In 2002, to rationalize oil and gas prices, the government reduced subsidies for LPG and kerosene, and dismantled the administered price mechanism that had determined prices for petroleum products. The shift to a market-based pricing system, however, has been incomplete and, in effect, there is still a retail price ceiling in this sector. Government-appointed expert committees have called for further reform, not just in the oil and natural gas sectors, but also in the coal sector, but their recommendations have not really been implemented. Legislation has succeeded in restructuring the power sector to an extent, but while it sought to limit power subsidies and cross-subsidies, it has not succeeded in eliminating them.

Another related issue is taxation. Energy is heavily taxed in India. For example, estimates indicate that levies and taxes on petroleum products – including state taxes, custom duties, and excise levies – constitute more than half the price the Indian consumer pays. A third of the Indian government's tax income is estimated to come from petroleum products. In addition, state governments also levy taxes at differing rates. There have been suggestions of rationalizing taxes in an integrated way across the energy sector, but any such plans might not bear fruit, especially since getting the states to agree on an integrated system is likely to be an uphill task. The states zealously guard their control over this revenue stream and are loathe to take direction from the centre on this – unless they are offered incentives. Complicating any such centre–state joint effort will be the fact that the political parties in power at the centre might be in the opposition in the states.

In the meantime, the government is at least using taxation to encourage or discourage the use of certain fuels, in addition to seeing it as a source for revenue generation. While there continues to be debate about ethanol blends – to encourage its use, for example, the central government reduced by half (to 5 per cent) the import duty on molasses[78] – the government is also considering re-categorizing ethanol as a 'product of importance' so that instead of states imposing various levels of taxes on it, which has discouraged its use, the central government can levy a flat 4 per cent rate.[79]

While India is the world's fourth largest producer of ethanol and the largest user of imported ethanol from Brazil, the ethanol has often been used for purposes more profitable than fuel use. To change this, the government started encouraging investment in ethanol production plants. It also made a 5 per cent ethanol blend mandatory from October 2007, with a required 10 per cent blend from October 2008.[80] The latter deadline was not met, and, currently, even the 5 per cent blending requirement, which did go into effect, is being questioned because of a decrease in the country's sugar output.[81]

Other fuel substitution efforts have involved proposals for use of a biodiesel blend, which the Indian Railways, for example, already utilizes. Sometimes substitution is instituted by fiat – for example, in the power generation sector, which is a large consumer of coal and gas, some state governments require power distributors to purchase a certain minimum amount of power generated from renewable sources.[82] Beyond governments, the judiciary has also played a role in encouraging fuel substitution, for example, by mandating the use of compressed natural gas in public transportation vehicles in major cities.

Some such efforts have also led to improved conservation and efficiency. Estimates indicate that by 2031–32, efficiency measures by end-users could reduce India's overall energy requirements by 5.3 per cent.[83] Official estimates indicate even higher potential energy savings of 20 per cent, and there has been some commitment, albeit mostly verbal, to increased conservation and efficiency.[84] The Bureau of Energy Efficiency (BEE) under the Ministry of Power, for example, runs education programmes, certifies energy auditors and managers, implements pilot programmes in select government buildings, formulates best practices for conservation, and drafts codes such as the Energy Conservation Building Code.[85] There has also been some visible progress on the roads, especially with regards to more efficient use of fuels. Authorities are working toward phasing out older vehicles in larger cities. The government has cut excise duties on small cars, and is also phasing in emission standards around the country, with a priority focus on the major metropolitan areas. At least three major cities are constructing metro rail projects to improve public transport.

These efforts have paid some dividends. Due to better roads and more efficient vehicles, gasoline and diesel consumption growth has slowed. Between 1980–81 and 2003–04, for example, the gasoline consumption growth rate stood at 7.4 per cent a year, while that of diesel was 5.7 per cent a year. Between 2000 and 2005, gasoline consumption grew at the rate of 6.9 per cent and diesel at 3.1 per cent annually.[86]

However, overall, conservation and efficiency remain orphan issues. The BEE, in theory, is responsible for coordinating overall efficiency efforts, but so far it has been fairly toothless, understaffed, and neglected. Some government officials believe the private sector should take the initiative – a former petroleum minister, when asked about conservation said, 'unfortunately this is not really a matter for my ministry. It's really more for those involved in automobiles or manufacturing to find out about energy savers of various kinds.' He added that he was not sure what the government could do beyond 'setting a good example'.[87] The Asian Development Bank has pointed out, however, that there is indeed a great deal the government can do, not least because the private sector in India is not likely to focus on conservation or energy efficiency measures without legislation requiring standards in these areas.[88]

International Implications

To aid its efforts overseas to supplement India's energy supply, and to mitigate the risk of its dependence on imports through diversification, the Indian government has been undertaking a more active diplomacy toward producers and even, to an extent, fellow consumers. This energy diplomacy, which is only one component of India's foreign policy efforts, aims to help Indian companies win deals, ensure secure supply, attract investment and technology, lay the groundwork for long-term cooperation, and gain a seat at the international table.[89] There is also a sense that in an energy crisis, relationships will count for more than ownership of assets. In pursuit of these aims, government officials have been wooing energy producers and attempting to coopt fellow consumers – conducting energy diplomacy through high-level visits, conferences, cooperative agreements, and offers of aid (military and economic).

While diplomats and energy officials point to instances where this diplomacy has borne fruit (Oman, Saudi Arabia, the USA, Venezuela), contrarians worry that the benefits of energy diplomacy are exaggerated. As a result of of the level of instability in a number of countries where it is being exercised, or the fragility of the agreements involved, critics argue that these efforts are unlikely to ensure stability, security, and sustainability of supply. They also question India's relative effectiveness, pointing out, for example, that during twin visits by the Saudi king to China and India, China got a better oil deal from Saudi Arabia than India. The government seems convinced for now, however, that the benefits of diplomacy make it worth the effort. In many regions it also sees energy diplomacy serving another purpose – advancing India's influence more generally.

Thus India's continuing (and increasing) dependence on imported energy, especially oil and natural gas, and on technology – especially for nuclear energy and alternative energy production, and cleaner and more efficient use of energy – will continue to have an impact on its international behaviour. When considering the implications of India's energy quest abroad, however, it is important to keep in mind that its energy-related activities beyond its borders are not shaped merely by energy imperatives. Similarly, India's foreign policy is spurred by a number of different drivers – with energy needs often neither the only, nor the primary, consideration.

Over the last decade and a half, a more confident Indian leadership has pursued an increasingly pragmatic foreign policy – based on what Prime Minister Manmohan Singh refers to as enlightened self-interest. Whereas one still hears voices espousing nonalignment, and emphasizing moral strength and leadership among developing nations in the corridors of power, India is now aiming higher. It has an expanded idea about the kind of power it wants to achieve strategically, militarily, economically, and culturally (though there are still questions about whether the country's decision-makers have a comprehensive sense of how to gain this power and influence). The focus is now on the country's interests, with the goal a strong, independent India with a seat at the international table, and increasing influence beyond its immediate neighbourhood.

Overall, India's foreign policymakers have become more flexible in pursuit of these aspirations. They seem to be guided by the mantra 'no permanent allies, lots of good friends', and have been entering into partnerships with a number of countries to serve multiple interests. This attitude will also be reflected in India's global behaviour in the energy sphere – it will consider, if not pursue, every option. India will develop its own energy resources, as well as act on its interests both nearer to home in Asia, and in the broader international community. The country will act cooperatively when it thinks it suits its interests, but also act competitively – in acquiring assets or pursuing partners – when it thinks that is what is required.

There are many indications, however, that India would prefer to cooperate rather than compete in its quest for energy. New Delhi would rather be – and be perceived as – a responsible stakeholder; in addition, most Indian officials realize that India still lacks the resources to win in a competitive atmosphere.

However, with whom should India cooperate? There are constituencies within the Indian government, including – but not exclusively – many members and supporters of the Communist parties in India, who advocate a tilt toward China and/or Russia or exclusive cooperation with other Asian countries. Ministers and officials subscribing to these views tend to be those suspicious of the West and a West-dominated international system, who believe that 'the global energy regime remains to be emancipated from [America's] hegemony'.[90] However, they are not the dominant faction in policymaking circles, and despite much speculation, India is unlikely to participate in an anti-west China–India–Russia 'axis of oil'.[91] India's desire to keep its options open applies as much to staying non-aligned from China and Russia, as it does the USA. Besides, each of the three countries has different energy interests – often competing ones – and distinct relationships with other Western countries (particularly so for the USA) and these relationships are likely to take precedence over the ones they have with each other.

The Sino–Indian relationship, for example, is infused with elements of both cooperation and competition. As mentioned above, Chinese and Indian companies agreed to work together – indeed they jointly hold assets – in Syria and Sudan. The motivation, according to a major advocate of Sino–Indian energy cooperation, was that the two countries had 'realized that when we compete in an unhealthy manner to acquire oil fields in third countries, we only end up driving costs for each other...We have ended up paying billions of dollars more by trying to outbid each other everywhere.'[92] However, the countries have more of an understanding than an agreement, which seems to operate on a case-by-case basis – even the advocate quoted above, a former minister, said that in practice the countries would 'in some cases bid against each other, in some cases bid together'. There was talk about setting up 'some form of a mechanism of mutual consultation regarding third-country properties', but this has not yet materialized.[93]

While India will attempt to collaborate with China, visions of 'complementary strategies executed by their state-owned energy enterprises, unique bilateral E&P programmes, specialized division of labour, [and] financial burden sharing' are premature.[94] The level of trust and institutional mechanisms required for that kind of cooperation do not exist at this stage. There is a tendency in some quarters to blame 'non-Asian interests' and private actors for the lack of trust between the two countries.[95] The distrust, however, is rooted in history and persists to this day, though to a lesser degree than in the past. Sino–Indian energy cooperation will continue, but on an *ad hoc* basis – and neither country will consider the relationship exclusive.

As for Russia, for years it (and the Soviet Union before it) was India's key strategic partner, but their bilateral relationship has never been an alliance. Even India's first prime minister, who helped establish the bilateral ties, was hesitant to grow too close to the Soviet Union, warning that it would demand or expect too much in return. More recently, as India increasingly pursues other partners, and the Russian government increasingly makes its presence felt in projects like Sakhalin, in which Indian companies have investments, strains between the two countries have become more evident.

More broadly, Indian energy cooperation could take the form of increased Asian coordination even, possibly, through an Asian collective mechanism to acquire more bargaining power and to coordinate import policies. However, despite some support for the idea of an 'Asian axis of oil'[96] – the subject of both hope and fear – this mechanism is unlikely to be 'an Asian counterpart to the International Energy Agency' outside the international energy system.[97] It is more likely that politics and proclivities will take a back seat to reality. India's decision-makers realize that the country cannot afford to be too picky, or to alienate potential partners outside Asia – after all, it has needs that can be met only in collaboration with the broader international community.

This desire for broader cooperation has been evident in India's efforts to seek technology abroad. It has, for example, joined the USA-led Clean Development Initiative with China, South Korea, Japan, and Australia.[98] India also participates in a consortium that includes the EU, China, Japan, South Korea, Russia, and the USA, as a partner in the International Thermonuclear Experimental Reactor (ITER) project, which will conduct R&D 'to demonstrate the scientific and technical feasibility of fusion power'.[99]

To build on these and other efforts, and to ensure that India's participation in the global energy system is more consistent and con-structive, the international community needs to address a prevailing reason for India's hesitation to cooperate with the West – resentment that India has been left out of international decision-making up to this point. Since India did not help create the current international energy order, there is a sense among the country's elite that India is, or could be, short changed by the current system. There is no guarantee, of course, that India will always play a constructive role on the interna-tional stage; among some policymakers, especially in the West, it has acquired a reputation of playing spoiler in international institutions like the World Trade Organization. However, India would be more inclined to cooperate if it were given a seat at the table and saw the benefits of cooperation at first hand. Without direct inclusion, Indian policymakers will only view the international system's institutions as a method for reducing their flexibility. Whether through creation of an 'energy halfway house' on the way to full membership in the IEA or some other solution, the members of the system should find a way to include India as soon as possible. India's energy decision-makers are going through a crucial learning phase, and the question of whether India becomes a spoiler or a supporter will depend not just on how New Delhi decides to respond to the international energy system, but on how the international energy system reacts to India.

Regardless, India's diversified energy diplomacy is here to stay. India may not go on a whirlwind buying spree for energy assets (and indeed it cannot afford to) but the government will continue to support Indian companies in their efforts, particularly because there is a feeling that they need to play catch-up. When faced with accusations that such support is unfair, the retort will always be that India is merely doing what the West did in decades past. In response to criticism from Western countries that in its quest for energy India is dealing with regimes that have poor human rights records, India will point to the American relationship with Saudi Arabia, and suggest that Western states have double standards.

The Indian government is, however, beginning to consider the indirect costs of investments in countries with unstable or politically-charged regimes. It is aware that diversification has associated costs as well as advantages. On the one hand, it allows India greater freedom in some cases by reducing its dependence on any one country or region. On the other, its relationships with some of these regimes can also limit India's flexibility (since India cannot afford to upset and subsequently lose an energy supplier unless it gains another). India is also aware that reaching out to these regimes to ensure a 'secure' supply has not proven so secure. Iran's reliability as a supplier, for example, came into question when it cancelled an LNG supply deal. As a result of these inherent instabilities, if India can be persuaded (rather than pressured) into believing that there are more secure means of attaining its energy requirements, it might gravitate toward them.

Today, almost all of India's major geopolitical relationships involve an energy dimension. However, India's energy interests will not trump its broader strategic goals: its international energy initiatives will have to fall in line with its efforts to become more influential globally. India will not completely reorient its foreign policy to gain (or maintain) access to energy sources. India's vote against Iran's disputed nuclear programme at the International Atomic Energy Agency while the USA–India nuclear deal was being negotiated made evident India's priorities. If New Delhi can be convinced that a certain path of action holds long-term strategic benefits – even if it hurts its energy interests in the short term – it is likely to follow that path.

Conclusion

As things stand, India's energy policies will continue to be formulated piecemeal by different agencies; the persistence of coalition governments at the federal level will make tough decisions on issues such as pricing and private participation in the sector politically unpalatable, and harder to propagate and implement; and abroad, India's broader strategic goals and its energy-related objectives will occasionally continue to clash. On the positive side, sectoral reform will continue, albeit at a slow pace; and, with increasing realization of the multi-pronged implications of its energy policies, coordination both within the government, and between the government and the corporate sector will improve.

Overall, as this chapter has made evident, India's decision-makers are faced with a Hydra-headed challenge in ensuring the supply of 'lifeline energy to all [its] citizens'. Coping with the challenge requires a Herculean effort that involves not just energy policymakers but also their counterparts involved in fiscal, environmental, and foreign policymaking, among others. After all, a decision made about gasoline prices, for example, reverberates in each of these realms – directly or indirectly affecting the bottom line of the state-owned oil companies (and thus the government), encouraging or discouraging the use of public transport, influencing India's attitude toward certain oil producers, and even affecting electoral rhetoric and possibly even results. Dealing with the energy challenge will thus require coordinated action that keeps in mind India's broader domestic and foreign policy objectives. Priorities will have to be clarified, and trade-offs will have to be weighed. The Indian government's recent efforts show a renewed activism in meeting the challenges it faces in this sector, but it has a long way to go, and has some tough decisions ahead that it might no longer be able to avoid.

As the Indian economy develops, the country will have a growing impact on global producer–consumer relations. India's increased energy consumption over time will help expand and diversify the market for oil and gas producers. Producer countries, in turn, will look to India to continue to be a source of investment for developing their energy reserves. If it feels that it is necessary, India will compete for these resources in energy-rich countries, or at least undertake activities that might be seen by other consumers as creating competition. However, India has also demonstrated a willingness to work with other consumers, like China and the USA, to coordinate policy. In the future, India's efforts to expand its international reach, both in the energy sphere and more broadly, could potentially open the door for cooperation with producers and consumers alike. Thus, while the rise of new consumers like India may make the producer–consumer framework more complicated and competitive, there will also be plenty of opportunities for cooperation.

Notes

1   Expert Committee on Energy Policy, *Report of the Expert Committee on Integrated Energy Policy*, Planning Commission, New Delhi, 2006, 1.
2   'India as an energy hot spot', *Indian Express*, 13 July 2005.
3   R. K. Pachauri, 'Oil in India's Energy Future', *Seminar* #555, November

2005, 54.

4   Kirit S. Parikh, 'Valedictory Address', to conference on 'India's Energy Security: Major Challenges', National Conclave, Observer Research Foundation, New Delhi, 14 February 2006.

5   Expert Committee on Energy Policy, *Report*, 54.

6   International Energy Agency, *World Energy Outlook 2007*, OECD, Paris 2007, 118.

7   British Petroleum, *BP Statistical Review of World Energy*, June 2008, 40–1.

8   I. P. Khosla, 'Introduction', in *Energy and Diplomacy*, ed. I. P. Khosla, New Delhi, Konark Publishers, 2005, 8. For amount consumed, see International Energy Agency, *World Energy 2007*, 600.

9   Ibid, 118

10 Expert Committee on Energy Policy, *Report*, 1.

11 KPMG, *India Energy Outlook*, 2006, 6.

12 Expert Committee on Energy Policy, *Report*, 59.

13 Rajiv Kumar, 'Energy Pipelines', in *Energy and Diplomacy*, Khosla ed., 69.

14 Energy and Resources Institute (TERI), 'New Exploration Licensing Policy: Will It Strike Oil?' static.teriin.org/energy/nelp.htm

15 Former petroleum and natural gas secretary S.C.Tripathi, remarks at conference on 'India's Energy Security: Major Challenges', National Conclave, Observer Research Foundation, New Delhi, 14 February 2006.

16 KPMG, *India Energy*, 8.

17 Rajat Gupta et al., 'Securing India's Energy Needs', *The McKinsey Quarterly*, 2005, 98.

18 Quoted in Daniel Yergin, *The Prize: The Epic Quest for Oil, Money & Power*, The Free Press, New York, 2003, 160.

19 Montek Singh Ahluwalia, 'Inaugural Address', to conference on 'India's Energy Security: Major Challenges', National Conclave, Observer Research Foundation, New Delhi, 14 February 2006.

20 Bani P. Banerjee, *Handbook of Energy and the Environment in India*, Oxford University Press, New Delhi, 2005, 175.

21 'Energy security calls for tax, pricing reforms', *The Times of India*, 6 October 2007.

22 Interviews with a government official and an economic analyst, February 2006

23 Pachauri, 'Oil in India's Energy Future', 56.

24 Government of India Press Information Bureau, 'PM Constitutes Energy Coordination Committee', press release, 13 July 2005, http://pib.nic.in/release/release.asp?relid=10163

25 Mani Shankar Aiyar, 'Interview', *Seminar* #555, November 2005: 59.

26 As of 2000, The World Bank, *World Development Indicators*, 2005, http://devdata.worldbank.org/wdi2005/Table2_5.htm

27 Anil Agarwal, 'Introductory Remarks', conference on 'India's Energy Security: Major Challenges', National Conclave, Observer Research Foundation, New Delhi, 14 February 2006. (Agarwal is president of ASSOCHAM, a business association.)

28 'India Hints at Removing Energy Subsidy', *UPI*, 22 May 2006.

29 Prem Shankar Jha, 'The Perils of Populism', *The Deccan Herald*, 3 May 2006.

30 'High oil prices to cut Asian economic growth: ADB', *Agence France Presse*, 4 May 2006.

31 Reserve Bank of India, *Handbook of Statistics on Indian Economy*, 201, Figures for 2006–07 are provisional.

32 Banerjee, *Handbook of Energy*, 209.

33 Debnath Shaw, *Securing India's Energy's Needs: The Regional Dimension*, Center for Strategic and International Studies, Washington, DC, 2004, 9.

34 India's CO_2 emissions grew 57 per cent from 1992 to 2002. See 'World Bank's 'Little Green Data Book 2006', www.noticias.info/asp/aspComuni-cados.asp?nid=176104&src=0

35 These figures indicate primary commercial consumption.

36 A large amount of the imported coal, though, is not necessarily used for energy production.

37 John Larkin, 'India's energy woes go deep', *The Wall Street Journal*, 11 July 2005, A11.

38 . 'GoM clears competitive bidding–based allocation of coal blocks', *The Press Trust of India Limited*, 23 July 2007.

39 International Energy Agency, *World Energy 2007*, 592 and 600.

40 International Energy Agency, *World Energy 2007*, 125.

41 International Energy Agency, *World Energy 2007*, 600.

42 Ibid., 171–172.

43 'Indian ONGC gets acting chairman following Subir Raha's exit', *Platts Commodity News*, 29 May 2006, 01:21.

44 Interviews, 2006, 2007.

45 'ONGC keen on setting up Kakinada refinery', *Business Line*, 28 June 2007, 3.

46 'India's ONGC, Mittal team up for energy projects', *AK&M Russia*, 25 July 2005.

47 'Reliance cements Ras Issa refinery stake', *Middle East Economic Digest*, 19 May 2006.

48 'ONGC–Mittal Joint Venture Lumbers On, Despite Growing Strains', *International Oil Daily*, 23 April 2007.

49 Ajish Joy in *ORF Strategic Trends*, April 2006.

50 'China Beats India for Angola Oil Deal', *CRI Online*, 19 October 2004, www.crinordic.com/2004/2004-10-19/87@160463.htm

51 'India May Build Gas Storage Facilities for Emergencies', *Dow Jones International News*, 15 March 2004.

52 KPMG, *India Energy*, 17.

53 Khosla, 'Introduction', 13.

54 Mani Shankar Aiyar, 'Energy Cooperation: India and Its Neighbours', in *Energy and Diplomacy*, Khosla ed., 27.

55 Argument laid out in Khosla, 'Introduction', 13.

56 Some have contended that Iran reneged on the deal as a result of India

voting against Iran at the International Atomic Energy Agency in 2005.

57 Dietl, 'Gas Pipelines: Politics and Possibilities', in *Energy and Diplomacy*, Khosla ed., 84.

58 Mahajan, 'Accessing Neighbourhood Energy' in *Energy and Diplomacy*, Khosla ed., 122.

59 Among others, former Foreign Secretary Salman Haidar.

60 'India as an energy hot spot', *Indian Express*, 13 July 2005.

61 'U.S.–India Deal May Spur Australian Uranium Sales, Howard Says', *Bloomberg*, 22 May 2006, www.bloomberg.com/apps/news?pid=10000081 &sid=aRAjcC4EvT9Y&refer=australia

62 'India is Planning to Invest $40bn in Nuclear Reactors', *Bloomberg*, 20 May 2006, (www.gulf-times.com/site/topics/article.asp?cu_no=2&item_ no=87386&version=1&template_id=48&parent_id=28).

63 Jyoti Malhotra, 'Russia to sell four N-reactors to India', *Live Mint*, 5 December 2008, www.livemint.com/2008/12/05000452/Russia-to-sell-four-Nreactors.html. 'France's Areva, India sign nuclear reactor deal', *Associated Press*, 4 February 2009, www.cbc.ca/world/story/2009/02/04/france-india. html

64 'Russia agrees India nuclear deal', *BBC News*, 11 February 2009, http:// news.bbc.co.uk/2/hi/south_asia/7883223.stm

65 Ahluwalia, 'Inaugural Address.'

66 Ibid.

67 The Committee on Vision 2020, *Report of the Committee on India Vision 2020*, Planning Commission, New Delhi, December 2002, 73.

68 Aiyar, 'Energy Cooperation: India and Its Neighbours', 42.

69 Kiran Yadav, 'Future Fuels', *Financial Express*, 14 May 2006, www.financialexpress.com/news/FUTURE-FUELS/168710/, 1 October 2007. For more details, see Avilash Roul, 'India's Solar Power: Greening India's Future Energy Demand', www.ecoworld.com/home/articles2.cfm?tid=418

70 'Solar loans light up rural India', *BBC News*, http://news.bbc.co.uk/2/hi/ science/nature/6600213.stm

71 The Committee on Vision 2020, *Report of the Committee*, 73.

72 2007 figures from Tim Sullivan, 'Coal is still king, but wind energy grows in India', Associated Press, September 27, 2007. 2004 figures from '3000 MW additional capacity energy to be installed in next two years', *Indian Business Insight*, 27 July 2005.

73 Expert Committee on Energy Policy, *Report*, 38.

74 The Committee on Vision 2020, *Report of the Committee*, 73.

75 Crude oil and Indian retail price data from Indian Petroleum Planning and Analysis Cell (http://ppac.org.in/OPM/Price_revision_other_cities_MS.htm and http://ppac.org.in/ppac_0506/international_price_0506.htm; US retail price data from EIA, 'Retail Gasoline Historical Prices', www.eia.doe.gov/ oil_gas/petroleum/data_publications/wrgp/mogas_history.html

76 'PM Stresses Need for India to Diversify Energy Supplies', *BBC Monitoring South Asia*, 6 August 2005.

77 N. Srinivasan, 'Energy Cooperation', in *Energy and Diplomacy*, Khosla ed., 52.

78 Biman Mukherji, 'Indian sugar mill stocks surge on new ethanol rules', *Reuters News*, 10 October 2007.

79 'Centre plans to introduce 4% uniform tax on ethanol', *Financial Express*, 24 September 2007.

80 Sanjay Jog, 'Mandatory Ethanol Blending from Oct Likely', *Financial Express*, 9 May 2006.

81 'Rethink on Ethanol Blend', *The Telegraph*, 3 March 2009 www.telegraph-india.com/1090304/jsp/business/story_10622031.jsp

82 'India Opens Green Energy Markets', *Energy Economist*, 1 August 2005, 29.

83 KPMG, *India Energy*, 7.

84 Power Secretary RV Shahi quoted in Yadav, 'Future Fuels'.

85 Expert Committee, *Report*, 82.

86 Expert Committee on Energy Policy, *Draft Report of the Expert Committee on Integrated Energy Policy*, Planning Commission, New Delhi, 2005, 11.

87 Aiyar, 'Energy Cooperation: India and Its Neighbours', 43.

88 Asian Development Bank, 'The Bank's Policy Initiatives for the Energy Sector – Energy Policy Issues', www.adb.org/Documents/Policies/Energy_Initiatives/energy_ini322.asp

89 The government is making a major effort to also encourage investment from producer countries in India's downstream sector to ensure that they are invested in the market.

90 Girijesh Pant, 'India and the Asian Energy Initiatives: Partnership in Development', in *Energy and Diplomacy*, Khosla ed., 91.

91 Jehangir Pocha, 'The New Axis of Oil', *In these Times*, January 31, 2005 www.newamerica.net/publications/articles/2006/the_new_axis_of_oil

92 M. K. Venu, 'India, China pump up the energy levels', *The Economic Times*, 13 January 2006.

93 Himangshu Watts, 'India aims to team up with China in oil asset race', *Reuters News*, 1 February 2005.

94 Steven Knell, 'India Views Partnerships Abroad to Service Soaring Energy Needs', *Global Insight Daily Analysis*, 8 August 2005.

95 Pant, 'India and the Asian Energy Initiatives: Partnership in Development', 106.

96 Siddharth Varadarajan, 'India, China and the Asian axis of oil', *The Hindu*, 24 January 2006.

97 M. K. Dhar, 'Iran and India's Energy Security', *Central Chronicle*, 25 May 2006.

98 'US Joins India, Australia, China, Japan, S Korea in Energy Pact', *The Press Trust of India*, 28 July 2005.

99 See ITER, 'The ITER Project', www.iter.org/

PART IV

CONCLUSION

CHAPTER 12

TOWARDS A MORE SUSTAINABLE GLOBAL ENERGY SYSTEM: INTEGRATING DEMAND-SIDE AND SUPPLY-SIDE POLICIES

Andreas Wenger

Few experts these days will disagree with the statement that the current global energy system is not sustainable. Recent changes in markets, politics, and the environment have brought about the need for a re-examination of the energy relationship between more assertive producers and more heterogeneous consumers. Current global energy markets are characterized by extreme price volatility and investment insecurity, which in turn have caused severe supply insecurity for consumers, and severe demand insecurity for producers. The political environment is now marked by an increasing nationalization of resources by producers, and by calls for energy independence from consumers. This situation means that political rhetoric could reduce trust between buyers and sellers, and in the worst case, could cause an energy security dilemma, in which traditional producers and consumers diversify away from each other, despite the obvious economic benefits of their energy relationship. Finally, the environmental consequences of current energy production and consumption patterns have made the present system unsustainable, and there is a growing consensus that carbon emissions will contribute to potentially catastrophic global warming in the long run.

The old energy system meant cheap oil and stable energy markets. It was created in response to the 1973 Arab oil embargo and was dominated by the traditional industrialized consumers in the West.[1] The stability of the system rested on three key factors: first, diversified supply provided consumers with a high level of security. For example, in reaction to the OPEC embargo, the Europeans increased oil production in the North Sea and invested in conservation, while the Soviet Union capitalized on OPEC cuts and expanded its energy deliveries to Europe, thus stabilizing supply. Second, traditional consumers were able to improve the coordination of their energy policies on the basis of the market principle. They established the International Energy Agency (IEA) in order to jointly monitor markets and share information, to encourage cooperation in the event of disruption and coordinate strategic stockpiles as a buffer against political pressure, and to strengthen their conservation efforts and lower the energy intensity of their economies.[2] Third, a strategic partnership between growth coalitions in the USA and Saudi Arabia, both biased in favour of the supply side, tied the producer–consumer structure into a firm political relationship. In return for US security guarantees, the Saudis provided the necessary excess capacity that allowed the USA to absorb major supply disruptions. A case in point was the 1991 Gulf War. The Saudis were also prepared to accept moderate prices to ensure stable, long-term demand, their thinking based on the technocratic logic that moderate prices would stimulate broad economic growth while constraining investment in alternative energies.[3] The USA, in turn, ensured Saudi Arabia's security, and maintained open access to waterways and to the Gulf, with its huge reserves of oil and low extraction costs.

However, since the beginning of the new millennium, the stability of the old energy system has been undermined, as energy issues have become inextricably linked to global market fluctuations and environmental concerns on the one hand, and to the geopolitical realignment resulting from the rise of new economic powers, increased demand for energy in Asia, and the accumulation of energy wealth in producing countries on the other. Yet while energy is linked to global market dynamics, it also affects local and global political conflicts. Access to affordable energy from abroad has been a critical factor in the peaceful rise of developing countries, including China which was once energy self-sufficient. High oil prices between 2003 and 2008 have also enabled producing states like Russia to strengthen their international positions, and to dispense with the notion that their cheap oil was, in effect, subsidizing the economic growth of others.[4] However, at the regional level, the often highly politicized management of pipeline infrastructures has reinforced asymmetric power relationships between neighbouring states, while at the local level, political violence in energy-rich states has often been closely linked to the negative effects of high rents from exports of natural resources, causing poor governance and creating structural barriers to economic innovation.[5]

Changes in the global financial and economic system have also caused significant shifts in global energy markets. Today's global oil markets are fraught with demand and supply insecurity, volatile prices, and considerable investment insecurity. Rapid economic growth in countries like China and India has brought new Asian energy consumers into the energy markets.[6] The surprisingly rapid increase in Asian demand for oil has led to reduced spare capacity, and this situation has been aggravated by low inventories of oil in OECD countries, and by the loss of Iraqi oil production after the US invasion in 2003. When economies were booming, the value of the US dollar was declining and energy markets were becoming tight; increased speculative activity connected to relatively low political risk quickly drove the oil price up to a staggering $147 per barrel in July 2008.[7] Generally speaking, high and volatile oil prices can damage economic growth – and oil price shocks often precede a recession.[8] Yet the current economic downturn was triggered not by oil but by the local crisis in the US mortgage market, which then quickly evolved into a global financial crisis, which in turn is now having serious consequences for economic growth in the USA, Europe, and Asia. When global demand for oil started to drop and reserves began to pile up at an alarming rate at the beginning of 2009, the oil price struggled to stay above $40 per barrel. This dramatic drop in oil price should act as a reminder that volatile markets and unpredictable prices can endanger the energy security of consumers and producers alike.[9]

The economic benefits of a relationship between traditional buyers and sellers have been seriously undermined by recent market shocks. Such insecurity has inevitably influenced the energy relationship between the more assertive producers and the increasingly heterogeneous consumer groups. Negative political rhetoric has brought about a looming energy security dilemma – a situation in which both traditional buyers and sellers are diversifying away from each other, only to leave each other in a worse position than before. On one side, consumers fear that producers may exploit the current situation to improve their political power. Two key trends have elicited this fear: first, the control of a large part of the global reserves has been shifting from international oil companies (IOCs) to national oil companies (NOCs).[10] This move began many years ago, but producers have recently increased the level of state control over their energy resources and have restricted the access of IOCs to their oil fields. Local elites in producer countries seem to believe that resource nationalism is the key to political stability and economic growth at home, and will also allow them to project power abroad. Second, the high concentration of known energy resources in the region stretching from the Middle East across the Caspian Sea to Western Siberia – one of the world's politically more volatile regions – has led to better armed and increasingly independent local and regional security actors. This has had negative geopolitical effects on the strategic interests of traditional consumer states. As a consequence, public debate in the USA and Europe has been dominated by calls for energy independence and for a drive towards greater energy diversity.[11] On the other side, the producers fear signs of a decline in consumption and have recast their energy policy rhetoric away from the traditional Western consumers to the consumers in emerging Asian countries; they have also complained that traditional consumers' attempts at diversification have undermined their own efforts to secure demand, and they have consequently decided to limit investment in new production capacity.

Energy relations between traditional and new consumers and producers have become more politicized over the past years. While the USA feels vulnerable because of its dependence on Middle Eastern oil, Europe feels vulnerable because of its dependence on Russian gas pipelines,[12] and when traditional consumers look to Africa, Eurasia, and Latin America to diversify their energy supply, they find themselves in growing competition with the new Asian consumers for access to and control of oil and gas.[13] Thus, energy security has become a key strategic concern for leaders in Washington, Europe, and Beijing alike,[14] and as long as traditional and new consumers decide to address their energy security dilemma primarily by focusing on the supply side, they are likely to face increased competition with other consumers and a more complex consumers' relationship with producers. If, however, traditional and new consumers decide to work more actively on the demand side, they will open up the potential that energy has as an element of cooperation in foreign relations between traditional and new consumers and producers. Narrow supply-side biased energy policies will lead to more competition over access to geographically more concentrated resources; it could also have a negative impact on the broader foreign policy relationships between key producers and consumers.

Further, as long as powerful growth coalitions dominate the domestic policy process, the supply-side bias of most consumers' energy policies is likely to persist. However, consuming countries in Europe and elsewhere are adopting domestic policies aimed at increasing efficiency and expanding the production of alternative energies, and the USA is now likely to do the same under the Obama government.[15] This renewed emphasis on demand-side approaches is being driven by an emerging consensus that current energy usage patterns are not sustainable, because of their long-term impact on the environment. It is now a well-established fact that the use of fossil fuels causes global warming.[16] Consequently, more and better cooperation that aims to increase energy efficiency and develop renewable energy is seen as essential to the reduction of carbon dioxide emissions. In fact, concern for the environment is having a growing impact on the way energy resources are used. Climate change is a serious issue for traditional and new consumers and producers alike; however, it also has the potential to bring all actors together in a common drive to cooperate in the interests of a more sustainable energy system. Moreover, new technologies can bring about economic benefits and open new markets, namely when countries decide to switch to a carbon-neutral energy mix.[17] The price of energy is clearly a key driver in the move toward improving the environment, and this means that the currently low price of oil will make it more difficult for leaders to muster the necessary political will needed for a strong internal response. However, the price of energy is likely to go up again when, in a few of years, the world economy rebounds from the current crisis, and this should be incentive enough for forward-looking governments to adapt their stimulus packages to a greener economy.

Political support for strong demand-side policies should be based as much as possible on environmental sustainability and encouraging any associated economic opportunities. However, moving towards a more sustainable energy policy will be difficult and expensive for many countries, not least because their current infrastructures are reliant on oil. Policymakers could therefore be tempted to justify a strong internal call for energy independence by framing energy as a national security issue. The most negative side effect would then be that the external elements of their countries' energy security would become more complex. Consumers must therefore realize that any effort to reduce dependence on imported energy and other non-renewable fossil fuels could negatively affect the demand security of producers. Consumers should point out to producers that their move away from oil and gas will be gradual. Moreover, they should offer expanded technology cooperation. This would improve the energy efficiency of producer states' own economies, thereby reducing carbon emissions and slowing down climate change; it would also extend the lifespan of their energy reserves, and prepare their economies for a time without hydrocarbons.

Three premises: Resilience, sustainability, politics

Reliable and competitive energy markets that are also environmentally sustainable can be achieved only if traditional and new consumers and producers acknowledge that energy security, economic growth, and environmental protection are interrelated issues that have to be addressed coherently and comprehensively. The development of a new producer–consumer framework that acknowledges the fundamental need to transform the old energy system should include the following three factors: first, traditional and new consumers and producers will need to accept that the energy system is a global construct. The scale and complexity of the global energy trade are rapidly increasing, as is the need to protect the entire supply chain. New consumers and new producers have entered global energy markets, where they now interact with a wide range of business actors, including powerful NOCs and flexible IOCs. These days, energy relations are more than simple producer–consumer relationships. Transit states have an important role to play and should not be left out of the energy equation. Oil, gas, and electricity markets are becoming more integrated, which means that energy policies need to go beyond gas and oil exploration and exploitation alone, to include electricity supplies and renewable energies. Producers and consumers alike should understand that the growing number of (inter-)dependencies in the global energy system require new efforts to increase the system's overall resilience.[18]

Second, traditional and new consumers and producers need to recognize that, given global warming, the current bias in favour of supply-driven energy policies is no longer sustainable. The need to manage factors that govern the demand side of global energy markets will gain in significance, as everyone's obligation to curb global warming increases. Traditional and new consumers should thus strengthen their commitment to energy efficiency and renewable energy industries.[19] Of course, overturning the domestic status quo, which favours supply-side solutions, will require considerable political will, significant economic investment, and a strong mix of public and private initiatives. An increase in the attention paid to reducing domestic consumption through improved efficiency should also be of interest to producers. Most producer economies are highly energy inefficient, as their domestic energy usage tends to be subsidized (for political reasons). Thus, a surge in efforts to protect the environment would not only benefit the global climate, but would also free up export potential, enabling producers to better meet their supply commitments. However, policies that limit domestic consumption (for example, increased domestic energy prices) and stimulate investment (for example, tax reduction and clear property rights) remain politically difficult to implement. Consumers and producers might, in fact, find it easier to balance their supply-side biased energy policies if they embedded these in a broader policy framework that combines the internal and the external aspects of their energy security. This would allow them to leverage the cooperative potential of demand-side policies in their energy relationships. Thus, all parties should understand that the environmental impact of current energy usage patterns necessitates new efforts to increase the sustainability of energy production and consumption.[20]

Third, traditional and new consumers and producers need to

recognize that they are unlikely to be able to separate their energy policies from their broader foreign and security policies. Both sides will have to deal with the fact that global energy politics will probably develop within a wider strategic framework that is influenced by values and interests unrelated to oil and gas. The ways in which countries manage their relations with one another in the future will influence their energy security. Conversely, energy politics are bound to have some geopolitical consequences, especially in the Caucasus, the Caspian, and the Middle East, where energy issues are closely linked to local conflicts, on the one hand, and to the strategic interests of great powers, on the other. Nevertheless, the geopolitical consequences of energy politics are likely to remain limited, because consumers and producers have a common interest in the long-term stability of world energy markets.[21]

Energy policies are most likely to evolve at the domestic level. This makes it unlikely that consumers and producers will agree any time soon on what represents a fair price for energy or on what role the state should play vis-à-vis markets. Consumers should acknowledge that energy nationalism in producing states reflects the fact that energy plays a significant role in the political and social development of these states, and also that the role of energy transcends the logic of market forces.[22] At the same time, producers have to realize that any attempts they may make to use their energy-derived power for political gain is unlikely to succeed, and could even backfire and have unintended side-effects.[23] Producers should also realize that calls for energy independence in consumer states can play an important role in mobilizing support for domestic environmental policies and specific foreign policy interests. In turn, consumers have to realize that independence from fossil fuel imports is an unrealistic goal, at least in the midterm, and producers and consumers should understand that the growing interconnection between energy issues and security issues demands better coordination between their energy policies and their foreign and security policies.

Stabilizing the global oil market

The stability of the oil market remains central to global energy security and to the smooth running of the global economy, at least in the midterm. Oil, natural gas, and coal make up more than 80 per cent of current global energy consumption.[24] Access to oil is not a geological problem yet, but it is linked to growing political and economic challenges.[25] From an economic perspective, oil remains critical to the stability of the global economy, not least because it dominates the transportation sector. Unlike gas, which is predominantly relevant in regional markets with fixed infrastructure, oil is a fungible, tradable, and easily substitutable commodity. As a result, the oil market is a global market. From a political perspective, however, there is no way around the fact that access to oil reserves is, to a large degree, under the control of a limited number of NOCs. Moreover, a large percentage of known oil reserves are in the Middle East.

The USA, China, and Saudi Arabia are the key drivers of the global oil market, so oil market stability depends on the policies of these three countries. Indeed, the primary interaction between the USA and global energy markets is through oil. Unlike Europe, the USA has limited interaction with regional gas markets. Further, the USA is the key guarantor of waterway safety, and only Washington has the global military capability to ensure open access to oil for all players in the global oil market.[26] Consequently, Washington's strategic partnership with Riyadh will remain critical to the stability of global oil markets, because Saudi Arabia is still the key market maker in the global oil trade, and Saudi oil is relatively inexpensive to get out of the ground compared to other sources. Saudi Arabia can balance its budget at a lower price than most other producers can, and it is also willing to maintain some spare capacity in order to retain leadership in global oil markets. Riyadh is also well aware that its swing-producer status ensures it a dominant role in OPEC and that this status can be used as leverage for gaining political influence in the region and around the world.[27] In comparison, China's emergence as a regional player in the Middle East, Central Asia, and Africa is closely tied to China's energy needs. In fact, access to oil from non-Asian regions has become critical for China's energy security, and Beijing's economic development has become – and is likely to remain – the key determining factor in the growth of global demand for oil. Chinese NOCs have become significant new players in almost all oil exporting regions, and China's impact on the oil market and on the oil industry is set to grow over time.[28] Despite these factors, stabilizing global oil markets will not be easy. There are strong reasons to believe that the global oil market will remain volatile for years to come, and will not return to the stability of the 1980s and 1990s. A series of cyclical and structural factors make it difficult to project – let alone agree on – the price of oil and the level of investment needed to ensure market stability. Short-term cyclical factors include huge demand insecurity due to recession and growth cycles, as well as speculative activity in opaque financial markets on the one hand, and the supply insecurity associated with political risks in producing countries, and situations in which producer states seek to wield political pressure through cartels and/or supply interruptions on the other. Longer-term structural factors include supply insecurity linked to the concentration of reserves in the Middle East, and to the growing control by states and their NOCs of their oil reserves, meaning less investment, less efficiency, and more politically-motivated subsidies to encourage domestic consumption. One can add the uncertain impact on demand of domestic efforts to protect the environment and curb global warming, and the impossibility of predicting what the future energy mix in key states like China will be.

The new energy system is likely to be characterized by price volatility and investment insecurity in global and highly interdependent oil markets. Stabilizing global oil markets in a transformed energy system will only be possible if supply-side and demand-side policies are better coordinated at the domestic level. The diversification of supply for consumers and of demand for producers will remain the bedrock of competitive and reliable oil markets. However, in order to make these markets more sustainable, diversification will have to include alternative energy resources such as nuclear energy, clean coal, and renewable energy. Simultaneously, the international governance framework that stabilizes global energy markets needs to be expanded in two ways: traditional and new consumers will need to enhance their energy security cooperation and coordination; and producers and consumers will have to move toward a new and expanded producer–consumer framework.

Diversification of supply, demand, and energy type

The diversification of supply will remain a key factor in ensuring the energy security of traditional and new consumers. Diversification shields consumers from disruptions, and guarantees them competitive markets. For example, Africa's energy resources have become increasingly important as a complement to dwindling oil production in the North Sea for European consumers, and as a source for China's expanding demand for foreign oil. As oil reserves are increasingly controlled by NOCs, and are concentrated in the Middle East, Africa is still relatively open to investment, and there is little competition between local needs and exports, because its domestic consumption is low.[29] In another key region, Russia has been relatively successful in controlling the flow of Caspian oil to Europe. However, alternative pipelines to Europe and China have increased export diversification somewhat.[30] Thus, the options for diversification open to traditional and new consumers are limited, and few fulfil the key requirements of providing stable, reliable, and affordable oil. Most transit routes and supplies are fraught with risks

– the complex geopolitical situation in the Caucasus and the Caspian, and resource nationalism and community activism in Africa and Latin America, serve as good examples.[31] In addition, high extraction costs and under-investment by state-controlled NOCs could create further barriers to the diversification of supplies.

At the same time, changes in global market forces have increased the diversification of demand. The entry of new Asian consumers into the oil market has increased the number of export options for producers. Countries like China do not make their cooperation and investment conditional on political demands, such as good governance or the protection of human rights; consequently, the emergence of new Asian consumers is an attractive alternative for many producers because it makes them more flexible in the way they handle their broader foreign policies.[32] However, producers' diversification options are also limited. New export infrastructures are expensive to develop, and the old ones have locked producers into dependencies with their traditional buyers. Moreover, it is often economically more viable to invest in the lucrative downstream markets of traditional consumers than to develop new markets in other world regions. Political considerations may further inhibit the development of alternative export markets.[33]

Diversification is a good energy strategy for both consumers and producers, because it protects their energy relationships against market and political shocks. This remains as true today as when Churchill introduced diversification as a key concept of Western energy policies. However, two recent developments necessitate a wider approach, to emphasize the diversification of resource type in order to ensure the sustainability of energy markets. First, the environmental consequences of current consumption patterns demand a shift away from fossil fuels. Second, the fact that sustainable energy markets are becoming increasingly integrated makes such diversification a more practical option for consumers. Diversification into markets for sustainable energy will add new weight to these forms of energy. It will also increase efforts in the area of efficiency, and investment in a new generation of nuclear power, carbon capture and storage (CCS) applications, and clean coal technologies.[34] These changes will work against oil markets in the long term, but change will be gradual and slow. The challenge will be to balance the short and long term energy interests of old and new consumers, and to move toward a new producer–consumer framework.

Expanded coordination between traditional and new consumers

Stability in the global oil market needs, first and foremost, a joint commitment from both traditional and new consumers to encourage open access and competitive markets. As a starting point, traditional and new consumers should acknowledge that there are differences in how they approach the oil market. China, for instance, seems to mistrust markets, and instead is focusing on gaining direct physical control over energy resources through investment in national companies. From Beijing's perspective, current market volatility is at least partly the result of unilateral US policies. The invasion of Iraq and the associated loss of Iraqi oil-production capacity, as well as the Wall Street meltdown, have had negative repercussions on the stability of the oil market. However, while China has to learn that access, and not control, is the guarantor of competitive markets, the West must recognize that Beijing will only learn to trust markets if it is integrated into the coordination mechanisms that govern these markets.[35] Future energy relations between traditional and new consumers should therefore have a focus on improving the resilience and sustainability of oil markets, and not on the division that tends to develop when one side pursues a market model, while the other pursues a mercantilist model in order to deal with a changing energy situation. Traditional consumers should be willing to expand their energy policy framework, and must find ways to tie emerging Asian consumers into the international networks that govern the energy trade.

Both traditional and new consumers have a strategic interest in a resilient global oil market. To this end, they should better coordinate their activities in the following three areas. Initially, they should jointly monitor markets and share demand and supply data. Information is critical for functioning markets, and it is imperative that the scale of investment and price insecurity is reduced to a level that allows the various participants to establish more reliable markets. Next, traditional and new consumers should coordinate their policies so they can better deal with supply disruptions. Improving the coordination of strategic reserves, and of the mechanisms designed to activate those reserves, is an essential factor in stabilizing volatile markets. Finally, consumers need to work together to create an environment that encourages investment in the energy sector. A joint assessment of future investment needs is an important means of curbing investment insecurity, and of overcoming investment bottlenecks.

However, better coordination across these areas is unlikely to be achieved through one instrument alone. Rather, many existing state and business institutions and mechanisms need to be strengthened. For example, traditional and new consumers need to develop their bilateral and multilateral institutions and instruments dedicated to energy issues.

While China is building strategic reserves and is becoming increasingly interested in coordination, traditional consumers should work hard to define ways to bring countries like India and China closer to a modernized IEA.[36] Formal membership will not be an option for China, however, because IEA members need to be committed to OECD standards. This means also that bilateral structures – for instance, the EU–China and the USA–China energy dialogues[37] – will remain important coordination mechanisms.

Another aspect of improving coordination would be for the traditional consumers to encourage new consumers to participate in the many global finance and trade networks that govern the global energy system. Increased transparency in financial markets is a critical component in the creation of a stable investment framework in the energy sector.

Additionally, traditional and new consumers should promote reciprocal business-to-business relationships. The fact that Chinese NOCs are not allowed to purchase American companies for political reasons is certainly not a helpful factor in a world where energy relations between traditional and new consumers need to improve.

Both traditional and new consumers have a strategic interest in improving the sustainability of global oil markets. There are three pressing reasons why the dialogue about the demand-side dynamics of the global energy market should be advanced. First, investment in efficiency and environmental protection will have overall economic benefits. For China, a reduction in demand could, in fact, become an attractive alternative to an expansion of the supply of fossil fuel, as this would limit its exposure to the volatility of global energy markets. For the USA, investing in solutions that reduce demand would, in turn, provide an opportunity for the country to establish itself as a leader in green technology innovation. Second, a shift towards efficiency and demand-side solutions makes sense for political reasons. Such a move would allow traditional and new consumers to limit their dependence on geographically concentrated oil resources, to protect themselves against the likely under-investment of producers and the resulting high oil prices, and to put pressure on producers, while at the same time offering producers the chance to cooperate with them in the areas of efficiency and renewable technologies. Third, demand-side solutions are becoming more and more attractive, as the public's awareness of the negative effects of climate change is growing. Traditional and new consumers have a joint interest in reducing carbon emissions. However, they have different opinions about who should be doing what. China, in particular, places the ultimate responsibility for reducing carbon emissions with the West.[38]

The adaptation of the demand side of the global energy markets is first of all a domestic challenge, but it will not be easy to turn around the current supply-side bias of most domestic energy policies. On the contrary, it will be expensive and time consuming, and success will depend on the right mix of state and private activities. In the end, political will is likely to be decisive, although the differences between various countries' policy processes will probably influence environmental progress directly.[39] The governments of relatively strong European states are more capable of raising taxes and regulating energy markets than the much weaker US government. In China, by contrast, most demand-side measures have been top-down, while bottom-up, market-based instruments for improving the economy's energy intensity are weak or non-existent. The fact that the differences in domestic energy policies are at least partly a function of state strength makes it plain that, in the area of demand-side policies, states should lead by example. Clearly, European states are most advanced in efficiency issues, and they also place more emphasis on renewable technologies, reflecting the particular institutional set-up of a multilevel governance system. In fact, the EU has taken on an agenda-setting role in demand policies, and its member states are committed to saving 20 per cent of their energy consumption, to increasing to 20 per cent the share of renewables in their overall energy consumption, and to cutting greenhouse gas emissions by at least 20 per cent by 2020.[40]

The development of US–Chinese relations will be critical in improving the coordination of energy supplies between traditional and new consumers. Europe will remain important to the demand-side dynamics between traditional and new consumers. However, the chances of a successful shift away from supply-side growth coalitions toward pro-efficiency, demand-oriented groups seem to be better than ever before, both in US and Chinese domestic politics. Clearly, the USA has reached a turning point in its energy debate. Domestic support for a green economy and for climate protection has expanded considerably. President Obama has pledged to invest in efficiency-enhancing technologies and environmental protection, and to significantly reduce national carbon emissions.[41] China's leaders have also begun to encourage demand-side efforts, and to promote green GDP. The political and social challenges associated with a move toward efficiency and energy reform remain huge; however, China has no alternative but to choose less energy-intensive development. Domestic change in China is also being driven by air and water pollution, by fears arising from its rapidly increasing dependence on global oil markets, and by growing international pressure on China – the world's biggest carbon dioxide emitter – to alter its domestic coal and oil trajectory.[42]

However, domestic measures alone will not force global consumption patterns onto a more sustainable path. Given the differences in progress between traditional and new consumers, Europe and the USA should attempt to exploit the economic and environmental potential of demand-side policies internationally. At the state level, governments should expand their dialogue about policies that work. They should consider best practices for energy efficiency and renewables, and they should provide incentives to stimulate investment by developing joint demonstration projects and joint R&D efforts. At the business level, corporations should consider exploiting joint development projects to spread their technologies throughout emerging markets.[43] A triangular relationship will be key to stimulating international action: EU countries are the world leaders in efficiency and conservation, and should lead by example. However, a successful turn-around toward a greener economy also needs US leadership and US innovation. As a large consumer and a large producer, the USA will remain a key driver in shaping global consumption patterns. Also, since China will account for almost 50 per cent of the world's carbon emissions by 2030, a more sustainable energy system may not be possible without major changes to China's domestic consumption. The biggest success for new technologies would be the modernization of China using these new and sustainable energy approaches.[44]

This brings us finally to politics. China's interaction with the world beyond Asia is tightly connected to China's energy needs. Beijing's rapid development from energy self-sufficient state to key player on global oil markets has dramatically extended China's foreign policy to Africa, the Middle East, Central Asia, and Latin America. China's energy policies will at times lead to friction in its foreign relations with other big consumers like the USA, the EU, Japan, and India, as other big powers also scramble for access to (and, in some cases, control over) scarce resources. China's policies – driven by competition for oil and gas – may sometimes undermine Western policies regarding these regions, for example, with regard to Sudan and Iran. Yet although China's approach to Africa and the Middle East has not been anti-Western, its policy of not interfering in domestic affairs points to the fact that China and the West are pursuing different development models in the region. The West would therefore do better to use the common interest in stability to draw China into stability-enhancing development and peace-building policies, instead of treating Beijing as a regional competitor.[45] Similarly, the traditional consumers should engage China in the protection of the whole energy supply chain. China depends on the maritime power of the USA to secure trade lines and energy infrastructures in the Middle East and Africa, and both the USA and China are interested in the prevention of transportation disruptions in the Straits of Malacca. Thus, the evolution of the US–Chinese relationship will arguably be critical for global peace and security. If the USA and China decide to work not only on the supply side, but also on the demand side of the energy equation, their energy cooperation could enhance their strategic relationship. The ways in which each side manages the supply and demand dynamics of its energy policy within the larger strategic framework will have important repercussions for their overall relationship.

Towards a new Producer–Consumer framework

Producers and consumers need to realize that the traditional producer–consumer framework will have to be adapted to take account of recent changes in the global energy system. Both sides should acknowledge the existing interdependencies within the global energy system, and recognize that market instability negatively affects both demand and supply security. It is unlikely that producers' and consumers' domestic and foreign policy interests – as these relate to energy – will converge any time soon. However, both sides should make sure that their energy rhetoric does not trigger an energy security dilemma, which leaves them both worse off energy-wise. Arab–Western relations have been going through a difficult period, and the public perception of both sides has been at a low point since 9/11 and the start of the war in Iraq. As a result, the energy debate relating to Middle Eastern oil has become highly politicized, especially in the USA. However, a move towards a new producer–consumer framework will only be possible if the traditional consumers acknowledge that the threat of politically-driven disruptions of oil flows from the Middle East are overstated, that calls for independence from Middle East oil are unrealistic, and that the Middle East has been a consistently reliable supplier of oil, with the exception of the 1973 Arab oil embargo.[46] (The embargo is a good example of the fact that using oil as a weapon can easily backfire and result in overproduction capacities and cheap oil.)

Both producers and consumers have a strategic interest in a strong global oil market. Although OPEC's structure and its internal divisions have a tendency to send mixed signals to the market, OPEC production cuts have usually been driven by market conditions. The 2008 decrease in demand and the subsequent dramatic fall of oil prices show that OPEC depends on Saudi Arabia accepting most of the production cuts, with other producers generally putting self-preservation first and keeping oil exports flowing above quotas.[47] Once the world economy starts to rebound, the oil price is likely to rise again, and the consequences of under-investment will then once more become apparent. Buyers and sellers thus need a better understanding of the nature of the interdependencies that link them to each other in the global oil market. Consequently, in order to stabilize oil markets, producers and consumers should strengthen their dialogue in four areas: First, they should improve their coordination of strategic reserves and define appropriate guidelines for the release of such reserves. Second, they should address the investment problem, which will reappear once economic growth returns, as early as possible. Middle East investment was stagnant in the 1980s and 1990s, leading to consumer fears that Middle Eastern producers may not be able to meet future demand. The 2008 demand drop has reversed this situation, but the fact remains that many states and their NOCs are reluctant to invest.[48] Further, the impact of domestic barriers on investment in producing states is an ongoing problem. Third, there is a danger in the current economic downturn that countries may adopt protectionist policies, thus weakening existing interdependencies in the energy system. Therefore, producers and consumers should try to create a political climate that encourages reciprocal investment opportunities in the upstream and downstream sectors. Fourth, producers and consumers should better coordinate their efforts to protect the whole energy supply chain.

To strengthen the producer–consumer framework, states and businesses will need to become involved. At the state level, increased dialogue and more extensive cooperation is required through a variety of bilateral and multilateral channels and mechanisms, including through global networks such as the IEA, OPEC, and the International Energy Forum (IEF), as well as through regional platforms such as the EU–OPEC Energy Dialogue and the EU–Russia Energy Dialogue.[49] It is especially important that the new energy consumers in Asia, including China and India, are integrated into these networks. Multilateral platforms often aim primarily at facilitating information exchange, data gathering, and integration, viewing these as a precondition of a functioning market. However, bilateral energy relationships remain important in the management of the political aspects of the energy trade. Markets alone cannot guarantee the smooth functioning of strategic reserves and investment flows, any more than they can guarantee the physical security of the whole energy supply chain.

At the business level, new models of cooperation between NOCs and IOCs are needed. The fact that NOCs control large parts of the global oil reserves means that IOCs will have to adapt their role, and shift their focus to non-conventional exploitation, and other aspects of the extraction business, such as refining, logistics, and retail. NOCs, on the other hand, under pressure from the global recession and with shrinking financial reserves, need access to IOC capital, technical expertise, and managerial know-how in order to overcome slumping production, and to develop new resources. If IOCs are prepared to accept a junior role more willingly, and if NOCs begin to develop from being purely national instruments into companies with an international outreach, there should be room for mutually beneficial joint ventures in the upstream and downstream sectors.[50] Business-to-business cooperation across the whole supply chain could strengthen the economic logic of mutual interdependencies, and could well be an essential element of oil market stability. Also, states have to find ways of keeping these markets open and allowing for reciprocal investments, and of increasing their transparency, so they can play a positive role for social development.

Traditional and new consumers, as well as producers, should be interested in improving the sustainability of global oil markets. However, good cooperation in promoting demand-side policies will be more difficult to develop between producers and consumers than between traditional and new consumers. This is because, from the perspective of producers, the environmental efforts of consumers undermine demand security. It is important that consumers accept the fact that income from energy is vital to the economic and political development of most producing countries. Yet consumers should also reassure producers that changes to their energy consumption patterns, as a result of changes to their demand-side policies, will inevitably be slow and gradual. At the same time, they should offer producers increased technology cooperation and should leverage the economic benefits of increased collaboration in the area of efficiency and alternative technologies. Increased domestic energy efficiency will enhance the overall efficiency of producer economies, and will open up new export potential to them. Moreover, increased technology cooperation in the area of efficiency and alternative energy sources will improve the lifespan of producers' fossil fuel deposits, while gradually diversifying their economies away from a dependence on oil and gas.

Finally, both producers and consumers have a common interest in fighting global climate change. If consumers place increasing emphasis on demand-side policies in order to curb global warming, rather than in response to calls for energy independence, they are demonstrating the one thing they have in common with producers: the desire to reduce carbon dioxide emissions. Producers should convince consumers that it makes sense to invest in CCS technologies as a means of dealing – in advance – with the environmental impact of future oil and gas consumption. Conversely, consumers should encourage producers to establish a regulatory framework that promotes emission reduction schemes. Expanding the producer–consumer framework with a focus on demand will thus enhance the long-term stability and sustainability of energy relationships between producers and traditional and new consumers.[51]

Politically, bilateral US–Saudi relations will remain critical to the stability of the global oil market and the producer–consumer relationship. Saudi Arabia is likely to remain the key market maker, and may also provide spare capacity because it wishes to maintain its leadership role in oil markets. The USA, on the other hand, is likely to remain the key security balancer in the region, and its policies on Iraq, Iran, and the Palestinian territories will critically affect the security of the whole region, including Saudi Arabia. Today, the USA and Saudi Arabia have a chance to increase their energy cooperation with China and mitigate the importance of Beijing's energy relationship with Teheran. Energy will also be central for both countries' political relations with Iran in general. While the current low oil price is putting economic pressure on Teheran, the prospect of long-term energy cooperation between Iran and the West could complement the West's political negotiation package.[52] Nevertheless, the political relationship between the West and Iran will continue to be dominated by such security issues as nuclear proliferation, regional stability, terrorism, and the future of Islamic fundamentalism, and this means that the short-term stability of oil markets will remain dependent on political stability in the Middle East, a fact that should persuade producers and consumers alike to pursue a broader and more robust framework for their energy relations.

Stabilizing regionalized gas markets

While the oil market is global, the gas market is still primarily regional. The two markets are connected, because the price of gas is linked to the price of oil. Over time, the two markets are likely to become even more interconnected, as pipeline infrastructure becomes more diversified, and liquefied natural gas (LNG) production expands. Yet these changes will be gradual and will take time, and in the meantime, most gas markets will remain pipeline markets that are controlled by sellers and buyers, with transit states in between. As gas is much more difficult to substitute than oil – for both producers and consumers – regional gas markets tend to be more politicized than global oil markets. At the regional level, the desire to dominate markets is often not distinguishable from the desire to secure political domination. At the same time, energy interdependencies are more likely to be part of broader trade and investment networks that link producers and consumers. As a result, the growing interconnection between energy issues, and broader foreign and security policy issues at the regional level, will remain a key challenge for producers and consumers.[53]

Russia and the EU are the key drivers of regional gas markets. Russia is the world's largest gas producer and holds one third of the global gas reserves, but it is not a global energy market maker, because the gas price depends on the price of oil. It is the main supplier of gas (and oil) to Europe, and controls most of the gas markets in the post-Soviet space. It is the sole exporter to Ukraine and Belarus, yet it also wants to reduce its dependency on these two key transit states. All major Eurasian gas pipelines run through Russia, but competition from China and Europe for Eurasian energy is likely to increase in the future. Although Russia aspires to the diversification of its exports and wishes to become a player in Asian markets, Europe will remain its central business partner for quite some time.[54] Conversely, Europe's domestic energy resources are disappearing quickly, and European states will have to rely on imports more and more in the future. Although Europe is committed to dramatically reducing its consumption of fossil fuels, gas and oil will still make up the majority of its energy mix for some time to come. Since oil is far easier to substitute than gas, Russian gas and Europe's energy relationship with Russia will remain the key energy concern for Europe.[55] By contrast, there is only very limited scope for a direct US–Russian energy partnership. There are no infrastructure interdependencies and only a limited number of common economic interests between Washington and Moscow.[56]

Bit by bit, the energy relationship between Russia and Europe has been moving towards an energy security dilemma in past years.[57] Although several European states have long-standing bilateral energy ties with Russia, most European states have viewed Russia as an unreliable energy provider that is prepared to use its energy power for political purposes. This negative perception is based on Russia's repeated cuts to the energy supply of various consumer states, its rejection of market methods, and its energy diplomacy, which has become more assertive beyond its traditional space in recent years. Russia feels unjustly punished for actions that make economic sense to Russian policymakers, such as its refusal to continue to subsidize post-Soviet economies with cheap energy, the diversification of Russian export infrastructure to Europe, and the construction of new pipelines that circumvent Ukraine and Belarus. Moscow has complained that Europe's talk of energy independence, its attempts to diversify its energy supplies, and its investments in efficiency-enhancing and renewable technologies undermine Russia's own efforts to secure demand. In response, the Kremlin has recast its energy rhetoric away from Europe and towards the East. In short, Europe worries about Russian supplies, and Russia worries about European demand.

Mutual dependencies, political challenges

Russia and European countries are unlikely to disengage from their energy partnerships. European buyers and Russian sellers look back on what was essentially a mutually beneficial energy relationship between producers and consumers, stimulated by economic logic and based on a durable physical connection. However, beyond their political rhetoric, policymakers on both sides would be well advised to recognize the existing interdependencies between Russia and Europe, as well as their limited diversification options. Yet adapting the European–Russian energy relationship will not be easy. There is a clear tension between the EU's liberal vision of energy governance and Russia's state-driven approach to energy policies. The intricacies of the policymaking process on both sides will further limit the options for negotiation and compromise in European–Russian energy relations. Moreover, energy issues cannot be addressed apart from the broader framework of the foreign policy relations between Russia and Europe.

Many European countries – some to a considerably greater degree than others – will remain dependent on Russian energy supplies in the medium to long term: Russia is close to Europe and has large reserves. Thus, although Russia's overall share of the European market is likely to decline, Russia will remain Europe's single most important source of hydrocarbons. Europe already has relatively diversified energy supplies in terms of types of energy, sources, and transit routes, thanks to the wide variety of national energy policies. Yet its options for diversifying by sourcing oil from stable and reliable energy flows in the Caucasus, North Africa, and the Middle East are limited and fraught with new risks, given the political volatility of these regions.[58] Conversely, Russia will remain dependent on Europe's energy demand for the medium to long term: Russia is locked into European pipelines, and thus its reorientation toward Asia will perforce be partial and gradual.[59] Russia is therefore likely to prioritize long-term contracts and down-stream investment in European markets, and the export revenues from the energy flows to Europe will remain crucial to its economic welfare and domestic stability. Also, as far as other markets are concerned, although there is a natural link between Russian resources and Chinese markets, Russia will continue to be slow in developing alternative export infrastructures to Asia and beyond.[60]

The biggest obstacles to stable and reliable European–Russian energy relations are the political decision-making processes in Russia and in Europe, and incompatible views regarding the role of the state in energy markets. The real threat, from a European point of view, is not that the Kremlin will play political games with its hydrocarbon supplies to Europe, but that Russia will be unable to maintain its current level of energy exports because of the negative effects of huge rents on the strategic and administrative capacities of the Russian state.[61] Russia's political elites have been unable to create the stable market environment with clear property rights that would stimulate long-term (foreign) investment, limit the growth of domestic energy consumption by increasing domestic energy prices, and encourage the effective management and good governance of Russia's energy sector. Although Russia's energy wealth has helped the country to stabilize its banking sector and the rouble, the current financial crisis highlights the sensitivity of Russia's economic welfare and political stability to hydrocarbon price swings.[62] Moreover, Russia has been unable to capitalize on OPEC cuts and increase its market share, due to a long-term lack of upstream investment. Once economic growth begins in Europe, investment bottlenecks are once again likely to plague European–Russian energy relations.[63]

It seems unlikely that Europe and Russia will be able to agree on energy prices, settle investment needs, and establish market transparency any time soon. This is due partly to decision-making processes in Moscow, and partly to the inability of the European states to speak with a unified voice, which in turn severely compromises Europe's position with regard to its energy relations with Russia. European efforts to create an internal energy market based on competition and common standards, and to expand this model to Russia, regularly come up against the different levels of energy dependency on Russia experienced by individual EU members and against EU members' disparate energy and foreign policy interests. Although the EU now sets the agenda with regard to competition, the environment, and technology, its individual members remain responsible for energy security, and for implementing national regulatory standards. Given the gap between EU policy formulation and the national implementation of EU policies, it is unlikely that internal market liberalization will advance quickly, or that Russia will feel compelled to ratify the Energy Charter Treaty.[64]

Towards a more robust energy partnership

Europe and Russia need to acknowledge that their long-term energy security depends on a functioning energy partnership. Both sides would do well to appreciate the existing interdependencies and the limits of their diversification options, and to recognize that price and investment insecurity negatively affect demand and supply security. While Russia needs to refrain from disrupting gas supplies in order to gain political power over its neighbours, Europe should reassure Russia that it is not striving for complete energy independence. It should also explain that its transition toward alternative energy and reduction of its energy use will be a gradual process.

The move toward a more robust and sustainable energy partnership requires Europe and Russia to better integrate the internal and external elements of their energy policies. Europe should take the lead, and affirm that its new focus on demand-side policies demonstrates the European polity's wish to include sustainability in all long-term energy policies. European policymakers should show that they understand the importance of the link between the domestic and foreign elements of European–Russian energy relations. While European environmental and efficiency efforts might quickly translate into demand changes, rapid consumption growth in Russia could cause supply shortages in Europe. More transparency and better information about the domestic and foreign features of Russian and European energy policies are preconditions for a stable and sustainable energy partnership.

Regarding the external elements of European energy security, the EU and its member states should not focus exclusively on their relations with Russia. Rather, they should aim for a partnership with Moscow that takes into account the current diversification of Europe's energy sources and the whole supply chain, including the interests of transit states. Interests in transit routes affect the EU's internal energy relations, as new pipelines around Central Europe inevitably result in a loss of individual EU member states' transit leverage within the EU, and in relation to their bilateral relations with Russia. External relations with countries such as Ukraine, Belarus, and Turkey also affect the EU's internal energy relations.[65] Thus, better relationships along the whole supply chain will only be achieved if the EU and its member states enhance their general foreign policy profile in the Caucasus, the Caspian, the Middle East, and North Africa.[66] Although Russia has so far been relatively successful in monopolizing gas flows from Central Asia and the Caspian, competition from pipelines to China will work in favour of Europe. Further, Europeans should also invest in their own pipeline projects to ensure competition, however modest. The key problem will be that Moscow will continue to focus its investments on building spoiler pipelines, rather than on the upstream sector.[67]

European energy policies for Russia should relax the market principle somewhat, and should also avoid insisting that Russia liberalize its internal gas markets quickly. At the same time, the Europeans should stress that their insistence on free market access is driven by their own internal market considerations, which are aimed at unbundling production. Russia is clearly interested in downstream investment and long-term contracts. The Europeans, however, should show that if their aim is reciprocal energy relations, access to European downstream markets must coincide with Russia's opening up its monopolistic market structures to European investment.[68] Increased reciprocal foreign direct investment could, in principle, play an important integrating role: It could create new avenues for the diversification of the Russian economy, on the one hand, and it could increase competition in Russia's domestic markets, on the other. Yet the engagement of foreign companies in Russia depends on Russia's ability to provide a stable regulatory framework – and in this area, progress has been, and will remain, slow.

In the meantime, state actors will have to rely on business-to-business relationships. Although state control over the Russian energy sector is likely to remain tight, private domestic companies are active, and international companies are allowed to participate in the sector as minority stakeholders. The dwindling financial reserves and increased political and social demands that are being placed on Russia's energy monopolies, through the global financial and economic crisis, have once again demonstrated the fact that Russia needs foreign companies to provide funds, technology, and management in order to maintain its energy output. Yet European and Western IOCs will have to learn to work as minority partners with big Russian NOCs. The best hope is that the private oil providers and small independent gas companies, which have been responsible for most of the country's output growth in past years, will eventually pave the way towards more liberal conditions in Russia's energy markets.[69]

For all parties, there is limited room for manoeuvre on the supply side. However, stronger cooperation on the demand side could yield considerable potential for a more sustainable and robust energy partnership. Ideally, the Europeans will seek ways to share and transfer know-how and technologies that promote energy efficiency and alternative energy industries. In Russia, energy efficiency is not as heavily politicized as the oil sector or the gas sector, as both these sectors are considered by the Russian state to be of strategic significance. However, interest in efficiency is growing among Russian elites.[70] The IEA estimates that Russia's domestic loss of flaring gas amounts to 60 bcm a year, which is four times the official figure provided by the Russian government.[71] Reducing domestic consumption through improved efficiency and alternative technologies would increase export potential, diversify the economy away from fossil fuels, and benefit global environmental protection policies. If Russia were to turn around its supply-side biased domestic energy policies and move towards a more sustainable development model, both Russia and Europe would benefit.

Electricity offers another promising path. It could help Russia and Europe to overcome their dependence on gas and oil exploration and exploitation; it could also help close the diversification rift between the two parties. Both Russia and Europe have experienced problems with the reliability and capacity of their electricity grids in recent years. The ongoing liberalization and privatization in EU markets, combined with the unbundling of Russia's internal electricity monopoly, should make electricity cooperation easier to establish than gas and oil cooperation has been.[72]

It is essential for the energy security of Europe and Russia that both parties establish a more constructive, comprehensive, and sustainable energy partnership. The energy-related networks, together with the trade and finance networks that link Russia with Europe, demonstrate that a foreign policy approach geared toward isolation is in no one's best interests. However, we can also realistically assume that the domestic and international effects of Russia's energy-related power will place limits on the cooperative potential of Russian–European foreign relations, and that security-related disagreements will at times overshadow energy relations. Russia's domestic stability depends on functioning energy markets and stable energy prices. Although Russia's macro-economic stabilization since 1998 has helped the Kremlin to deal with the current global financial crisis, Russia's ability to diversify its economy, and its administrative capacity for managing the negative effects of huge oil and gas rents on its domestic political development, remain limited. The Russian state and its political system will be dominated by small and highly fragmented elites, with ubiquitous corruption linking politics and business.

Russia's ability to shape the global political agenda will also depend on its energy-related power. As a regional power with global ambitions, Russia could be tempted to leverage its energy-related power as a means of achieving larger foreign policy goals, in particular in the post-Soviet space.[73] In order to anticipate the inevitable – if limited – geopolitical fallout of Russia's energy power, the Europeans will have to enhance their foreign policy profile along the European periphery, on the one hand, and define, with the USA, a more coherent strategy for engaging Russia at the global level, on the other. While the West is well advised to exercise caution when considering expanding NATO to include Ukraine and Georgia, and should take Russia's concerns into account, Moscow needs to understand that if it puts unilateral economic and military pressure on the fragile states along its southern borders, its relations with the West will suffer.[74] Further, at the global level, the West should attempt to make the best use possible of cooperation opportunities in the areas of nuclear arms control, missile defence, the Iran nuclear crisis, and the stabilization of Afghanistan.

Conclusion

Changes in markets, politics, and the environment have undermined the stability of the global energy system. As a result, relations between the more assertive producers and increasingly heterogeneous consumer groups have become more politicized and less stable. The transformation of the global energy system has created new challenges and opportunities, and the ways in which producers and consumers redesign their domestic energy policies and readjust the producer–consumer framework at the international level will have important repercussions for their larger strategic relationships. As fossil fuels are concentrated in unstable regions, narrow, supply-side energy policies will tend to increase competition for access and control, and this could have potentially negative consequences for the foreign policy relationships between consumers and producers. If, on the other hand, consumers and producers decide to expand and complement their energy relationships, with a new focus on demand-side policies, then energy cooperation could become the catalyst for a broader strategic cooperation in the relationship between traditional and new consumers and producers.

The successful transformation of the old energy system depends on the better integration of the internal demand-side and the external supply-side aspects of sellers' and buyers' energy policies. Moving towards an efficient, robust, and sustainable energy system will only be possible if the new system meets the needs of the new and traditional consumers, as well as those of producers. A balanced energy system can be achieved through investment, and will primarily be the result of decision making at the domestic level, and of the right mix of private and public initiatives. However, the way in which producers and consumers prioritize their investments – in the downstream sector or in the upstream sector, in distribution capacities or in production capacities, in extraction and exploitation or in efficiency and environmental protection, in fossil fuels or in alternative resources, in energy or in other social projects – will have international repercussions. National solutions that differ depending on the strength of each state and on the level of fragmentation of each state's energy policymaking process will not suffice to overcome the supply-side bias of the current energy system. To stimulate action, international incentives, through a variety of multilateral institutions and bilateral mechanisms, are also needed. State and business leaders in efficiency and alternative energies should proactively exploit the international cooperative potential of demand solutions.

Traditional and new consumers and producers have a common interest in improving the resilience of global energy markets. The scale and complexity of the global energy trade have expanded rapidly, and will keep increasing in the future. Markets are tight and highly interconnected. Both producers and consumers feel the need to protect themselves against energy-flow disruptions resulting from market and political shocks. The diversification of demand and supply structures will hence remain the bedrock of the energy security of both consumers and producers. However, diversification is not enough. Coordination between traditional and new consumers needs to be increased, and the producer–consumer framework needs to be readjusted and broadened. To increase the resilience of the global energy system, all parties will have to share information and jointly monitor markets, improve the coordination of strategic reserves and the mechanisms for activating reserves, jointly assess future investment needs and create an environment for continuing investment in the energy sector, and enhance coordination and make a bigger effort to protect the whole energy supply chain.

Traditional and new consumers and producers have a common interest in a sustainable global energy market. It will not be easy to overcome the power of domestic growth coalitions in many consumer countries and the fear of producers that increased environmental efforts will undermine their demand security. Global warming, in particular, highlights the long-term negative environmental impact of current energy consumption patterns. Thus, both consumers and producers will have to move toward a less energy-intensive development model, and shift their energy mix away from fossil fuels in order to successfully deal with the long-term challenge of global warming. With the future in mind, consumer states should assist producers in improving the efficiency of producers' energy sectors, which will free up additional export potential. Expanding technology cooperation in the area of efficiency and alternative energy resources will also help producers to extend the lifespan of their hydrocarbon deposits, while they gradually diversify their economies away from gas and oil.

Finally, traditional and new consumers and producers must recognize the importance of the links between their energy policies and their larger foreign and security policies. The growing interconnections between energy security, economic growth, and environmental issues demand better coordination between the energy policies and foreign policies of states. Narrow national security strategies must be complemented by policies that focus on improving the human security of individuals in energy-rich regions on the one hand, and on improving the sustainability of global market structures and of the global environment, on the other. Narrow energy policies – still too often driven by growth coalitions and biased toward supply-side solutions – must be extended to engage a global network of public and private stakeholders in an effort to maintain efficient and robust (energy) markets that are environmentally sustainable.

Notes

1 On the history of oil, see, for example, Daniel Yergin, *The Prize: The Epic Quest for Oil, Money, and Power*, Simon & Schuster, New York, 1991; Leonardo Maugeri, *The Age of Oil: The Mythology, History, and Future of the World's Most Controversial Resource*, Praeger, Westport, Conn., 2006.
2 On the history of the IEA, see, for example, William F. Martin and Evan M. Harrje, 'The International Energy Agency', in *Energy and Security: Toward a New Foreign Policy Strategy*, eds. Jan H. Kalicki and David L. Goldwyn, Woodrow Wilson Center Press, Washington, 2005, 97–116.
3 Joe Barnes and Amy Myers Jaffe, 'The Persian Gulf and the Geopolitics of Oil', *Survival* 48, no. 1, 2006, 143–62.
4 On the interaction between Russia's energy power and its broader foreign policy, see Jeronim Perovic, Robert W. Orttung and Andreas Wenger, eds., *Russian Energy Power and Foreign Relations: Implications for Conflict and Cooperation*, Routledge, London, 2009.
5 See, for example, Terry Lynn Karl, *The Paradox of Plenty: Oil Booms and Petro-States*, University of California Press, Berkeley, 1997; Ian Bannon and Paul Collier, *Natural Resources and Violent Conflict*, World Bank, Washington DC, 2003; Macartan Humphreys, Jeffrey D. Sachs, and Joseph E. Stiglitz,

eds., *Escaping the Resource Curse*, Colombia University Press, New York, 2007.

6   See, for example, International Energy Agency (IEA), *World Energy Outlook 2007: China and India Insights*, OECD/IEA, Paris, 2007; Adam E. Sieminski, 'World Energy Futures', in *Energy and Security: Toward a New Foreign Policy Strategy*, ed. Jan H. Kalicki and David L. Goldwyn, Johns Hopkins University Press, Washington, DC, 2005, 21–50.

7   For a history of the oil price: Energy Information Administration (EIA), World Crude Oil Prices, http://tonto.eia.doe.gov/dnav/pet/pet_pri_wco_k_w.htm

8   See Chapter 4 in this volume. See also Donald W. Jones, Paul N. Leiby, and Inja K. Paik, 'Oil Price Shocks and the Macro-economy: What has been learned since 1995', *Energy Journal* 25, no. 2, 1–32.

9   See, for example, Cambridge Energy Research Associates, 'Recession Shock': The Impact of the Economic and Financial Crisis on the Oil Market (executive summary), 19 December 2008, p. 5, www.cera.com/aspx/cda/public1/news/pressReleases/pressReleaseDetails.aspx?CID=10002

10 See, for example, the case studies written for 'The Role of National Oil Companies in International Energy Markets', a project jointly sponsored by the Japan Petroleum Energy Center and the James A. Baker III Institute for Public Policy, Rice University, Houston, March 2007, www.rice.edu/energy/publications/nocs.html. See also Anthony Sampson, *The Seven Sisters: The Great Oil Companies and the World They Shaped*, Viking Press, New York, 1975.

11 See, for example, John Deutch and James R. Schlesinger, *National Security Consequences of U.S. Oil Dependency*, Council on Foreign Relations Independent Task Force Report no. 58, 2006, www.cfr.org/content/publications/attachments/EnergyTFR.pdf

12 See Chapters 8 and 9 in this volume.

13 See Chapters 5, 6, and 7 in this volume.

14 See Chapters 8, 9, and 10 in this volume.

15 See Chapters 8 and 9 in this volume.

16 See, for example, Kevin A. Baumert, 'The Challenge of Climate Protection: Balancing Energy and Environment', in *Energy and Security: Toward a New Foreign Policy Strategy*, ed. Jan. H. Kalicki and David L. Goldwyn, Woodrow Wilson Center Press, Washington, DC, 2005, 485–508.

17 See, for example, Melanie A. Kenderdine and Ernest J. Moniz, 'Technology Development and Energy Security', in *Energy and Security: Toward a New Foreign Policy Strategy*, ed. Jan. H. Kalicki and David L. Goldwyn, John Hopkins University Press, Washington, DC, 2005, 425–59.

18 See, for example, Daniel Yergin, 'Ensuring Energy Security', *Foreign Affairs* 85, no. 2, 2006, 69–82.

19 See Chapter 3 in this volume.

20 See, for example, Nathan E. Hultman, 'Can the World Wean Itself from Fossil Fuels?' *Current History* 106, no. 703, November 2007, 378–9.

21 See, for example, Jan H. Kalicki and David L. Goldwyn, eds., *Energy and Security: Toward a New Foreign Policy Strategy*, Johns Hopkins University Press, Washington, DC, 2005.

22 Consumers have an interest in helping Middle Eastern and African producers to overcome their governance deficits (rentier state symptoms) and
to cope with the structural weaknesses of their economies (Dutch disease
symptoms). See, for example, Erika Weinthal and Pauline Jones Luong,
'Combating the Resource Curse: An Alternative Solution to Managing
Mineral Wealth', *Perspectives on Politics* 4, no. 1, 2006, 35–53; William Tompson, 'A Frozen Venezuela? The "Resource Curse" and Russian Politics',
in *Russia's Oil: Bonanza or Curse?*, ed. Michael Ellman, London, Anthem,
2006, 189–212; Egil Matsen and Ragnar Torvik, 'Optimal Dutch Disease',
Journal of Development Economics 78, no. 2, 2005, 494–515; Benjamin Smith,
'Oil Wealth and Regime Survival in the Developing World: 1960–1999',
American Journal of Political Science 48, no. 2, 2004, 232–46.

23 The link between energy and politics is more pronounced in regional gas
markets, where pipelines establish a physical link between different territorial
sovereignties. Nevertheless, even disruptive action at export choke points,
such as the straits of Hormuz or Malacca, is likely to result in short-term
political effects rather than in a long-term realignment of political power.
On the limits of the utility of the Middle East energy weapon, see Chapter
4 in this volume; see also Dennis Blair and Kenneth Lieberthal, 'Smooth
Sailing: The World's Shipping Lanes Are Safe', *Foreign Affairs* 86, no. 3,
2007, 7–13; Caitlin Talmadge, 'Closing Time: Assessing the Iranian Threat
to the Strait of Hormus', *International Security* 33, no. 1, 2008, 82–117.

24 International Energy Agency, *Key World Energy Statistics 2008*, IEA, Paris,
2008, 6.

25 For studies taking an alarmist view, see, for example, Kenneth S. Deffeyes,
Beyond Oil: The View from Hubbert's Peak, Hill and Wang, New York, 2005;
Richard Heinberg, *The Party's Over: Oil, War and the Fate of Industrial Societies*,
revised and updated edition, New Society Publishers, Gabriola Island, 2005.

26 See Chapter 8 in this volume. See also Stephen J. Randall, *United States
Foreign Oil Policy since World War I*, McGill Queen's University Press, Montreal,
2005.

27 See Chapter 4 in this volume.

28 See Chapter 4 in this volume. See also Indra Overland and Kyrre Elvenes
Braekhus, 'Chinese Perspectives on Russian Gas and Oil', in *Russian Energy
Power and Foreign Relations: Implications for Conflict and Cooperation*, ed. Jeronim
Perovic, Robert Orttung, and Andreas Wenger, Routledge, London, 2009,
201–22.

29 See Chapter 6 in this volume.

30 See Chapters 5 and 9 in this volume. See also Julia Nanay, 'Russia's Role
in the Eurasian Energy Market: Seeking Control in the Face of Growing
Challenges', in *Russian Energy Power and Foreign Relations: Implications for Conflict
and Cooperation*, ed. Jeronim Perovic, Robert Orttung, and Andreas Wenger,
Routledge, London,2009, 109–31.

31 See Chapters 5, 6, and 7 in this volume.

32 Although the development of Russian energy exports to China has been
and will remain slow, the West should acknowledge that there is a natural

match between Russian resources and Chinese markets, not unlike the link between Russia and Europe. Russian supplies carry strategic significance for Beijing because China has no independent capabilities to ensure energy imports via waterways. Strong domestic and international forces will push these two countries toward energy cooperation in the long term. See, for example, Kyrre Elvenes Braekhus and Indra Overland, 'A Match Made in Heaven? Strategic Convergence between China and Russia', *China and Eurasia Forum Quarterly* 5, no. 2, 2007, 41–61.

33 See Chapter 5 in this volume.

34 Yergin, 'Ensuring Energy Security'.

35 See Chapter 10 in this volume.

36 See, for example, William F. Martin and Evan M. Harrje, 'The International Energy Agency', in *Energy and Security: Toward a New Foreign Policy Strategy*, ed. Jan. H. Kalicki and David L. Goldwyn, John Hopkins University Press, Washington DC, 2005, 97–116; Joe Barnes and Amy Myers Jaffe, 'The Persian Gulf and the Geopolitics of Oil', *Survival* 48, no. 1, 2006, 143–62.

37 See, for example, Hongtu Zhao, 'Some Thoughts on Sino–U.S. Energy Cooperation', in *Energy and Conflict Prevention*, ed. Greg Austin and Marie-Ange Schellekens-Gaiffe, Gidlunds Forlag, Hedemora, 2007, 88–107.

38 See Chapter 2 in this volume.

39 See, for example, G. John Ikenberry, 'The Irony of State Strength: Comparative Responses to the Oil Shocks of the 1970s', *International Organization* 40, no. 1, Winter 1986, 105–37.

40 For an overview, see European Union Activities: Energy, http://europa.eu/pol/ener/overview_en.htm

41 See Chapters 8 and 3 in this volume.

42 See Chapter 10 in this volume. See also Jonathan Sinton et al., *Evaluation of China's Energy Strategy Options*, The China Sustainable Energy Program, Berkeley, 2005. Available from http://eetd.lbl.gov/ea/china/china_pubs-policy.html; Liu Xuecheng, *China's Energy Security and Its Grand Strategy*, The Stanley Foundation Policy Analysis Brief, The Stanley Foundation, Muscatine IA, September 2006, www.stanleyfoundation.org/publications/pab/pab06chinasenergy.pdf; Jin Liangxiang, 'Energy First: China in the Middle East', *Middle East Quarterly* XII, no. 2, 2005, www.meforum.org/article/694; Kenneth Lieberthal and Mikkal Herberg, 'China's Search for Energy Security: Implications for U.S. Policy', in *NBR Analysis 17/1*, The National Bureau of Asian Research, Seattle, WA, April 2006, 13–19, http://nbr.org/publications/analysis/pdf/vol17no1.pdf.

43 See, for example, Patrick Avato and Jonathan Coony, *Accelerating Clean Energy Technology Research, Development, and Deployment*, World Bank Working Paper no. 138, The World Bank, Washington DC, 2008.

44 See Chapters 8, 9, and 10 in this volume.

45 See Chapter 6 in this volume. See also Jennifer Giroux, 'Africa's Growing Strategic Relevance', *CSS Analyses in Security Policy* 3, no. 38, 2008, www.isn.ethz.ch/isn/Digital-Library/Publications/Detail/?ots591=0C54E3B3-1E9C-BE1E-2C24-A6A8C7060233&lng=en&id=56968; Bates Gill,

Chin-hao Huang and J. Stephen Morrison, 'China's Expanding Role in Africa: Implications for the United States', Center for Strategic and International Studies, February 2007, www.csis.org/component/option,com_csis_pubs/task,view/id,3714/type,1/

46 On the limits of the utility of the Middle East energy weapon, see Chapter 4 in this volume. See also Bassam Fattouh, *How Secure Are Middle East Oil Supplies?*, Oxford Institute for Energy Studies Paper, WPM 33, Oxford Institute for Energy Studies, Oxford, September 2007, www.oxfordenergy.org/pdfs/WPM33.pdf

47 See, for example, Bassam Fattouh, 'OPEC Pricing Power: The Need for a New Perspective', *OIES Working Papers WPM*, no. 31, Oxford Institute for Energy Studies, Oxford, March 2007 www.oxfordenergy.org/pdfs/WPM31.pdf

48 See Chapter 4 in this volume. See also Valérie Marcel, *Investment in Middle East Oil: Who Needs Whom?*, Chatham House Reports, Chatham House, London, February 2006, www.chathamhouse.org.uk/files/3304_vmfeb06.pdf

49 See, for example, Robert Skinner, 'Energy Security and Producer–Consumer Dialogue: Avoiding a Maginot Mentality', OIES Background Paper presented at the Government of Canada Energy Symposium, Sheraton Hotel, Ottawa, 28 October 2005, www.oxfordenergy.org/presentations/SecurityOfSupply.pdf

50 See Chapters 2 and 7 in this volume. See also Amy Meyers Jaffe, 'The Changing Role of National Oil Companies in International Energy Markets', Presentation at the James A. Baker III Institute for Public Policy, Rice University, 1 March, 2007, www.rice.edu/energy/publications/docs/NOCs/Presentations/Hou-Jaffe-KeyFindings.pdf

51 See Chapter 3 in this volume.

52 See Chapter 9 in this volume.

53 See, for example, Andreas Wenger, 'Russia's Energy Power: Implications for Europe and for Transatlantic Cooperation', in *Russian Energy Power and Foreign Relations: Implications for Conflict and Cooperation*, ed. Jeronim Perovic, Robert W. Orttung and Andreas Wenger, Routledge, London, 2009, 225–44.

54 On the Russian energy situation, see Chapter 5 in this volume. David Lane, ed., *The Political Economy of Russian Oil*, Rowman & Littlefield, Boulder, 1999; John D. Grace, *Russian Oil Supply: Performance and Prospects*, Oxford University Press, Oxford, 2005; Jonathan Stern, *The Future of Russian Gas and Gazprom*, Oxford University Press, Oxford, 2005; Michael Ellman, ed., *Russia's Oil and Gas: Bonanza or Curse?*, Anthem Press, London, 2006.

55 See Chapter 9 in this volume. See also Stacy Closson, 'Russia's Key Customer', in *Russian Energy Power and Foreign Relations: Implications for Conflict and Cooperation*, ed. Jeronim Perovic, Robert W. Orttung and Andreas Wenger, Routledge, London, 2009, 89–108.

56 See, for example, Peter Rutland, 'US Energy Policy and the Former Soviet Union: Parallel Tracks', in *Russian Energy Power and Foreign Relations: Implications for Conflict and Cooperation*, ed. Jeronim Perovic, Robert W. Orttung, and

Andreas Wenger, Routledge, London, 2009, 181–200.

57 See, for example, Andrew Monaghan, 'Russia–EU Relations: An Emerging Energy Security Dilemma', *Pro et Contra* 10, nos. 2–3, 2006, English version available at: www.carnegieendowment.org/files/EmergingDilemma1.pdf

58 See, for example, Andrew Monaghan, *Russia and the Security of Europe's Energy Supplies: Security in Diversity?*, Special Series 07/01, Conflict Studies Research Centre, Swindon, 2007, http://se2.isn.ch/serviceengine/FileContent?servi ceID=10&fileid=E01719FD-5CEE-6B5D-EF48-181E39EDFC83&lng=en

59 See, for example, Nina Poussenkova, 'Russia's Future Customers: Asia and Beyond', in *Russian Energy Power and Foreign Relations: Implications for Conflict and Cooperation*, ed. Jeronim Perovic, Robert Orttung, and Andreas Wenger, Routledge, London, 2009, 132–53; Nina Poussenkova, *The Wild, Wild East: East Siberia and the Far East–A New Petroleum Frontier?*, Economic and Energy Policy Working Paper, no. 4, Moscow Carnegie Center, Moscow, 2007, www.carnegie.ru/en/pubs/workpapers/77259.htm

60 See Chapter 5 in this volume.

61 See, for example, Andreas Wenger, Jeronim Perovic, and Robert W. Orttung, eds., *Russian Business Power: The Role of Russian Business in Foreign and Security Relations*, Routledge, New York, 2006.

62 See, for example, Philip Hanson, 'The Sustainability of Russia's Energy Power: Implications for the Russian Economy', in *Dealing with an Assertive Russia: Power, Perceptions, and the Role of Energy*, ed. Jeronim Perovic, Robert Orttung, and Andreas Wenger, Routledge, London, 2009, 23–50.

63 See, for example, Daniel Simmons and Isabel Murray, 'Russian Gas: Will There Be Enough Investment?', *Russian Analytical Digest*, no. 27, September 2007, 2–5, available from: www.res.ethz.ch/analysis/rad/

64 See, for example, Pami Aalto, 'European Perspectives for Managing Dependence', in *Dealing with an Assertive Russia: Power, Perceptions, and the Role of Energy*, ed. Jeronim Perovic, Robert Orttung, and Andreas Wenger, Routledge, London, 2009, 157–80; Sanam S. Haghighi, *Energy Security: The External Legal Relations of the European Union with Major Oil- and Gas-Supplying Countries*, Hart, Portland, 2007, especially 37–64; Janne Halland Matlary, *Energy Policy in the European Union*, Palgrave Macmillan, London, 1997.

65 See, for example, Andrew Monaghan, *Russia and the Security of Europe's Energy Supplies: Security in Diversity?*, Special Series 07/01, Conflict Studies Research Centre, Swindon, 2007, http://se2.isn.ch/serviceengine/FileContent?servi ceID=10&fileid=E01719FD-5CEE-6B5D-EF48-181E39EDFC83&lng=en

66 See, for example, Aad Correlje and Coby van der Linde, 'Energy Supply Security and Geopolitics: A European Perspective', *Energy Policy* 34, no. 5, 2006, 532–43.

67 See Chapters 5 and 9 in this volume.

68 See, for example, Andreas Heinrich, 'Gazprom's Expansion Strategy in Europe and the Liberalization of EU Energy Markets', *Russian Analytical Digest*, no. 34, February 2008, 8–15, available from: www.res.ethz.ch/analysis/rad

69 See, for example, Daniel Simmons and Isabel Murray, 'Russian Gas: Will

There Be Enough Investment?', *Russian Analytical Digest*, no. 27, September 2007, 2–5, available from: www.res.ethz.ch/analysis/rad/

70 See, for example, Petra Opitz, 'Energy Savings in Russia–Political Challenges and Economic Potential', *Russian Analytical Digest*, no. 23, June 2007, 5–9, available from: www.res.ethz.ch/analysis/rad. On the issue of energy efficiency, see also the contributions in the *Russian Analytical Digest*, no. 46, September 2008.

71 IEA, *Optimising Russian Natural Gas: Reform and Climate Policy*, OECD/IEA, Paris, 2006, 141–66.

72 See, for example, Susan Wengle, 'Power Politics: Electricity Sector Reforms in Post-Soviet Russia', *Russian Analytical Digest*, no. 27, September 2008, 6–9, available from: www.res.ethz.ch/analysis/rad/; William Tompson, *Restructuring Russia's Electricity Sector: Towards Effective Competition or Faux Liberalization*, OECD Economics Department Working Paper, no. 4003, OECD, Paris, 2004.

73 See, for example, Svante E. Cornell and Niklas Nilsson, eds. *Europe's Energy Security: Gazprom's Dominance and Caspian Supply Alternatives*, The Central Asia–Caucasus Institute & Silk Road Studies Program, Stockholm and Washington DC, 2008, www.isdp.eu/files/publications/scornell/sc08europesenergy.pdf

74 Jeronim Perovic, 'Caucasus Crisis: Implications and Options for the West', *CSS Analyses in Security Policy* 3, no. 39, 2008, www.isn.ethz.ch/isn/Current-Affairs/Policy-Briefs/Detail/?lng=en&id=90955

INDEX

Date Due
